MORAL THEOLOGY
IN AN AGE
OF RENEWAL

MORAL THEOLOGY IN AN *Age* OF RENEWAL

A Study of the Catholic Tradition since Vatican II

PAULINUS IKECHUKWU ODOZOR, C.S.Sp.

University of Notre Dame Press

Notre Dame, Indiana

Manufactured in the United States of America

Library of Congress Cataloging-in-Publication Data
Odozor, Paulinus Ikechukwu.
Moral theology in an age of renewal : a study of the Catholic
tradition since Vatican II / Paulinus Ikechukwu Odozor.
p.   cm.
Includes bibliographical references and index.
ISBN 0-268-03469-9 (alk. paper)
ISBN 0-268-03470-2 (pbk. : alk. paper)
1. Christian ethics—History—20th century.   2. Catholic Church—
Doctrines—History—20th century.   I. Title.
BJ1249.O355   2003
241'.042—dc21
2003009027

∞ *This book is printed on acid-free paper.*

to

Livy, Caje, Ekwy, Anne, Eunice, Justina, Leo, Hygy, & Oluchi,
and to all their little ones,
who make their lives and mine happier,

with love and gratitude

contents

PART TWO
The Nature of Christian Ethics

PART THREE
Norms, Contexts, and Method

PART FOUR
A Living Tradition

acknowledgments

I first thought of writing this book sometime soon after the publication of *Veritatis Splendor,* the encyclical of His Holiness, Pope John Paul II, in 1994. I was unable to begin work on the project until 1999, owing to heavy teaching and administrative responsibilities at the Spiritan International School of Theology, Attakwu, Enugu, Nigeria, where I was then. I started researching and writing the book only when I moved to the University of Notre Dame in the fall of 1999. Since I began work on the text, I have received so much assistance from many people, and it is thus my pleasant duty here to express my gratitude to the many individuals who have facilitated this work in various ways.

I owe immense gratitude to my community, the Congregation of the Holy Spirit (the Spiritans), Province of Nigeria, for allowing me time to undertake this work. I thank my Provincial Superior and friend, Fr. Gabriel Ezewudo, C.S.Sp., for generously extending my study leave. Thanks immensely to the Most Rev. John O. Onaiyekan, the Archbishop of Abuja, my father in faith, and a friend whose wise counsel and constant support and encouragement have been crucial to the success of this project and to many other endeavors of my life. In like manner, I must acknowledge the friendship and love of Fr. Daryl Rybicki, my host at St. Adalbert Parish, who provided me with a conducive living environment for my research.

Several members of my religious family were particularly helpful to me during this period in ways I cannot even begin to mention here. Among these are Frs. Mike Onwuemelie, C.S.Sp., Eugene Uzukwu, C.S.Sp., Casmir Eke, C.S.Sp., Lawrence Teteh, C.S.Sp., Jude Ogbenna, C.S.Sp., Ernest Ezeogu, C.S.Sp., Fr. Peter Damian Akpunonu, and James Okoye, C.S.Sp. Fr. Okoye read an initial version of this text and, as is usual with him, offered very insightful comments on the structure and content of the book. Thank you all.

The Department of Theology at the University of Notre Dame deserves my special gratitude. Special thanks to Professor John Cavadini, the Chair of the department, who welcomed me into the department and has done everything in his power to make me feel at home. John's generosity is infectious. It sustained me in more ways than he knows, as I did this work. Like John Cavadini, so the rest of the department. I want to express my thanks to the following colleagues in the department who read this manuscript or portions thereof. First on this list is Professor Jean Porter, John A. O'Brien Professor of Christian Ethics. Jean generously read the entire manuscript at least two times and provided me with useful ideas that certainly made the book a lot better. Professor Maura Ryan also found time to read the material and offer useful advice, in spite of her busy schedule in the department and as Associate Provost of the University. Professor Cathy Kaveny and Professor Mike Baxter, C.S.C., read the entire text as well and provided me with useful critical input, as did Professor Jennifer Herdt who made some very useful suggestions on several chapters. I sincerely thank these colleagues. Their suggestions helped lift the book several notches higher than would have been the case, by preventing me from making more errors than I did.

As usual, my family and friends provided me with such steady and sure support that I do not know how even to begin to express. Thanks to them all. Special thanks to Livinus Odozor, my brother; Ekwy, my sister-in-law; and all my brothers and sisters and their families. Among these younger ones, I thank Ezinwanne and Uzodimma, who helped with reformating my bibliography. Thanks in a most special way to the following friends and their families for the tremendous help and support they offered me while I worked on this book: Fabian Udoh and his wife, Francesca Udoh, their children Kufere and Uyime Udoh, Nkechi Azie and Okey Azie, Ebere Igboko, Abel Ekpunobi, Doi Mbanefo, Laeticia Ofodile, Linda Shaw, Dolores Cieselski, K.C. Kanu, Ogo Kanu, Kelechi Dibie, my cousin, and Sr. Caroline Mbonu, H.H.C.J.

This book could never have materialized without the help of two special friends: Professor Joseph Boyle of the University of Toronto, and Jeffrey Gainey, Associate Director of the University of Notre Dame Press. Professor Boyle helped me conceive this project and, in spite of his rather heavy workload as a teacher and Principal of St. Michael's College at the University of Toronto, found time to read the manuscript and offer useful suggestions. Jeff was his usual supportive self throughout my work on this project. I hope the outcome of this book rewards his optimism. Finally I thank Barbara Hanrahan, Director of the University of Notre Dame Press, Rebecca DeBoer, Managing Editor, and all the other staff of the Notre Dame Press for their many kindnesses to me and the diligence they have shown not only with this book but also with the two other books I have published with the University of Notre Dame Press. Thank you. Thanks to Margo Shearman for her excellent editorial work on this book.

Finally, this book is dedicated to my siblings. There are no better relatives anywhere than these. God bless you all.

Paulinus I. Odozor, C.S.Sp.
Department of Theology
University of Notre Dame

introduction

Special care is to be taken for the improvement of moral theology.
Its scientific presentation, drawing more fully on
the teaching of holy scripture, should highlight the lofty
vocation of the Christian faithful and their obligation to
bring forth fruit in charity for the life of the world.

—Optatam Totius, 16

When the Second Vatican Council issued the above directive, it was not trying to single out moral theology for its pre-eminence over the other theological disciplines.[1] The Council was rather reacting to the long-standing discontent which many people in the Church in general as well as in the moral theological community had been expressing over the state of the discipline. Although this displeasure had become especially noticeable in the years leading up to the Council, its roots were indeed very deep. For example, in 1899, Fr. Thomas J. Bouquillon, the first professor of moral theology at Catholic University of America, wrote that moral theology had become obsolete, a pathetic poor cousin of other theological specialties as a result of its inability to keep up with the times.[2] Moral theology, he said, had failed "to put itself in touch with new currents of thought; failed to anticipate the problems of life and to win consideration for the solutions it offers." The result was that "modern civilization has forced to the foreground serious problems which properly belong to the domain of Moral Theology, but the world has not asked that science for guidance in meeting them . . ."[3]

1

Bouquillon pointed to a number of external and internal factors which had adversely affected moral theology. One of the most important was the secularizing trend in European universities at the turn of the twentieth century. In this secular atmosphere, faculties of theology were eliminated in most state-sponsored universities in Europe. Moral theology, like all other theological specialties, was no longer taken seriously as a branch of learning. The secular climate permeated everything religious, literary, and academic, and led to the suppression and secularization of universities and to the confiscation of ecclesiastical properties and benefices which had enabled so many priests to devote themselves to study. In such a climate an ethic with a theological orientation counted for very little.

Bouquillon blamed the demise of moral theology on a number of internal factors as well. An important element here was the separation of moral theology from dogmatic theology. This separation destroyed the organic unity between these two branches of theology. Detached from revelation, which is its real source of information, moral theology lost vitality and influence. Consequently, other disciplines made inroads in areas once the preserve of moral theology, a fact which contributed to making moral theology vacuous. Devoid of any real content, moral theology was "forced to confine itself to the laws of private life alone,"[4] thus neglecting areas for which the discipline had been known since St. Thomas Aquinas and other notable theologians of the past:

> Nothing is written on habits. In the treatise on laws, the essential theological position regarding the law of God is very often neglected. The external and canonical character is most insisted upon, while the obligation of civil law is studied in a superficial manner. The study of conscience is reduced to a minimum and then literally absorbed into the question of probabilism or equiprobabilism. Finally, the virtues, vices and sin are incompletely studied. As far as studied, they are superficially treated or reduced to pure casuistry.[5]

The sorry state of moral theology at that time had also to do with the intellectual and general theological climate in the Church. This general situation was evidenced by Jansenism and Rationalism, which caused the creation of forms of polemical literature which broke the unity and harmony of theological science; the gradual neglect of the Summa of St. Thomas in moral theology; the separation of moral theology from dogma;

the tendency to separate principles from their application; the intense controversies in the sixteenth and seventeenth centuries between legalism and rigorism, a rivalry which was fully played out in the manuals of moral theology; the principle of probabilism, wrongly understood and misapplied, which led to the neglect of truth; and a too frequent and unnecessary recourse to Roman congregations for decisions, when there was no necessity whatsoever for so doing.[6] A renewal of moral theology was now necessary, Bouquillon said. Although this renewal should begin with a return to the works of St. Thomas Aquinas, it would also include "a more intimate union with the theoretical truths of revelation . . . , so that the laws of right living may be seen to spring from the very heart of dogma." Bouquillon called for a return to Scripture as a wellspring of the Christian moral life: "Critical study and extended research into the development of the fundamental ideas and principles of moral life and their application, not alone in Christian lives, but in OT times as well and back to the beginning of humanity, must be made." He believed that the intelligent application of these principles to the problems of modern individual, social, religious, and civil life was essential to the renewal of moral theology, "as is also a more constant contact with the other social sciences from which, rightly understood, only good can come." He believed there was reason to hope that the coming century, the twentieth, would see this done, "for the impetus has already been given in the admirable encyclicals of Pope Leo XIII."[7]

The coming century, that is, the twentieth century, did indeed witness many attempts to renew moral theology.[8] The impetus for this renewal came from various quarters, including the encyclical *Aeterni Patris*, which was published by Pope Leo XIII in 1879,[9] and the promulgation of the new code of canon law under Pope Benedict XV in 1917. As John A. Gallagher notes, the titles of the manuals of moral theology which appeared at this time "frequently claimed that their contents were 'Based on St. Thomas Aquinas and the Best Modern Authors' or '*Juxta Constitutionem Apostolicam Deus Scientiarum Dominus.*' Others noted that their teachings had been developed in relationship to the new code of canon law."[10] Gallagher points out as well that these neo-Thomistic texts of moral theology which were in use up until the eve of the Second Vatican Council shared many of the characteristics of their seventeenth- and eighteenth-century predecessors. Like these predecessors, "they intended to provide the theological basis for a pastoral ministry focused on the sacraments. The manuals of moral theology were seminary texts devoid of wider systematic and theological concerns of university theology. They addressed theoretical and

systematic issues only to the extent necessary to resolve issues of casuistry."[11] Richard McCormick also describes pre-Vatican moral theology in
similar words: "It can be pointed out that in the 40s and 50s Catholic
moral theology was the stepchild of the *institutiones theologia moralis* of
Genicot, Noldin, Prümmer, Aertnys-Damen, et al. Concretely, it was all too
one-sidedly confession-oriented, magisterium-dominated, canon law–
related, sin-centered, and seminary-controlled."[12] Although McCormick
quickly adds that notwithstanding the above, these texts tended also to be
"very pastoral and prudent, critically respectful, realistic, compassionate,
open, charitable, and well-informed,"[13] his summary captures succinctly
much of what was wrong with pre–Vatican II moral theology. However, he
found the worldviews of these texts too restrictive and sometimes down-
right quaint. The reason for the restrictive worldview found in these texts
is not hard to fathom. First of all, as has already been noted above, because
they were influenced by the basic parameters of Scholastic theology, they
exhibit remarkable uniformity in many ways. "They all treat the same
topics—often in the same sequence—and they tend to share a similar position on issues."[14] Henry Davis, author of one of the most widely used
moral manuals of this period, insists that there can be no originality in
moral discourse since everything that needs to be said had already been
said. Says Davis, "A writer on moral theology today must be indebted
beyond measure to the labor of past writers, for the matter is one that has
been treated with the greatest acumen and scholarship during the well-
nigh three centuries, and there is no room for originality."[15]

Beside being the product of the revival of Scholasticism decreed by
Pope Leo XIII in *Aeterni Patris* in 1789, these texts were also marked by the
philosophical rationalism which had characterized Catholic theology in
general, at least since the beginning of the eighteenth century.[16] Rationalism as a philosophical approach to knowledge goes back to Descartes. It is
a system of thought which stresses reason in opposition to experience.
Descartes was primarily a mathematician, and the system he developed
was intended as a model of study in that discipline more than in theology
or biology or history. Rationalism stresses certitude as an objective. Thus,
as Germain Grisez says, it is not totally conducive to a system of knowing,
such as theology, where growth in understanding (in faith, for example) is
gradual. As a system which emphasizes clear and distinct ideas, rationalism
"tends to distract users of the method from the complexity and richness
of the human condition," making them inattentive to the many meanings
inherent in linguistic expressions. Consequently, "rationalists almost in-

evitably misunderstand the relational character of the language used to talk about God."[17] Another point about rationalism is its tendency to focus on the intellectually knowing subject. The human person is his mind, so to speak. As Descartes himself put it, "I think, therefore I am." The corporeal and other dimensions of being human are almost totally ignored. Grisez notes the tendency of the theologian using rationalism to ignore many aspects of revelation for this reason and to stress the communication of prepositional truths. Thus, at its extreme, this tendency leads to a conception of faith as "acceptance of a certain amount of correct information rather than as a personal relationship of hearing and adhering to God revealing himself." This is exactly what happened with the moral manuals that were in use prior to Vatican II. Also, rationalism not only focuses on the intellectually knowing human person; it makes a sharp distinction as well between the knowing subject and the things known. Thus, "it tends to be unsuited to practical reflection, in which one thinks about oneself and shapes one's thought. A rationalist approach tends rather to look at what is known as if it were a detached object . . . ." Finally, rationalism takes little account of history and of people in their existential and historical dimensions, with varied abilities, diverse needs and opportunities, and as living in actual relationships with others.

John Mahoney, in his seminal work on the making of moral theology, has clearly shown that the limitations of moral theology were a direct result of the circumstances under which the discipline was founded and nurtured in the first place. As Mahoney has shown, "the single most influential factor in the development of the practice and of the discipline of moral theology is to be found in the growth and spread of 'confession' in the Church."[18] This involvement with confessions marked moral theology severely and left it with a pessimistic anthropology, the tendency to exaggeration of one aspect of the moral life—the sin aspect—to the detriment of all others, a negative orientation toward the world, an individualistic approach to moral matters, and a stress on legalism, for which the discipline came to be known until recently.[19] One other telling criticism of the pre–Vatican II moral theology manuals, as has already been indicated, was that they saw morality primarily in terms of law. This legalistic tendency was brought to bear on every aspect of life, including the formulation and interpretation of Church teaching. It led in turn to an obsession with "seeking eternal truths" and with searching for "immutable essences" with little regard to the human subject as a historical being and the subject of moral deliberations. Moral theology had in fact become a type of moral philosophy with little relevance to Christians as human beings who were seeking to live an authentic existence in this world. By the Second Vatican Council, dissatisfaction with this kind of theology had become very noticeable. It is this climate of discontent that prompted the Second Vatican Council to issue the call for the renewal of all theological studies, especially moral theology.[20]

The call of the Second Vatican Council for the renewal of moral theology has indeed borne much fruit thanks to the efforts of so many scholars all around the world. Various studies of the work of some of the individual theologians who shaped the period under study have already appeared.[21] What remains to be done is to try to offer a more comprehensive study of the entire period. As far as I know, no such work exists in English. The fine historical studies done by John Mahoney, S.J.,[22] and John A. Gallagher[23] attend to this period only in passing. They pay more detailed attention to the period leading up to the Council than they do to the time after it. The fine works of Bernard Hoose[24] and Lucius Iwejuru Ugorji[25] attend to a particular issue under discussion at this time, albeit in a historical manner. My own book on Richard McCormick, like some others, attends to just one of the significant players at this time.[26] So far, the most comprehensive attempt to assess the theological efforts to renew moral theology since the Council comes from Pope John Paul II in *Veritatis Splendor*, the encyclical which he issued in 1994 on moral theology.

Aims

Anyone familiar with moral theology in the Catholic Church since the Second Vatican Council will agree that the discipline has been alive with debates and arguments. "What began as mere dissatisfaction with some aspects of the method employed by most moral theologians [before the Council] has turned into a major debate over every aspect of the discipline . . . every aspect of the method, content, and goal of Catholic moral theology has come into question and become the subject of long and sometimes acrimonious debate." The issues involved range from the nature of moral obligation to the manner of determining it. "They include specific questions such as birth control, moral norms, abortion, the role of authority (that is, scriptural, magisterial, or natural law), and so forth."[27] These have been interesting times indeed. They have been marked not only by debates, but also by a manifest plurality of views which have intrigued many people, given the near complete uniformity of views which characterized moral theology until recently.

This book has two important aims. The first is to offer a systematic presentation of some of the major debates as well as an assessment of the diversity and pluralism in moral theology since the Second Vatican Council. Diversity and pluralism in a particular tradition presuppose a certain degree of agreement. This is no less so in Catholic moral discourse since the Council. In spite of our diversity and pluralism many of us in the Church do agree on the essentials of what one can regard as the provisional *telos* of the Church, to borrow from Jeffrey Stout.[28] In other words, there is, despite our diversity and pluralism, a real and significant agreement on the good. It is this agreement which makes our diversity and pluralism possible. The debates over contraception, or moral norms, for example, are not possible without this basic agreement. A second important aim of this work is therefore to identify the significant and real agreement on the good which, despite our diversity and the plurality of our views, makes Catholic moral theology unique as a form of moral discourse, as well as to try to ascertain the bases of such agreement on the good.

John Mahoney has observed that it would not be difficult to show that much of the ethical controversies in society today are not about the ethical importance of freedom and responsibility, peace and justice, the sanctity of human life and the quality of that life, for example. The controversy is usually at the level of practical decision and action and in the face of competing values, choices, priorities, and approaches. It is here that moral consensus usually breaks down or becomes difficult to achieve.[29] I believe that it is at this point too that one can discover in a clearer way the goods which the defenders of a particular position want to preserve as well as the goods which all the interlocutors in a particular debate hold in high regard. Therefore it is part of my intention to identify the goods which the many divergent and plural voices in postconciliar moral theology agree on and which they seek to preserve.

Pluralism and Diversity

The plurality and diversity which characterize the post–Vatican II situation in moral theology can be accounted for on several grounds. First, as Karl Rahner pointed out some time ago, the postconciliar Church has truly become a world Church in which diverse modes of acting and being in the world are all struggling to find a home. Second, the Church's desire to be open to the influences of modernity through dialogue with the sciences, humanities, and behavioral sciences has produced new challenges to the faith in recent years. Christian ethics is a systematic attempt to extend into these areas the abiding insights of the Christian tradition in a disciplined and persuasive manner. Since the Council, this has meant taking a fresh look at a number of old issues and trying to come to terms with new ones. The result has been a marked pluralism and diversity in moral discourse in the Catholic tradition to an extent that was not hitherto the case. For some, this is nothing short of chaotic. For others, it signals a birthing process which must be carefully managed if we are to have a healthy new baby. Consider, for example, the plethora of views on such issues as the place and role of Scripture in morality, the relationship of authority and the individual in moral determination, and method in morals, to name a few. However one looks at the current situation, I believe the pluralism and diversity in the Catholic and other Christian communities show that these communities today must not be regarded as a "faithful moral remnant in society and the custodian of rejected values"[30] but as traditions in the best sense of that word. As Thomas Gilby and Alasdair MacIntyre have each stated, arguments are a characteristic of traditions which are truly alive. Since the goods which constitute such traditions are never totally settled, arguments are ways such living traditions try to determine the nature of the goods in question. Arguments also help to preserve and nourish the goods in order to help the tradition itself continue to stay alive and continue to provide meaning and purpose in an ever-changing world to those who anchor their lives around their world of meaning.

Much of the diversity and pluralism in Catholic moral theology since the Council is therefore directly a result of the attempt by many theologians, in obedience to the call of the Council, to extend the abiding insights of the Christian tradition into all facets of human existence and to let earthly reality in turn enrich and expand the goods which constitute this tradition.

Postconciliar moral theology is not just diverse in terms of the interlocutors, the variety of issues they discuss, and the divergences in the solutions they proffer; it is diverse in relation to what went before it prior to the Council. We are certainly moving away from the type of moral theology which has been described as seminary-controlled, legalistic, individualistic, and sin-centered. It is on this ground that Enda McDonagh has argued that moral theology in the classical sense is dead given that the interests, language, and presuppositions of moral theology since the Council have undergone such drastic changes which make the discipline nearly unrecognizable from its manualist past.[31] Elsewhere I have taken issue with McDonagh on his claim that moral theology is dead and that what we have since the Council is something other than moral theology. My response, briefly, is that the past lives on in the present. Moral theology continues to live in its renewed postconciliar counterpart as a legitimate and much more complex offshoot of a more monolithic forebear,[32] thanks, as I already stated, to the work of so many scholars in the Church today.

Strictures

The reactions to the efforts at renewal have not been all positive. For example, Pope John Paul II in *Veritatis Splendor* gives much of postconciliar moral theology less than a pass-mark—at least in certain areas. The pope characterizes much of the theological effort in the period following the Second Vatican Council as distorting and denying some important Christian truths. He speaks of "certain trends" in theological thinking, of philosophical affirmations which are "incompatible with revealed truth" (*VS*, no. 29), and of a remarkable lack of harmony "between the traditional response of the Church and certain theological positions encountered in seminaries and faculties of theology, with regard to questions of the greatest importance for the Church and for the life of faith of Christians, as well as for the life of society itself." Some of these disharmonies are evident, according to the pope, in the various answers which some postconciliar theologians have been giving to the recurrent questions of context versus principles, faith versus reason, the individual subjective conscience versus authority, and the question of the existence of intrinsically evil actions. As far as the pope was concerned, these theologians have gone too far from what should be considered authentic renewal in moral discourse.

The pope is not alone in his dissatisfaction with some aspects of postconciliar moral theology; some theologians are unhappy too. For example, in a book published initially in French in 1985, the Belgian Dominican theologian Servais Pinckaers expresses, even more strongly than the pope, his dissatisfaction with much of postconciliar moral theology. He states that the openness to the world, which had been encouraged by the Second Vatican Council, has led to regrettable results.

Freedom of conscience, ecumenism, dialogue with other religions, attention to science and politics—all this has produced in many Christians and theologians a strong reaction leading them from one extreme to the other; they have developed an allergy to traditional positions. Obedience to law had at times been servile or infantile; now the priority has become defense of the rights of the subjective conscience. The teaching on natural law has been demolished by ethicists themselves and readily abandoned in the name of science. Sudden openness to modern thought in the areas of philosophy, psychology, sociology, and history has caused an explosion. All moral theology and religion has been subject to rethinking in light of Hegel, Freud, Marx or Nietzsche.[33]

In other words, moral theology since the Council is, for Pinckaers, little more than a wasteland of relativism. In Pinckaers's words: "The Catholic attachment to orthodoxy and theological and dogmatic truth was soft-pedaled in the climate of research, dialogue, and pluralism, open theoretically to all opinions but in fact excluding the orthodox one. Love of truth yielded to a taste for novelty, variety, relativity, adaptation." Pinckaers also states that a good number of ethicists have changed their minds on some of the hotly debated issues of the day such as abortion, euthanasia, contraception, and the problem of the existence of intrinsic evil. These ethicists have been engaged in the revision of fundamental principles of Catholic morality which had hitherto been useful in solving cases of conscience. The end result of all this, as Pinckaers sees it, is that *"the rock of moral theology has been dashed by the powerful waves of the world and of history, which threaten to break and shatter it"* (emphasis added).[34]

These are indeed very weighty allegations. The question, though, is whether they represent the true situation of postconciliar moral theology and whether "the rock of moral theology" has been so shaken by current and adverse modes of thought that moral discourse and morality in general in the Catholic Church are about to break and shatter under this influence. One wonders as well whether such positions as that expressed by Pinckaers in *The Sources of Christian Ethics* present rather simplified views of a complex situation. Are these strictures on postconciliar moral theology too bad to be true, as some people contend, or do they contain valuable insights regarding the validity of some of the elements characterizing moral discourse in the Catholic Church since the Council?

Plan of Work

There are four major parts to this work. The first section, made up of the first three chapters, provides historical, ecclesial, and theological dimensions to the renewal of moral theology in the post–Vatican II era. The first chapter is devoted to the study of the moral theology of the Second Vatican Council. Since it was Vatican II that introduced the spirit and content of moral theology in the past thirty-five years or so, the Council therefore has provided the context for a more comprehensive discussion of the renewal of moral theology in this period as well. This chapter raises the question of the contributions of Vatican II to the renewal of moral theology. The answer can be found in the documents of the Council, but especially in *Gaudium et Spes, Lumen Gentium,* and *Dignitatis Humanae.* The second chapter is a study of *Humanae Vitae* and its aftermath. Richard A. McCormick, one of the leading authorities in moral theology in this period, has written of the importance and effect of this encyclical in this way: "I can think of no moral issue or event in this century that impacted so profoundly on the discipline of moral theology."[35] In this chapter, I try to put the issues surrounding the controversy over *Humanae Vitae* in perspective and to show the ramifications of these debates and their impact on the entire discipline of moral theology. The third chapter is a discussion of two key theological developments which in some ways predated the call for the renewal of moral theology but which have had an enormous impact on moral theology in the period under study. These are the movement for the renewal of biblical studies in the Catholic Church, and Karl Rahner's theology of grace especially as it pertains to non-Christian religions. The effects of the biblical renewal movement are evident in the call by the Council for the centrality of Scripture in the moral life, and in the debates on Scripture and ethics which have been among the most enduring in Catholic moral theology since the Council. The effects of Rahner's position on non-Christian religions is evident as well, both in the discussion on the distinctiveness of Christian ethics and in the discussion on freedom.

The second section is dedicated to issues in metaethics and ethical epistemology. Thus the focus here is on the nature of Christian ethics, as understood by those who explicitly identify themselves with the task of constructing a moral theology, which was truly Christian, following the directives of Vatican II. The questions in this area are legion and have also been asked in various ways. What does faith add to the moral life and discourse? What does revelation add to moral insights? What is the source of the moral ought? If Christian ethics is mostly a matter of natural law, why should morality be of any specific interest to Catholics? Why should there be any question on magisterial authority in moral matters? This second section comprises four chapters. Chapter 4 discusses the question of the distinctiveness of Christian ethics, an important discussion in Catholic moral theology in the years following the Council. The fifth chapter on Scripture and morality reviews the postconciliar debate on the role of Scripture in ethics, while chapter 6 considers the question of natural law in Christian ethics in the work of theologians of this era. The section concludes with a discussion of the role of the magisterium as moral teacher in the Catholic community since the Council.

The third section is devoted to the question of method in recent Catholic moral discourse. Chapter 8 focuses on the debate over moral methodology and moral norms between traditionalists and proportionalists which went on in the Church following the publication of Peter Knauer's article on the revision of the principle of double effect in 1965 and the publication of *Humanae Vitae* in 1968. In the past fifteen years or so, the debate on method in the Church has actually widened to include others. Thus the ninth chapter will discuss two alternative approaches to decision making which have become more and more prominent in moral theology in recent years as many theologians have become disillusioned with the great norms debate of earlier decades.

My intention in the fourth and final section of this work is to suggest what I think are the benchmarks of Catholic Christian moral discourse. The assumption here, as I stated above, is that Catholic Christian ethics since the Council is identifiable with some goals which are indeed sometimes variously articulated. I will try to provide a broad overview of the areas of agreement and to search for the reasons that support this consensus, especially those which stem from the Catholic imagination.

The eleventh chapter constitutes a sort of epilogue to the whole book. It studies two important recent papal documents from the pontificate of Pope John Paul II which are devoted to ethical issues and to moral theology. These documents (*Veritatis Splendor, Evangelium Vitae*) provide us not only with authoritative insights regarding the outcome of the movement for renewal of moral theology; they are important signposts to the future as well. That is why I locate the discussion on them at the end of the book.

*   *   *

This study is a search for significant trends and achievements in moral theology during the postconciliar period. The search for what is significant is of course driven by the historian's belief that certain events or persons sometimes provide foundations on which so much is built and meaning is sought for a particular trend or movement in the period. The question is asked why such and such happened. In reply, the historian would want to say, such and such happened as a result of such and such. This search for historical causality could be read in various ways. For example it could be understood to mean that there is historical progress. One thing happens and then another and another and then another . . . all in a logically coherent form. Another interpretation could be that one thing happens which creates other effects or establishes other trends, whether planned or not, but in a random manner that does not necessarily imply either progress or decline. Yet this significant event is so because it explains—that is, throws light on—some other subsequent event or trend. I indicated above that this work is one theologian's effort to read the moral theological landscape of the post–Vatican II era in the Roman Catholic Church. *Veritatis Splendor* tried to do that from a papal point of view. This work is not being undertaken either to refute or to confirm the claims of *Veritatis Splendor*. The reference to this encyclical is made basically because it points to a project that was long overdue: a comprehensive assessment of the renewal of Catholic moral theology after the Council. Finally, this is a book on fundamental moral theology. Therefore, as much as possible, I shall limit myself to only those issues which traditionally belong to this aspect of moral theology.

part one

The Quest for Renewal: Historical, Ecclesial, and Theological Contexts

The Second Vatican Council and the Renewal of Moral Theology

The Second Vatican Council offered no systematic teaching on the basic questions of fundamental moral theology even though it treated certain moral questions such as marriage, family, war, and peace in some detail. Even on these issues the Council's treatment tends to be brief and unsystematic.[1] This notwithstanding, it is important, for various reasons, to take a look at the teachings of the Second Vatican Council, especially those pertinent to the development of moral theology in recent years. Since it was the Council that mandated the renewal of all theological disciplines, including moral theology, it is necessary to find out whether the Council itself left any hints regarding the direction such an exercise should take. Furthermore, the influence of the Council on the life of the Church has been enormous. This is especially evident in the way many authors and indeed the magisterium have tried to relate their work to, or claim warrants for their words and actions from, the Council. The intention in this chapter then is to discuss the Council's contribution to the renewal of moral theology. We will explore the ways the Council itself tried to update moral discourse in the Catholic tradition, as well as the ways it provided the impetus for developments in postconciliar moral discourse.

As we saw in the introduction, the impetus for the renewal of moral theology, and indeed of all theology, did not originate with Vatican II. Rather, it arose from within the Church and then gave rise to the Second Vatican Council and its developments. I tried to provide a general picture of the situation of moral theology before the Council in the introduction. So much has been written on this issue that it does not bear repeating in any detail here. Therefore what I intend to do here is to provide a general picture of how the treatment of issues by the Second Vatican Council has influenced the development of moral theology since the Council. There are two aspects to the contribution of the Council to theology in general and moral theology in particular. One contribution is in the tone that was set by the Council to theological discourse and to pastoral practice. The other contribution has to do with specifics, that is with the actual teaching and directives from the Council.

The Achievement of Vatican II

One important characteristic of the Second Vatican Council is its general affirmation of the world as a created reality. In the previous texts of moral theology, all moral ultimates were formerly referred to everlasting happiness. The section on *De Fine Ultimo* criticized all other rival human values and encouraged a flight from the world as the only way to salvation. "Life in this world appeared only as a testing period *(in hac lacrimarum valle)* [in this valley of tears]. A more or less emphatic *contemptus mundi* [contempt for the world] was the orientation of Christian asceticism and moral theology."[2] The now-famous commitment of the Second Vatican Council to secular reality stands in stark contrast to the mood before the Council. One of the enduring achievements of the Council is the reversal of this type of Platonic flight from the real into an ideal world. The Council took seriously the hopes and anxieties of all peoples, including very basic interests that have no obvious religious content. *The Pastoral Constitution of the Church in the Modern World (Gaudium et Spes)*, for example, emphasizes that the Church can learn from the world and must help in critically evaluating what the world has to offer. The important thing is that this critique must be made from a positive understanding of the values under discussion. The Council recognizes that the modern world labors with imbalances and limitations. It notes too that despite much scientific and technological progress, more and more people are raising very basic questions about life and its meaning, and sometimes in a dramatically new way. "What is man? What is this sense of sorrow, of evil, of death, which continues to exist despite so much progress? What is the purpose of these victories, purchased at so high a cost? What can man offer to society, what can he expect from it? What follows from this earthly life?" The situation of modernity is not to be seen as reason for abandoning the world, but rather as a challenge for the Church to find creative and meaningful ways to engage the world in dialogue for the good of all. It is the Church's belief that Christ can, through his Spirit, offer humanity the light and the strength to measure up to what is proper human destiny and therefore to achieve its deepest aspirations. It is the task of the Church then to help bring the saving light of Christ to the world as well as to show the world that "beneath all changes there are many realities which do not change and which have their ultimate foundation in Christ, who is the same yesterday and today, now, and forever."[3]

Like the Church itself, the individual Christian also has a moral obligation to the world. The Council insists that no one should be indifferent to the course of events in the world for whatever reason, or indulge in merely individualistic morality. Everyone has a duty to work for justice. And "the best way to fulfil one's obligation of justice and love is to contribute to the common good according to one's means and the needs of others, and also to promote and help public and private organizations devoted to bettering the conditions of life."[4] Indeed, one of the contributions of Vatican II to moral theology lies not just in this stress on a Christian moral obligation to the world, but also in the intrinsic link it establishes between what is done here on earth and the life to come. The Council maintains that the self we construct here on earth by the things we do is an ultimate component of the life to come. The world we construct here is intrinsically connected to the world to come. This is at the heart of the humanism the Council so often speaks of. Consider numbers 38 and 39 of *Gaudium et Spes,* for example. Here the Council teaches that the word incarnate, Jesus the Christ, has revealed to us that God is love. By his life and teaching he has shown that love is the only way that leads to universal brotherhood. Love for Jesus is not something which is reserved only for important matters. It is something which "must be pursued chiefly in the ordinary circumstances of life." Christ himself has shown by his life that love can lead to the cross. However, "Christ is now at work in the hearts of people through the energy of His Spirit." This Spirit is making it possible for people to put aside all love of self and to devote themselves with all their energy and resources to working to bring about that future "when humanity itself will become an offering acceptable to God." Although it is true that we have no lasting city here, "the expectation of a new earth must not weaken but rather stimulate our concern for cultivating this one. For here grows the body of a new human family, a body which even now is able to give some kind of foreshadowing of the new age." Although the Council cautions against equating earthly progress with the growth of the kingdom, it states nonetheless that "to the extent that the former can contribute to the ordering of human society, it is of vital concern to the Kingdom of God." What we do here is taken up into the kingdom and purified. Thus our lives here are part of the fabric of the kingdom. "For after we have obeyed the Lord, and in His Spirit nurtured on earth the values of human dignity, brotherhood and freedom, and indeed all the good fruits of our nature and enterprise, we will find them again, but freed of stain, burnished and transfigured. This will be so when Christ hands over to the Father a kingdom eternal and universal" (*GS*, 39). The Council sees a new humanism at work in the attempt people are making in the world to master the major problems of humankind, whether those efforts pertain to war and peace, the economy, politics, justice, international relations, culture, marriage, and so on. Furthermore, the Council provides certain warrants for this secular commitment. These include: the fundamental goodness of creation, the dignity of the human person, "the diaconate of charity, 'recapitulation' in Christ, his example, and the cosmic relevance of the Resurrection" (AA7; *GS*, 43, 45, 58).[5] As I have already indicated, this sense of optimism, realism, and the necessity of the "worldly" reality which comes out of the Council is in stark contrast to the pessimism of the moral manuals which viewed the world and human beings with mistrust. For these manuals the world as a whole was synonymous with danger, "hence the incentives to *fuga mundi,* flight from the world."[6]

It bears remarking that the Church has always worked for the good of the world in one way or another. So in that sense the Second Vatican Council introduced nothing new or different. What is really different about the Council is the way it makes Christians understand that the world is not synonymous with evil and depravity but is rather a legitimate and good field of human activity which Christians can and must be part of to be authentically human and Christian. The change here is both in substance and tone. The Christian must engage the world because it is good, it is our home, and God expects everyone to make it a habitable home for all. The Christian has a lot also to learn from the rest of the world as he or she journeys to the kingdom of God.

So much has been written of other ways in which the Council introduced a fresh and different tone into moral theology than was previously the case. Scholars have pointed out the Council's regard for particular cultures and situations, its stress on the historicity of human institutions and laws, its stress on the balance between the personal and social dimensions of morality, and its disdain for legalism in all its forms. Here, for example, is how Antonio Moser and Bernardino Leers put the matter: "Vatican II, not in a few texts but in all its texts, not in its texts alone but in its whole context, in this way lent fresh impetus to efforts at surmounting a whole series of characteristics: eternalism—through the principle of historicity; dualist pessimism—through recovering confidence in the human race; terror of sin—through confidence in grace; legalism—through stressing the theme of the covenant; privatism—through assigning value to earthly realities."[7] However, apart from the general tone which it created in contradistinction to what was there before, the Second Vatican Council also made certain specific contributions to moral theology as theology through its specific teachings in the areas of fundamental theology. The Second Vatican Council was very much an ecclesiological council. As such, what it says about the Church is essential to understanding what it teaches about morality in its various ramifications. The Council's teaching on fundamental theology is enormous and not really part of what can be called the moral doctrine of the Church. Therefore, we are interested here with only those aspects of this teaching which have had considerable impact on the development of moral theology since the Council finished its work in 1965.

The Ecclesiology and Fundamental Theology of Vatican II

Since Vatican II, moral theology has embraced ecclesiology rather closely. Although this closeness was exacerbated, as we will see, by the debate which was engendered by the publication of *Humanae Vitae,* much of that debate was carried on in terms supplied by the Second Vatican Council itself. The Council's description of the Church is indeed significant. It describes the Church as a sacrament, a sign and instrument of humanity's communion with God. The Spirit guides the Church in the way of all truth, unites it in fellowship and ministry, and bestows upon it different hierarchical and charismatic gifts (*LG,* 4). In the second chapter of the Dogmatic Constitution on the Church, *Lumen Gentium,* the Council describes

the Church as the new Israel, made up of both Jews and Gentiles. It is the
new people of God, made up of those who believe in Christ. Those who
believe in Christ are reborn through the word of the living God and from
water and the Holy Spirit. Thus, they are established as "a chosen race, a
royal priesthood, a holy nation, a people for his possession . . . who in
times past were not a people, but now are the people of God" (1 Pet
2:9–10). The people of God "possess the dignity and freedom of the
daughters and sons of God"; its destiny is the kingdom of God. The people
of God is "the seed of unity," the hope and salvation of the whole human
race, "the instrument for salvation of all," sent into the world as "the light
of the world and the salt of the earth" (*LG,* 9). The baptized, by regenera-
tion and the anointing of the Holy Spirit, "are consecrated as a spiritual
house and a holy priesthood" (*LG,* 10). The Council also stresses the
common priesthood of all the faithful: "The common priesthood of the
faithful and the ministerial or hierarchical priesthood are none the less
interrelated; each in its own way shares in the one priesthood of Christ"
(*LG,* 10).

The people of God—that is, the whole body of the faithful who have
received an anointing which comes from the Holy One (see 1 Jn 2:20,
27)—cannot be mistaken in belief. Such infallibility is manifest when
"from the bishops to the last of the faithful" the people "manifests a universal consensus in matters of faith and morals" (*LG,* 12). The Council
uses several metaphors to describe the Church: the Church as sacrament,
the Church as servant, the Church as collegial, the Church as ecumenical,
the Church as an eschatological reality, among others.[8] The collective result of these ways of expressing the reality of the Church marks a departure from much of pre–Vatican II ecclesiology. Here is how Edward
Schillebeeckx describes the notion of the Church which was prevalent before the Second Vatican Council. The Church, he says, was construed in a
Neoplatonic-hierarchical manner. In this conception, "the Church forms a
pyramid, a multi-stage system: God, Christ, the pope, the bishops, priests,
deacons. Below these were the religious and then the laity; first were the
men and finally the women and the children."[9] By speaking of the Church
in concentric terms as people of God, with Christ at the center, rather than
in pyramidal terms, the Council showed another face of the Church. As
Schillebeeckx points out, it is only after talking of the people of God on
the way to consummation does the Council take up consideration of the
various particular elements which constitute the organic structure of the
people of God. Thus, "the differentiations in ministry among the people of

V2 - concentric
s - a crisis : hierarchy still there

God do not affect the rights of the people of God as the objects of being-the-church. All ministries are there for the people, as service."[10]

The Church's mission can be hindered or helped by its self-understanding. Theologians have also written extensively on some of the implications which the change from a pyramidal to a more concentric understanding of the Church entails for moral discourse. Richard McCormick points out, for example, that the very self-definition of the Church can be tremendously influential in determining the nature and function of moral argument. McCormick believes that "if the prevalent notion is highly juridical, drawn up according to the pyramidal model, then this easily leads to a notion of unity intolerant of differences in moral analysis and conclusions. Arguments are viewed as wrong or unimportant because they lead to a difference of opinion at a very detailed and concrete level. In a juridical model of the Church, this is viewed as divisive and intolerable, and the analysis that led to it as somehow mistaken."[11] Thus, if the new way of construing the Church, which followed the teaching of Vatican II, has had tremendous positive impact on moral theology since the Council, it has also been a source of tremendous tensions. Some of these tensions are evident in the debates over competences: the place of the laity in the government and administration of the Church; the role of the individual conscience in moral matters vis-á-vis the magisterium of the Church; the relationship between the universal and the particular/local churches.[12] We will return to a number of these issues in subsequent chapters. The intention here is simply to note that there is still ongoing struggle to appropriate fully the insights of the Council many years after the event. This is not surprising. For, after all, we are still plumbing the depths of the Council of Nicaea and Chalcedon and other such monumental councils.

The Council also speaks of a Church on pilgrimage on earth, which has to grope for answers for many of life's problems. "The Church . . . will receive its perfection only in glory in heaven . . . However, until the arrival of the new earth in which justice dwells, the pilgrim Church, in its sacraments and institutions, which belong to this present age, carries the mark of this world which will pass and it takes its place among the creatures which groan and until now suffer the pains of childbirth and await the revelation of the children of God" (*LG,* 48). Finally, and following from the above, the Council emphasizes the competence of the laity. Secular duties and activities, the Council says, are mainly the domain of the laity. They are to strive to excel in what they do and to cooperate with other people who have the same objectives.

It is their task to cultivate a properly informed conscience and to im-
press the divine law on the affairs of the earthly city. For guidance and
spiritual strength let them turn to the clergy; but let them realize that
their pastors will not always be so expert as to have a ready answer to
every problem, even every grave problem, that arises; this is not the
role of the clergy: it is rather the task of lay people to shoulder their
responsibilities under the guidance of Christian wisdom and with
careful attention to the teaching authority of the Church. (*GS*, 43)

In an early commentary on this passage, McCormick remarked that the
Council was asking theologians, directors of souls, and the magisterium to
leave "prudential elbow room for both professional lay competence and
the individual conscience in its existential situation," contrary to what obtained in the past where moral theology had been approached by many as
the source from which they could dot every "i" and cross every "t."[13] Generally, it was evident that the Council considered all believers as co-
responsible for the Church on the basis of their baptism by water and the
Holy Spirit. Schillebeeckx maintains that this co-responsibility, as envisaged by the Council, includes participation of all believers in decisions relating to Church government. The Council, he says, "also gave at least
some institutional encouragement towards making this universal participation possible: the Roman synods, the national councils, the Episcopal
conferences, the council of priests, the diocesan and parish councils of lay
believers and the frameworks of many Catholic organizations."[14]

The description of the Church which the Council gave has turned out
to be a very powerful influence on the development of moral theology in
the Church ever since. The idea of the Church as a sacrament has continued to motivate many people in the Church to see the need for the
Church to continue to search for ways to bear effective witness to Christ in
the world. A sacrament is both a sign of God's presence in the world and a
cause of salvation. A sacrament causes by signifying. And it can only be an
effective sign to the extent that it is true to the mind of its Lord and master.
One of the effects of this way of viewing the Church is the growing recognition of the need to fight all the situations and structures of sin which may
have crept into the life of the Church itself or which may have been historically fostered by the Church either actively or passively. In recent years, for
example, Pope John Paul II has found it necessary to apologize on behalf of
the Church for some historical wrongdoing which Christians had either
created or had passively acquiesced in. The pope has apologized to Afri-

cans for the role of Christians and indeed of the Church itself in the trans-Atlantic slave trade. During the Jubilee 2000 celebrations, the pope also apologized for the sins of the Church against the Jews during the Nazi era. On a trip to Greece, in 2000, the pope issued an apology to the Greek Orthodox Church for the role of the Western Church in sacking Constantinople. In short, following the Council, there has arisen in the Church a greater awareness that, as a later Roman synod puts it, "everyone who ventures to speak to people about justice must first be just in their eyes."[15]

As Josef Fuchs points out, the world as understood by the Council is a world of people.[16] And even though the Christian must remember that we have no lasting city here, he or she has tremendous obligations to the world and its peoples. First of all, the Church to which the Christian belongs is intimately and eternally linked with humanity and its history (*GS*, 1) even though it has a saving and eschatological purpose that can be attained only in the future world. The Church "serves as a leaven and a kind of soul of human society" (*GS*, 40). Although the role of the Church is primarily a religious one, from this religious mission comes "a light and energy which can serve to structure and consolidate the human community according to the divine law" (*GS*, 42). The Church is always to remain a religious institution directed toward the kingdom and in the service of the kingdom. "But the kingdom is partially realized in history, and the Council calls the Church to fulfill its religious ministry in a way that protects human dignity, fosters human rights and contributes to the unity of the human family."[17]

Another theological teaching of the Second Vatican Council which has influenced moral discourse in the Catholic Church since then concerns the understanding of the universality of the invitation to holiness, which God issues to all humanity in Christ. The Son is sent by the Father to restore all things in himself (*LG*, 2). The Holy Spirit which is the Spirit of the Father and the Son convokes the Church and dwells in the Church as in a temple (*LG*, 3). The Church is a *sheepfold, God's building, the new Jerusalem, spouse of the Lord, mother,* and so forth. The Church on account of its association with God is holy. "Therefore, all in the Church, whether they belong to the hierarchy or are cared for by it, are called to holiness" (*LG*, 39).[18] This call to holiness is for salvation (*LG*, 40). As the Council's Dogmatic Constitution on Divine Revelation puts it, revelation, the self-disclosure of God and God's purposes to humanity, is "a summons to salvation" (*DV*, 1). The Church, which is "a communion with God and the entire human race," is charged with fulfilling Christ's mission of salvation in the world. The

Church is "the kingdom of God already present in mystery," and through it, Christ's mission of salvation is continued in the world through the work of the Holy Spirit sent by Christ to sanctify the Church continuously "so that believers may have access to the Father through Christ in the one Spirit," to guide it in the way of all truth (*LG, 4*).

Although there are many tasks and forms of life, there is only one holiness and this is achieved through obedience to the Father's voice in truth and by following Christ "poor and humble in carrying his cross" (*LG, 41*). Charity "by which we love God above all things and our neighbor because of him" is the surest way to and sign of holiness. However, martyrdom is "the highest gift and supreme test of love." While martyrdom is a gift given to only a few, all must be prepared "to confess Christ before humanity and follow him along the way of the cross amid the persecutions which the Church never lacks" (*LG, 42*). Christian moral life is therefore a following of Christ on the way of the cross, an invitation to imitate Christ, who emptied himself, "taking the form of a servant . . . and became obedient unto death" (Phil 2:7–8) and for our sake "became poor, though he was rich" (2 Cor 8:9). "All the faithful are invited and obliged to try to achieve holiness and the perfection of their own state" (*LG, 42*).

The Christian moral life had for a long time been understood as comprising two separate parts—one concerned with the demands of the natural law and the life of the commandments, the other with the life of perfection. The first was studied by moral theology, while "the spiritual life" or life of perfection was the concern of spiritual theology. Striving for perfection was the calling of the religious who were vowed to the evangelical counsels as well as priests and bishops. The laity just managed to get by. The effect of this was that some Christians never seemed to think, for example, that conjugal morality, besides forbidding adultery, also imposed certain obligations and restrictions on the use of sexuality even within marriage. This was also true of the use of material things. For many centuries Christians were taught that poverty meant a different thing for the vowed religious and for the laity. It was often forgotten that all Christians were called to practice the beatitudes.

The Council's teaching on universal holiness did two things. First is the very obvious point that the call to holiness is universal. There is one holiness and not two levels of holiness as the manuals had taught. The routes to this one holiness might be divergent, but holiness remains the gift of the Holy Spirit and is realized in charity which is in conformity with the will of God.[19] "Christians are called to be holy—and nothing less. They are invited to a life of prayer and of self-giving love for God and for other persons."[20] "Loving or not, is determined by its relation to the order of persons."[21] The Council thus stresses that moral life is a unity. All the faithful are called to holiness. Whatever way this holiness is manifested, it can be founded only on a life of charity. "Love, as the perfection and the fullness of the law (see Col 3:14; Rom 13:10), directs and gives meaning to all the means of sanctification and leads them to their goal. Hence the true disciples of Christ are noted both for love of God and love of their neighbor" (*LG*, 42). In *Gaudium et Spes*, the Council further speaks of the unity between faith and praxis: "One of the gravest errors of our time is the dichotomy between the faith many profess and their day-to-day conduct . . . Let there, then, be no such pernicious opposition between professional and social activity on the one hand and religious life on the other" (*GS*, 43). The second thing the conciliar teaching on universal holiness did was to help bring moral theology and spiritual theology into closer harmony and to a greater realization that morality and spirituality are indeed two sides of the same coin. As Charles Curran has noted, the Council's call to holiness has had significant effects on moral theology since then through the insistence in recent theology on the moral growth and development of the person. In the work of Bernard Häring (and others), for example, it led to an insistence "on the importance of conversion—a fundamental change of heart and the need to deepen and grow through continued conversion." Karl Rahner developed an anthropology which distinguishes the core freedom of the person from categorical freedom. The emphasis on the subject and the person also, in Charles Curran's words, "changed the understanding of the important Catholic distinction between mortal and venial sin and the understanding of the sacrament of penance."[22]

The Anthropology of Vatican II

Another important orientation, which the Second Vatican Council provides to moral theology, is the teaching on the origin, nature, vocation, and destiny of the human person. The starting point of this anthropology is the restatement of the traditional teaching that all men and women are created in the image of God. Thus, they are made able to know and love their creator who has set them over other earthly creatures, "that they might rule them, and make use of them, while glorifying God" (*LG*, 12). God did not create us as solitary creatures. God rather created man and woman in partnership, a partnership that constitutes the first form of communion between people. The human person is thus a social being whose very development and existence is impossible if he or she does not enter into relationships with others (*GS*, 12). The Council therefore links humanity's likeness to God to the existence of humanity as male and female, or in other words, with sexuality. But this connection of human sexuality to the human creature's likeness of God "involves the fact that human sexuality goes beyond the merely natural phenomenon of reproduction, rising to the level of dialogue in psychological and spiritual love, and according to the level of a love that involves the whole person."[23]

Creation in God's image has other important implications. In the first place, the human person is a creature not the creator. As the Council says, "Men and women were created in God's image and were commanded to conquer the earth with all that it contains and to rule the world in justice and holiness; they were to acknowledge God as maker of all things and refer themselves and the totality of creation to him, so that with all things subjected to God, the divine name would be glorified through all the earth" (*GS*, 35a). I have already shown above that the Council affirms the importance of human activity which betters the world as being in accord with God's mandate to human beings to subject the world to themselves and to govern the world with justice. David J. O'Brien and Thomas A. Shannon point out also that for the Council the subjugation of all things to humans is a form of worship: "This then is the moral norm for individuals: in accordance with the divine will, they should harmonize with the genuine good of the human race and allow persons as individuals and members of society to pursue their total vocation and fulfil it."[24] A corollary point is that despite their eminent dignity, "human beings are not God and only resemble him: they are literally created in the image of God, in other words, as dependent on him, with the task of reflecting him, and therefore of being something other than God."[25] Third, the creation of man and woman in God's image has implications for human rights as well. In the Council's view, since all men and women are endowed with a rational soul and are created in God's image, "they have the same nature and origin and, being redeemed by Christ, they enjoy the same divine calling and destiny; there is here a basic equality between all and it must be accorded ever greater recognition" (*GS*, 29a). In summary, the dignity of the human person does not depend on some social convention but on God himself. All human beings share the same nature and origin—God himself—all of them, regardless of gender, race, social standing, religion, or any other particular characteristics, are destined for life with God. This is the source of all human equality and the basis of all human dignity and rights. The concept of the human person as being gifted with infinite worth and absolute value as an image of God, not only makes it possible to affirm the rights of human beings everywhere, it also makes it possible to develop a truly Christian anthropology and humanism "in which all persons are equally worthy of esteem, respect and love, especially the poorest and the weakest, and even one's enemies."[26] Human beings not only possess certain rights (*GS*, 26), they are not to be treated in certain ways, given who they are.[27]

In the order of creation, the human person is superior to other created things. Although made of body and soul, he is not a duality. He forms a unity of body and soul. He is one. The Council in this regard stresses the beauty of human corporeality. We cannot despise our bodies nor the created world in which we find ourselves in spite of the stirrings of rebellion which we feel in our bodies as a result of our being wounded by sin. The human person is superior to bodily concerns and by his interior qualities outstrips the sum of mere things. Human beings have the power of introspection. And by this very power "to know themselves in the depths of their being they rise above the entire universe of mere objects" (*GS*, 14). Human intelligence is capable of knowing truth and moving beyond merely observable data to arrive at metaphysical certitude, "though in consequence of sin, that certitude is partly obscured and weakened" (*GS*, 14).

body & soul

intellect

Human beings are created free. And it is God's intention, the Council says, that men and women should be left free to make their own decisions so that they might of their own accord seek their creator and freely attain their full and blessed perfection by cleaving to God. Human dignity requires that men and women should act out of conscious and free choice, as moved and drawn in a personal way from within, and not by their own blind impulses or by external constraint (*GS*, 17). Human beings have not always used their freedom well. Enticed by the evil one, "they have raised themselves against God, and tried to attain their good apart from him. They did not glorify him as God, but their hearts were darkened, and they served the creature rather than the creator" (*GS*, 13).

freedom

Sin is therefore a very important element in the anthropology of the Second Vatican Council. In this regard the Council speaks of an interior struggle within the human person. This struggle is between good and evil, light and darkness. It is a struggle people can win only with the help of Christ's grace. "People find that they are unable of themselves to overcome the assaults of evil successfully, so that everyone feels as if in chains. But the Lord himself came to free and strengthen humanity, renewing it inwardly and casting out 'the prince of the world' (Jn 12:31), who held it in the bondage of sin" (*GS*, 13). The effects of sin are not only individual. They

sin

affect every facet of human life and activity and can be seen everywhere—in a disordered hierarchy of values where good and evil intermingle, and in the self-centeredness of individual persons and societies. "So it is that the earth has not yet become the scene of true amity; rather, humanity's growing power now threatens to put an end to the human race itself" (*GS*, 37). Even though damaged by sin, human freedom is still an essential constituent of the human person. However, only with the grace of God can we bring our relationship with God, and thereby with the whole of creation, to full flower. Gregory Baum faults the Council's teaching on sin as incomplete in some ways. He points out that while the Council acknowledged the presence of personal sin in society, especially in the neglect of the poor, it said hardly anything about social sin, the structural result of past and present personal choices. He argues that since it is people who create ghettos and encourage racism, sexism, homelessness, and the spread of disease through their choices, neglect, and inattention to certain negative trends which eventually turn into oppressive and dehumanizing conditions and into structures of injustice, the Council could have done more to identify and condemn such existing conditions.[28]

Rounding off the list of anthropological constants, as the Council sees them, is the fact of death. The human being is a creature that experiences the dissolution of his being by death. As the Council puts it, in the face of death the riddle of human existence becomes even more acute. This anxiety over death is not calmed by technological advancement, for the prolongation of biological life cannot satisfy that desire for a higher life which is inescapably lodged in the human heart (*GS*, 18). Although the mystery of death utterly beggars the imagination, says the Council, "the Church has been taught by divine revelation, and herself firmly teaches, that the human person has been created by God for a blissful purpose beyond the reach of earthly misery" (*GS*, 18).

The impact of the Council's teaching on the human person on moral theological discourse has been tremendous. Since the Council, more attention has been focused on the dynamic of moral growth and development of the human person. Sinfulness is mostly understood in a new way: as a fundamentally negative orientation toward the Supreme good—God. In moral decision processes, there have also been tremendous efforts to base the determination of moral norms not merely on the realm of nature but on a consideration of the integral good of the whole human person in his or her dimensions. This stress on the integral good of the human person is certainly one of the greatest contributions of the Council to moral discourse in the Catholic tradition in recent times. We will return to this issue later in chapter 10.

The Moral Teaching of Vatican II — content

In this section I will try to piece together some elements that can be said to constitute the teaching of Vatican II in the area of fundamental moral theology. I will mention a few of these elements in what follows. Whereas we dealt with orientations in the preceding sections, here we are dealing with content. A very important teaching of the Council is on love. Christian morality as a response morality starts with the basic premise that God is love (1 Jn 4:8). The law of love is "the basic law of human perfection and hence of the world's transformation" (*GS*, 38). The way of love is the means to universal communion. Love is not something to be reserved for very special occasions but must be pursued in the ordinary circumstances of life. The faithful have a lofty vocation and obligation "to bring forth fruit in charity for the life of the world" (*OT*, 16). Christians engaged in modern economic and social affairs are required, in obedience to Christ, to seek first the kingdom and to draw from the kingdom the motivation "for helping all their brothers and sisters and for accomplishing the task of justice under the inspiration of charity" (*GS*, 72). There are two issues to note quickly here. The first is that the conciliar teaching on the centrality of love in the moral life was a hard-won battle against those like Frs. Hürth, S.J., Gillon, O.P., and Lio, O.F.M., who had been asked to prepare the pre-conciliar schema *De Ordine Morali*. Not only was there no mention of charity in this text, following the well-known opposition of casuistic moral theology to the inclusion of this concept in the study of moral theology; but the authors expressed a fear that "a moral theology of charity would mean no more than verbalism, sentimentalism and an abandonment of moral precepts."[29] These authors lost out to the fathers of the Council themselves who taught that the Christian moral life must bear fruit in love. The second point is that the conciliar insistence on the importance of love in moral theology reflects the impact of a new generation of moral theologians in the Church just before the Council. The most influential work in this was *The Primacy of Charity in Moral Theology*, by the French Jesuit Gérard Gilleman, who was a professor at the Jesuit faculty of theology in Kurseong in India. This book, which was in fact the author's doctoral dissertation, which he had presented to the Institut Catholique of Paris, had appeared in French in 1954 and was later published in English in 1959. The thesis of Gilleman's book was that "we can draw from the New Testament and Tradition a core of teachings and of practical attitudes which reveal a certain spirit, a vital moral choice, the source of all further systematization." The very soul of the moral life is expressed "in the fundamental law of love." Gilleman laments that this truth had been neglected by the classical treatises (the manuals) of moral theology. Gilleman's express aim in his book was therefore "to work out a method of exposition in which charity will play the role of a vital principle" in the moral life,[30] that is, to formulate a Christian morality "which will always be kept under the primacy of charity." Gilleman did not claim that his insights were entirely new. He thought of his work as an attempt to rediscover the hidden treasures of the Catholic moral tradition which lie hidden beneath the rubble of the more recent manualist tradition. Gilleman's book, along with Bernard Häring's three-volume *The Law of Christ* (1961–1966), were the most widely read moral theology texts in the years immediately before, during, and after the Council.

The teaching of the Council on love has had a major impact on the Church since Vatican II through the Council's teaching on marriage and has provided the frame of reference for the postconciliar debate on contraception by recasting the relationship of the unitive and procreative dimensions of sexuality. An important contribution of *Gaudium et Spes* to this debate is summarized in the following famous lines from the document: "When there is a question of harmonizing conjugal love with the responsible transmission of human life, the moral aspect of any procedure does not depend solely on sincere intentions or on an evaluation of motives. It must be determined by objective standards. These, based on the nature of the human person and his acts, preserve the full sense of mutual giving and human procreation in the context of love" (51). This passage has been variously interpreted. And, depending on the interpreter's frame of mind, it has been used to support either a more permissive view of contraception or a more restrictive one. Whatever be the case, however, there is unanimous agreement that this passage decisively cast the consideration of marriage and human sexuality in more personalist terms than had been done previously. The morality of human relationships was to be determined on a much wider canvas than on simply the human act. Love was at the center of all human relationships including marriage and sex.

The Council reminds us how interconnected we are, especially in our families. Thus the well-being of everyone is connected intimately with the healthy state of marriage and family. It notes, however, that many facts of life obscure the beauty of marriage and thus blur its capacity to be a locus for human nurturing and growth. *Gaudium et Spes* mentions some of these as polygamy, divorce, free love, adultery, selfishness, pleasure-seeking, and wrongful practices against having children. The Council speaks of Christian marriage in these terms: a covenant, brought about by an irrevocable consent, an intimate sharing of life and love, instituted by the creator and regulated by God's laws; a stable institution made so by divine ordinances, establishing a bond which is not dependent on human decision. Marriage is endowed with various values and purposes and is aimed at the good of the couple and their children. Marriage is vital for the continuation of the human race and necessary for the personal development and eternal destiny of the individual members of the family. As an intimate union of man and woman, in marriage a man and woman are no longer two but one flesh. Thus marriage creates an indissoluble union. Marriage is directed to the begetting and upbringing of children. Marriage requires complete faithfulness between partners. Marriage is blessed by Christ and made by him to be a reflection of his union with the Church. In matrimony, God encounters Christian couples. God abides with them and helps them to love each other with everlasting fidelity in their dedication to each other. Marriage is a sacrament which sanctifies the Christian partners to fulfill their duties as parents and to attain perfection. The Council also speaks of the role of children in marriage. They are a gift from God, the supreme gift of marriage. Thus, marriage as a means for transmitting life is also an important aspect by which couples cooperate with God in the work of creation. Thus, the Council urges parents to realize that in regard to transmitting life they cannot just do as they please. They must rather make their decisions before God and be ruled by a conscience which is in conformity with divine law.

One of the important points made by the Council was its insistence, almost contrary to Augustine, that marriage is not instituted just for procreation. There is more to marriage. It is instituted for love. Sex in marriage is also for expressing love for each other. It is in this regard that *Gaudium et Spes* speaks of marriage as an intimate communion of life and love. It is a sharing. It is a communion. It retains its beauty, and it remains a communion of love even if children are not coming. In other words, infertile marriages are no less marriages just because there are no children involved.

The teaching of the Council on the centrality of love in marriage has not been easy to absorb in all its aspects. Theodore Mackin has shown some of the legal struggles following the Council and in the course of the

revision of the canon law to incorporate the teachings of the Council into
canon law. In pursuance of the spirit of Vatican II, the new code does not
speak of marriage in terms of ends, as was the case, following Augustine,
before the Council. It tries to incorporate the concepts of covenant while
retaining the idea of contract in its description of marriage. Understanding
and incorporating the Council's theological/pastoral visions of marriage
into the language of the law has not been easy for the lawyers and judges in
the Church's courts. Two important problems have troubled them. First,
whether the Council did indeed intend its understanding of marriage as
community of life and love to be part of the legal language of the code of
canon law. If this is so, what is it that anyone who enters into marriage
must share and must be able to share to contract marriage validly? The
second problem is how to understand the notion of the consent that creates marriage. If it is consent that creates this community of life and love,
can consent once given be withdrawn, and can marriage once validly established by a free consent go out of existence because the parties to the
marriage have withdrawn their consent as a result of the death of love in
such a situation?[31] These questions arose from real-life cases. In one of
these cases a lower ecclesiastical court in Utrecht, Holland, ruled that "according to the teaching of the bishops at Vatican II in *Gaudium et Spes,* a
marriage is an intimate community of life and of married love. Therefore,
because both the community can disintegrate and the love can erode and
vanish, the marriage itself can erode, disintegrate and come to an end."[32]
This ruling was overturned subsequently by a higher court, the signatura.
In reversing the ruling of the lower courts, the signatura emphasized the
act that creates a marriage and the object that this act bears upon.

> It is a bilateral and free act of the will, in the nature of the contract, al-
> beit unique, of its kind. It is also in the words of *Gaudium et Spes* "a
> marital covenant of irrevocable personal consent." The object of this
> consent is the spouses themselves: "The human act by which the part-
> ners mutually surrender themselves to one another." To say this an-
> other way, the persons of the spouses, under the specific marital
> aspect, constitute the object of consent. It is the nature of this consent
> that once it has been legitimately posited it produces its effect once for
> all, the juridical effect of giving and surrendering. This effect contin-
> ues throughout the entire life together of the spouses, independently
> of and impervious to any subsequent revocation on the part of the
> spouses. This effect, understandable also as a bond, does not cease to

exist if later love between the spouses ceases, or if the intimate communion of life and marital love, with its so-called existential nature,
ceases.[33]

same source, diff. conclusions

It is instructive that both of these rulings try to find justification from
the Second Vatican Council and indeed from the same passages in *Gaudium et Spes*. The way these various ecclesiastical courts ruled on this issue
after the Second Vatican Council in contradiction to each other reflects the
tension in the teaching of the Council itself on marriage and shows how
untidy some aspects of the Council's teachings really are. This untidiness
is reflected as well in many other positions which claim warrant from the
Second Vatican Council on some contentious theological questions in recent times.

A second important element in the conciliar discussion of morality *CONSCIENCE*
pertains to conscience. The conciliar teaching on this question is very traditional and comes right out of the work of St. Thomas Aquinas. In
Gaudium et Spes, the Council speaks of conscience as the concrete call to
what is good and as inner light, which aids human persons to discover "a
law, which they have not laid upon themselves." Conscience is the tribunal that teaches people to obey this law which is inscribed in human
hearts by God. In line with traditional Catholic teaching, the Council asserts the existence of an objective moral law the essence of which is to do
good and avoid evil. The dignity of all human beings rests in their observ-
ing the law inscribed in their hearts. It is by these laws that all human beings shall be judged. People encounter God in their consciences, which
the council refers to as their most secret core, their sanctuary. "There they
are alone with God whose voice echoes in their depths." Loyalty to conscience is said to be the common ground on which Christians join others
in the search for truth and for the right solution to so many problems that
arise both in the lives of individuals and from social relations.

A correct conscience is an antidote against group egotism and individual bad choices, so to speak. It is indeed a guide to conformity to "the
objective standards of moral conduct." However, conscience can go astray
for several reasons. Conscience can be misguided due to invincible ignorance. In this case it does not lose its dignity. The case is different where
persons take little trouble to find out what is good and true "or when conscience is gradually almost blinded through a habit of committing sin"
(*GS*, 16). In the *Declaration on Religious Freedom* the Council speaks of the
dignity of each individual to follow his or her conscience faithfully "in

every sphere of activity so that they may come to know God who is their last end." Thus the individual has a right not be forced to act against his or her conscience especially in religious matters (*DH, 3*).

The conciliar teaching on conscience must be considered against the stress in Catholic theology on the law of God as the norm by which human life and conscience itself will be judged.[34] As Charles and Maclaren point out, there is an understanding of a moral law which is eternal, objective, and universal. By this law, "God orders, directs and governs the whole world according to a plan conceived in his wisdom and love." In line with traditional Catholic teaching, the Council also assumes that the human person participates in the divine law in a way suited to his nature—that is, through natural law. Thus, for example, after speaking of the divine law in the third paragraph of *Dignitatis Humanae* as eternal, objective, and universal, and as a means by which God governs and directs the whole world, the Council asserts that God has enabled the human person to share in this law, so that "under the gentle disposition of divine providence, many may be able to arrive at an even deeper knowledge of unchangeable truth" (*DH, 3*). In this same document, the Council also speaks of "the principle of the moral order which springs from human nature." The point here is that the Council continues the traditional teaching on natural law as the participation of the human person in the divine objective and universal law, a teaching that evokes the thoughts of St. Thomas Aquinas on the same subject.[35] It should also be noted that while the Council stresses the need for the human person to follow his conscience, as well as the right of conscience to freedom of thought and expression, it states, within the same vein, that conscience is regulated by the law of God which is the norm that regulates human life and activity. "Conscience is by definition subjective. It may honestly tell me to do what is in fact against God's law. If so, it must be followed. But Christians should strive to do God's will, not their own."[36]

If conscience is the proximate norm of morality, then, there exists an objective moral order from which conscience must draw. For example, we saw above that in speaking of the right use of marriage, the Council asserts that "when it is a question of harmonizing marital love with the responsible transmission of life it is not enough to take only the good intention and the evaluation of motives into accord: Objective criteria must be used, criteria drawn from the nature of the human person and human action" (*GS, 51*). This objective moral order is knowable to any human being in any place or time. Thus, anyone with a properly formed conscience can come to knowledge of truth. The Church has a special place in the formation of conscience of the faithful, and since the Church is, by the will of God, the teacher of truth, the faithful are bound to pay careful attention to her teaching. It is the duty of the Church "to proclaim and teach with authority the truth which is Christ's and, at the same time, to declare and confirm by her authority the principles of the moral order which spring from human nature itself."[37] As we will see in subsequent chapters in this book, one of the most contentious issues in recent Catholic moral theology has had to do with the relationship between the individual conscience and the Church as teacher of truth.

There is another aspect to the teaching of the Council on the freedom of religion which is interesting because it seems to break new ground. This is the teaching on religious freedom. In the second paragraph of *Dignitatis Humanae,* the Council states: "All human beings, because they are persons, that is, beings endowed with reason and free will and therefore bearing personal responsibility, are both impelled by their nature and bound by a moral obligation to seek truth, especially religious truth" (*DH,* 2). The "especially" here is important for two reasons. It indicates, first, that the right to seek the truth, though a right that pertains eminently to religion, does not stop there. Second, it helps establish the duty to seek religious truth as a moral norm. This moral norm is predicated on two things: the dignity of the human person, and the nature of the act of faith. The first falls to natural law, in the sense that the common principles of morality knowable by all are grounded in an understanding of the human agent as intelligent and free. To be a moral act, an act must be human—that is, it must proceed from human reason and will. Thus, what makes an act moral is that we know what we are doing and we freely do it. Any serious lack on the side of either freedom or knowledge makes an act the act of a person, not a human act. The same goes for faith. Faith that is forced is no faith. It is faith only when it proceeds from free human volition. The right to seek religious truth leads to the norm to live by that truth when it is found. One who grasps the nature of faith and freely refuses it condemns himself. Those who do not grasp it do not reject it as such, and their ignorance may not be culpable.

The teaching of the Council on religious liberty gives rise to a normative question: Do people have a right to force others in religious matters? Does political society have a right to use its power to force a religion? Forty years after the Council these questions are still very pertinent in many parts of the world, especially in some Islamic countries where there seems to be an increasing tendency in recent times to force people to convert to the faith and to use the powers of coercion available to the state to force people to convert to the faith. The difficulty in answering these questions arises from the fact that although political society is not justified in commanding religious belief, there can be extreme situations where for reasons rooted in the nature of the good of religion itself, a religious community can be prevented from conducting its affairs. The Second Vatican Council itself teaches as follows: "The practice of religion of its very nature consists primarily of those voluntary and free internal acts by which human beings direct themselves to God. Acts of this kind cannot be commanded or forbidden by any merely human authority."[38] Political community may therefore not use its power of coercion to command religious allegiance or to impede religious activity. But that is not all. "Political authority," as Joseph Boyle points out, "is morally obliged to create the social space for people to fulfill their moral obligation to seek the truth in religious matters and live accordingly." This cannot be done "if political life is conducted as if a certain outcome of this inquiry—whether a particular type of belief or unbelief—were correct." Such political action, Boyle continues, "skews public life in ways that hinder rather than facilitate this inquiry, and inevitably and unfairly coerces some to support actions whose rationales are incompatible with deep elements in their worldview."[39]

Finally, the most important statement of the Council on moral theology is the now-famous call of the Council for the renewal of moral theology. The conciliar directive was issued as part of a larger call for the revision of ecclesiastical studies for clerical students in the seminary. Theological studies in the seminaries have to be preceded by a reasonably thorough immersion in the humanities, including philosophy, and the sciences so that "with a proper understanding of the present age, they will be equipped for dialogue with people of their time" (*OT,* 14). Speaking of theological studies, the Council gives pride of place to Scripture, which it refers to as the soul of the theology in the theological curriculum. Students should be carefully initiated into exegetical method and be made to "study closely the main themes of divine revelation and find inspiration and nourishment in daily reading of the sacred books and meditation of them." Next, the Council discusses dogmatic theology. Here as well, scriptural themes come first, and the overall goal is to teach students "to use the light of divine revelation in seeking the solution to human problems, to apply its eternal truths to the changing condition of human life, and to communicate these truths in a way the modern world can understand." Then come the now-famous words about moral theology: "Special care is to be taken for the improvement of moral theology. Its scientific presentation, drawing more fully on the teaching of scripture, should highlight the lofty vocation of the Christian faithful and their obligation to bring forth fruit in charity for the life of the world" (*OT,* 16).

This rather terse passage on moral theology speaks volumes. First of all, it contains a programmatic intent on the part of the Council fathers regarding which direction postconciliar moral theology must take. Moral theology must be scientific. In other words, it must employ, in its own way, acceptable standards of academic inquiry. Like all other branches of theology, it must not lose contact "with its own times" but rather, by collaborating with other fields of learning, it may help lead people "to a deeper knowledge of the faith" (*GS,* 62). Second, the Council stresses the need for a Scripture-based ethic. This means that sacred Scripture should determine the fundamental orientation and conception of moral theology. "It would appear, too, that the Council had in mind not just a scriptural moral theology but rather a basically scriptural outlook that would guide and permeate it. In this way the desired connection with the mystery of Christ and the history of our salvation would be suitably effected."[40] A third related component of the conciliar injunction is the stress on the Christ-centeredness of moral theology. Lastly, the Council spoke of the goal of moral theology as making explicit in a scientific way the vocation of the Christian, which is to bear fruit in charity for the life of the world. Josef Fuchs summarizes the Council's injunctions this way:

> The Council requires that moral theology shall be taught not only and not primarily as a code of moral principles and precepts. It must be presented as an unfolding, a revelation and explanation, of the joyful message, the good news, of Christ's call to us, of the vocation of believers in Christ. This means that Christ and our being-in-Christ are to be its center and focus; the fundamental characteristic of Christian morality is a *call,* a vocation, rather than a *law;* Christian morality is, therefore, responsive in character; it is a morality *for Christians;* its *exalted nature* must be made clear in the manner of its presentation.[41]

In an article written shortly after the Council to explain the conciliar position on moral theology, Josef Fuchs pointed out that for the Council, God is the goal and end of the human person and therefore "the ultimate basis of moral norms and obligations." A Christ-centered moral theology should thus bring out "the fullness and richness of the relationship between God and man-in-Christ." As a theological discipline concerned with the vocation of the faithful to follow Christ, moral theology has the task of explaining "that man is called personally in Christ by the personal God." This call is a gift from God for our salvation. But it implies, on the other hand, "a life conformable to salvation, a life actuated by that perfect love which characterized the life of Christ, and it obviously implies also those Christian activities through which each of us, according to his situation, strives for perfection in Christ."[42] It is God who takes the initiative in his relationship with us. We respond to this initiative by the quality of our lives and by this ensure a constant dialogue between God and ourselves. The notion of morality as being responsive conveys the fact that moral theology is concerned with more than bare compliance with a set of moral principles. Moral theology must of course teach "everything that goes to the making of the Christ-like life—obligations deriving from general principles and obligations arising from claims on particular individuals." However, says Fuchs, that is not the reason it should assume the character of "a hide-hound collection of laws and of neutral and impersonal obligations" as though "literal observation of such obligation was all that was necessary to be a good Christian."[43]

The moral theology that the Council wanted to see, according to Fuchs, is one that would explain and illustrate the Christian's high vocation in Christ and what this implies in practice. This moral theology although Christian is the one morality there is for all human beings because "man according to all God's decrees, is simply and solely man called in Christ. It is merely incidental that not all of mankind know and accept the divine call with the same explicitness." Non-Christians share both the "natural" and the "supernatural" contained in Christian morality. Christians, in other words, are merely custodians of a common human patrimony to which all peoples, even atheists, have a right, even if they are not conscious or capable of perceiving the grace that flows to them through Christ. It is thus the task of the moral theologian, faithful to the injunctions of the Council, to present the Christian moral message to everyone as a joyful message.[44]

It is the task of moral theology not only to point out the exalted nature of the Christian vocation, but also to show the faithful how to bear fruit appropriate to their vocation. The chief constituent of this fruit is Christian charity. This charity is primarily concerned with "the life of the world" in Christ, and its object is to make this world of ours a friendlier place to live in; in this way the various social virtues, "imbued with the spirit of Christian charity, will constitute the fruit of the Christian vocation."[45] In another article on the same Christian morality of Vatican II,

Fuchs summarizes the characteristic features of the conciliar teaching on moral theology in these words: "Christian morality is a morality of call-in-Christ; Christian morality is a morality of the Church; Christian morality is a morality for the world today."[46] The Council enjoins the faithful to overcome the individualistic view of morality for "the life of the world." The primary and fundamental element in the fruit of the Christian vocation for the life of the world is love for all humanity. Love of neighbor is "the very soul of all the works done by the faithful 'for the life of the world.'" It is the task of the theologian, then, to show that Christ's call to us to love the Father also means that "we must give nothing more and nothing less, for the life of the world than our love for the world and for all who are in it."[47] Fuchs is thus not only sure that there is a Christian morality, one espoused by the Council itself; he believes it is the only morality there is. All other moralities, even if they did not know it, would indeed be Christian moralities.

Fuchs would make a remarkable shift from this position later on when he began to claim that for the Council, contemporary human questions have nothing to do with "our salvation" because although they are human questions, they are part of the innerworldly behavior of the human person. He tries to make a distinction between the lived human reality, what he refers to as innerworldly behavior, and the salvation of the moral agent. As we shall see in the chapters ahead, this distinction has become a staple of his theology, especially from the mid-1970s. But whether he can read this kind of dichotomy into the work of the Council is another matter. Fuchs himself did not seem to think so in the articles he wrote earlier on the moral theology of the Second Vatican Council. In one of those articles he argued, among other things, that the Christian morality envisaged by the Council was not a private morality of the individual with Christ, or "an inner Church morality without regard for the world." On the contrary, "a right viewpoint and mastery of the world" is essential to Christian morality. Christian morality being a morality of call-in-Christ means that the vocation of the Christian is above all else gift and grace. It is also a command and a challenge "to live as one redeemed—liberated . . . and to live as one called to salvation in Christ," a fact which is meant to bear fruit in our Christian living and which determines our life "from our innermost thoughts and love to the shaping of our world-view."[48]

In this chapter, I have tried to present some of the elements of the Council's teachings that are of significance to the development of moral theology in the period under study. Some of these elements were intended by the Council itself to influence the direction of Catholic moral discourse.

Others have for various reasons since then had an appreciable impact on the development of postconciliar moral theology. Although the Council did not give a systematic treatment to moral theology, it provided some general directions along which it believed moral theology should proceed. It is evident, for example, that the Council believed there was an ethic that was distinctively Christian in origin, orientation, and content. There is a consensus as well among the pope and the fathers of the Council that the magisterium of the Church has a role in teaching morality. In short, as has been demonstrated above, there is more to the contribution of the Second Vatican Council to moral theology than providing Catholics with new and unreserved access to Scripture, the liturgy, and the spiritual and patristic traditions of the Church. There is also more to the Council's contribution than just a renewed attitude to the world.[49] Richard McCormick provides a fine summary of some of the gains attendant to and consequent upon the contribution of Vatican II to moral theology. These include the rejection of legalism in moral matters, the understanding of Christian morality as a profound personal response to God in the yes of faith, the understanding of the social character of the moral life, the centrality of the human person in moral thought, and the nature of the moral magisterium, among others.[50]

The Council has sometimes been criticized on several grounds. Andrew Greeley, for example, has argued that the Council spent too much time on institutional reform, doctrinal propositions, and sexual morality. Greeley asserts that the Council "did not produce a positive statement on sexuality and did not debate the question of human reproduction," and that it paid very little attention, if any, to catechetical style for presenting the Christian gospel to people today.[51] No one can claim that Vatican II cured the Church or moral theology of everything that ailed it. It was never the Council's intention to do so. Nor would it have been possible to do so, assuming even that it tried. However, as one bishop is reported to have said, were it not for the Second Vatican Council, "the Church would have been like the Loch Ness monster: rumored to exist, of venerable antiquity, actually seen by some, but not of much relevance in the contemporary world."[52]

And as is well known, the meaning and intention of the Council is sometimes in dispute. Moreover the attempt to construct a moral theology which is historically conscious, as opposed to one which is founded on eternalism; a moral theology which has confidence in the human race, as opposed to that which is pessimistic about the prospects of the human race; a moral theology which is built on confidence in grace, as opposed to one which is founded on the terror of sin; a moral theology which stresses the theme of the covenant rather than legalism; a moral theology which assigns values to earthly realities rather than one which stresses only private piety and sins—this attempt has not been without frictions. The rest of this book is a study of how the Catholic moral tradition has tried in recent years to rediscover itself in line with the directives of and under the impetus of the Second Vatican Council.

Humanae Vitae and Its Aftermath

Anyone who wants to study the course of moral theology in recent times must, in addition to a study of the Second Vatican Council itself, take a serious look at the effects of the birth control debate on the course of moral theology since the Council. The debate on this issue has contributed in no small measure to the development of moral theology since the Second Vatican Council. The history of the debate over the moral evaluation of contraception is well documented and will not detain us here.[1] Although the discussion on contraception is almost as old as the Church itself, this debate intensified in the twentieth century for various reasons. These include: (*a*) rapid growth in world population and the attendant fear of an overcrowded planet having neither enough food and material resources nor enough living space for everyone; (*b*) the change in the status of women, which for many women, in the Western world at least, meant a certain measure of equality with men in economics, politics, the professions, educational opportunities, and so on, since the latter half of the nineteenth century;[2] (*c*) the rising financial cost of raising large families. Children's education was becoming solely the responsibility of parents, who had to pay more for raising children and for their education. Social expectations and an increasingly technical society made it necessary for the children who could attend secondary school or college to do so in order to acquire the education needed to find work. This formal education could be expected to last sixteen or more years. It became increasingly difficult for parents to balance the theological doctrine that the primary purpose of marriage was the procreation and education of children, with the economic and personal costs of bearing and raising large numbers of children.[3]

Other factors shaping the contraceptive debate were new discoveries in biology, psychology, sociology, philosophy, and so on.[4] For example, the human ovum was discovered in 1827; in 1875 understanding of the joint role of both the ovum and the spermatozoa was also gained, and in 1923 it came to be known that "fecundation was possible only in a fraction of the menstrual cycle." These new discoveries were challenging older notions about the purpose of sexual intercourse which themselves had been largely based on clearly obsolete biological assumptions. In psychology too, there were new insights which strongly suggested that sexuality went far beyond the old theological focus on distinct genital acts to the whole of the human personality. These findings cast a new light on the interaction of persons in marriage and on the place of sexual intercourse in their relationship. In sociology and anthropology as well, new data were emerging which would force the discussion of human sexuality, marriage, and family beyond the traditional categories. And in philosophy, a personalist conception of the natural law was replacing the essentialist approach to morality. Taken together, these factors, in the words of John T. Noonan, Jr., "created a world of data and of mental attitudes different from the world in which contraception had been analyzed since the second century after Christ."

The debate on contraception also benefited from the creation of more Catholic universities, a greater flowering of theological speculation, and an increasingly vocal and educated laity which was seriously concerned with the teaching of the Church. Of even greater significance for the analysis of contraception was the voice of women. Better educated and more economically independent than had hitherto been the case, they offered testimony that was not just from the perspective of married people, "but of those who bore the children." Lastly, there was the example of other Christian churches. On August 15, 1930, the Lambeth Conference of the Anglican Church officially endorsed the use of contraception. The Anglicans were to be followed at various times between then and the 1960s by the Lutherans, the Calvinists, and other major Christian confessions. Such consensus among other Christian denominations in an age when ecumenism was being stressed was bound to be felt in the Catholic Church.

In *Casti Connubii*, the encyclical on marriage issued on December 31, 1930, Pope Pius XI responded to the endorsement of contraception by the

Lambeth Conference. The pope condemned contraception as "shameful and intrinsically immoral" because it was "against nature" as was every act of direct sterilization. Christian doctrine, said the pope, "establishes, and the light of reason makes it clear, that private individuals have no power over their bodies than that which pertains to their natural ends." And, except in cases where no other provisions can be made for the good of the entire body, they are not free "to destroy or mutilate their members, or in any other way render themselves unfit for the natural functions."[5] The pope located the ecclesial doctrine on contraception within the general right of the Church as moral teacher. This was a right given to the Church by Christ. And it includes the power to teach, regulate, and guide the human race without error in the matters of religion and moral conduct. It was the duty of the faithful to subject their minds and hearts to the guidance and teaching of the Church on all counts and in all circumstances.[6] Pope Pius XII would later add that this obligation would not be lessened even by the mode of teaching. That is, whether the matter is infallibly proposed in a solemn declaration or put forward in an encyclical through the pope's exercise of his ordinary teaching authority, it still calls for total obedience. For, argues the pope, "these matters are taught with the ordinary teaching authority of which it is true to say: 'He who heareth you, heareth me.'"[7]

As indicated above, several important scientific developments helped keep the debate on birth control alive during the period between the publication of *Casti Connubii* and the Second Vatican Council. Two of these must be mentioned here, albeit very briefly. The first development has to do with the discovery, already alluded to above, that fecundation was possible only during a fraction of the menstrual period. As a result of the work of the Japanese researcher Kyusaku Ogino (published in 1924) and the Austrian doctor Hermann Klaus (published in 1929), it became clear that ovulation occurred sixteen to twelve days before the next menstrual period. Therefore, it was possible to avoid pregnancy by avoiding sexual intercourse at the time when fecundation of the egg might occur. These studies led many people in the Church to believe that they had at last found the solution to the problem of contraception.[8] Thus, when Pope Pius XI stated that it was permissible for couples to engage in sexual intercourse, "even though, through natural causes either of time or of certain defects, new life cannot thence result,"[9] many people took that to mean a papal endorsement of the so-called Ogino-Klaus (or rhythm) method. The truth, however, as John Noonan points out, is that there was nothing in the pope's words which really dealt with systematic avoidance of births by

use of the rhythm method. It was Pius XI's successor, Pope Pius XII, how- P /2
ever, who eventually spoke of the rhythm method in a systematic way. In $+$
his famous address to a group of Italian midwives in 1951, Pius XII spoke rhythm
of the rhythm method as one which is open to all couples with serious
motives—eugenic, medical, economic, or social. On these grounds, said
the pope, the observance of "the sterile period can be licit" for couples
who want to regulate birth.[10] Pope Pius XII made other subsequent statements in which he restated his support for the use of the rhythm method
for couples who had serious reasons to avoid procreation. Noonan correctly points out that even though this papal position was not an earth-
shaking event, it marked a new attitude toward birth control in the
Church.

A second related scientific development which affected the debate on
birth control in a significant way was the birth control pill. With the development of the pill in the late 1950s the debate on birth control was re-
cast significantly. Although Pope Pius XII had condemned the pill in 1958
because it created a "temporary sterilization," some Catholic theologians
embraced the new discovery. For example, in an article published in 1963,
Louis Janssens, moral theology professor at the Catholic University of
Louvain in Belgium, maintained that the new pill acted much like the
rhythm method and was therefore not morally different from that method
which had come to be accepted by the Church. According to Janssens,
"Rhythm positively excludes procreation: it creates an obstacle of a temporary sort by exclusively choosing the time for sexual relations during
periods of sterility." One advantage of the rhythm method is that it does
not put any spatial barrier between husband and wife as all other mechanical forms of birth control do. The same is true of the pill. "It does not
destroy anything. The pill is more like the rhythm."[11]

The debate on contraception in the Catholic Church reached an important and critical point with the publication of the encyclical *Humanae
Vitae* on July 28, 1968. *Humanae Vitae* had been in the making for a long
time. Its history dates back to the now famous birth control commission
which had been secretly set up to consider the threat of overpopulation
by Pope John XXIII a few months prior to his death in 1963. This commission was subsequently enlarged by Pope Paul VI with a wider mandate
to examine all aspects of the teaching of the Church on birth control, including population, family, and childbirth, and to make recommendations
to the pope on the issue. In 1966 the commission presented its report to the
pope (or rather reports, for it subsequently became known that there was

division between the members of the commission which led to two reports on the issue).

In its final report, comprising eight short chapters, the papal commission distinguished between a selfish and sinful "contraceptive mentality," and interventions in physiological processes as an application
of objective moral criteria; and it concluded that "it is impossible to
determine exhaustively by a general judgment and ahead of time for
each individual case what these objective criteria will demand in the
concrete situation of a couple." The cardinals and bishops of the papal
commission prefaced the technical report with a pastoral introduction
in which the Church's *magisterium* was described as in "evolution" on
the subject.[12]

In short, the report urged the pope to change the received teaching on
contraception which had prohibited the use of contraception and to allow
the use of artificial birth control under certain circumstances. The report
tried to consider the question of contraception from the point of view of
the totality of the marriage—that is, from the point of view of what is
good for the marriage, and not from consideration of the sexual act or the
sexual faculty. "Therefore, the morality of sexual acts between married
people takes its meaning first of all and specifically from the ordering of
their actions for a fruitful married life, that is one which is practiced with
responsible generous and prudent parenthood. It does not depend on the
direct fecundity of each and every particular act." The idea here was to get
the pope to acknowledge the force of circumstances in the determination
of the value of moral norms, at least concerning the use of artificial contraception. John Gallagher points out that the authors of the "majority report" believed they were being faithful to the tradition by suggesting a
situationist approach to the use of contraception. "They hold that the values which the Church in the past protected by a universal exclusion of artificial contraception can now be best protected by allowing it in certain
cases." The authors seem to be distinguishing two levels of moral norms.
"On one level are basic values which are seen to endure from century to
century. On another level are the more specific rules by which values applied in particular times and situations." The teachings on this second
level are subject to change as conditions change and new information becomes available on the issue.[13] And since, in the words of the commission's
report, "moral obligations can never be detailed in all their concrete particularities," the personal responsibility of each individual "must always be

called into play." These lines of reasoning made the report of the commission unacceptable to a group of dissenters, who issued a contrary document which has since come to be known as the "minority report." This report argued for the retention of traditional teaching on birth control, as had been expressed most recently by *Casti Connubii*, on the ground that the prohibition against contraception was one which "until the present decade was constantly and authentically taught by the Church." Furthermore, it observed that "for the Church to have erred so gravely in its grave responsibility of leading souls would be tantamount to seriously suggesting that the assistance of the Holy Spirit was lacking in her." The report also reviewed the various lines of philosophical argument employed by those who supported relaxing the teaching on contraception, and it concluded that the question is not merely or principally philosophical. It is rather a question of human life and human sexuality "as understood theologically by the Church."[14]

Humanae Vitae: The Text

The document which Pope Paul VI issued on July 28, 1968, five years after the birth control commission was set up by his predecessor, basically concurred with the "minority report" by reaffirming the traditional teaching that it was unlawful and intrinsically wrong for couples to engage in any sexual intercourse "which is deliberately contraceptive."[15] *Humanae Vitae* opens by noting some of realities of the modern period which pose new and serious challenges to the Church's teaching on human sexuality. Some of these challenges are: the rapid increase in human population throughout the world, a situation which had caused many to fear "that world population is growing faster than available resources"; a new understanding of the dignity of women and of the place of women in society; a new understanding of "the value of conjugal love in marriage and the relationship of conjugal acts to this love." Most remarkable, however, was the "stupendous scientific and technological progress which has given humanity the ability to dominate and rationally organize and control the forces of nature," including "the laws that regulate the transmission of human life." The encyclical notes that these realities have given rise to a number of questions from many people concerning the validity of existing moral norms, including those which regulate human sexuality. Some of these questions the encyclical says stem from some sort of understanding of the principle of totality, asking "if it could not be accepted that the intention to have a less prolific but more rationally planned family might transform an action which renders natural processes infertile into a licit and provident control of life." The argument here, according to the pope, is that procreative finality applies to the totality of married life rather than to each single sexual act.[16] In responding to these arguments the pope takes up the doctrine of the Second Vatican Council expressed in *Gaudium et Spes* (51) on the twofold objective of the marriage act, an objective that serves to unite husband and wife and a procreative objective. He affirms that these two objectives are inseparably connected and that it is therefore unlawful to attain the former by excluding the latter. The central point of *Humanae Vitae* lies in this reaffirmation taken essentially from *Casti Connubii:* "The Church, nevertheless, in urging men to the observance of the precepts of natural law, which it interprets by its constant doctrine, teaches that each and every marital act must of necessity retain its intrinsic relationship to the procreation of human life."[17]

The teaching of *Humanae Vitae* stated here is based on the ancient tradition which asserts that certain acts are against nature. Marriage acts which are contraceptive are considered to be against life and thus against nature. They are intrinsically evil and no circumstances can excuse them. The pope adds however, that "the Church does not consider at all illicit the use of those therapeutic means necessary to cure bodily diseases, even if a foreseeable impediment to procreation should result therefrom— provided such impediment is not directly intended for any motive whatsoever."[18] He upholds the obligation of responsible parenthood by the spouse: such birth control must be generous, prudent, and can use only the rhythm method. "If there are well-grounded reasons for spacing births, arising from the physical or psychological condition of husband or wife, or from external circumstances, the Church teaches that married people may then take advantage of the natural cycles immanent in the reproductive system and engage in marital intercourse only during those times that are infertile, thus controlling birth in a way which does not in the least offend the moral principles which We have just explained."[19] The birth control methods which offend moral principles include direct abortion, even for therapeutic reasons; "direct interruption of the generative process already begun"; direct sterilization whether of the man or the woman; and finally, any action "which before, at the moment of, or after sexual intercourse, is specifically intended to prevent procreation— whether as an end or as a means." Finally, *Humanae Vitae* reaffirms the positive value of the marital act as an expression of conjugal love. In the words of the encyclical, "The sexual activity, in which husband and wife are intimately and chastely united with one another, through which human life is transmitted, is, as the recent Council recalled, 'noble and worthy.' It does not, moreover, cease to be legitimate even when, for reasons independent of their will, it is foreseen to be infertile."[20] In the closing section of the encyclical, Pope Paul VI urged priests to give sincere internal and external *obsequium*[21] to the magisterium of the Church by teaching with frankness the Church's view on marriage in its entirety. Like Pope Pius XII, he stated that the faithful were bound to obey the teachings of the Church because the Pastors of the Church enjoy a special light of the Holy Spirit in teaching the truth. And this, rather than the arguments they put forward, is the reason for such obedience.

A few things need to be noted right away. First, as a document on marriage *Humanae Vitae* was essentially a grandchild of *Gaudium et Spes*. Like *Gaudium et Spes* it speaks of marriage as the wise and provident institution of God the creator which God established to effect his loving design. "As a consequence, husband and wife, through the mutual gift of themselves, which is specific and exclusive to them alone, develop that union of two persons in which they perfect one another, cooperating with God in the generation and rearing of new lives."[22] *Humanae Vitae* lists four characteristics of conjugal love. It is human, a compound of sense and spirit, not only instinct or emotion but also and above all an act of free will. Conjugal love is total, "a special form of personal friendship in which husband and wife generously share everything, allowing no unreasonable exceptions and not thinking solely of their own convenience." Conjugal love is exclusive of all until death. And conjugal love is fecund. Here *Humanae Vitae* quotes directly from *Gaudium et Spes*: "Marriage and conjugal love are by their nature ordained toward the procreation and education of children. Children are really the supreme gift of marriage and contribute in the highest degree to their parents' welfare" (9). The spirit of *Gaudium et Spes* looms large over this text in two ways: by way of inspiration, making the encyclical view of marriage from a much wider perspective than had hitherto been the case, and by being the direct source of the teachings contained in the encyclical itself. Another noteworthy point is that *Humanae Vitae* did not teach anything new on contraception. In its main statement on contraception, it merely restates the teaching of *Casti Connubii*. The question here then is why the encyclical caused the kind of uproar it did when it was simply restating what everyone knew was the traditional teaching on the issue. The answer seems to be that the encyclical did not meet the expectations of those who believed that the received teaching on this matter was ripe for change for many reasons, including improved knowledge of human biology. We will return to this question later.

A third noteworthy issue is that there are two parallel logical structures in *Humanae Vitae* by which the encyclical supports its central claim regarding the intrinsically evil nature of artificial contraception. Let us refer to the first as the separability argument. The separability argument states that when a man and a woman are engaged in the act of sexual intercourse they are united in one body and thus one purpose—to procreate. The unity of bodies and the procreative goal cannot be separated because God has willed their inseparability. It should be noted here that the operative background premise seems to come from Augustinian theology on the ends of marriage. In this theology, we may recall, marriage has both primary and secondary ends. The primary end is the procreation and rearing of children. Anything that violates this primary end is contrary to the creator's will for marriage and thus sinful. Artificial contraception is wrong because it effects the separation of what is meant by God to be inseparable—the uniting of man and woman in sexual intercourse and the intention to procreate through this union. Another logical structure by which *Humanae Vitae* supports its ban on contraception is based on the fact that to do otherwise would not only amount to ignoring the "inseparable" connection between the unitive meaning and openness to new life, but would also ignore what has been a constant teaching of the Church on the matter. Finally, it must be noted that *Humanae Vitae* is in agreement with the position of the "majority" report and the Second Vatican Council on spousal love. However, as has already been noted, it differs from the "majority report" on whether there can be circumstances which would violate the general norm by allowing the use of artificial contraception. *Humanae Vitae* could not easily have made the break from past Church teaching on this matter. *Humanae Vitae* is in many ways, therefore, a direct refutation of many of the assertions of the "majority report," and thus it was joined in battle against many people who have since come to believe in the soundness of the position of the authors of that report.

Reactions

The reactions following publication can be likened to a theological earthquake of the most intense form. Many bishops' conferences around the world issued pastoral letters to their people either to show support for the encyclical, to suggest how the encyclical should be read, to clarify aspects of the text, or to urge restraint by the faithful in the face of mounting criticism of the encyclical.[23] While some theologians wrote in support of the encyclical, many more reacted against it. Reaction to the encyclical was so intense and so acrimonious because of the practicality of the problem of birth control, because many people felt the encyclical signaled a backtracking from some important contributions of the Second Vatican Council, and because a number of the questions it raised go to the very heart of some important dogmatic assumptions of the Church. Thus, soon after the publication of *Humanae Vitae* the debate over birth control quickly turned into a debate over almost everything about the Church and its faith. Here is how a group of theologians gathered at Marquette University in August 1968, barely one month after the publication of the encyclical, summarized the debate which the encyclical engendered:

> (1) In the areas of human understanding which are proper to human reasoning, such as natural law, what is the function of the Church as the authoritative teacher of revelation? (2) What are the sources for the formulation of binding moral doctrine within the Christian community? (3) What is the precise role of the Pope as authoritative teacher in these areas? (4) What is the role of the bishops, of the body of the faithful, and of the Church's theologians in formulating such moral teaching? (5) What qualifications may be attached to the individual Christian's assent to admittedly fallible statements of the merely fallible magisterium, especially when this involves practical judgments of grave consequences?[24]

This statement is remarkable in many ways and is therefore a good example of how *Humanae Vitae* stirred up issues which go far beyond contraception. Notice that there is no mention at all of birth control as an issue. The emphasis is on authority to teach doctrine, the extent of that authority, and the composition of the ecclesial magisterium. Birth control continued to be an issue after the publication of *Humanae Vitae*, but especially as a neuralgic center in a complex doctrinal web. One thing which was left unsaid here but which was actually brought forward by the drafters of the minority report was the question of the status of doctrines which have been taught with constancy by the Church's magisterium but which have not been formally declared infallible. Were such doctrines really open to abrogation?

What about those who have modeled their lives on such doctrine? Had the Church been in error all along? How are we sure that the present set of propositions to which the Church now gives adherence constitutes the truth? Germain Grisez and John C. Ford would in 1978 go on to argue, with specific reference to the teaching on birth control, that the teaching on this issue amounts to an infallible teaching because it met all the criteria established for infallibility of doctrine in *Lumen Gentium* 25.[25]

In order to illustrate the type of controversy which followed the publication of *Humanae Vitae* we will take a look at the case of Fr. Charles E. Curran. Fr. Curran's case is important because it leads to some of the most pertinent questions elicited by the publication of the encyclical on birth control.

The Case of Fr. Charles E. Curran

Fr. Charles E. Curran, priest of the diocese of Rochester, New York, was a professor of moral theology at Catholic University of America in Washington until July 1986 when he was told by the Sacred Congregation for the Doctrine of the Faith (CDF) in Rome that he "would no longer be considered suitable nor eligible to exercise the function of a professor of Catholic theology." Fr. Curran was subsequently removed from his teaching post at the university. Curran's case is very well documented; therefore we need not discuss it in great detail. It is mentioned here because it illustrates clearly the nature of the dissent that followed the publication of *Humanae Vitae* as well as what was at stake in the reactions which followed the publication of this encyclical.

Curran had been a seminary professor during parts of the Council. During this period, at the end of 1963, he followed closely the nascent debate over the Church's traditional teaching on birth control. He describes his preoccupation with this debate in the following words: "I followed the debates and reported on them sympathetically in an article published in the summer of 1964 in *Jubilee*. Shortly thereafter I became convinced of the need to change the teaching of the Roman Catholic Church on birth control and before the year was out wrote an article to explain my change and gave addresses on this topic."[26] Curran states that his contact with people during his weekend ministries had forced him to rethink the inherited teaching on contraception.

As a moral theologian teaching in a diocesan seminary and as a priest helping out weekends in a parish, I came into contact with a large number of young married couples. Often I was asked in those days to give talks to parish groups on questions of marriage. Likewise, many couples were sent to me by others to talk about their problems. I was jarred by the discrepancy between theory and practice. These couples who were practicing artificial contraception did not seem to be sinning. At first I had justified their position by saying that objectively what they did was sinful, but subjectively there was no sin. They were showing all the signs of a good Christian life. What was wrong with what they were doing? I was also troubled by the fact that many other couples who were trying to follow the teaching of the Church seemed to be under difficult pressures and tensions in their lives.

These experiences forced Curran to rethink the reasons which had been proposed by the Church against contraception. He found it particularly difficult to accept the natural law basis of this teaching as well as the teaching authority of the Church on the matter. In a 1964 article he stated his doubts:

> Any thoughtful discussion of the question of artificial contraception must face the question of natural law and the teaching authority of the Church. These were the two areas I discussed in that article. The teaching against artificial contraception seemed to be based on only one aspect of the human—the biological. Research for my thesis helped me to show that the Catholic teaching was proposed at a time when all thought the seed the only active element of human reproduction, so that every single act of sexual intercourse was open to procreation. Today we know that this is not true. In the section on the teaching authority of the Church I pointed out the possibility of change in the light of the change in other Church teachings and also based on the changing understanding of human sexuality and reproduction.[27]

There are a number of things to note here. Even before *Humanae Vitae* was issued, Curran had concluded on the erroneousness of the traditional Catholic doctrine which taught that the use of contraception was wrong. He was not alone in this. We have already noted the position of Louis Janssens on this issue. Nor was he alone with regard to the reasons he gave for reaching such a conclusion. Curran had also concluded that the magisterium of the Church had no particular competence over or special insight concerning issues pertaining to natural law. Finally, he had also come to believe in the right of the individual "to dissent from authoritative non-infallible teaching of the Church."[28] As Curran himself points out, this latter aspect became even more pronounced following his participation in and indeed leadership of the organized theological dissent against the papal condemnation of artificial contraception in 1968.

Prior to the publication of *Humanae Vitae* Curran had worked tirelessly "to raise enough publicity to prevent the issuance of any encyclical" on birth control. He believed that "an encyclical . . . reaffirming the older teaching would be catastrophic" because it was certainly going to meet with opposition from all segments of the Church, including priests and laity. Thus, even before the publication of the encyclical he had made plans "to formulate a response to the encyclical which was rumored to be imminent." Thus, when the encyclical on birth control was issued on July 29, 1968, Curran was ready with a response.

> On Sunday evening, July 28, it was reliably reported on radio and television that an encyclical would be issued on Monday, July 29th. The encyclical was released in Rome on that Monday morning (at 4:30 A.M., New York time). I already had contingency reservations to fly back to Washington about noon on Monday. After numerous phone calls Sunday evening and Monday morning, a meeting was set for Caldwell Hall (my residence) at Catholic University that afternoon for a group of theologians to assemble and discuss a response to the encyclical. Copies of the encyclical were promised to us at that time. Other calls were made to theologians around the country telling them that a statement would be forthcoming and asking them to sign the statement. A group of about ten theologians met in Caldwell Hall, read the encyclical, and discussed a response. I insisted that the statement could not hedge, but would have to meet head-on the question of dissent. After a fruitful discussion I typed out the final draft with help from Dan Maguire, but the whole enterprise had been the fruit of the contributions of those present at the meeting.[29]

The response Curran speaks of came in the form of the so-called Washington Declaration, which was eventually signed by over six hundred theologians. This declaration was significant especially as a precedent-setting attitude to magisterial authority in the Catholic Church and for its content as well. It both summarized the reasons for the dissent by some theologians up to that point and provided the grounds for those who in the future would dissent from magisterial teaching on birth control and other moral issues. Because this text is a critical document for understanding the problem of dissent since the Council and for assessing the course the renewal of moral theology took after the Second Vatican Council, I reproduce it here in its entirety.

As Roman Catholic theologians, we respectfully acknowledge a distinct role of hierarchical magisterium in the Church of Christ. At the same time, Christian tradition assigns theologians the special responsibility of evaluating and interpreting pronouncements of the Magisterium in the light of the theological data operative in each question or statement. We offer these initial comments on Pope Paul VI's encyclical on the regulation of birth.

The encyclical is not an infallible teaching. History shows that a number of statements of similar or even greater authoritative weight have subsequently been proven inadequate or even erroneous. Past authoritative statements on religious liberty, interest-taking, the right to silence, and the ends of marriage have all been corrected at a later date.

Many positive values concerning marriage are expressed in Paul VI's encyclical. However, we take exception to the ecclesiology implied and the methodology used by Paul VI in the writing and promulgation of the document. They are incompatible with the Church's authentic self-awareness as expressed in and suggested by the acts of the Second Vatican Council.

The encyclical consistently assumes that the Church is identical with the hierarchical office. No real importance is afforded the witness of the life of the Church in its totality; the special witness of many Catholic couples is neglected.

It fails to acknowledge the witness of the separated Churches and the ecclesial communities; it is insensitive to the witness of many men of good will; it pays insufficient attention to the ethical import of modern science.

Furthermore, the encyclical betrays a narrow and positivistic notion of papal authority, as illustrated by the rejection of the majority view presented to the commission established to consider the question, as well as by the rejection of the conclusions of a large part of the international Catholic theological community.

Likewise, we take exception to some of the specific ethical conclusions contained in the encyclical. They are based on an inadequate concept of natural law: the multiple forms of natural law theory are ignored, and the fact that competent philosophers come to different conclusions on this very question is disregarded. Even the minority report of the papal commission noted grave difficulty in attempting to present conclusive proof of the immorality of artificial contraception based on natural law. Other defects include: overemphasis on the biological aspects of conjugal relations as ethically normative; undue stress on sexual acts and the faculty of sex viewed in itself apart from the person and the couple; a static worldview which downplays the historical and evolutionary character of humanity in its finite existence, as described in Vatican II's Pastoral Constitution on the Church in the Modern World; unfounded assumptions about the evil consequences of methods of artificial birth control; indifference to Vatican II's assertion that prolonged sexual abstinence may cause faithfulness to be imperiled and its duality of fruitfulness to be ruined; an almost total disregard for the millions of human beings brought into the world without the slightest possibility of being fed and educated decently.

In actual fact, the encyclical demonstrates no development over the teaching of Pius XI's *Casti Connubii,* whose conclusions have been called into question for grave and serious reasons. These reasons, given in a muffled voice at Vatican II, have not been adequately handled by mere repetition of past teaching.

It is common teaching in the Church that Catholics may dissent from authoritative, non-infallible teachings of the Magisterium, when sufficient reasons for doing so exist.

Therefore, as Roman Catholic theologians, conscious of our duty and our limitations, we conclude that spouses may responsibly decide according to their conscience that artificial contraception in some circumstances is permissible and indeed necessary to preserve and foster the values and sacredness of marriage.

It is our conviction also that true commitment to the mystery of Christ and the Church requires a candid statement of mind at this time by all Catholic theologians.[30]

This statement was unique, as much for the fact that it was issued in the first place and in a nontheological secular paper, the *New York Times,* as for its content. A few important points from the declaration need to be highlighted for our purposes here. The first concerns the nature of the teaching authority of the Church. The Washington Declaration all but gives theologians total oversight of magisterial pronouncements. The theologians have the role of evaluating these pronouncements to ascertain their theological soundness. The declaration does not even speak of a situation where theologians and the magisterium are co-learners, with the magisterium as final arbiters of the validity and authenticity of a particular teaching because of a special charism that is particular to the magesterium as such. Second, the declaration argues that *Humanae Vitae* is not an exercise of the infallible teaching authority of the magisterium. Rather, its teaching belongs to the authentic noninfallible magisterium whose teaching is reformable because it is open to error and is indeed inadequate and erroneous with reference to birth control. Third, the Washington Declaration considers *Humanae Vitae* erroneous on three particular grounds: ecclesiology, natural law, and tradition. The declaration faults the ecclesiology of *Humanae Vitae* on the grounds that it is informed by a certain self-understanding which makes it possible for the pope to promulgate a doctrine contrary to the views of the Christian Churches, the international Catholic theological community, and the consensus of believers on the issue. The declaration considers *Humanae Vitae* to be a break from at least the immediate past tradition, notably the Second Vatican Council, on sexuality and family. Finally, the declaration faults the concept of natural law which is found in *Humanae Vitae* as inadequate, narrow, and contrary to the conclusions of competent philosophers, theologians, and the consensus of believers on the issues.

The papal encyclical, as Curran himself remarks, has continued to echo in the life of the Roman Catholic Church and "basically set the future agenda for moral theology in four important areas—sexual ethics, natural law, the existence and grounding of norms, and dissent from authoritative hierarchical teaching."[31] In the rest of this chapter, I intend to take up the discussion on sexual ethics. Questions concerning the magisterium as moral teacher, natural law, and the grounding of moral norms will be taken up in subsequent chapters.

Sexual Ethics

The criticism of the teaching on sexual ethics contained in *Humanae Vitae* can be grouped under three broad and overlapping headings: the teaching of the encyclical on the inseparability of the procreative and unitive aspects of human sexuality, the doctrine of the encyclical on the twofold "meaning" (*significationes*) of marital intercourse, and the analyses or argumentation employed by the encyclical for its conclusions. A lot has been written on these issues by many theologians since the publication of the birth control encyclical. Since it is impossible to consider everything written on these issues, I have chosen one theologian to speak for the many others who share the same view. Where necessary, I have brought in other voices for support or as conversation partners.

The Inseparability of the Procreative and Unitive Aspects

Soon after the publication of *Humanae Vitae* Bernard Häring wrote a critique of the teaching of the encyclical on the inseparability of the procreative and unitive aspects of human sexuality.[32] Because this article captures the essence of much of the criticism of the encyclical's teaching on this matter I will report it here at some length. Häring points out that the position of *Humanae Vitae,* which argues for the inseparability of the procreative and unitive elements in the conjugal act, is based on the long-standing assumption that each conjugal act is by its very nature procreative and could only fail to be so accidentally. He argues that this assumption has been overturned in recent times by the discovery that there is a certain natural rhythm which itself sets limits to fecundity and separates the procreative and unitive functions of sexual intercourse by restricting biological fecundity to few conjugal acts only. The implication of this discovery is that "the procreative good" which *Humanae Vitae* speaks of can be obtained only at times in the month—during the fertile period. This discovery led to the reluctant change in the Church's long-standing opposition to sexual intercourse in marriage when there was neither hope nor desire for procreation. Häring notes that *Humanae Vitae* affirms the positive role of marital love as an expression of conjugal love. However, he argues, when the encyclical maintains that "every marriage act must remain open to the transmission of life," it fails to take the changed historical and scientific situation of today into sufficient account. Häring argues that this expression originated at a time when scientific theories on infecund periods were limited. And in that period it was taken literally and absolutely. However, the expression refers today to a very different reality. *Humanae Vitae* teaches that the calculated use of the infertile period is not contraceptive. The rhythm method keeps sexual intercourse open by following "the natural laws and rhythms of fecundity which of themselves cause a separation in the succession of births" (no. 13). The encyclical still asserts the openness of the sexual act to pro-

Häring
on HV
↓

creation by couples using the rhythm method.[33] Häring contests this assertion. He argues that notwithstanding the fact that "the openness remains as
long as the 'laws of the generative process' (no. 13), 'the natural laws and
rhythms of fecundity' (no. 12), are observed," and considering that the
rhythm method is undertaken to avoid a new pregnancy, it is wrong to
state that every act of sexual intercourse must be "open to new life" since
scientific calculations might literally eliminate the possibility of the transmission of life during the infertile period. By endorsing the rhythm method,
the encyclical allows the exclusion of the transmission of new life as effectively as possible.[34]

Humanae Vitae confines the procreative meaning of the marital act to
the faithful observance of biological laws and rhythms, thus implying that
God's plans are revealed in the spouses through these physiological laws.
Häring maintains that it does not follow that God governs the human person through the same biological laws as animals. Nor are human beings
ruled by instincts. "The absoluteness of biological laws apply to the
human person to the extent that he knows them; he has to observe them,
even against the prodding of passion." In other words, the human person
is not to be absolutely subjected to biological laws and rhythms, but
should rather be the wise administrator of his generative faculties. Thus
even though it may be correct to assert that any arbitrary interference in
the generative process is against the natural moral law, such an assertion
does not warrant the subordination of the whole human person and the
institution of marriage to the absolute sacredness of biological laws. These
laws are not immutable. These laws are constantly subject to change.[35]

According to Häring, when *Humanae Vitae* refers to the human person
as "minister of the Creator's design," it is simply saying that the human
person must submit to biological "laws and rhythms" at least insofar as
"each and every marriage act must remain open to the transmission of
life." Thus it is not human reason but human biology which determines
whether a conjugal act is to become fruitful or not, "even at times and in
situations when a new pregnancy or total continence would destroy persons or the marriage itself."[36] Häring argues that this is wrong. He believes
that although medicine endorses interference in and even destruction of
biological functions for the well-being of the human person, "the final
perspective of an anthropologically grounded medicine is not the mere
restoration of the *organism* but the wholeness of *a person* in community."[37]
The same interest in the good of the whole person should inform the
Church's teaching on sexuality as well since the modern person thinks

more in terms of the good of the whole person rather than in terms of
absolutely sacred but often dysfunctional "natural laws and rhythms."
Häring therefore insists that it is difficult to understand the distinction the
encyclical makes between "recourse to infecund periods" and "the use of
means directly contrary to fecundation." It is hard as well for anyone to
understand how sexual intercourse can really remain open to the transmission of life when a calculated use of the rhythm method "guarantees no
new life in the marriage act." Furthermore, he maintains that it is impossible to see any moral difference between an act which interferes in the organism with a view to restoring the organism or correcting the improperly
functioning rhythm method and the responsible use of other means of
birth regulation with even less interference in the biological function. In
short, the question here is why a "pill that fixes the date of ovulation and
guarantees the loss of the ovule" should be considered "more Catholic"
than a "pill which preserves the ovule which, here and now is not needed
because procreation would be irresponsible. Should heavy and very dangerous burdens be shouldered by couples who simply cannot rely on natural rhythm while others go justified because they can operate 'safely'
within such bounds and thereby avoid pregnancy?"

Although Häring concurs with the injunction of the encyclical that
the human person should not abdicate responsibility in his sexual life and
rely instead on technology, he insists, however, that it would be wrong
only if a person were to rely solely on technology. The argument in *Humanae Vitae* runs differently because it speaks of technical means relative
to "natural processes" as destructive of the integrity of conjugal love. As
far as Häring is concerned, such a statement has no basis in human experience but rather is based on the assumption that biological laws and
rhythms best protect the dignity of the human person as well as his capacity for love, if dutifully followed. For this reason, Häring believes that
the wording of the encyclical concerning the relationship between the unitive and procreative meanings of human sexuality was a mistake which
could have been avoided had the issue been studied a little further by the
drafters of the encyclical. As it is, the encyclical appears, for example, to
let adulterers "who use the rhythm method [and] with the greatest skill
and certainty observe the biological laws and relate the unitive and procreative meaning in the unrealistic and tenuous sense of 'openness to the
transmission of life' as emphasized in *Humanae Vitae*" off lightly. This is
wrong from a personalistic point of view; the adulterers have divorced the
two meanings of the sexual act since "they do not bind themselves in a

covenant uniting the conjugal and parental vocation. Indeed, they have fully neglected both meanings while respecting the biological laws and rhythms."[38] In other words, a marriage can both fulfill the unitive meaning of sex and not the procreative aspect, and vice versa. However, both functions may be present in which partners truly consider each other as spouses and love each other in a way that would keep them open for parental responsibility, if possible. It is this general openness to procreation which should count and not the per se possibility that each act of sexual intercourse could result in a pregnancy. On the other hand, homosexual unions cannot count as a union of two persons since they are opposed to any kind of parental vocation. The same goes for premarital sexual intercourse because it separates the procreative and nurturing functions of human sexuality.

> Both the communicative-unitive good of the marriage and the good of the children impose certain sacrifices on the spouses who strive incessantly to do their best for the family. These sacrifices cannot be determined and motivated by a biological understanding of natural law or by mere respect for badly functioning rhythm. There are higher, more demanding but less frustrating criteria of "natural law." I am referring to the very nature of the persons as persons and the meaning of the acts of the persons.[39]

Thus, a couple who strive as much as possible to grow in mutual affection, to promote the unity and stability of the marriage as better to fulfill the parental vocation with regard to good education and readiness to desire as many children as they can responsibly accept, preserve the human connection between the two meanings.

Some of Häring's views here merit closer attention. First, his claim that the Church had taught that without the hope or desire for procreation marital sexual intercourse is wrong cannot be supported with credible evidence in the tradition. Although Augustine influenced Church teaching and discipline in many ways, including marriage theology, that does not make his teaching the teaching of the Church. Second, Häring's remark that the encyclical seems lenient toward adulterers if they could with greatest skill and certainty observe the biological laws which relate to maintaining the unitive and procreative aspects of sexual intercourse is a bit disingenuous. Adultery is wrong and condemnable on other grounds even if the adulterers do manage to keep together the unitive and procreative aspects of the

sexual act. Therefore, the issue of the separability or otherwise of the unitive and procreative aspects of sexual intercourse cannot in any way relate
to the question of the justification of adultery. Finally, the idea that contraception needs to be shown to be distinct from natural family planning in
morally decisive ways remains one of the hard issues on which the last
word has yet to be written. As we shall see below, many of the arguments
put forward today to show the moral difference between both procedures
appear unpersuasive. However, it is wrong to suggest as Häring seems to
do that the teaching that the sexual act "is by itself destined" for procreation means or once meant in Church teaching that the act ought to be
causally capable of procreation. If the sterile are to perform marital acts
and if marital acts are by themselves destined for procreation (not mutual
masturbation, for example), then to say that an act must of itself be destined for procreation does not and did not mean what Häring says it was
thought to mean in the tradition.

It is obvious that there are real issues about how to read the tradition.
Since one of the major contentions of this book is that much of the diversity and pluralism in postconciliar moral theology stems from rival readings of the same Catholic tradition, we will revisit this issue later in this
chapter and in the last chapter of this book. Meanwhile, we must return
to the question raised by Häring on whether natural family planning
(NFP) is distinct in any decisive way from artificial contraception.

Dietrich von Hildebrand argues that the sinfulness of artificial birth
control is rooted "in the arrogation of the right to separate the actualized
love union in marriage from a possible conception, to sever the wonder-
ful deeply mysterious connection instituted by God. This mystery is
approached in an irreverent attitude." In other words, in artificial methods
of birth control, we are confronted with "the fundamental sin of irreverence toward God, the denial of our creaturehood, the acting as if we were
our own lords." This is a basic denial of the *religio,* of our being bound to
God: it is a disrespect for the mysteries of God's creation. On the other
hand, the intention of avoiding conception through the natural family
planning method does not imply irreverence since there is no active interference to cut the link between the conjugal act and a possible conception.
"The fact that conception is limited to a short period—is itself a God-
given institution." In other words, the natural family planning method is
itself "a grateful acceptance of the possibility" granted by God himself of
avoiding conception when this is desired "without preventing the expression and fulfillment of spousal love in the bodily union."[40] The value and

meaning of the conjugal act is not affected by the couple's certainty that the act cannot lead to conception. On the contrary, the fact that conception is limited to a period of time implies "a word of God." It both confirms that the bodily union of the spouses has meaning and value in itself apart from procreation while making it possible at the same time to avoid conception for serious reasons. "The sin consists in this alone: the sundering by man of what God has joined together—the *artificial, active* severing of the mystery of bodily union from creative act to which it is bound at the time. Only in this artificial intervention, where one *acts against* the mystery of superabundant finality, is there the sin of irreverence—that is to say, the sin of presumptuously exceeding the creatural rights of man."[41]

Hildebrand's position hinges on a certain understanding of nature in which he makes a distinction between nature as "purely factual order of creation, especially material and biological creation," and nature as signifying "the essence of profoundly significant relations endowed with a high value."[42] Hildebrand tries to explain the difference between these two conceptions of nature:

> That the time between the conception and birth of a man is nine months and not eight or ten months is merely a factual datum. It could just as well be otherwise, and this fact bears no significant value. That the openings of the esophagus and the windpipe are so close together in man that one can choke easily is certainly a fact, but it is not a deeply meaningful relation which has a value. On the contrary, injuries could be averted were this not the case. But quite different, for instance, is the fact that love brings happiness. This is not something merely factual; it is deeply meaningful and bears a high value. This is also true of the fact that a deep union of two persons is constituted in mutual love. Indeed, it is of meaning and value that this reciprocal love is the only path leading to a spiritual union that is much deeper and more authentic than any amalgamation, any fusion, in the impersonal world. This fact, which is rooted in the nature of love and the personal I-thou communion, is the bearer of a high value.

The essential difference between the two conceptions of nature lies in the fact that in one "relations are deeply meaningful and possess a high *value*, and in the other they are only factual."[43] Even though both kinds of nature proceed from God and are therefore to be treated reverently, according to

value - intervention not OK

nature < fact - intervention OK

Hildebrand, nature in the factual sense is a proper area of human activity in which intervention is required and sometimes is obligatory on reasonable grounds for seeking a change when necessary. Intervention in nature in the secondary sense—that is, in the sense where "meaning and value are grounded in the essence of a thing"—is a different case altogether. In this case, "nature contains in its very meaning and value a unique message from God and calls upon us to respect it."[44]

The view of nature espoused by Hildebrand is very problematic. First, the division of nature into two aspects seems disingenuous and calculated to protect certain aspects of human activity from human reason. *dualist physicalist* Second, this theory is thoroughly physicalist. It almost deifies raw nature. Third, the division of nature into two aspects is too theoretical and neglects the fact that value is often assigned to a thing by human beings, or by human beings reading the mind of God through revelation.

Unlike Häring and Hildebrand, Germain Grisez, Joseph Boyle, John Finnis, and William E. May do not base their position on contraception and natural family planning (NFP) on nature or natural processes, but mostly on the intention of the moral agent. First of all, they point out that not all natural family planning is morally right. They note that NFP can also be chosen with contraceptive intent. It can, on the other hand, be chosen "without the contralife will that contraception necessarily involves." The difference between NFP which is contralife—that is, contraceptive— and therefore wrong, and that which is acceptable as a means of family planning lies in the intention of the couple. Natural family planning can become contralife if it is considered by the couple as a convenient way to avoid the inconvenience involved in other forms of birth control.

> To see that NFP can be chosen with a contralife will, imagine a married couple who rightly judge that they should not have another baby. But they feel that they are entitled to regular satisfaction of their sexual desire and so are not willing to accept long-term abstinence. They choose to use some form of birth prevention. Looking into methods, they find something they do not like about each of them. IUDs and pills can be dangerous to a woman's health. Condoms and diaphragms interfere with the sexual acts and pleasure. Jellies and lotions are messy and often ineffective. And so on. Then they hear about NFP. They will have to abstain a longer stretch than they would like but still will be able to have intercourse during a week to ten days each cycle. Even the abstinence will have its advantages from their point of view.

They know it will increase desire and intensify their pleasure. So they decide to use NFP as their method of contraception. For them, choosing to use NFP is not essentially different from choosing any other method of contraception.[45] *critique of NFP as one among many types of be*

Only natural family planning which is undertaken without contraceptive intent can be considered non-contralife and thus acceptable. How is NFP chosen without contraceptive intent different from NFP which harbors a contraceptive goal? Our authors provide some criteria for making such a distinction. The first step in determining when NFP is noncontraceptive and thus acceptable is to become aware of the reason not to have another baby. The reason not to have the baby must not include "the very not-being of the baby." It must include "only the burdens that having another baby would impose with respect to other goods, and/or the benefits that might flow from avoiding those burdens." Grisez, Boyle, Finnis, and May recognize, however, that the reason to engage in NFP when avoiding the consequences of a possible baby's coming to be might equally be the same reason to use contraception. The question then is how the use of contraception in such a case and the practice of NFP are different from each other.

For our authors, the difference lies not in the reason for the choices which are motivated. The difference lies in the choices which motivate "and in those choices' relationships to the benefits and burdens which such a reason represents." When NFP is chosen with contraceptive intent, the choice is made as a way to impede the coming to be of the baby "in order that the goods represented by it be avoided." When NFP is chosen noncontraceptively, the choice stems from a decision to abstain from intercourse that would likely result "in both the baby's coming to be and the loss of goods and/or occurrence of evils represented by that same reason in order that the goods represented by that reason be realized or the evils represented by it be avoided." While contraception is a choice *to do something*— against the baby's coming to be and against all the goods which could have been realized or evils to be avoided by the coming to be of the baby—NFP is a choice *not to do something*—that is, not to engage in possibly fertile sexual intercourse, "with the intent that the bad consequences of the baby's coming to be will be avoided, and with the *acceptance as side effects* of both the baby's not-coming-to-be and the bad consequences of his or her not-coming-to-be." Such a decision does not represent a choice against life because those who consider choosing to do something for a certain good but refrain from doing it in order to avoid certain side effects

do not as a result reject the good they do not pursue. In fact such a decision not to realize a good which offers of itself a reason for its realization
can be in harmony with reason.

It is apparent that two issues inform the position of Grisez, Boyle, and
their collaborators here. First, it is evident that this position presents a
philosophical rationalization of the teaching of Pius XII on the use of the
rhythm method. Recall that Pius XII justifies the use of this method on
certain eugenic, medical, and social grounds. What these authors have
done, especially in the light of later debates on abortion, is to try to exclude the possibility of co-opting NFP in the fight against life, what Pope
John Paul II would later describe as a culture of death. Second, the position of these authors must be understood against the background of their
teaching on the basic goods (see chapter 8). According to this theory, one
must not go against any of the basic goods. To engage in contraceptive
intercourse is to go against the basic good of marriage. This is wrong
because it goes against an absolute prohibition. On the basis of this reasoning it would seem more consistent to me to disallow even the use of
NFP or to avail of the infertile period altogether. Why? The reason is that
all NFP involves a certain unwillingness to allow the baby to come to be.
It is true that some particular practices of NFP might signal a greater unwillingness to do so than others. However, by allowing intentions and
motives to determine the wrongness or rightness of a particular practice
of NFP, our authors are guilty of the commensuration between goods
which they accuse the proportionalists of engaging in. For, let us face it,
NFP practiced by whatever intention is still NFP—it is materially the
same as any other NFP. If the difference in the various practices of NFP is
in the intentions and motives, as our authors suggest, what it means then
is that although all measures which prevent pregnancy from happening
are wrong, such measures might sometimes be right, given the right intentions and motives. This is the same structure of argument which proportionalists would employ to justify such a case, an argument which our
authors, as we shall see, would normally condemn when used to justify
any actions which are designated as objectively wrong.

The Meanings (Significationes) of Marital Sexual Intercourse

A second contentious issue with regard to *Humanae Vitae* on human sexuality is the question of the meaning or meanings of marital sexual intercourse. As we have seen, Häring seems comfortable with the doctrine of
two aspects of human marital sexuality, even though he is opposed to the

teaching of the encyclical that these two aspects or meanings of sex in marriage can be sundered by the use of contraception when necessary. There are other theologians, on the other hand, who reject the theory of the two significances of marital sexuality as reductionist and unrepresentative of authentic Catholic tradition. We have already noted the views of the signatories to the Washington Declaration on this. Joseph Selling, a one-time student of Louis Janssens and professor of moral theology at Louvain, has also consistently argued that the teaching of *Humanae Vitae* on the two meanings—the procreative and the unitive meanings of human sexuality—"constitutes a departure" from and represents "an innovation" in the teaching of the magisterium on conjugal morality. According to Selling, "One searches in vain to find a teaching characterized by 'constant firmness.' One finds no evidence of a teaching before *Humanae Vitae* that proposes a 'twofold meaning' (*significationes*) for marital intercourse . . . Instead, what one finds is that in light of the teaching of Pius XII on periodic continence, the so-called doctrine of the 'ends of marriage' was in shambles by the opening of Vatican II."[46] The Council teaches that marriage is a covenant based on conjugal love which is "human, total, faithful and exclusive." It also urges couples to approach the issue of fertility with generosity and prudence and in the understanding that a childless marriage is no less a marriage than one that is blessed with children. Thus, the Council put a stop to the emphasis which had characterized Catholic theology since Augustine on the "ends of marriage." One question which arises from Selling's position is this: If the ends of marriage can no longer be understood in terms of the procreative potential of marriage, what then can serve as anchor for embodying a love which is total, human, faithful and exclusive? Selling argues that the Council fathers recognized marriage and conjugal love *together* "as an appropriate condition for the realization of human procreative potential." They also recognized that "the demand to respect life . . . and the process by which life is transmitted, could sometimes come into conflict with the demand to safeguard conjugal intimacy for the good not only of the couple and their union but also for the good of any children that they had or might have in the future." When such is the case, the Council fathers propose the resolution of such conflict through what they refer to as "objective standards based upon the nature of the person and his or her acts" (*GS*, 51).[47] Such a criterion is meant, again in the words of *Gaudium et Spes*, "to preserve the full sense of mutual self-giving and human procreation in the context of true love," that is, to take into account the demands both of conjugal love and of responsible parenthood. Selling contends that the Council merely provided a skeletal structure for working out the meaning of marriage and conjugal love upon which marriage is based by teaching that conjugal love is total, faithful, exclusive, and human. However, the ways the specifics of these characteristics are to be realized are, according to Selling, left to the "worthy customs of various cultures" (GS, 47 and 48). Thus, for the Council, according to Selling, "it is marriage and conjugal love that are potentially fertile and not necessarily the individual sexual encounter. Procreation is seen neither as an end nor a purpose— nor even a 'meaning'—but rather as the 'ultimate crown' (GS, 48) or the 'supreme gift' (GS, 50) of marriage and conjugal love."[48] Humanae Vitae is thus an arbitrary attempt by Pope Paul VI to assign "meanings" to human sexuality contrary to Catholic teaching and tradition. Selling writes thus of the role of Pope Paul VI in this regard: "In his effort to ground his position on the use of contraception, Paul VI invented yet another teaching, another innovation which, rather than pushing forward the developments of the conciliar teaching, stopped the development in its tracks and resorted to a terminology reminiscent of the—now discarded—teaching on the ends of marriage. The teaching on the twofold 'meanings of sexual intercourse,' the unitive and the procreative, is neither constant nor conciliar."[49]

How many "meanings," then, does "sexual intercourse" have? How are these to be determined? Selling replies that the answer to this question has been given by many theologians at different times based on various criteria. For example, Augustine believed that there was just one acceptable meaning to sexual intercourse: procreation. Even so, Augustine himself recognized that a spouse who gives in to a sexual request from the other spouse who is requesting sex for reasons other than procreation is not committing a sin (only the requesting party is) but is rather paying the marital debt. Following Augustine, most medieval theologians added the concept of the remedying of concupiscence as another reason or meaning of sexual intercourse. Over the years, various popes have added to or emphasized the meanings or purposes of sexual intercourse in marriage. The 1917 code, for example, speaks of three primary and secondary ends or purposes of marriage. Pope Pius XI expanded the secondary ends to include "marital love" as grounds for sexual intercourse which is known to be infertile, and Pope Pius XI added yet another ground, "moderate pleasure," as a possible motivating factor for marital sexual intercourse. Selling concludes therefore that there has been an expanding understanding of the meaning of human sexuality in the Catholic tradition up until the publication of Humanae Vitae. The question then is why Humanae Vitae shrank this expanding understanding of the meaning of sexuality. Selling argues that the position Paul VI took in his encyclical on birth control was a "safe" position. This position was inspired by what the pope feared would be the disastrous consequences of withdrawing the Church's condemnation of contraception. "Without the breaks of moral questionability, it was feared that governments facing severe overpopulation would impose contraception on their people without the slightest hesitation—a scenario that is not without reason or even complimentary precedents."[50]

Selling ends with two notable assertions in contradistinction to the position of *Humanae Vitae* on the inseparability of the procreative and unitive meanings of human sexuality. First, he asserts that sexual meanings do not reside in nature or in mere physical things. Meaning is rather "the result of personal social construction that is attributed to experience uniquely by human beings. Without persons there are no 'meanings,' only things." Thus a slap in the face could "mean" any number of things in particular contexts—such as the heat of an argument, a liturgical celebration of confirmation, and so forth. Human sexuality could in fact have "meanings" which are recognized variously in different cultures of the world and are thus understandable only when one understands the context in question. Second, seen from a much wider experiential and scriptural context, human sexuality has a multidimensionality of goods and meanings. "The meanings include among others not only intimacy ('unitive') and fertility ('procreative') but also pleasure, recreation (play), relief, affirmation, receptivity, self-acceptance, forgiveness, reconciliation, gratitude and, of course, respect. They would stretch, as well, beyond the personal experience of the couple to the social, institutional, political and religious meanings that can only be appreciated in those respective contexts."[51] In short, human sexuality has "meanings" which cannot be inferred only from the physiological or biological aspects of sex. Selling believes that the Bible shows us that human sexuality always begins with relational context and is concerned with sexual behavior "only insofar as it has a bearing on the integrity of individual and social relationships." The relationality of sexual behavior is also governed by the virtue of justice and the respect of the human person and not just by biological and institutional criteria. To achieve sexual justice we need to go beyond biology and physiology to the needs of the human person adequately considered.

Selling is certainly right that the twofold signification ascribed to human sexuality is new in Catholic theology. However, this "new" insight itself involves a recognition that marriage itself involves something else other than procreation. *Humanae Vitae* uses novel language but sticks to the traditional bottom line on contraception. This is to say that while employing language which recognizes more than one meaning to sexual intercourse, the encyclical still sticks to the traditional position which prohibits contraception. Whether this amounts to stopping the development of the tradition on sexuality in its tracks is still open to debate. The conclusion that Pope Paul VI is imposing an arbitrary understanding of human sexuality on the Church follows if one shows or assumes that the traditional rejection of contraception is not itself one of the norms based on the objective standard of a person's nature and acts. Some might indeed argue that contraception is wrong based precisely on these standards. Finally, Selling notes that between the 1917 code and Pope Paul VI there was an expansion in understanding with regard to the meanings of human sexuality. This is indeed the case, as he has shown. The problem, though, is whether it is right to say that rejecting contraception in *Humanae Vitae* shrank the meaning of marital intercourse. That rejection was taken as given in these older teachings, and contradicting this part of the teaching is hardly expansion. As has already been stated, a very central issue is that of the interpretation of the tradition. Who is reading the authoritative tradition, especially as stated in Vatican II, correctly? What constitutes legitimate "expansion" or, on the other hand, illegitimate shrinkage of the tradition? We will return to these questions later.

Argumentation in Humanae Vitae

A third basis for dissent from the teaching of *Humanae Vitae* on sex in marriage is couched in terms of the rejection of the analyses which the encyclical employs for its argumentation and conclusion. In his first detailed reaction to the encyclical, Richard McCormick noted that *Humanae Vitae* considers that intercourse is a single act with two aspects or inner meanings, the unitive and the procreative, which are by divine design inseparable, so that one who deliberately renders sexual intercourse sterile "attacks" its meaning as an expression of mutual giving. He also pointed out that *Humanae Vitae's* teaching that contraceptive intercourse amounts to depriving sexual intercourse of its meaning and purpose (13) is the very basis of the encyclical's analysis and conclusion regarding the intrinsically evil nature of contraception. He notes that such analysis is not new. Since the publication of *Casti Connubii* the question of sexual intercourse as an expression of marital love had been a matter of constant debate. What had

McCormick

become clear through these debates was the incompleteness of the approach taken by *Casti Connubii*. Even theologians who supported the basic position of the encyclical had subsequently come to realize that contraceptive intervention could not be seen as a merely biological intervention but as "one which affected the very foundation of the act as procreative and hence as unitive of persons; for by excluding the child as the permanent sign of the love to be expressed in coitus, one introduced a reservation into coitus and therefore robbed it of that which makes it objectively unitive."[52] In response to *Humanae Vitae* McCormick stated that he now believed that although such analysis was indeed a genuine advance, it rested on the supposition that "every act of coitus has and therefore must retain a per se aptitude for procreation" as *Humanae Vitae* teaches. McCormick argued that the difficulty with such a position is that it was founded on an "obsolete biology" which "attributes meaning to all coitus on the basis of what happened with relative rarity." Like Häring he believed that *Humanae Vitae* itself reflects some form of contradiction when it teaches that sexual intercourse during infertile periods is legitimate even when, for reasons independent of the will of the husband and wife, "it is foreseen to be infertile." The clear implication then is that sexual intercourse during the infertile period cannot be said to be destined for procreation—because it is not possible. The procreative and unitive aspects of sexual intercourse are separable in the infertile periods, and the encyclical itself acknowledges this separation during the infertile periods. In conclusion, therefore, McCormick insists that the teaching of the encyclical on the per se aptitude of sexual intercourse as the basis for determining the moral rightness or wrongness of human action is extremely difficult to sustain. Such an approach is wrong because it determines the meaning of the act by examining its physiological structure. It is the human person, not some isolated aspect of the person which should be the basis for determining the meaning of human action. McCormick insisted that he was not questioning the fact that sexuality is founded on biological realities, or that sexual intercourse, "materially considered," has some orientation toward fecundation. Rather, he is suggesting that "the meaning of sexual activity cannot be derived narrowly from biological materialities: for this does not take account of the full range of meaning of human sexuality. It is not the sexual organs which are the source of life, but the person."[53]

One of the interesting things about Richard McCormick's position here is that it represents a total about-face from that which he held right up to the eve of the publication of the birth control encyclical. As a

HV as poor analysis based on obsolete science

similar to Cahill

younger theologian, McCormick had insisted that in exercising its right to teach, the magisterium of the Church was not bound always to come up with "persuasive" arguments in order to be believed or obeyed. In a review of Louis Dupré's *Contraception and Catholics,* he objected to the author's proposal that one could hold a dissenting position if the arguments supporting the position of the Church on the matter were unpersuasive:[54] "What if the arguments have not been and are not likely to be decisive? Is the Church muted on that account in the area of morals? Can she not take a truly authoritative position when there exist not decisive arguments but only Rahner's 'reasonable theological justification.'"[55] The point to note here is that the birth control encyclical, for some reason, seems to have radicalized even some of the most conservative theologians in the Church around the time of its publication. Considering that the teaching of the encyclical was really not new in the main, this situation is most intriguing. As we go along in this book, I will try to piece together some of the reasons for this change of heart by so many people.

Related Issues

Our understanding of human sexuality has been challenged in recent times not only by the separation of sexual expression and procreation through effective contraception, but also by the achievement of procreation apart from sexual expression through several forms of reproductive technologies, such as in vitro fertilization (IVF), artificial insemination, using either the semen of the husband (AIH) or donated semen (AID), surrogate motherhood, and possibly human cloning. These procedures and practices, like contraception, raise profound questions concerning the nature and meaning of human sexuality and of family. While *Humanae Vitae* dealt exclusively with contraception, later documents from the Vatican have tried to grapple with the challenges to our understanding of human sexuality posed by these recent reproductive technologies. In all, the principle employed to answer these challenges has been basically the same: human sexuality has a nature, a telos, and inherent meaning which the human person cannot ignore or treat with levity.

In 1987 the Congregation for the Doctrine of the Faith issued a document on reproductive technologies in answer to the requests from various episcopal conferences, individual bishops, theologians, scientists, and others, "concerning biomedical techniques which make it possible to intervene in the initial phase of the life of a human being and in the very processes of procreation and their conformity with the principles of Catholic morality."[56] Some of the biomedical techniques in question included IVF (in vitro fertilization), artificial insemination, using either the semen of the husband or that of a donor, and surrogate motherhood. The position of *Donum Vitae* is that IVF is immoral because "it is contrary to the unity of marriage, to the dignity of the spouses, to the vocation proper to the parents, and to the child's right to be conceived and brought into the world in marriage and from marriage." Heterologous artificial fertilization, or AID, constitutes an affront on the unity of the marriage, the dignity of the spouses, and their exclusive right to become father and mother only through each other because it introduces a third partner whose sperm is used in the fertilization of the egg. Homologous artificial fertilization or IVF with the husband's sperm is also wrong because it separates the unitive and procreative aspects of marital sexuality. In this procedure semen is typically obtained through masturbation. "Such fertilization is neither in fact achieved nor willed as the expression and fruit of a specific act of the conjugal union. In homologous 'in vitro' fertilization and embryo transfer, therefore, even if it is considered in the context of the de facto existing sexual relations, the generation of the human person is objectively deprived of its proper functioning: namely, that of being the result and fruit of a conjugal act in which the spouses can become 'cooperators with God for giving life to a new person.'" Artificial insemination in all its forms— that is, either with donated semen or with the semen of the husband—is morally wrong as well. The child has a right to be conceived in marriage. The same affront to the unity of marriage occurs in the case of surrogate motherhood. The Instruction characterizes this procedure as "an objective failure to meet the obligations of maternal love, of conjugal fidelity and of responsible motherhood."

Donum Vitae provides six general criteria by which the morality of the various forms of reproductive technologies can be judged. These include respect for persons, avoidance of harm, respect for the rights of the unborn child and the man and the woman as parents, and fidelity to the spouses. Thus, in consonance with recent Catholic moral tradition, *Donum Vitae* bases its prescription on the notion of the centrality of the human person in moral determination. Thus it speaks of rights and dignity of the individual human person, it speaks of promoting the integral good of the human person, and of the sacredness of life, and so forth. Lisa Cahill and Thomas Shannon argue that the crucial question is to determine what all these terms and ideas mean in the concrete. They believe that the starting point

for determining the meaning of these terms and ideas is the cultural experiences as well as the presuppositions and religious practices of the
community and the scientific information available to the community in
question. "Particularly, in the realm of specific sexual and procreative acts,
the foundation in natural law of these acts cannot remain at the level of abstract principle. It must be determined which among the specific procreative options are morally acceptable in practice and in relation to the
concrete circumstances that make some options possible and not others."[57]

A special key to the moral evaluation of the various forms of reproductive technologies which are discussed in the Instruction is found in the following passage which the Instruction takes directly from *Humanae Vitae:*

> The Church's teaching on marriage and human procreation affirms
> the inseparable connection, willed by God and unable to be broken
> by man on his own initiative, between the two meanings of the con-
> jugal act: the unitive meaning and the procreative meaning. Indeed,
> by its intimate structure the conjugal act, while most closely uniting
> husband and wife, capacitates them for the generation of new lives ac-
> cording to laws inscribed in the very being of man and woman. This
> principle, which is based upon the nature of marriage and upon the
> goods of marriage, has well-known consequences on the level of re-
> sponsible fatherhood and motherhood.[58]

*   *   *

In this chapter I have tried to discuss the impact of the debate on birth
control on the renewal of moral theology. The debate on contraception
and sex in marriage since the publication of *Humanae Vitae* has often been
acrimonious precisely because the stakes are very high indeed, not only
with regard to the teaching on human sexuality but in relation to other
issues as well, as the rest of this work will show. In the latter part of this
chapter, I tried to show that this debate as it specifically relates to human
sexuality has been waged for the most part on very narrowly defined
grounds such as the meaning/meanings of human sexuality, the analyses
employed to arrive at these meanings, and the soundness of the theological and scientific argumentation which support such conclusions. I will
try to show in the last chapter of this work how these arguments reflect
certain deeply shared assumptions within the Catholic tradition about the
human person and his or her nature, among other things. However, it

seems necessary here to point out the role of history in the debate on birth control in the Catholic tradition.

It is quite striking the way history, personalities, and the social reality of clerical and hierarchical life play in relation to the propositional and dialectical realities of arguments, Church teaching, and so on. I began this chapter by retelling the story of Fr. Charles Curran's protest activity with regard to certain aspects of the teaching of the Church on birth control. Curran was a child of the 1960s. The history of the 1960s is relevant to the debate over contraception. How much of the prevailing zeitgeist of protests and demonstrations and disdain for authority and tradition could account for the posture and style of Curran and the signers of the Washington Declaration, for example? How much of the personality of Pope Paul VI contributed to the way the encyclical was received? If he had not moved back and forth on the issue of birth control but had gone on instead to publish his views soon after receiving the various reports, would things have been different? No one will ever know all the answers to these and similar questions. In any case, I do not think that these are idle or speculative questions, considering that the central thesis of *Humanae Vitae* on contraception was already a long-held position in the Church. The document itself overall contained a refreshing advance in the theology of marriage. Under normal circumstances there should not have been the kind of uproar that accompanied the publication of the birth control encyclical. But the 1960s, and especially 1968, were really not "normal" times, as anyone who remembers the period knows.

The controversy over the teaching of *Humanae Vitae* is also concerned with history at an even deeper level. Basic to this controversy is the question of how to read the history of the Catholic moral tradition and how to read the significant authors of the past. The question is: Who do we canonize today among those ancient authors and who do we demote from their privileged positions, and on what grounds? We have seen appeals made to Augustine, to the various councils and various popes. Every one of the interlocutors believes himself to be the rightful heir to this common past, and the perfecter of our inherited tradition. This in itself is not bad. In fact, it is my contention throughout this book that such debates are indicative of a tradition that is alive. However, the question is whether there is a limit to how much disagreement any tradition can take without losing its soul, and if so, how to determine when such a limit has been reached, and who should make such a determination. We will be contending with this question in subsequent chapters of this book.

Some Theological Supports for the Renewal of Moral Theology

The renewal of moral theology has also been aided, prepared for, or supported by other developments in Scripture and dogmatic theology. In this chapter we will examine some theological developments which preceded the Council but which helped to shape moral theological discourse after the Council. Three issues are of special importance here: the movement for the renewal of biblical studies in the Catholic Church; the question of non-Christian religions; and the issue of freedom.

Catholic Biblical Renewal

The concern for the renewal of moral theology coincided with the renewal of biblical studies in the Catholic Church. The renewal of biblical studies, which had started with Pope Leo XIII's encyclical *Providentissimus Deus* in 1893, was given great impetus by Pope Pius XII in his encyclical *Divino Afflante Spiritu*, issued in 1943 on the fiftieth anniversary of Pope Leo's encyclical. Pius XII urged Catholic biblical scholars to embrace, among other types of scriptural exegesis, the historical critical method. They should, he said, "with all care and without neglecting any light derived from recent research, endeavor to determine the peculiar character and circumstances of the sacred writer, the age in which he lived, the sources oral or written to which he had recourse and the forms of expression he employed." What the ancient writers wished to express in their writings, the pope said, cannot be determined "by the rule of grammar and philology alone, nor solely by the context." The interpreter "must, as it were, go back wholly in spirit to those remote centuries of the East and with the aid of history, archeology, ethnology and other sciences, accurately determine what modes of writing, so to speak, the authors of that ancient period would likely use, and in fact did use."[1]

The pontificate of Pius XII was a golden age for biblical studies in the Catholic Church. As some commentators have put it, this period "inaugurated the greatest revival of interest in the Bible that the Catholic Church has ever seen."[2] Signs of this renewal were evident in many ways, including the new attitude from the Pontifical Biblical Commission, which had in 1941 condemned the distrust of modern approaches to biblical research among some Catholic biblical scholars. Catholic biblical scholarship had reached a nadir as a result of the modernist crisis in the Church at the beginning of the twentieth century. As a result of the restrictions put on Catholic scholarship in general following the publication of *Pascendi* and *Lamentabili* by Pius IX, Catholic biblical scholarship had neither the courage nor the resources to join the new approaches to the study of the Bible which had been inaugurated by German Protestant scholars in the previous century. For example, due to warnings from the Sacred Congregation for the Consistory in 1912 for his use of the modern critical method, M. J. Lagrange, the leading Catholic biblical scholar of his day, decided to give up further study of the Old Testament until shortly before his death in 1938. The modernist crisis left Catholic biblical scholarship in a sorry state from which it would only begin to recover in the pontificate of Pope Pius XII.

As Thomas Aquinas Collins and Raymond Brown put it, "The encyclical *Divino Afflante Spiritu* of 1943 was a Magna Charta for biblical progress . . . The stress on the use of the principle of literary forms to solve historical problems and the encouragement to make new translations of the Bible from the original languages (rather than from the Vulgate), were an invitation to Catholic scholars to begin writing freely again and to catch up with Protestant scholarship which had greatly out-distanced them during the preceding years of 'trials and struggles.'"[3] As Vincent MacNamara points out, the influence of the biblical renewal on moral theology was enormous, as many works of high quality appeared on the general subject of biblical morality as well as many monographs on individual topics. These were mostly the work of biblical scholars which were quickly taken over by the moral theologians. This movement had its finest hour in the now-famous recommendation of the Second Vatican Council to make Scripture the heart of all theological studies.[4]

The gains to moral theology from the revival of biblical studies have been very many indeed.[5] For example, the historical critical method which was championed by *Divino Afflante Spiritu* has unearthed many social and cultural concerns which to a large extent shaped the various theological positions in the Bible as well as the diversity in Scripture itself. Furthermore, it has come to show that "revelation and the cultural-cum-historical expression of it are not to be had separately."[6] Nor is the reception of revelation to be divorced from the faith of the receiving historical community. One of the results of this situation is the discovery that the Bible itself harbors so many theologies on several key questions such as war and peace, marriage and sexuality, and so forth. Edward Schillebeeckx has noted the effects that the discovery of the historical-cum-cultural context has on the way the New Testament, for example, tried to articulate the reality of God expressed in Jesus Christ.

> Within the New Testament as it stands there is a motley whole of varying interpretations of Jesus that go back to the first local communities of Christians: the thing is done one way in Mark, differently in Matthew and Luke, differently again in the case of Paul and in the Johanine gospel. Via the gospels and Paul it is possible to reconstruct, with a fair degree of certainty, a number of yet primitive variations: a Hebrew and Judeo-Greek Jerusalem Christology, a pre-Pauline, a pre-Marcan, a pre-Johanine one and, finally, the Christology of the Q community, where the Christological confession is often less developed though never totally absent.[7]

Part of the gain to moral theology from the biblical renewal is therefore the realization that since scriptural revelation was conditioned by its historical circumstances, the moral teaching of the Bible was itself also conditioned by those circumstances. For example, in an essay he wrote in reaction to the book *Human Sexuality,* co-authored by Anthony Kosnik and some others as a project of the Catholic Theological Society of America, Eugene LaVerdiere advised caution in the way we rush to conclusions concerning what the New Testament taught concerning human sexuality or what that teaching means now.[8] LaVerdiere reaffirms a general principle of biblical scholarship which recognizes the importance of a historical critical approach to the study of the Bible. With specific reference to the study of the teaching of the Bible on human sexuality, with a view to developing a contemporary ethic of sexuality, LaVerdiere suggests a two-tier approach: the first step would be an exegetical investigation which tries to reach the meaning of the text in its ancient context; the second would confront the ancient text with our modern situation in order to translate it into contemporary theology. LaVerdiere tries to show how the teaching of the New Testament on human sexuality was influenced by the various stages of ecclesial development in the New Testament. The stages in question include the earliest stage when the Church was primarily a movement characterized by a strong apostolic and evangelical emphasis; the second stage coincides with the period during which the emerging Christian communities had developed into consolidated Churches with a clearly defined sense of their identity in relation to the greater world and the challenge of history. LaVerdiere shows how the sexual ethics of the New Testament emerged in relation to the various contexts of the New Testament formation. He explores the relationship between the Church today and the first stages of its emergence in New Testament times. In the end, he concludes that any hermeneutical interpretation of the teaching of the New Testament on human sexuality must respect the nature of the various documents of the New Testament and their histories. Our task, he says, "is to discern the position of the Church today in relation to that which underlies the various letters and Gospels which we accept as challenging and normative for Christian living." The significance of New Testament ethical teaching for modern life should emerge in light of this relationship.[9] Since the study of the New Testament has shown that ethical issues emerging in a particular historical context often do so in response to definite historical situations, neither the teachings of Jesus nor those of the early Christian community can be understood apart from their "social and political contexts and the challenges these periods posed."[10] This need to understand and interpret the Scriptures in their historical context has led to the study of the moral teachings of the Catholic Church in the light of their historical contexts, as the above example from LaVerdiere shows.

As we shall see below, this particular approach to the use of Scripture has led to several debates on the import of using the Bible as warrant for teaching in particular areas in ways which are at variance with the "experience" of several people or groups in the contemporary world. The issue

SS as authority

here is that, as Allen Verhey points out, "to say scripture is an authority is not yet to say what moves are authorized in an argument 'from the Bible to the modern World.'" Therefore, an important first step toward methodological clarity in this regard would be to distinguish between "authority" and "authorization." Says Verhey, "The question of *whether* (and within the believing communities, the agreement that) scripture is a source and canon for moral discernment and judgment must be distinguished from the questions of *what* this source provides or *how* this canon functions as a norm. In spite of the agreement that scripture is an authority, there are widespread disagreements about the authorization for moving from scripture to moral norms."[11]

Also, with the study of the moral teachings of the Church in their historical settings in Scripture has come the realization that ethical pluralism is at the very foundation of Christian faith, at least on some issues. Such pluralism is evident, for example, in the way the early Church resolved the debate over the eating of forbidden foods.[12] The resolution of this issue in the writings of Paul was very nuanced, taking into account the need to protect the freedom of the individual Christian from ritualism and legalism, while allowing room for the genuine feeling of those who felt that such things as food taboos, ascetic practices, and ritual observance were important to their standing before God.[13] John R. Donahue argues therefore that an important contribution of the biblical renewal to moral theology is the realization that "New Testament ethics does not exist in a technical sense; the New Testament is not and does not contain a systematic treatise on the principles and practices of the Christian life." Biblical scholars thus use such terms as "ethos" or "the moral world" of the New Testament, for example, when they describe the behavior of early Christians.[14] The goal of the New Testament, especially, is to communicate a world to which it invited everyone. One of the tendencies among Catholic scholars especially in the years around the Second Vatican Council was to isolate one term or concept as an organizing principle which they believed to encapsulate this scriptural invitation and to build around it what they thought was a biblical moral theology. For example, in speaking of the gains to moral theology from the biblical renewal, Charles Curran insisted that the biblical renewal had shown that Christian morality was a religious ethic in which the Christian is considered as one who responds to the activity and call of God. Christian moral life is a response of the human person to the saving work and word of God in Jesus Christ. For Curran, the operative category which reinforces this call-response motif is the concept of *covenant*.[15] In the Old Testament, this covenant is summed up in the oft-repeated refrain from the prophets "I will be your God, and you will be my people." It is summed up in the New Testament in the paschal mystery of Jesus' life. Like Curran, Richard Gula also believes that "the covenant gives us our basic identity as the people of God and it affirms that out of our identity we are to decide and act. The basic requirement of covenantal existence is to respond to God's offer of love by living with God as the center of our heart's desire."[16]

Curran maintains that the biblical renewal has shown that Scripture argues against the primary insistence on either the teleological or deontological models in Christian ethics. "The biblical renewal with its emphasis on covenant and love of God runs somewhat counter to the supremacy of the deontological model which has been a staple of the Catholic tradition." It points out the secondary role of law in the life of Christians. Although the Ten Commandments were now viewed as law in themselves, they were seen within the context of the covenant as expressions of personal commitment and relationship with God. "The renewal of biblical theology showed the subordinate and relative position of law not only in the Old Testament but also in the New Testament. The ethical teaching of Jesus was seen primarily in terms of conversion, *agape,* or the following of Christ and not primarily in terms of law." In this regard, biblical studies have reminded moral theology that the life and death of Jesus is the model for daily Christian living. What this amounts to is a dissolution of the dichotomy between the heroic life of saints and people with a special vocation, as in the case of those professed to the evangelical counsels, and a lesser ethic which was thought to be meant for ordinary Christians. As the Second Vatican Council puts it, all are called to holiness. The call to perfection is made to all and is not a particular preserve of those who receive the vocation to follow the evangelical counsels. This greater awareness that the call to perfection is for all occasioned a change in format of moral theology. It was no longer limited to training judges who would distinguish between grades of sin. Rather, it became a discipline that considers "the life of Christians who are called to be perfect even as the heavenly father is perfect." Following from this realization that the call to be perfect is meant for all is the further realization that the moral life can no longer be viewed in terms of passive conformity to minimalist laws but should be seen in terms of growth and development. In turn, this has led to a greater appreciation of the virtues "and the creative aspects of the response of the Christian to God."

From the biblical renewal, moral theology has also learned a greater appreciation for interiority and the totality of the human person, with a corresponding lessening of emphasis on the individual external act itself. Since the Scriptures view the human person primarily in terms of the faith relationship with God, individual acts are considered to be manifestations of the person's basic attitude to this relationship. Thus, the theme of conversion has assumed a new importance in post–Vatican II moral theology not only because it "interiorizes" the moral response of the total person, but also because it has a social and cosmic dimension as well.[17]

The effects of the renewal of biblical studies on moral theology have not been all comforting, however. The discovery of biblical diversity has led to questions about the nature of biblical authority, about the significance of this diversity, and ultimately about how to understand the canonicity of the Bible. Is the Bible as a whole canonical, or is that designation reserved just for a part? How do we determine which parts of the Bible to consider canonical? In chapters 4 and 5 we shall return to discuss these and some other questions which the discovery of biblical diversity raised for theology in general and for Christian ethics in particular.

Karl Rahner on Non-Christian Religions

The second issue to consider here is the theology of grace which was developed by Karl Rahner in his treatment of the problematic of non-Christian religions, especially that aspect of Rahner's theology which was appropriated by Catholic moralists in the years after the Council.

Christianity has always had to exist alongside a world of non-Christianity. There was first the world of Judaism within which it was born and which "expanded" to include the entire Greek and Roman world. The movement which took its rise from the carpenter from Nazareth has had constantly to think and rethink, define and redefine, its place in this world and its relationship with other worldviews (religions and philosophies) which it has had to encounter increasingly as its world expanded. In other words, the fundamental Christian belief that there has occurred a definitive and unrepeatable self-disclosure of God in Jesus and that it (the Christian community) is the custodian of the truth of this self-disclosure and the one dispenser of the fruits therefrom has, as it were, imposed on Christianity the obligation to say something about the other worldviews which make rival or similar claims. That need has arisen more and more in modern times as the world continues to "shrink" as a result of globalization and as Christians discover more and more the values in other religions and worldviews.

It is not my intention to discuss fully the Christian response to the issue of non-Christian religions. I am interested here only in the response to this issue by Karl Rahner, for Rahner's response to the question has had serious and lasting echoes in moral theology since the Second Vatican Council, as we shall see.

There are four important elements in the Roman Catholic theological evaluation of non-Christian religions. The first is the notion of God's universal salvific will and, as a corollary, of a general and salvific history deriving from this. The second is the notion of the unique and indispensable personality of Jesus Christ with regard to salvation. Third is the unique reality of the Church in relation to salvation. Finally, there is also the issue of grace and, especially for Rahner, of the transcendence of the human spirit. These four elements all come into play in Rahner's theological evaluation of non-Christian religions. Rahner is particularly concerned with the age-old Christian claim that "outside the Church there is no salvation." The question for him is whether indeed the Christian can believe even for a brief moment "that the overwhelming mass of his brothers, not only those before the appearance of Christ right back to the distant past (whose horizons are being constantly extended by paleontology) but those of the present and of the future before him, are unquestionably and in principle excluded from the fulfillment of their lives and condemned to eternal meaninglessness."[18] Rahner rejects such a prospect, arguing instead that the Scriptures show conclusively that God wants the salvation of every human being (see 1 Tim 2:4). But if it is true, according to Catholic doctrine, that there is no salvation outside the Church, that salvation is of Christ the Lord, and given that the overwhelming mass of humankind has never acknowledged Jesus and may never explicitly acknowledge Jesus Christ, what then is going to happen to them? Answers to this question constitute the core of Rahner's theological thinking on non-Christian religions.

Rahner prefaces his treatment of this issue with the assumption that Christianity is the absolute religion. This implies that Christianity "is the noblest of all living religions . . . God's own self disclosure, completely valid for all men in whatever age they may be living, essentially definitive, never to be superseded."[19] The absoluteness of Christianity is self-evident neither to Christianity itself nor to other religions. Thus, Christianity can come to this knowledge about itself only "when it enters with existential power and demanding force into the realm of another religion and—judging it by itself—puts it in question."[20] The absoluteness of Christianity is structurally mediated, through Christ's continuing presence (the Church) which is the religion that "binds men to God." It is also historically realized. "The Christian religion as such has a beginning in history . . . It has not always and everywhere been the way of salvation for men . . . at least not in its historically tangible ecclesio-sociological constitution . . . It must come in a historical way to men, facing them as the only legitimate and demanding religion for men."[21] The question here is whether this demand is made validly once and for all, for every people everywhere and in every age, or whether each people, nation, religion, age, and every person has their own demanding encounter with this demanding religion. What is the status of the non-Christian religions prior to their encounter with Christianity? Is there any possibility of salvation for a person in his or her non-Christian religion before the encounter with Christianity?

Rahner's answer is that non-Christian religions are lawful and valid religions. For Rahner, a valid and lawful religion is an institutional religion "whose use" by people at a certain time "can be regarded on the whole as a positive means of gaining the right relationship with God and thus for the sake of attaining salvation, a means which is therefore positively included in God's plan of salvation."[22] In a valid and lawful religion God acts on human beings and freely reveals himself to them. The non-Christian religions, prior to their encounter with Christianity, contain both elements of a natural knowledge of God and "supernatural elements" arising out of the grace which is given to human beings as a gratuitous gift on account of Christ. This grace is here understood by Rahner to be "God himself in his forgiving and divinizing love." It is no mere substitute for salvation nor a means of salvation. "It is salvation (God) communicated in and through Christ."[23] The conclusion then is that since God communicates himself (acts) in the non-Christian religions, God is also saving human beings through these religions. Thus these other religions can be regarded as valid and lawful. There is no way we can escape this conclusion, Rahner says, if we are truly Christian and believe in the "universal and serious salvific purpose of God" toward all human beings.[24]

Hence, Rahner is faced with the problem of reconciling this claim about God's serious salvific purpose toward all people with the idea that this concept is Christocentric—that is, that it cannot be had without faith in Jesus Christ. The problem is rather acute when viewed statistically, as we have indicated above. Most human beings never did, do not, and perhaps never will profess Christianity. Does God not intend their salvation too? We have already seen that Rahner teaches that God intends the salvation of every human being. He tries to explain how this is possible in and through the non-Christian religions. Every human being, Rahner says, "is really and truly exposed to the influence of divine, supernatural grace which offers an interior union with God and by means of which God communicates himself whether the individual takes up an attitude of acceptance or of refusal towards this grace."[25] Every individual is also offered "a genuine possibility" in his or her life of partaking in a genuine saving relationship with God. In view of the social nature of the human person, this offer had to be made and accepted or rejected socially—within a religion. Thus, to obtain salvation, the human person had to be *homo religiosus,* and in the concrete religion in which people lived and had to live at the time. "If, however, man can always have a positive, saving relationship to God, and if he always had to have it, then he has always had it within that religion which in practice was at his disposal by being a factor in his sphere of existence."[26] Such religion, the depravity it may contain notwithstanding, can be called an absolutely lawful religion for the person concerned.

If it is true that God desires that all human beings should be saved and that this salvation cannot be found outside the Church, then, Rahner argues, every human being must somehow be capable of being a member of the Church, really and in a historically concrete way.[27] I have already noted above that Rahner considers pre-Christian religions to be avenues by which God can communicate grace (himself) to human beings, offering them salvation. Rahner argues further that if it is true that the salvation thus proffered is Christ's salvation given through the Church because there is no other, "then it must be possible to be not only an anonymous theist but also an anonymous Christian, and this (since the Church of Christ is not only purely interior reality) not in any merely intangible way, but also with certain making visible and tangible of the anonymous relationship."[28] Says Rahner, the anonymous Christian is "the pagan after the beginning of the Christian religion, who lives in the state of Christ's grace through faith, hope and love, yet who has no explicit knowledge of the fact that his life is orientated in grace-giving salvation in Jesus Christ."[29]

It is part of traditional Christian teaching that supernatural faith is indispensable for salvation, and that baptism is essential for membership in the Church.[30] If so, the question is how one who is visibly without this faith and therefore unbaptized can be termed Christian, even if anonymously. It must be noted that it is also the teaching of the Second Vatican Council that "God in ways known to himself can lead those inculpably ignorant of the gospel to that faith without which it is impossible to please him (Heb 11:6)."[31] In *Gaudium et Spes,* the Council addresses the issue of how the pagan could receive supernatural faith by saying that "the Holy Spirit in a manner known only to God offers to every human being the possibility of being associated with the paschal mystery."[32] In these passages we have not only an acknowledgment of the necessity of faith for salvation, but also of the possibility of receiving this faith outside "normal channels," so to speak. We have, above all, a remarkable admission of ignorance with regard to how this faith is or can be given outside the visible structures of the Church. Rahner considers it the task of the theologian to continue where the Council left off and to try to find out how faith is given to the non-Christian. Otherwise, the Church's teaching would be laid open "to the objection that it was simply self-contradictory in that it asserted both that salvation was possible for all men and that faith was necessary."[33]

Rahner's own attempt to find a solution hangs on two concepts. We have noted the idea of the universal salvific will of God. The other idea has to do with the capacity of the human spirit for unlimited self-transcendence:

> Because the universal and Supernatural will of God is working for human salvation, the unlimited transcendence of man, itself directed of necessity towards God, is raised up consciously by grace, although possibly without explicit thematic reflection, in such a way that the possibility of faith in salvation is thereby made available. Thus, one can speak of genuine faith on condition that a man freely accepts his unlimited transcendence which is raised up by grace and directed to the immediate presence of God as its final goal.[34]

Every human being, whether he or she is conscious of it or not, or likes it or not, is always and inevitably involved with God in his or her secular awareness. So long as each person freely accepts his or her unlimited self-transcendence, he or she implicitly accepts God. So long as the individual freely and genuinely follows his or her conscience, he or she affirms as well "the possibility of such a radical option which is implicitly bound up with this decision, i.e., he affirms God."[35] The individual's transcendence makes this reference to God imperative. The question then is whether this implicit affirmation of God also includes a reference to Jesus Christ and in what way. Rahner answers that it does.

> If one takes it seriously that God has become man, then—it must be said—man is that which happens when God expresses and divests himself. Man is . . . that which God becomes if he sets out to show himself in the region of the extra-divine . . . Conversely, . . . man is he who realizes himself when he gives himself away into the incomprehensible mystery of God. Seen in this way, the incarnation of God is the uniquely supreme case of the actualization of man's nature in general.[36]

We have so far discussed Rahner's view on supernatural grace as the condition of the possibility of salvation. This supernatural grace, according to Rahner, is God himself in his forgiving and divinizing love (i.e., salvation), an offer which can be rejected or accepted. We know too that for Rahner, the religions are the structural channels through which this offer is made. This grace, though an ontological reality beyond the scope of consciousness, brings with it a new, a priori formal object: "the radical nature of the unlimited transcendence of man itself which is consciously known, though not necessarily perceived as an object or fully thought out."[37] God is the proper goal of this transcendence to which it is directed by the transforming power of grace. The process by which this human transcendence is directed to God, even if it defies individual human conceptualization, is universal in time and place since God's saving will is universally operative. Rahner sees in this free self-communication of God and the conscious, if unthematically reflected, grasping of this communication by the individual, a realization of the two conditions essential for supernatural revelation. This supernatural (transcendent) revelation can only be grasped and understood through the grace of faith—that is, through "the self-communication of God to the human spirit in the depths of his being." This, and the new, supernatural formal object given by grace, the unlimited transcendence of the human person, constitute what Rahner refers to as "the transcendental factor in revelation." He says that if a person by a free act in which he accepts himself unconditionally in his radical reference to God raised up by grace, also accepts the basic finality of his spirit, even without reflection, then he is making a genuine act of faith. This finality already means revelation. If this supernatural finality is freely accepted, without explicit reflection, then there exists what can be termed anonymous faith.

Human transcendence is of course mediated historically, according to Rahner, through a mediating "categorical objectivity" which could be either an explicit religious act or a particular moral decision in which a person is responsible for himself and accepts or rejects himself. Thus, for example, an atheist who is absolutely obedient to his conscience manifests the acceptance of his human transcendence in faith and so accepts himself and God, at least unreflectively.[38] Rahner therefore concludes thus:

> It is possible, then, to envisage a man who is in possession of that self-imparting of God called grace as the innermost heart and center of his existence, one who has accepted in unresolved faithfulness to his existence . . . in other words, a man . . . who even as a "pagan" already possesses the blessing of salvation . . . which ultimately speaking is the sole point of Christianity . . . Now if this is true, then, I cannot see why we should not call such a man an anonymous Christian . . . For after all he does possess, even though in a way hidden to himself and to others, that which constitutes the essence of what it is to be a Christian: the grace of God which is laid hold of in faith.[39]

So far, the position of Rahner on the issues discussed here raises a host of further questions about the Church. What is the relationship between the historical structural Christianity and the anonymous faith which is also Christian? What relevance has the Church? What about Christian missionary efforts—what use do they serve? Rahner answers by contrasting explicit and implicit Christian faith. Explicit Christianity must be seen as "the process, willed by God in his saving providence and demanded by human nature, by which the transcendent revelation becomes present to itself . . ."[40] Implicit Christianity is destined to be explicated by the word of Christ. According to Rahner, such explication is demanded by two things: "(1) by the incarnational and social structure of grace and Christianity and (2) because the individual who grasps Christianity in a clearer, purer and more reflective way, has, other things being equal, a still greater chance than someone who is merely an anonymous Christian."[41] The Church's missionary activity is therefore a summons and the extension of an offer which is meant to bring the world of non-Christianity to "explicit consciousness of what already belongs to it as a divine offer or already pertains to it as a divine gift of grace accepted unreflectively and implicitly."[42]

If during his life a person is offered, "in a manner credible to him," the chance to explicate that which is implicit in him, the chance of "supernatural elevation," and if this person rejects this possibility, then this person "is deliberately denying his grace-filled transcendence as well. It is not possible to have 'anonymous faith' when its thematic expression in the Christian belief in revelation is culpably rejected."[43] Therefore, one may add, it is not possible for such a person to be saved. This, I believe, is how Rahner understands the dictum "outside the Church there is no salvation." Thus, for Rahner, the Church should not be regarded as an exclusive club of people who alone are destined to be saved. Rather, it should be thought of as "the historically tangible vanguard" of what is also but implicitly present outside the Church.

Rahner's position on the salvation of non-Christians has raised a lot of questions concerning the way people can be "the willing recipients of the grace of Christ whom they either do not know or have, for one reason or another, rejected but in whose name alone man can be saved."[44] Thus, Rahner's position has been condemned by some as "patronizing" toward non-Christian religions. John Macquarrie believes that the term "anonymous Christian" is a misuse of language which erodes the distinction between the Christian and the non-Christian.[45]

In reacting to Rahner, it must not be forgotten, as John Mahoney reminds us, that neither modern theology nor Karl Rahner was "the first to adumbrate a theology of the influence of Christ, and not just of a Unitarian God, at work in the thinking and lives of unbelievers."[46] There has always been an optimistic strain running through Scripture with regard to humanity's status before God and in positive appreciation of humanity's extrabiblical religious experience and institutions.[47] God knows no partiality (Rom 2:6, 10–11) but desires the salvation of all humankind (1 Tim 2:4–6). Following Paul, Christians link the fate of the whole of creation to Adam's fall in Genesis. The consequence of that fall has been universal. As a result, the fruits of the redemption wrought by Christ are also universal. Christ came to take away the sins of all (Heb 9:26–28) and brought about a universal grace that knows no consideration. As early as the second century, St. Justin Martyr concluded that it is the belief of Christians that "those . . . who strive to do the good which is enjoined on us have a share in God . . . Christ is the divine Word in whom the whole human race shares, and those who live according to the light of their knowledge are Christians, even if they are considered as being godless."[48] Justin, Origen, Clement of Alexandria, and many others saw the *logos* present in a hidden way, even in the pagan religions which predated Christianity; hence they talked of these

religions as imbued with *logoi spermatikoi* or *rationes seminales.* Clement
and his school even went further, refusing to accept the popular opinion
that paganism was an invention of the devil, and insisting instead that it
had actually been willed and planned by God—as the law of the Jews had
been—in guise of a *paidagoges,* or a slave who leads the truth-seeker to
Christ.[49] The non-Christian religions were therefore preparations for the
gospel, the slave son who was only holding the fortress until the heir appeared.

In Rahner's articulation of this ancient strain in the Christian religion
we see a few important elements which were to be very influential in the
debates in moral theology after the Council. First is that God's grace is on
offer, through Christ, to all people in their particular situations and context. Within these contexts, human beings can be saved or damned. The
second point follows from this: human beings have the freedom to say yes
or no to God. Rahner was not per se a moral theologian; however, his
work has had tremendous impact on the work of moral theologians since
the Council especially on the question of the distinctiveness of Christian
ethics and the question of human freedom.

Following from Karl Rahner's work many moral theologians have
drawn the conclusion that since grace is a universal gift within the reach
of everyone, moral insights as consequences of the action of grace are not
the preserve of any one religion. To put it more specifically, many questions of Christian morality are not merely Christian but universally
human questions. Josef Fuchs would argue, for example, that to the extent
that moral norms proclaim truth, "they are universally human and therefore also Christian—hence, not distinctively Christian."[50] Christianity has
nothing specific to contribute to ethics, nothing to teach people which
could not be known by people in non-Christian religious contexts.

Karl Rahner on Transcendental (Fundamental) Freedom

The second and perhaps most potent element in the theology of Karl Rahner which we have so far discussed has to do with his position on freedom. I have already indicated that for Rahner, the offer of divine self-
communication (the supernatural existential) presents us with a decision:
for or against God. "This decision is not with reference to the God of the
distant, receding horizon of our spiritual nature, but the God of infinite
closeness."[51] This decision implies what has already been stated several

times in this chapter regarding an important element of Rahner's work: the belief that every human being is always and inevitably involved with God in his or her secular awareness and is free to reject or accept God, and in fact exercises either option to the extent that he or she accepts or denies his or her unlimited self-transcendence. By exercising this freedom either way the individual decides him- or herself. This is what in Rahner's theology has come to be understood as transcendental freedom.

Transcendental freedom is not a faculty by which a human person can do this or not do that through arbitrary choices. For Rahner, freedom is first of all the subject's being responsible for himself or herself. It has to do "with the subject as such and as a whole." It is the capacity of the subject "to decide about himself in his single totality."[52] Freedom is transcendental because, as Ronald Modras points out, "it is not an object of experience nor merely the quality of an action, but a mode of being."[53] The actualization of this freedom is not done merely through categorical acts because freedom is not "an individual datum of human experience which is immediately and empirically observable in time and space."[54] Although the subject in his original experience of himself as subject knows who he is, the subject cannot know with absolute certainty the moral quality of the individual actions of his life. Rahner does not deny that individual concrete human acts have a moral quality. What he emphasizes is that we cannot tell exactly what that quality is because we do not know how we stand before God just on the basis of an individual act here or there. These acts may be indicative of who we are. But no one can know that for sure since no one can exactly know when an act chosen is an indication of the rejection or acceptance of God and of human unlimited self-transcendence. To understand what Rahner is saying here, we must repeat what has already been stated above. God is the object of the core of transcendental freedom, its infinite ground and horizon, the source of human freedom. For, says Rahner, if there were no such infinite horizon, the human agent would be locked up within itself, "in a definite and intrinsic limitation . . . and would not be free."[55] God as object and term of human transcendence cannot be a matter of indifference to the subject as knower. This is why freedom is "the freedom to say yes or no to God." Rahner is aware that there are all sorts of false notions of God out there and all sorts of ideas pretending to come from God. Therefore he speaks of what a real rejection, a real saying "no" to God means: "As a being of freedom . . . man can deny himself in such a way that he really and truly says 'no' to God himself, and indeed to God himself and not merely to some distorted or childish notion of God. To God himself, not merely to some innerworldly norm of action which we rightly or wrongly call 'God's law.' "

We cannot know exactly when this "no," this rejection of God, really happens in a person's life because such a "no" to God is not originally merely the moral sum which we calculate from individual good or evil deeds. This is to say that in our individual existence, we can never with certainty indicate "a definite point in our lives and say: precisely here and not somewhere else a really radical 'yes' or 'no' to God took place." What we certainly know is that "the entire life of a free subject is inevitably an answer to the question in which God offers himself to us as the source of transcendence."

What we have just said in the last paragraph raises one further question about the relation between the categorical choices we make every day, the acts we posit as moral agents every day, and this basic freedom which Rahner writes about. Rahner believes that the object choices we make, what he refers to as our categorical freedom, has an influence on our transcendental freedom and is influenced by that freedom as well. In other words, as Josef Fuchs, who is often credited with domesticating this theory for moral theology, puts it, even though the free commitment of ourselves as persons in fundamental freedom is more than any particular action or actions and more than any sum of them, "it underlies them, permeates them, and goes beyond them, without ever being one of them." Ronald Modras captures the essence of the relationship between human categorical choices and fundamental freedom in Rahner's work when he notes that "it is out of the innermost core of our beings that we make those basic decisions of transcendental freedom (fundamental option) which lead to or away from God. But because freedom extends formally to the whole person, free actions can arise from outside the inmost core which do not affect us as acts of transcendental freedom do."[56]

Rahner's Influence on Moral Theological Discourse

The influence of Rahner's theory of fundamental freedom on moral theology in recent times has been enormous. First of all, it has changed the way many moralists treat the question of sin. In this regard the question is asked whether the traditional classification of sin is still applicable or not. The tradition had always classified sin into various forms—mortal and venial. A sin was said to be mortal if the matter in question was a grave one and if the agent knew it was grave and deliberately performed the action. In other words, mortal sin involved grave matter, full knowledge, and freedom of choice on the part of the agent. Although for some moralists the moral psychology of Karl Rahner put the classification into question, for others it has become an opportunity to re-evaluate the meaning of mortal and venial sins and the process by which one arrives at these classifications. Bernard Häring is one of those theologians who insists on keeping the traditional classification of mortal and venial sins but who argues that the meaning of these terms must be understood differently in light of the theory of fundamental freedom. Mortal sin occurs, Häring writes, if the free decision of the moral agent penetrates to the inner depth of this free person. "Given sufficient knowledge and commensurate freedom, man realizes that it is a matter of decision that sets final orientation to his life; thus he declares himself against friendship with God, against solidarity in good in favor of solidarity in evil. The decisive element of a mortal sin, therefore, is the fact that the act arises from one's deepest being, from one's own malice of heart, and with such knowledge and liberty as to represent a real self determination against God. If I say 'the act' I do not think of an isolated act, but on the whole development that constitutes the decision for total alienation."[57] This constitutes a significant shift from the traditional position in that it places greater emphasis on the disposition of the moral agent rather than on the act performed. First of all, it implies that the small act here and there, the apparently "insigificant" acts of the moral agent, may indeed be indications of a much bigger life orientation, a tip of the iceberg, so to speak. Also, Häring tries to steer a middle course between the notion of the moral act as a spontaneous, almost thoughtless action, and the idea of the moral act as involving deliberation, freedom, and choice. Thus one who commits murder would have planned, thought about it in many respects, and gone ahead to kill. Murder in this sense is a whole process brought to culmination. Häring also retains the notion of venial sin but insists that it is sin only in an analogous sense. He argues that the best of the Catholic moral tradition has always held that there is a qualitative difference between mortal and venial sins. While mortal sin deprives the person of God's friendship, venial sin never has the power to do so, "although it can cause most serious dangers of alienation."[58]

Richard McCormick has written about the pastoral implications of the *McC.* theory of fundamental option. First of all, he maintains that this theory suggests that the moral life must be seen as a growth process, a general unfolding of our being as Christians: "The transformation of faith into love (charity-option) is what the Holy Spirit is operating within us. Seen from this perspective, the moral life is a progressive deepening, stabilizing, rendering more dominant and facile of our charity."[59] Second, the discussion on fundamental freedom is also partly responsible for the renewed emphasis on conversion in the moral life. Just like a decision against God, a person can also change and opt for God though conversion. "This is a change of the person, and is achieved only by a free self-disposition of the person." Such change involves the act of freedom as a fundamental decision which is not wholly open to analytic reflection and is often a continued process. This is why we speak of continued conversion. The radical decision for God once made is verified by the "ongoing integration of the whole reality of our lives into the profound disposition of ourselves."[60] Third, the theory of fundamental freedom calls into question what constitutes "serious" matter in mortal sin. McCormick claims that while serious matter was identified with a whole host of things in traditional theology, with the notion of fundamental freedom at the heart of the moral act, serious matter is understood as "that concrete human choice which is apt to occasion a self-disposing response."[61] Fourth, the notion of fundamental freedom, as we have already seen, recasts the whole discussion on the distinction of sins.

The idea of fundamental freedom as presented above has not gone down well with everyone. Germain Grisez argues that this notion overlooks the existential dimension of free choice and rather attributes self-determination to fundamental option. He believes that the proponents of this theory hold that one could freely choose "in a way inconsistent with one's fundamental option without altering that option." Finally, Grisez has a problem with the idea of fundamental option or some explanations of it because he believes that it does not adequately explain the difference between light and grave matter. It cannot account for why some matters are likely to subvert a good fundamental option and others cannot do so.[62]

Other criticisms of this theory have come from official Church documents. We will look at what Pope John Paul II says on this matter later on in the book. The point here has been to describe in some detail some of the theological ideas which have influenced moral theology in a considerable way in the years after the Council. How all these ideas in their various combinations played out in this period is the subject matter of the rest of this book

As I pointed out earlier, the need to make Scripture source and center of Christian ethical reflection had been felt in the Catholic tradition long

MT based in SS

before the Council. Thus, when the fathers of the Second Vatican Council decreed that Scripture must be made the center of ethical discourse, they were really not saying anything new. For at least two decades before the Council scholars who had become tired of the "Christian" morality offered by the neo-Scholastic moral rationalism of the manuals had been trying to "Christianize" moral theology. This effort received a tremendous boost from the conciliar call for a more scripturally oriented moral theology. Theologians in the 1960s and early 1970s read the Council's injunction as a call to revolt, so to speak, against the neo-Scholastic natural law morality of the manuals. These scholars who had all along considered the moral theology of the manuals "too pagan"[63] also saw in the Council's call an opportunity to insist on the specifically Christian character of Christian morality.[64] They insisted that the morality of Christians, to be Christian, must be dependent on revelation and be biblical through and through. As Josef Fuchs put it then, "The Council requires that moral theology shall be taught not only and not primarily as a code of moral principles and precepts. It must be presented as an unfolding, a revelation and explanation, of the joyful message, the good news of Christ's love to us, of the vocation of the believers in Christ." For Fuchs, then, Christ and our being in Christ must be the center and the focus of a renewed moral theology.[65] The theologians argued as well that moral theology must center its attention on the key themes of the Bible and not just be satisfied with random quotations to bolster positions arrived at philosophically. "It must recognize that the reality of the kingdom creates new values; that the kerygma contains moral doctrine—a paschal mystery—which is necessarily bound to the mystery of Christ; that the Bible shows us what our life is like when it is based on the mystery of Christ and the salvation brought by Christ; that it gives us not only general moral bearings but guiding principles and even definite and concrete norms."[66] The assumption was that the revealed ethics taught by Jesus Christ and proposed by the Church differ from merely human morality. The problem was to show in what way this was the case. Certain events both within and outside the Church forced theologians to raise this question, and, as Vincent MacNamara has so well shown, made the attempt to Christianize morality soon run into difficulties from which the discipline has not quite recovered. Thus, any discussion on the question of the nature of Christian ethics after the Second Vatican Council must include the debate over the distinctiveness of Christian ethics which ensued soon after the conciliar call for the renewal of moral theology, as well as the debate over the use of Scripture in ethics which was part of this larger debate.

Finally, although we will return to the question of the distinctiveness of Christian ethics in the next chapter, it must be noted right away that Rahner's position on the universal availability of God's grace and on everyone's grace-aided ability to do good led many theologians, as we have already remarked, initially to hold that Christian morality is human morality par excellence and ultimately to deny that there is any specificity to Christian ethics.

part two

The Nature of
Christian Ethics

The Distinctiveness of Christian Morality

The problem of the specificity of Christian ethics has always been a part of Christian moral discourse. This problem becomes particularly acute whenever Christianity encounters a new cultural situation, as was the case, for example, when the apostolic fathers and the apologists were obliged "to highlight the newness of Christian ethics with respect to the moral ideal of the pagan world."[1] This was itself part of a larger problem of the relationship between faith and reason which needed the genius of Clement of Alexandria to bring to some resolution, at least for the Christian mind.

Prior to Clement of Alexandria, most Christian writers considered philosophy (reason) an enemy of or worthless to the faith. What has Jerusalem to do with Athens? Tertullian had asked. Even Paul had warned his converts against the dangers of philosophy. Clement, however, did not consider philosophy (reason) an enemy to faith and revelation. On the contrary, for Clement philosophy is an ally of faith. God, says Clement, is the cause of all things. God is the primary cause of both the Old and New Testaments as well as philosophy. While God revealed himself to the Hebrews through the Scriptures, "philosophy was given to the Greeks directly and primarily, till the Lord should call the Greeks." Philosophy was a schoolmaster to bring the "Hellenic Mind" to Christ. Therefore, philosophy was a preparation, "paving the way for him who is perfected in Christ." There is only one way to truth, says Clement. "But into it, as into a perennial river, streams flow from all sides" (*Stromata*, 1, V).

Philosophy is characterized by investigation into truth and the nature of things. This, according to Clement, is the same truth of which the Lord had said, "I am the truth." Philosophy is necessary for coming to the knowledge of this truth. "Some who think themselves naturally gifted, do not wish to touch either philosophy or logic; nay more, they do not wish to learn natural science. They demand bare faith alone." Such people, according to Clement of Alexandria, are misguided. The mind must travel various routes to reach the absolute truth. "So, I call him truly learned who brings everything to bear on truth; so that from geometry, and music, and grammar, and philosophy itself, culling what is useful, he guards the faith against assault" (*Stromata*, 1, IX). Philosophy, being the search for truth, contributes to the comprehension of truth not as the cause of truth, but a cause, along with others, of truth. For "while truth is one, many things contribute to its investigation." Even though philosophy contributes to the discovery of truth, the truth of philosophy is distinct from the truth of faith, "both in respect of external knowledge, certainty of demonstration, divine power, and the like." In other words, "faith and reason are distinct forms of knowledge, with different objects and finalities; therefore, they do not elude unification, but come together in a superior knowledge, the gnosis, which includes both."[2]

Clement's achievement lies in his insistence on a rapport between Christian faith and human knowledge. Faith builds on and conserves knowledge. Faith and knowledge are distinct forms of knowledge with different objects and goals. Human knowledge has nothing to fear from faith. They are not necessarily in competition since they have different objects, although they have the same source. As Battista Mondin remarks, "Clement has made one of the most significant moves in the bimillenary history of Christianity; after him, Christianity, at least in the Catholic line, will no longer line up against, but for reason—will no longer fight against man, but for him."[3] But that does not mean that reason (philosophy) would always embrace faith as an ally or readily accept its contributions to human knowledge, whether theoretical or practical. Thus, the question of the distinctiveness of Christian ethics is often a question put to the Christian faith by philosophy, broadly so-called, to provide rationally acceptable grounds for its moral assertions and doctrines.

In what follows, I will discuss the factors which prompted and continue to fuel the debate on the distinctiveness of Christian ethics. This will be followed by a survey of the main positions on the issue. The chapter concludes with a brief reflection of my own.

Contemporary Contexts of the Problem

The question of the rational justification of Christian moral claims is being exacerbated in modern times in part by globalization. Globalization has been defined as "the intensification of worldwide social relations which link distant localities in such a way that local happenings are shaped by events occurring many miles away and vice-versa." As Anthony Giddens further says, "Whoever studies cities today, in any part of the world, is aware that what happens in a local neighborhood is likely to be influenced by factors—such as world money or commodity markets—operating at an indefinite distance away from the neighborhood itself."[4] Malcolm Waters also speaks of globalization as a social process "in which the constraints of geography on social and cultural arrangements recede and in which people become aware that they are receding."[5] In the words of Roland Robertson, a leading authority on globalization, the world is more and more becoming "a single place."[6]

There is no unanimous agreement among scholars on the factors causing the shrinkage of the globe. Is it the mass media and mass communication (including faster and easier means of commuting from one part of the globe to another)? Is globalization a result of the increasing hegemony of transnational corporations? Is it a combination of factors, and in what ratio and order? Whatever is fueling it, the world is clearly becoming more of a single place than it was fifty years ago.

Globalization has repercussions in fields as diverse as economics, marketing, communication, science and technology, politics, culture, and religion. The global field is a highly pluralistic one in that "there is a proliferation of civilizational, continental, regional, societal and other definitions of the global human condition as well as considerable variety in identities formed in those respects without direct reference to the global situation."[7] Thus, in addition to the compression of the world, one of the main consequences of globalization is "an exacerbation of collisions between civilizational, societal and communal narratives."[8]

At the root of the issue of the distinctiveness of Christian ethics is the issue of cultural and religious pluralism. Not only does globalization imply a pluralistic consciousness, it also highlights the inadequacy of any single answer concerning human values and human life or even the sameness in the answers proffered for some shared human concerns. The participants in the discussion on the distinctiveness of Christian ethics since the Second Vatican Council are aware of this. This is why, as we shall see shortly, they were initially determined to show that the Christian is indeed the human, and vice versa.

Globalization has also affected the discussion on the nature of Christian ethics through the spread of a culture of secularism. As Peter Berger puts it, a secular culture is one in which "the supernatural as a meaningful reality is absent or remote from the horizons of everyday life of large numbers, very probably of a majority of people . . . who seem to manage to get along without it quite well."[9] In such a culture, various aspects of human life are no longer determined by religion. On the contrary, individuals and whole societies assert their independence and adulthood with regard to religion and the transcendent.[10] Therefore one of the attendant results of secularization is a growing sense of human autonomy. The madman in Nietzsche's *Gay Science* exults after announcing the death of God, "The sea, our sea, now lies open!"

Autonomy could be understood to mean a movement of emancipation of human culture, science, and ideas and a desire by human beings to be treated as adults in matters pertaining to God and religion. However, as Jean-Marie Aubert points out, human autonomy can also signify respect for God's creative intentions toward humanity and the universe. In this sense, the world and human beings are respected for what they are, and the natural and profane structures are seen as signs of God to be read in the context of faith. This is what the Council means when it speaks of the autonomy of earthly realities.[11] Thus, emphasis on human autonomy has many positive and valid aspects. However, in epistemology, and by extension morality, it explicates a problem that goes back to ancient Greek philosophy.

Socrates and Plato introduced a polarization between opinion and knowledge in Western thinking. From them, many people learned to regard knowledge as that which the individual can apprehend or test for herself. Opinion is belief which the individual takes over from the community. This polarization was adopted by both the Renaissance and the Enlightenment. For the latter, especially, critical thought starts only when the individual begins to doubt or cease to consider as true whatever views or insight are inherited from parents, teachers, or the community into which one is born.[12] Thus, the modern individual is suspicious or even opposed to authoritative or religious directives regarding what to know or

knowledge ⟶ opinion

believe or how to act. As is true with respect to other values, and so also with respect to the ethical value, the modern person tends to want to withdraw "from the guardianship of religion and, with the help of his own reason and experience, resolve the moral problems of his intramundane existence and his activity in history."[13] An extension to this mentality is that this person, having come of age, to paraphrase Dietrich Bonhoeffer, is conscious of the fact that in the face of common human problems of the day, such as war and peace, disease, poverty, injustices, and other evils, reference to the gospel does not seem to yield different or quicker solutions than is the case with people who are not working from any faith propositions. In the open dialogue which ensued between the Church and others, in the open atmosphere fostered by the Second Vatican Council, it became clear that Christians and non-Christians seemed to share many of the same ethical values. Working side by side with other people for the same social causes and ethical concerns, many Christians felt in harmony with the solutions which originated from their non-Christian friends.[14] Thus they wondered whether it was not arrogant and pretentious of Christians to speak of a Christian ethics as if there were an arcane source of moral knowledge available only to them.

academic theology

The world of the postconciliar era did not just seek to emancipate itself from religion and God, it actively went to war against these. One area where this culture war was being fought was the academy. In this setting many scholars questioned openly the credentials of theology as an academic discipline. In some universities which were started in the first place as schools of theology, some scholars actively campaigned for the suppression of the theology faculty, or at least its merger with the school of religion where religion would be studied as a merely phenomenological reality. The effect of this way of thinking on religious ethics of all kinds was dramatic. Many moral philosophers have felt free in recent years to dismiss religious ethics as fallacious and therefore unworthy of serious academic study.[15]

As much as by the epistemological and practical concerns, if not more so, the problem of the nature of Christian ethics has been exacerbated since the Council by internal theological factors as well—some as ancient as the Church itself, some relatively new. Germain Grisez points out that almost from its very beginning, "Christian moral thought has been impeded by an unresolved, underlying tension between the supernatural and the natural, between the sacred and the secular." These questions had not arisen in either Jewish or pagan antiquity. The distinctions arise from

[handwritten margin notes: ongoing Docetism, Arianism]

the distinctions introduced by the gospel. "Birth as a human person is distinguished from rebirth as a child of God; flesh is distinguished from Spirit; the things of Caesar distinguished from the things of God."[16] Despite the best efforts of Chalcedon and Nicaea, the Docetist heresy remains a constant temptation. Indeed, so is Arianism. It has always been difficult to maintain a balance.

[handwritten margin note: manuals]

The manuals had no problem as regards the nature of Christian ethics. Even though what was right and wrong was inscribed in nature, which in turn was knowable by human reason, nature itself was in fact a viceroy for God. Thus, natural law morality was ultimately in some sense a religious ethic, for behind all creation was the great artificer, God, and in all nature was written his intention and purpose for the world. As we shall see below, many people found this type of reasoning unacceptable because it seemed to them to leave little room for human initiative in morality. The

[handwritten margin note: still a problem]

problem then was to find a way to include the human without throwing out the divine. In spite of sincere efforts on the part of many moralists after the Council, this attempt proved rather difficult and indeed remains so even today. Another important internal factor which contributed immensely to the question about the distinctiveness of Christian ethics was the publication of the encyclical *Humanae Vitae* in 1968. As we saw in chapter 2, the discussion on the encyclical soon moved from the issue of contraception to almost every other aspect of ethics and theology. Some people wondered whether revelation (the kerygma) contains moral teachings which are peculiar and known only to people who believe in the revelation of God contained in the Bible. The question ultimately had to do with the basis for the conclusions that the encyclical reached to what is a common human problem. Is this conclusion drawn from some moral teachings which are specific to the Lord Jesus and which ought to make a difference in the way the Christian lives in and construes the world, or is it arrived at on the basis of common human experience? If so, why do so many other persons of integrity, learning, and goodwill have opinions contrary to the conclusion of the encyclical? Is there, therefore, a distinctively Christian ethics, as opposed to, say, philosophical, other religious, or merely human ethics?

One final factor which has helped to determine the way the question of the nature of Christian ethics has been raised in the post–Vatican II era has to do with the people involved in these debates and their theological background. For example, it is not by accident that this question in its earlier manifestations appeared as a discussion on the relation of revelation and reason (natural law). During this first phase of the discussion in the 1970s and early 1980s, the categories as well as the terms of reference in this debate were almost entirely Catholic. The discussants themselves were mostly people, especially priests, who had been very thoroughly immersed in the natural law tradition and had come to see morality almost entirely in its categories. Following the Council, many theologians tried, in accordance with conciliar directives, to help in finding solutions to the world's problems—social, economic, scientific, and so forth. This desire to be relevant in the contemporary world and acceptable to the men and women of their day led many moral theologians to try to present a Christian morality which was not esoteric, reserved only to believers, and warranted only by the Bible. This desire was not just a way to achieve cheap public relations goals for the Church or to appear modern; it was indeed fueled by a genuine theological rethinking by the Second Vatican Council of the problematic of non-Christian religions as means also of salvation and the possibility of salvation for inculpable atheists, who led good lives. We have already seen the influence of Rahner on this discussion and his view of non-Christian religions as valid and lawful religions through which God offered the grace of salvation as well. Thus, pluralism, and the conciliar teaching regarding the sufficiency of ethical systems other than the Christian to inform people's lives here on earth, helped to make some of the earlier proponents of a distinct Christian ethics rethink their position.

The second phase of the debate on the nature of Christian ethics centered more explicitly on the place of Scripture in ethics—a discussion to which we shall turn in the fifth chapter of this book. During this phase we are dealing not only with the motivation provided by the directives of the Council or by other theological developments in the Catholic Church, such as the movement for scriptural renewal. We are also dealing with the impetus provided by Protestant writers whose influence had become increasingly felt in the Catholic Church through the increasing exchanges between Catholic and Protestant theologians, and through the impact of their work on younger Catholic theologians. Many of these younger theologians had acquired their education in Protestant theological institutions all around the world or had been taught by some of the Protestant theologians hired to teach in Catholic theological schools after the Council. In the United States, for example, the influence of theologians like James M. Gustafson, Stanley Hauerwas, and Paul Ramsey, to mention just a few, is still being felt through their former students who since the early 1980s have become very prominent in the field.

We must be careful, however, not to exaggerate the difference between the two phases which have been mentioned above. For, after all,
Bernard Häring had wondered about the way to make moral theology
more scripturally based even before the Council, and Jean Porter has continued to write about the importance of natural law in moral theology and
its relationship to Scripture nearly forty years after the Council. However,
the point remains that the interlocutors in the debate on the distinctiveness of Christian morality phrased the question differently at different
times after the Council because they were also motivated by slightly different concerns to raise the question in the first place. As has already been
indicated, we are concerned in this chapter with the question of the distinctiveness of Christian ethics as it was raised and discussed in the first
phase of the debate on the nature of Christian ethics.

We will next turn to the substance of this initial debate on the distinctiveness of Christian ethics. There were basically two sets of interlocutors
to the debate: those who propounded an autonomous ethic position, and
others who defended a faith-ethic (*Glaubensethik*) position. These two positions were defended or propounded by some of the most prominent
theologians of the period. In what follows, we will discuss in detail the
work of some of the more prominent contributors to the debate: Alfons
Auer, Josef Fuchs, Bruno Schüller, and Richard McCormick, for the autonomous ethic position; and Joseph Ratzinger and Phillipe Delhaye, for
the faith-ethic position.

The Debate

The Autonomous Ethic School in Moral Theology

Alfons Auer
One of the earliest exponents of the notion of autonomy in Catholic ethics
was Alfons Auer of the University of Tübingen. Auer's position was initially presented in a collection on the conciliar text on the *Pastoral Constitution of the Church in the Modern World.*[17] Réal Tremblay summarizes
Auer's position in this way: First, Reality is the foundation of ethics (the
morality of being). Second, morality consists in a "yes" to Reality's request.
Third, this "yes" is autonomous because it arises from the human person's
capacity to think through existence and human action in this world or because it does not arise from an "explicit knowledge of God." Fourth, for
the Christian, however, this "yes" of the autonomous human being to Re-

ality does not happen without "the active help of God." This means that the free (autonomous) "yes" exists as such in the relations with the transcendent relations (*a*) of origin (protologue: God-Logos) and (*b*) of meaning and end (soteriology/ecclesiology—eschatology: God-Christ-Kyrios). This is the "horizon of meaning" which constitutes the Christian *proprium.* This "horizon of meaning" which is proper to the Christian faith has an impact at the level of the autonomous search for moral norms (function of integration, of stimulation, and of criticism) and at the level of Christian action in the world (invincible courage in commitment). However, it must be noted that it has no influence on the material determination—that is, on the content of the moral act which depends only on the human person and on human reason.[18] This thesis of an autonomous morality was basically accepted and furthered by some notable European theologians such as Hans Küng, Edward Schillebeeckx, Bruno Schüller, and Josef Fuchs, to name a few.

Josef Fuchs

A German Jesuit who taught for many years, from the 1950s up until the late 1980s, at the Pontifical Gregorian University in Rome, Josef Fuchs has more than anyone else carried forward the program of the autonomous school. Fuchs's initial concern in the question of the distinctiveness of Christian morality was to find out whether Christian morality is different from, or even contradictory in content to, the daily morality of men and women everywhere.[19] His conclusion was that there are very few concrete directives in the Scriptures which can be said to be native to the Bible alone. Instead, "much of what we find in scripture, in Christian tradition and the Church's teaching authority is universally human morality."[20] Fuchs refers to human morality as "the morality of man as man" which excludes "everything that we know only from God's revelation about man as he is." This is the same thing as the morality of the natural law.[21] If this is the case, the question is whether there is anything distinct about Christian morality.

According to Fuchs, Christian morality as the morality of those who have found ultimate hope for life and their expectation of salvation in Christ is made up of two complementary yet different elements. Fuchs refers to these as categorical conduct and transcendental attitudes. Categorical conduct refers to action or conduct "in which categorical values, virtues and norms are realized—values, virtues and norms of different categories, such as justice, faithfulness, and purity." Transcendental attitudes, on the other hand, refer to "attitudes and norms, which inform various ethical categories and go beyond them, virtues such as faith, love, allowing oneself to be redeemed, living as a sacramental person, following Christ."[22] Fuchs states that whereas Scripture speaks frequently about transcendent and Christian attitudes as specifically Christian attitudes, it rarely speaks about "the particular, categorical approaches to the various spheres of life (social attitudes, family and conjugal morality, etc.) and is less clear about their meaning and application to various historical periods."[23] The question about the specificity of Christian morality is therefore concerned with whether there are distinctively categorical Christian ways of life—that is, whether there are ways of being just, pure, and faithful which are specifically Christian, or whether "genuinely human attitudes and life styles in various areas of life are not also those of non-Christians." Fuchs argues that the specificity of Christian morality does not lie in the "particularity of categorical values, virtues and norms or various human activities." Rather, it can be located in the fundamental decision of the believer to accept God's love in Christ and respond to it in faith and love and with a sense of responsibility for life in this world in imitation of Christ.[24] It is this Christian decision and fundamental attitude which Fuchs refers to as "Christian intentionality."

There are two aspects to Christian intentionality. In the first instance, it refers to the "full personal, enduring decision, a being-decided in each particular situation" of the Christian. In the second place, Christian intentionality refers to the actual presence of Christian decision and fundamental conduct in the various concrete situations in life. "Christian attitude is brought to bear consciously in the daily shaping of life and the world, so that this daily life in its manifold particularity represents at the same time and in its depths the living, conscious and free actualization of the decisiveness of Christian intentionality."[25] There are two aspects to morality as well. In the one sense, morality refers to the making concrete of a moral value—for example, justice, kindness, faithfulness—through human action. On the other hand, morality refers to the human person's actualization or realization of him- or herself before the Absolute (God) in the light of specific values. In other words, through specific acts, individuals realize not only specific values but themselves as well. It is possible, and is indeed usually the case, that individuals reflect more or less on particular categorical aspects of their lives in a thematic way. The story is different on the transcendental level. There, by choosing certain specific values "ultimately in the light of the Absolute," the individual achieves self-realization or actualization. This form of actualization, according to Fuchs, "tends to the thematic reflection: indeed, it cannot properly be accessible in the center of the 'I' to a full thematic reflection. Nevertheless we are conscious of this self-realization as person before the Absolute, as flowing from the concept of self-realization as an aspect of freedom." Objectively, says Fuchs, it is this latter, the aspect of the individual's self-realization before the Absolute, which constitutes the essence of the moral act, more so than the categorical act, say, of justice or realization of faithfulness. Here we are at the heart of the theory of basic freedom or fundamental option, which has been championed by Fuchs and other theologians of the autonomous school, a theory which as we have already noted in chapter 3 was developed by Karl Rahner. It must be recalled that according to this view, morality must not be thought of in terms of the rightfulness or wrongfulness of particular acts. Rather, what is morally right or morally wrong is decided on the basis of the more basic choice a person makes with respect to the whole moral order. Morality, in this view, "is the free determination of oneself with regard to the totality of existence, a fundamental choice between love and selfishness, between ourselves and God our savior. It is the fundamental acceptance or rejection of the grace that is the person of Jesus into my life at the invitation of the Father. It is our acceptance or rejection deep in our persons of God's enabling love."[26]

In both the categorical and transcendental aspects, Christian intentionality is actually present in the Christian's daily moral conduct as "actual decision for Christ and the Father of Jesus Christ." However, although Christian intentionality pervades and completes "the particular-categorical conduct" of the Christian, it does not determine the content of morality. The reason why this is so, according to Fuchs, is that categorical Christian morality is basically a *humanum*, "that is, a morality of genuine being-human." This implies that "truthfulness, uprightness and faithfulness are not specifically Christian, but generally human values in what they materially say, and that we have reservations about lying and adultery not because we are Christian, but simply because we are human."[27] Since it is the human person who believes existentially, she or he must live and express this belief "in the genuine realization of being-human, of the *humanum*." Christian ethics is thus human ethics. The mission of the Christian within the sphere of morality is to be truly human. In this quest, the Christian "may find help in the sources of revelation." This help does not provide a distinctively Christian morality but rather a genuine understanding of the human person and of human morality.

As Vincent MacNamara points out, Fuchs bolsters his position on this issue with three points which have since become a staple of the autonomy school. The first is the classical position, which has come down from Aquinas, that revelation did not add any new moral precepts which could not be known by reason. Says Fuchs, "The operative moral norms of the new law of Christ are . . . according to Aquinas, determined by reason." What this amounts to is that "there does not exist a moral law added by Christ, which in its material content could be 'specifically' Christian."[28] Second, many biblical authors have shown that "in the law given to us by our savior there is nothing which is not of natural law except those things which pertain to faith and sacraments."[29] Finally, as we have already seen, Fuchs maintains that "many non-Christians follow a morality not only of basic duty but of high ideals—they love enemies, practice non-violence, sacrifice themselves, etc."[30] The task of Christians, as Christians, is "to understand their being-human and the corresponding *humanum* of genuinely human morality."[31] In the search for the *humanum,* Fuchs cautions that we must avoid two pitfalls. On one hand, we must not think of the *humanum* as purely human reality in contrast to or separate from a transcendent morality. On the other hand, we must not perceive "man and his world either—pantheistically or mythically—as 'divine,' or as a world of humans on whom a detached, external God *also* imposes a moral law—his will." God's will is rather the desire of God that human beings exist and live. It is thus left for the human person to discover how to live as human being in this world.[32] Fuchs claims to find support for his position here in the teaching of St. Paul (see Rom 2:1ff.;12:1; 1 Cor 10:32; 1 Thes 4:12) and in the work of St. Thomas Aquinas (*ST,* I-IIae, 108, 2). These, he says, presume that the moral conduct of Christians is materially identical in content to that of non-Christians.[33]

Just as there is a *humanum* of Christian morality there is also a *Christianum* of Christian morality—the distinctively Christian element in the concrete categorical conduct of Christians. This *Christianum* of the *humanum-Christianum,* as Fuchs puts it, is constituted by such realities as the person of Christ, the Spirit of God at work among us, the Christian community, the hierarchical Church, the sacraments, and Christian anthropology, among other things. These realities, which we recognize and accept in faith, constitute part of our very being as Christians. Thus, they must be taken into consideration in our daily lives if we wish to be true to our faith.[34] But how do these realities orient our concrete conduct beyond the *humanum*? Fuchs speaks of a twofold influence. First, the meaning of

— motivation

the *Christianum* for Christian living is to be found in its *motivational power*. This motivational power provides human conduct with a deeper and richer meaning.[35] Second, the *Christianum* has meaning for the conduct of Christians since it also determines the ways of human conduct in their content, through the religious-cultural relationship of the human person *— rel w/* with God. The believer's familiarity with the life and work of Christ and *JC + church* with the basic elements of Christian anthropology, and the general ethos of the Christian community, will influence his life and awaken him to the ethos of the Church and community. At bottom, it will be an ethos of *humanum Christianum*. Fuchs cites several examples: the significance of renunciation and of the cross, the meaning of Christian virginity, obedience to the personal guidance of the Holy Spirit, to the necessity of religious and cultic life, and so on.

Fuchs claims to find support for his position even in the teaching of the Second Vatican Council. He argues that when the Council speaks of human behavior in the world it is not dealing with morality in the strict sense, but rather with the problem of the correctness of the active shaping of the world of people by people. He argues that the Council was aware that the individual is obliged by his or her personal morality both to assume responsibility for the world of people and consequently to set out in search of right or correct action in the world, so as to behave according to the solution he or she has found. This has nothing to do with salvation. It is morality in the real sense of the word. Personal morality or morality in *V2 morality* the real sense in the work of the Council is "an interior openness and readiness to work for the good of the others (*GS,* 39), concern for the right shaping of the world of humanity (*GS,* 39), a tendency towards right action and truth of life (*GS,* 42), readiness to contribute to the temporal world (*GS,* 43), motivation for a right ordering of the world (*GS,* 4)."[36] Morality in the strict sense, Fuchs says, applies to free persons and not to actions as such. These have nothing to do with salvation. Rather they refer to "the right ordering of things in this world." Although faith may be of help in finding solutions to these issues, they are not connected with human salvation. Instead, they have everything to do with what Fuchs in his later writings came to refer to as moral rightness in this world.

Thus another approach to understanding Fuchs's position on the distinctiveness of Christian morality lies in the distinction between the horizontal and the vertical aspects of the human person. The horizontal aspect refers to the person being and acting in the world. It refers to the proper disposition of the realities of this world. It refers to the moral rightness or

horizontal — vertical

wrongness of human conduct. Moral rightness has to do with norms derived from natural law which stem not from revelation but from human
insight.[37] The arena of moral rightness/wrongness, which is the level of
morality properly so called, is neither distinctly Christian nor an area of
competence of the magisterium of the Church. This is because rightness
of "the horizontal realization" of the world of the human person is quite
different from "the goodness of the vertical realization of the person as
person." Although moral rightness is not totally unrelated to moral goodness, they are different. Moral goodness, says Fuchs, refers to the moral
agent, to his or her salvation. "Salvation is the moral goodness of the person as person, given by grace. Salvation as grace brings about the moral
goodness of the person. Moral goodness is both effect and sign of the
grace of salvation. What can be said about the moral goodness of the person is therefore the truth of salvation."[38] Thus, moral goodness is morality
in an analogous sense. Being the area that is concerned strictly with revelation and with salvation, it is the area of the Church's competence. The
following two quotations clearly illustrate Fuchs's position on this issue:

> The question of the "rightness" of acting within this world is not in
> itself a question of the moral goodness of the person, but rather a
> morally neutral question. What is right for the horizontal human
> world: going to the moon or not going? What daily timetable best
> suits a mother who has to go out to work? What kinds of sexual life
> are appropriate for human sexuality as understood in its totality and
> in the richness of its different aspects? Can there be an interruption of
> pregnancy that is the "right" thing to do, taking into account all the
> rights and needs involved? What, under certain circumstances, is the
> right proportion between religion and worldly activity?[39]

Concerning "moral goodness," here is what Fuchs says:

> The judgement as to the rightness of innerworldly actions is not di-
> rectly concerned with salvation. Thus he who realizes all that is
> "right" in this world and avoids what is "wrong" is not yet, therefore,
> necessarily "good" and within the realm of "salvation." Perhaps he is
> an egoist and only wants to be noticed (cf. 1 Cor 13: but if he does
> not have love, he is not in the realm of salvation). On the other hand,
> he who really, as a person, is morally "good" but is not successful in
> his serious search for "right" behavior and therefore does not incar-

nate his goodness in right behavior, can nevertheless be within the realm of salvation.[40]

→ Keenan addresses this

How can a person be "wrong" and still be saved? What then is the relation between the ordinary choices we make in life and the eternal destiny of the human person? Of equal concern to me here as well is Fuchs's attempt to read his dichotomy between moral rightness and moral wrongness as separate areas of the human personality into the works of the Second Vatican Council. I do not believe that this is a warranted assertion. Fuchs himself did not seem to think so in the articles he had written earlier on the moral theology of the Second Vatican Council. In one of those articles he argues, among other things, that the Christian morality envisaged by the Council is not a private morality of the individual with Christ, or "an inner Church morality without regard for the world." On the contrary, "a right viewpoint and mastery of the world" is essential to Christian morality. Christian morality being a morality of call-in-Christ means that the vocation of the Christian is above all else gift and grace. It is also a command and a challenge "to live as one redeemed-liberated . . . and to live as one called to salvation in Christ," a fact which is meant to bear fruit in our Christian living and which determines our life "from our innermost thought and love to the shaping of our world-view."[41]

In this early evaluation of the teaching of the Council, Fuchs, I believe, was certainly right. As I tried to show in the first chapter, the morality that came out of the Council encompassed the individual and social dimensions of the life in this world. It was a morality with repercussions for the eternal well-being (salvation) of the acting person. If how I order my sexual life or what decisions I make in regard to the unborn under any circumstances do not have some relation to my eternal destiny (salvation), I wonder what else does. As I have argued elsewhere, the moral goodness/ moral rightness distinction runs the risk of introducing an unacceptable dualism into human experience. Without impinging on the rightful autonomy of earthly reality, it can be said that "one result of the incarnation is the merging of the orders of creation and redemption. Thus, every action of the Christian has eternal implications. This is why such 'mundane' actions as feeding the hungry or clothing the naked assume eternal spiritual significance." Therefore, the question is to what extent an act can be analyzed in abstraction from the goodness or the badness of the agent. "Is contraception, for example, totally an issue of moral rightness and thus completely unconnected to the salvation of the agent? Or can it not also

citation?

be indicative of the agent's disposition toward the absolute. If so, to what extent can we rule the Church out of it?"[42] When Fuchs classifies the decision whether or not to interrupt a pregnancy as an issue of moral rightness, an innerworldy behavior which might have little or nothing to do with our salvation, he touches on one of the objectionable aspects of his moral theory, one which goes against the belief that certain human actions by their very nature mark our lives and affect our eternal destiny for good or for ill, and therefore ought not to be done at all.

Bruno Schüller

Another theologian who has been at the center of the autonomous ethics debate is Bruno Schüller. Schüller maintains that the notion of an autonomous ethics is not an attempt by some theologians in recent years to renounce the Catholic moral tradition. Rather, it is an effort to win fresh recognition for what has always been there in the tradition.[43] According to Schüller, autonomous ethics is natural law ethics by another name since it is built on the same two characteristic features of natural law. Like natural law, autonomous ethics considers moral demands to be morally right or wrong (φύσει δίκαιον) and thus shuns all moral positivism. Also, "it ascribes the logically original insight into the moral demand to reason (*ratio*), insofar as reason is gnoseologically distinguished, in the Augustinian sense, from faith (*fides*)." It maintains that knowledge of what constitutes morally right conduct or of what it means to be good "can be disclosed to human beings only by their understanding it on their own, and not by, say, leaning (in faith) upon an authoritative assertion from someone else."[44] Like Fuchs, Schüller tries to reach back into the Catholic moral tradition in the manuals and beyond to prove his assertion that autonomous ethics is just a new name for natural law ethics[45] and that it even has a basis in Scripture itself.

Schüller has always maintained that prior to being addressed by God in revelation the human person is an ethical being and, as such, is capable of comprehending moral goodness "in its utterly axiological character." Thus, in the discussion on the distinctiveness of Christian ethics the question is to find out what contributions divine revelation in Scripture makes to this natural situation. Schüller prefaces his discussion on this issue by distinguishing between exhortation and normative ethics. He asserts that although it might appear that Christian ethics has a foundation which is peculiarly its own, it is not really so. Biblical ethics is hortatory. This paranetic character is evident everywhere, including the Decalogue and all of the New Testament. As a statement about the moral goodness of God and of how this goodness makes itself known to human beings, the gospel uses the language of morality when it speaks of the demands of morality on the sinner. However, this language is exhortatory.

The gospel deals with ethical goodness as something real. Insofar as the gospel is embodied in the action of Jesus Christ, it proclaims a moral goodness that has become a reality through perfect obedience. And insofar as it is addressed to Christians, the gospel again has in view a moral goodness that becomes a reality through obedience: Christians have died to sin as is required of them, and have become servants of righteousness as is required of them. As a proclamation of the action of Jesus Christ, and of Christian existence, the gospel is dealing with the requirements that are still to be fulfilled. Thus, it becomes clear, once again, that in the relationship of gospel and law there can be no question of normative ethics, that is, of determining and articulating the content of the requirements of morality.[46]

The normative character of the gospel as the revelation of God's action and purposes in the world and of Christ's action for the salvation of the world is the normative character of a model. A model is normative on the grounds of its exemplarity—that is, of an exhortative example of what it means to fulfill the demands of morality. Jesus Christ is presented as an exemplar, a *norma normata,* "whenever the New Testament presents his life and death as the exercise of obedience or the fulfillment of the Father's will." Yet this normativity of Jesus must not lead to "Christonomous positivism," as if to say that the action of God or of Christ constituted the concept of moral goodness. To think like this is to assume implicitly that to act in a morally good way is "to act like God" or "to act like Christ," even though neither the word "God" nor the word "Christ" contains "to be morally good" as a distinct element in its meaning. The normativity of Jesus can only be expressed in hortatory terms. And the exemplarity of Christ is not to be understood in the sense of Christ being the standard of what it means to be morally good but in the sense that he provides the standard of the exercise of moral goodness.[47]

When the Scriptures bring up the requirements of morality in connection with future judgment, we have exhortation. This exhortation "finds expression in ethical statements the truth of which is taken as self evident." This does not mean that exhortation is not something to be taken seriously. For although exhortation, of itself, does not convey any new moral insights, its intention is intimately to touch the person addressed and move her or him to conversion, penance, and a change of life, "to act as he knows he ought to act." Thus,

> exhortation is to be valued not primarily in terms of its truth-value but in terms of its effect-value, that is according to whether it is effective or ineffective, whether it succeeds or fails. We would form a very inadequate idea of exhortation if we looked for it only in catalogues of virtues and vices or in lists of commands and prohibitions such as the decalogue and the rules for house-holds. No, exhortation may also be given through stories, parables, metaphors and narratives.[48]

Since Jesus perfectly fulfilled the demands of morality in his own life and authentically interpreted them in his preaching, the believer's unconditional reliance on Jesus as infallible authority in morality is well placed, Schüller says, provided it is not assumed that the demands of morality as lived and interpreted by him "take us beyond the realm of knowledge accessible to reason." Schüller maintains that, theologically speaking, "the requirements of morality, insofar as they are accessible in principle to reason, are commandments of the Creator." If this is kept in mind, he says, "it is not clear how anyone can show that Jesus did not intend simply to revalidate the commandments of the Creator against possible misunderstanding."[49]

A number of issues arise here. The first has to do with Schüller's view on how we come to know right and wrong. His view is very rationalistic in that it does not address the particularity which is the source of our knowing. Thus, for him it seems that a Muslim born in Somalia and a Christian teaching in Germany know the same way and if they are rational enough would always come to the same conclusions as to what is right and wrong as a Christian living in South Bend. All that would distinguish a Christian in this situation would be that he would be motivated by the life of Jesus to do good and avoid evil. But this attitude to moral knowledge misses an important insight in recent moral discourse which shows that "there is no other way to engage in the formulation, elaboration, rational justification, and criticisms of accounts of practical rationality and justice except from within some particular tradition in conversation, cooperation, and conflict with those who inherit the same tradition. There is no standing ground, no place for enquiry, no way to engage in the practices of advancing, evaluating, accepting, and rejecting reasoned argument apart from that which is provided by some particular tradition or other."[50] What this amounts to with specific reference to Christian ethics is that it derives its status and specificity from a narrative structure which is founded on belief in what Joseph Sittler refers to as "God's engendering deed" in Jesus Christ. This narrative structure provides a basis on which the believer is able to comprehend reality and to live in relation to that reality. It also provides the basis on which moral theology can be regarded as theology. The crisis of pre–Vatican II moral theology results precisely from its failure to remain attached to its Christian roots. Thus in the end what resulted was a "theology" which was rendered contextless and which ultimately turned into everything else but theology. A second issue arising from Schüller's attempt is that by rendering the person of Jesus vacuous as a moral teacher it fails to take account of the innumerable people in history who saw Jesus as more than a model of good behavior, but as indeed a moral teacher from whom one can take specific directives about what to do on a day-to-day basis concerning the concrete categorical choices every human being has to make in life.

Richard McCormick

Richard McCormick presents what may be regarded as a mitigated form of the autonomous ethics theory. Like Schüller, he presents his understanding of the specificity of Christian ethics against the background of the Church's teaching on natural law. As we shall see in chapter 6, natural law in Catholic tradition is understood to imply that "moral values and obligations are grounded in a moral order known by human reason reflecting on experience."[51] Consequently, knowledge of the moral law is not based directly on faith or Church teaching or limited to Christian tradition since it is disclosed through the order of creation which reflects the reason of God. This order being available to rational analysis implies that the teaching office of the Church is not the sole but only the authentic interpreter of this mind of God—and this because what is available in creation has received special articulation in the incarnation to which the Church is an infallible authority. Lastly, this traditional view of natural law holds that "nature" is immutable and essentially the same always and everywhere. McCormick is basically in agreement with the substance of this natural law tradition, but he insists that for Church teaching, biblical revelation provides the starting point for various interpretations of natural law. Biblical revelation contributes three basic elements to moral discourse: the notion of God's gift of himself to humankind, the centrality of love in morality, and the understanding of moral action as an empowered (graced) response.[52] These elements, and indeed the entire gospel, lead to a "profound relativising of basic human values."[53] And since they affect "our way of perceiving basic human values and relating to them" through shaping "our whole way of looking at the world," they should protect us against the tendency "to meet persons functionally" by sensitizing "us to the meaning of persons, [and] to their inherent dignity regardless of function-ability."[54]

There is therefore a dialectical tension between biblical morality and natural law. For although the revelation of the word of God in the Scriptures represents a full articulation of the mind of God, "man's [moral] obligation is founded on man's being."[55] And thus biblical morality would be incomprehensible to the believer if he were not, prior to the revelation of God's Word in Scripture, an ethical being.[56] In *The Critical Calling*,[57] Mc-Cormick argues that although, as the Second Vatican Council would say, "faith throws new light on everything,"[58] and although religious faith "stamps one at a profound and irrecoverable depth," affecting one's perspectives, analyses, and judgments, Christian moral judgments are not essentially different from the moral judgments of non-Christians or even of nonbelievers. That is, they are not exclusive or particular to Christians as a matter of special and particular revelation.[59] Therefore, McCormick affirms the autonomous existence of a natural moral order grounded in the being of the human person as human person, though he argues that this affirmation says very little and leads to two types of interpretation and to two different understandings of the basis of moral obligation.[60]

McCormick's position on this issue was eventually anchored on the division of ethics on various levels. Following Nobert Rigali,[61] McCormick states that there are four levels at which the term "ethics" can be understood: essential ethics, existential ethics, essential Christian ethics, and existential Christian ethics. The level of essential ethics is that of norms which are applicable to everyone, the level where "one's behaviour is but an instance of general, essential moral norm." Thus, for instance, keeping promises, killing, contracts, and so on, are all issues whose rightness or wrongness is rooted in the dignity of every human person *qua* person. This is the level at which obligations can cut across the entire human spectrum, irrespective of stature, station, or affiliation. The second level, that of existential ethics, refers "to the choice of the good that the individual should realise, the absolute demand addressed to an individual," and which requires that the individual make a concrete ethical choice based on his or her welfare, growth, inclination, background, talent, and so forth. Essential Christian ethics, on the other hand, refers to the ethical choices a Christian *qua* Christian has to make. For example, it includes such choices as those about regarding his fellow workers as brothers and sisters in Christ (not just as autonomous, to-be-respected persons), providing a Christian education for one's children, belonging to a particular worshipping community, and so forth. It is an ethic which stems from the fact of Christianity as a Church with pronounced and preordained structures and symbols. And fourth, Christian existential ethics refers to the ethical decisions which the Christian as an individual must make, such as whether to become a priest, a nun, or not, whether to concentrate on this or that political issue or not.[62]

ecclesial factor

Natural law ethicists speak on the level of essential ethics.[63] And even though it is true that "religious faith stamps one at a profound and not totally recoverable depth," thus affecting one's perspectives, analyses, and judgments,[64] and even though it should be readily granted that revelation and one's faith do influence one's ethical decisions at the last three levels,[65] it is also true here that "one's conclusions will not be substantially different from those yielded by objective and reasonable but non-religious analyses."[66] As McCormick himself puts it, the Christian community is a storied community, that is, a community which speaks out of a particular memory.[67] In the process of reasoning about its story, the Catholic community claims to disclose "surprising and delightful insights about the human condition as such." Reasoning about the Christian story thus claims to reveal the deeper dimensions of what it is to be human. And even though this reflection cannot and does not add to human ethical self-understanding as such—in terms of a material ethical content that is "strange" and "foreign" to man as he exists and experiences himself in this world—the Christian story represents a "privileged articulation, in objective form, on this experience of subjectivity. Precisely because the resources of scripture, dogma, and Christian life ('the storied community') are the fullest available objectifications of the common human experience, the articulation of man's image of his moral good that is possible within historical Christian communities remains privileged in its access to enlarged perspectives on man."[68]

sounds like Fuchs' motivation but more nuance

The point here is that Scripture is related to the natural law as a privileged articulation and objectification. And even though Scripture can and does influence the formation of people's conscience, yet in matters relating to concrete moral decisions, the substantive results are not in any way particularistic, exclusive, or unreasonable on the essential (most important) level.

I referred earlier to McCormick's position as a mitigated version of the autonomous ethic position. The reasons are clear. Although he believes in the autonomy of the human person to make choices, he is careful to work into this understanding the influence of the faith or particular traditions and beliefs which the individual inhabits. The individual does not come to moral decision making as a *tabula rasa*. Nor is the sphere of the faith as clear and that of the otherworldly realities as clear-cut as it appears in the works of Fuchs. This position would influence, as we shall see later on, what McCormick would say about the Church's competence in certain moral matters. The difference would be that unlike Fuchs he would not rule the Church out of contention in most moral matters. Rather, he would suggest a more modest ecclesiastical pronouncement in these matters, especially in those matters like contraception which he believes do not warrant an absolute prohibition from the magisterium since they are matters pertaining to natural law.

The theologians I have presented here are not the only ones who defend an autonomous ethic position in postconciliar moral theology. A fuller picture would have to take into account the works of J.-M. Aubert, Franz Böckle, Charles Curran, and many others. The views of the theologians presented here fairly represent the mainstream in this movement. The theologians of the autonomous ethics movement in Catholic moral theology do not consider themselves as advocates of autonomy in the secularist sense. Rather, they see themselves as heirs of the call of the Second Vatican Council for a proper respect for the autonomy of earthly things. They consider themselves furthermore as continuing in the footsteps of St. Thomas when they insist that it is only human reason (even if enlightened by faith) which concretizes ethical obligation. The human person has direction for his life and is delegated by God to take charge of it through the use of his reason and of his liberty. Human theonomy supposes a liberty which leaves to human reason, created by God for that, the mission to find ways of acting ethically as a Christian.[69] Ethical autonomy is thus situated within concrete norms of action. It is a relational autonomy which is not absolute but is united to the theonomy on which it is founded. Autonomy is thus discovered and assumed by the faith to a level which puts it on a new horizon of signification and comprehension.[70] The divine transcendence penetrates the human being with its power and raises human liberty and potentials in a way that their historical and ethical development become not only their doing but that of God as well.[71] "Human autonomy can therefore only be understood as a gift of God. This communion with God gives a salvific value to the profane action of the Christian and makes the ethical engagement of the Christian a participation in the action of God in history."[72]

The Faith-Ethic Position

As we have seen so far, no theologian denies that there is some relationship between faith and morality. What is being debated is the precise nature of this relationship. The faith-ethic nomenclature refers to the position of the theologians who, in contradistinction to the autonomous ethic position, hold that "part of Christian ethics is not only revealed but specific and therefore closed to unbelievers. Since this is found primarily in the Bible, approach to morality, they say must be through the Bible."[73] Joseph Ratzinger regards it as basic to the discussion on the specificity of Christian morality to determine what is specifically Christian in view of the changing historical forms of Christianity. The faith-ethic position thus makes direct appeal to the Bible both as a source of moral norms and values, and as a source of faith—"of beliefs, stories, symbols—which influences discernment and which leads the Christian in any age to moral judgments that are specific."[74]

For many theologians, the position of autonomous ethics constituted a reversal of the renewal for which so many had worked for so long. G. Emercke, an early advocate of renewal, was among the first to react in bewilderment to the position of the autonomous ethic theologians. He reproached the autonomous ethicists for being immanentist and argued that they were in danger of espousing a form of utilitarian subjectivism. He insisted that motivations alone cannot account for what is specific in Christian ethics. Christian ethics is also made up of specific concrete norms. He maintained that if the human person is elevated to the order of salvation and grace, that should also translate to full normative content and a unique way of acting in the world. The influence of grace cannot just be limited to intentionality alone.[75] B. Stöckle, in reacting against the autonomous ethic position, in 1975 began with contesting the idea of autonomy itself. He believed the concept was too ambiguous and smacked of opposition to the notion of transcendence. The human person cannot be the subject of transcendence, he said; God is. In the incarnation, God transforms the

imperative (you should love) to an indicative (you are loved). Like Emercke, Stöckle contests the limitation of what is specific to Christian ethics
to merely the level of motivation.[76]

As anyone who is familiar with the literature knows, reaction to the
autonomous ethic position runs wide and deep. That reaction has been
well documented by Vincent MacNamara and Eric Gaziaux in their books
on the debate over the nature of Christian ethics. There is no need to go
into all the details here. I shall only present in some detail the views of two
of the most vocal and influential critics of the autonomous ethic theologians: Joseph Cardinal Ratzinger and Phillipe Delhaye.

Joseph Ratzinger

Joseph Cardinal Ratzinger is the prefect of the Congregation for the Doctrine of the Faith in the Vatican. Ratzinger was for many years professor of
theology at Feising, Bonn, Münster, and Tübingen. In 1969 he became
dean of the theological faculty at Tübingen; in 1976 he was made archbishop of Munich. He was made a cardinal in 1977.

In his discussion on the distinctiveness of Christian ethics Ratzinger
has two goals in mind: first is to show that there is a definite and distinct
content to Christian morality; second is to demonstrate that the magisterium of the Church has authority to teach in matters of right and wrong.
For Ratzinger, the originality of Christian morality does not lie in the sum
of principles, which have no parallel elsewhere. "Christian originality consists rather in the new overall conception in which man's quest or aspiration was directed by faith in the God of Abraham, in the God of Jesus
Christ. The reference of morality to pure reason is in no way proved by
the fact that the moral teaching of the Bible has its origin in other cultures
or philosophical thought. . . . What is decisive is not the fact that these
principles can be found elsewhere, but only the problem of the place they
do or do not occupy in the spiritual structure of Christianity."[77] Ratzinger
insists that it is incorrect from the historical point of view to assert that
Christianity took over at all periods the morality of its environment—that
is, the degree of moral knowledge reached by reason. There was no ready-
made morality to be taken over to begin with. "We see rather that, amid
tensions that were often highly dramatic, the elements of the juridico-
moral tradition of the surrounding world were divided into those which,
corresponding to the figure of Yahweh, could be assimilated by Israel and
those which, on the basis of the representation of God, had to be rejected.
In the last analysis, the battle of the prophets is connected with this prob-

lem."[78] In other words, there has always been a close connection between faith and ethics. And, "the option for one God or for the gods is in every case a life decision."[79]

Ratzinger offers three examples of the union of faith and morality. The first is the Ten Commandments. These commandments were pivotal in the relationship of God and Israel. They have also been a source of renewal for the morality of Israel and the Church. It is true that the commandments have models both in Egyptian lists of crimes and in Babylonian texts, yet the very words which preface the commandments—"I am the Lord your God"—give them a new significance and indicate their connection with the God of Israel, the God of the covenant and his will.[80] The Decalogue shows the nature of God, who God is, and with whom God is in alliance— a fact which indicates the particular connection between God's holiness and morality. It is thus clear from the Bible that Yahweh's being-quite-different, his holiness, is a moral greatness to which the moral action of the human person must correspond according to the Ten Commandments. "The conception of holiness as the specific category of the divine, merges, even in those ancient strata of tradition to which the Ten Commandments belong, with the conception of morality, and this is precisely the novelty, the singularity of this God and his holiness. But here, too, lies the new value that morality acquires, which determines the criterion of choice in the dialogue with the ethics of peoples, until there arises that lofty concept of holiness which, in the Old Testament, anticipates the divine figure of Jesus."[81]

A second example which Ratzinger offers concerning the union of faith and morality comes from early Christianity. He stresses the fact that the very conception and even the very name "Christian" were understood by the early Christians as a "conspiracy to do good." The name "Christian," he says, "means communion with Christ, but for that very reason, the willingness to accept the martyrdom of good. Christianity is a conspiracy to do good. The theological and moral qualities are inseparably bound up with the name and, even deeper, with the essential concepts of Christianity."[82] Finally, Ratzinger argues that the union of faith and morality is very much evident in the apostolic teaching of the early Church. Paul, for instance, did not just take over pagan philosophical morals. Faith and imitation of the apostle, which is imitation of Jesus, are characteristics of the preaching of Paul, for example in 1 Thessalonians 4:1 and in the following verses. Ratzinger maintains that when in this text Paul urges the Thessalonians to continue to live in a way that pleases God, the "live" in this passage belongs to tradition. The order comes from the Lord Jesus and not from anywhere else, and the specifications which Paul gives as to how the Christian should live are taken from the Ten Commandments, which are explained in a Christian way and adapted to the specific situation of the Thessalonian Christians. The same is true of all other passages in which Paul urges Christians to imitate him and to keep doing what they have heard or seen him do, as, for example, in Philippians 4:9 or Philippians 2:5, where he urges his audience to be "of the same mind as Christ." In these instances, says Ratzinger, we find a necessary connection between Jesus' way of thinking and the Christian existence. We find, moreover, nothing like the carryover of pagan philosophical morals into Christianity. Thus we are not dealing here with exhortation, the intention of which is merely to awaken Christians to what is considered good by reason. There was in fact "not a precise position of research on good, which could be taken over" by Christianity. There was, instead, "a confusion of contradictory positions of which Epicurus and Seneca are only two examples." Consequently, it was not possible to proceed by accepting these positions. "It was necessary, on the contrary, to make a decisive and critical separation in which the Christian faith formed its new option in accordance with the Old Testament standards and with the way of thinking of Jesus Christ. These options were condemned by the outside world as 'conspiracy,' but were all the more resolutely considered as the real 'good' by Christians themselves."[83]

Also, for Paul, says Ratzinger, conscience is true only when it says the same things as God said in the covenant with Jesus, revealing what is abiding and leading necessarily to the way of thinking of Jesus Christ. It is clear especially in the letter to the Romans, that Paul sees a real connection between morality and the conception of God. Lack of the conception of God "brings about the moral deficiency of the pagan world; conversion to God in Jesus Christ coincides with conversion to the imitation of Jesus Christ." In Ratzinger's opinion, therefore, "the apostolic preaching is not a moralizing appendage the contents of which could be changed, but is the concrete designation of what faith is and therefore linked indissolubly with its central point." Paul in his teaching does not theorize about human rationality. Rather he "sets forth the inner necessity of grace." His teaching is magisterial and guaranteed by the Lord. It is not a mere variable accessory to the gospel. Paul shows that "the line of demarcation drawn by God's grace in regard to the life of those who know God is quite clear: it is abstention from wantonness, greed, envy and quarrelsomeness; inclina-

tion to obedience, patience, truth and joy: in these attitudes the fundamental command of love is unfolded." As in Paul's day, so today. The magisterium of the Church has the task of explaining the apostolic doctrine in
a way that is suited to the situation. It is obvious from the New Testament,
says Ratzinger, that the ecclesial magisterium does not end with the time
of the apostles. The Church remains apostolic, and it is still its task to see
to it "that the successors of the apostles defend the unchangeability of the
apostolic doctrine."[84]

As Vincent MacNamara points out, the conclusion from Ratzinger's
position is clearly that faith includes judgments of content. It is therefore
the task of Christianity "to continue to elaborate moral norms from faith
and refuse to capitulate to reason. In doing so it is to remember that the
clear content of biblical morality is a constant of Christianity and not a
variable."[85] In the words of Joseph Ratzinger himself, "The practice of faith
belongs, in fact to Christian faith. Orthodoxy without orthopraxis loses the
essence of Christianity: the love that comes from grace. At the same time,
however, it is admitted that Christian practice is nourished by Christian
Faith: by the grace that appeared in Christ and was admitted to the *Sacramentum Ecclesiae*. The practice of faith depends on the truth of faith, in
which man's truth is made visible through God's truth and is raised one
step higher."[86]

The problem with Ratzinger's position is that it fails in some sense to
address the real question which some of the autonomous ethic theologians are raising. This question is whether the Christian faith adds any
concrete elements to the moral code which are not discoverable by reason
or which are knowable only by faith. The issue here is very tricky given
the Church's espousal of natural law. The trick arises especially in the context of the debate which arose in regard to contraception in the Church.
As we have pointed out already, some of these theologians assumed that
since this was a teaching based on natural law the Church had no business legislating on the matter. The answer to that charge lies in the
Church's self-understanding which can only be accepted in faith, namely
that in some sense natural law is the reverse side of the revealed truth of
which the Church is guardian. It is in that sense the word of God, and
thus an area of ecclesial competence as well. Thus even if there are no
moral precepts which are known only by faith, morality and faith are still
inextricably intertwined. Faith still has a moral component. Morality is
sustained by faith. The magisterium has competence to elaborate on matters of right and wrong in this world.

Phillipe Delhaye

Phillipe Delhaye insists that it is important to ask what we mean by the specificity of a morality, what attributes that make a morality constitute a species, and why a particular morality is original, if we must get the right answer about the specificity of Christian morality. He notes that although there is certainly extensive concordance between the different religions and philosophy on a lot of practical moral issues, there is also alongside this material concordance a radical difference of inspiration, "the one religious in the form of the covenant, the other philosophical if not political."[87] These divergences become apparent only when a comparison is made between what some call "ancient morality" and "new morality" in connection with areas such as abortion, fidelity in marriage, premarital relations, revolution, and so forth. It is the tendency of the so-called new morality, Delhaye says, to reject all predetermined, fixed, and objective moral rules. These thinkers assert that "only relations exist" instead of universally applicable principles, and they state that there are moralities instead of a morality by which all are bound. Delhaye believes that given this situation, the distinction made by Josef Fuchs between transcendental morality and categorical morality becomes useful in showing that "the specificity of the ethics of Aristotle and of Kant also situates on the transcendental level much more than on the categorical level." Thus, even if one assumes that there are no divergences between Christian categorical and philosophical categorical levels of morality—an assumption Delhaye rejects—yet "the specific situation of the ethics of Christianity would not be a situation of so rare a character."[88] Greater attention has to be paid, however, to the meaning of the categorical contradictions between the "new and classical moralities," especially at the level of the transcendental.

> In all the concrete problems of the new morality, it is evident that, at bottom, what makes the difference is an option for the "lived experience" against principles (inspired by faith or reason), for a demand of total freedom against the idea of duty (based on the life of Christ or on human dignity), for the absolute creation of values against their transcendental objectivity, for cultural models determined by the historical state of each society, indeed by its economic condition, against a moral "project" based on a God who transcends time and on a human structure a certain permanence of which is recognized.[89]

The negation of a specific Christian morality is quite often based in part on the rejection of the classical theology of revelation. Delhaye argues that such a negation is understandable if one shares the views of Bultmann and others that revelation is not the manifestation of the mystery of the will of God. However, such a view of revelation is inadequate. Indeed it is wrong. The correct thing is to assert, as did the Second Vatican Council, that the Church has its life and support in revelation which is also the soul of theology, especially moral theology, which must, in the words of the Council, "be thoroughly nourished by scriptural teaching."[90] Delhaye notes that Christian morality has always been presented as the morality of faith in the Scriptures,[91] in the work of the fathers of the Church,[92] and in the work of the Scholastics, especially Thomas Aquinas.[93] He also notes the link in the texts of the Second Vatican Council between faith and morals.[94] The popes also have always emphasized the bond between morality and revelation. Pope Paul VI makes the matter clear, emphasizing that Christian morality is "a manner of living according to the faith, that is to say, in the light of the truth and of the example of Christ such as they are related to us in the gospel and in the first echo of Christ given by the apostles in the New Testament."[95]

The First and Second Vatican Councils distinguish between the revelation of mysteries, properly so called, which transcend human intelligence and the revelation of natural verities. The revelation of mysteries is absolutely necessary for salvation. However, salvation which is on offer is not given without acceptance and collaboration on the part of the human agent. What is involved here is a newness, the like of which does not exist anywhere else. The life of the Christian is new. And this newness lies in love: "A new commandment I give you, that you love one another. By this all men will know that you are my disciples, if you have love for one another." Some writers of the autonomous ethic school would deny that there is newness in this commandment. However, Delhaye wonders whether there is not in this command "a new extension in as much as nobody can be excluded, a new sense in as much as Christian love is connected to Christ who gave his life for his friends (Jn 15:13) as well as for his enemies." Human love is before all else "a desire for reciprocity whereas Christian love is essentially a gift offered even to those who, as enemies, have no value in our eyes (Mt 5:43–48)."[96] Charity introduces specificity to Christian ethics not only at the transcendental level but at the categorical level as well. It is impossible to love well without keeping the commandments (Jn 14:15; 1 Jn 5:3). But, on the other hand, we cannot be possessed by charity without adopting precise rules of conduct. Delhaye points out as well how Paul has shown that charity commends specific virtues and forbids specific vices when he enjoins his listeners to certain forms of action: "Be patient, render service, be not envious, boast-ful, or arrogant, do nothing that is ugly, seek not your interest, be not irri-table or resentful, rejoice not at wrong, but rejoice in the right, forgive all things, believe all things, hope in all things and endure all things." The fact is, according to Delhaye, that even though these practical attitudes can be discovered by reason, "revelation has integrated them so that all persons can have access to them with greater facility and greater sure-ness." Thus, we must, in line with the First and the Second Vatican Coun-cils, attribute to revelation the fact that "those religious truths which are by their nature accessible to human reason can be known to all men with ease, with solid certainty, and with no sense of error, even in the present state of the human race."[97] Delhaye warns that while it is proper to take proper cognizance of the philosophical and human arguments which are presupposed in these verities, we must not forget the specific Christian consideration which Paul advances therein. In other words, the desire to emphasize human authenticity should not end in the loss of Christian identity. Such a situation would play into the hands of those who believe that Christian involvement in the human city constitutes a threat to human authenticity.[98]

Delhaye insists that in order to understand the demand for a Christian morality, it is necessary to go back to what revelation and the magisterium say on the vocation of the human person. A first dimension of this voca-tion is the divinization of the human person.[99] In line with the Second Vatican Council, Delhaye argues that this incorporation does not destroy the *humanum.* Rather, by the revelation of the mystery of the Father and his love, Christ, the final Adam, "reveals man to himself and makes his supreme calling clear." Catholic tradition acknowledges that grace acts in unseen ways in the hearts of all people of goodwill, and this does not ex-clude all that which belongs to the secular and natural dimension of the human person from this unique divine vocation. The *contemptus mundi,* which had in past ages created the conviction that to be fully human one had to disengage oneself from the divine, is not the stand of Catholicism. Catholicism believes in the intrinsic worth of human cultural, economic, and social affairs. The human person is not divided into the divine and human aspects of his or her vocation. The Church, even though it is a so-ciety of those "who are fastened to Christ," casts "the reflected light" of the divine life over the entire earth. It has pleased God to unite all things in Christ. This, however, does not deprive the temporal order of its inde-pendence, its proper goals, laws, resources, and significance. Rather, it perfects it in its intrinsic strength and excellence, raising it "to the level of man's total vocation on earth."[100]

critique of Fuchs

According to Delhaye, one of the shortcomings of the position of Josef Fuchs on the specificity of Christian morality is its failure to consider the incidence of divine life on human life through grace, on the categorical level, as he has done with regard to the transcendental level. The specificity of Christian morality is incomprehensible outside the frame of Christian life and grace. The imperatives of the life of the human person divinized in Christ are the very consequence of the presence of the Spirit. This is precisely why "the fruits of the Spirit (Gal 5:22), faith, hope, charity (Rom 5:5), are before all else the action of God in us. All the categorical injunctions that flow from it, and not only in some exceptional cases as Fr. Fuchs thinks, all the most trivial sectors of life, all the action of a Christian ordained to effectuate the humanization of his person, of others, of the cosmos, are always under the prompting of the grace of Christ."[101] It is for this reason then that Christian morality has, throughout its history, transformed the categorical morality it took over from different civilizations, especially from ancient Greece and ancient Rome. These mutations have not always been sufficiently catalogued thematically on the level of principles.[102]

*   *   *

In this chapter, we have discussed some of the postconciliar debates on the very assumption of a distinctive Christian morality. I have tried to show some of the underlying motivations of this debate, as well as the specific contributions and presuppositions of some of the major interlocutors on this issue. Certain features of this debate must be kept in mind. One of these is the sometimes overlapping positions of the interlocutors who otherwise are opposed to each other on some other fundamental issues, and the differences in the positions of some of those who are thought to belong to the same camp, so to speak. Let me explain.

Although McCormick and Ratzinger are basically on opposite sides of the discussion on the distinctiveness of Christian ethics, they also have a good deal in common insofar as both of them suggest that the true distinctiveness of Christian ethics is a distinctiveness of its narrative embedding. McCormick speaks of the Christian community as a storied community, while Ratzinger draws attention to the place that particular moral principles occupy in "a new overall conception" brought by faith in

similarities: McCormick + Ratzinger

Christ and attends to the specific contributions made by the prophets and other teachers in the Bible, such as Paul. The positions of these two authors contain a very important insight. Revelation teaches moral truths which are not without resonance in general human experience but which we cannot completely grasp without the light of revelation. This implies that although revelation does not teach us everything, it does not teach us nothing. It is false to hold an absolute position on this matter. A position like that of Schüller, which denies all content to Christian morality and reduces it to merely inspirational or paranetic, is unjustifiable. Schüller could arrive at such a conclusion because he holds a very restrictive view of morality which limits morality to rules and obligations. A wider view of morality, such as that seen in the work of Richard McCormick, and especially in the work of virtue ethicists, whom we will consider later in this book, would consider morality as including also the disposition, vision, or the moral agent. Given this widened view, what one should consider in the question on the distinctiveness of Christian ethics is not just "the individual elements of morality, but the overall conception into which the Christian's quest and aspiration are directed by faith, the spiritual structure of Christianity." It is in this overall structure that one discovers the vision and perspective of Christian morality, "its spirit and disposition, its open-ended character."[103]

There are of course some serious differences between McCormick and Ratzinger, insofar as McCormick wants to highlight an ethical arena which is not subject to control by the magisterium, while Ratzinger insists that the magisterium's teaching authority does not have such limits. This debate will of course form the basis of discussion in chapter 7 of this book. The pertinent issue here is whether Ratzinger's two goals, that of insisting on the distinctiveness of Christian morality and that of insisting on the teaching authority of the magisterium, must hang together. For one could also hold, closer to the position of Delhaye, that the teaching authority of the magisterium is required not because the ethic of Christianity is unique, but simply because human reason is corrupt, so that the magisterium must teach authoritatively even in matters pertaining to natural law. On this latter issue, Ratzinger and Delhaye are farther apart. Whereas Ratzinger has more of a historicist sensibility, and attends to the context within which distinctively Christian ideals emerged, Delhaye seems intent on denouncing historicism and insisting that Christianity teaches absolute values which are not in any way historically or contextually shaped.

Euro + clerical

The mostly European nature of the debate on the distinctiveness of Christian ethics has to be kept in view, as does the clerical nature of its participants. The initial European character of the discussion can easily be explained by several factors. First, up until the time of the Council, it is safe to say, Catholic theology was mostly European theology. The agenda and the actors were mostly European since, as was shown earlier in the chapter, the issue of distinctiveness arose particularly out of the need for the European Church to make sense of the cultural pluralism which had become a feature of European life by the 1960s and to which the Church had to respond to stay relevant. Second, the scriptural renewal which had begun with *Divino Afflante Spiritu* was also mostly felt in Europe, which up until then had the most prestigious centers of theological learning in the Catholic world. Thus, it was no accident that the main players were from Louvain, Paris, the Gregorian University in Rome, Catholic theological faculties in Munich, Freiburg, Tübingen, and other theological faculties in Europe. And they were mostly clerical. Since theology was mostly a clerical pursuit at the time, this should not be surprising. However, by the mid-1970s things had begun to change. The debate expanded to include especially theologians in North America and to address the more precise question of the relationship of natural law and revelation or Scripture and the specific contribution of the latter to Christian ethics.

The debate on the specificity of Christian ethics has meanwhile continued in other forms. Many younger Catholic moralists seem to have *young MT?* taken the view that Christianity has a distinctive content as a narratively embedded discourse. These moralists argue that the distinctiveness of Christian ethics, or any form of moral tradition for that matter, lies in the way it shapes character. Thus, by ordering our values, the Christian tradition as a tradition of moral discourse delineates our perspective, shapes our loyalties, and indicates ways through which the central symbols of the community can be brought to bear on our particular moral problems as members of the particular community in question.[104] According to this view, our moral judgments are incarnations of more basic normative positions which have their roots in spontaneous, prereflective inclinations. Although these inclinations are prior to acculturation they are nonetheless culturally conditioned. "We tend toward values as perceived. And the culture in which we live shades our perception of values . . . In other words, decisions are made, policies set not chiefly by articulated norms, codes, regulations, and philosophies, but by 'reasons' that lie below the surface."[105] Thus different traditions are influenced by different stories which make them able to shape the worldviews of the people who inhabit or are informed by the traditions in question. Here lies the distinctiveness of any moral tradition, including the Christian moral one.

The crucial question which those who espouse this view still face is whether the moral positions or the conclusions which people from a particular tradition adopt on a given issue are open to them only on account of their particular stories and to no one else. Let us take abortion or euthanasia or suicide, for example. Is the Christian story the only way to know that committing abortion or suicide is a wrong thing to do? Can human reason working independently of revelation and in another tradition come to such a conclusion? We must conclude that it can. This is also the view of the Catholic tradition as we shall see when we treat the question of natural law in the Catholic tradition. Natural law in this tradition, as we will see, is understood to imply that moral values and obligations are grounded in a moral order known by human reasoning reflecting on experience.[106] Consequently, knowledge of the moral law is neither based solely on any faith nor limited to any one tradition since it is disclosed through the order of creation which reflects the reason of God. The point then is that although the various traditions to which we belong shape our perceptions of the world and of the moral order, they neither have exclusive hold on our reasoning nor do they offer exclusive insights into normal moral dilemmas and problems.

Scripture and Ethics

Another aspect to the discussion on the distinctiveness of Christian ethics concerns the place and role of Scripture in ethics. The Bible is believed to be the revealed word of God among Christians. Although the Catholic Church has for much of its history since the thirteenth century espoused a natural law ethic, it has always considered the Scriptures to be normative for its life and mission. We have seen how inadequate the use of Scripture was in the moral manuals prior to Vatican II. We discussed as well the conciliar injunction to make Scripture the center of moral discussion and how this interest in the importance of Scripture was preceded and to a large extent motivated by the biblical renewal movement which was afoot in the Catholic Church in the early to middle part of the twentieth century. One of the great gains from the biblical renewal movement is the recognition of biblical diversity. This recognition of the diverse cultural concerns and theological positions in the Bible has in turn given a new twist to the discussion on biblical authority. The questions on this issue can be broadly grouped into three categories. The first question concerns the significance of biblical diversity for the canon. At issue is whether the entire Bible or just parts of it are canonical, and thus authoritative. And even if it is granted that Scripture is authoritative for the Churches, how have Catholic theologians seen this authority, especially in regard to ethics? The Churches for which the Bible is authoritative are made up of members who, as Lisa Sowle Cahill puts it, "have a number of overlapping identities

(cultural, political, familial), providing multiple understandings of themselves and their world."[1] The question is whether and how Scripture can
be authoritative to all these people in their various particularities.

The second question concerns how to make the move from authority
to authorization. How can Scripture be used as the norm for particular
doctrinal and/or ethical judgments, with reference especially to specific historical, cultural, and sociological situations? The third question has to do
with whether Scripture alone is authoritative. In other words, the issue is
the relationship between Scripture and other sources of ethical wisdom.[2]
The first two questions will occupy us in the rest of this chapter. We will
illustrate the problems and the solutions offered using two significant approaches to Scripture in recent times. The third question will be discussed
in the following chapter on natural law.

The Authority of Scripture in Christian Ethics

Attitudes toward the authority of Scripture vary among scholars. There are
those who simply insist that every word in the Bible is inspired and thus
identical with the word of God.[3] Although he believes that the historical
critical method presents serious challenges to the unity of the Bible, Brevard Childs remains committed to the idea of the entire Bible as canonical
and thus normative.[4] Raymond Brown also endorses the unity of the
canon by arguing that the meaning of the Bible is to be found not in isolated passages, but in the passage taken in the context of the entire book
in question and ultimately of the entire Scripture.[5] Thus, for example, to
understand what Proto-Isaiah meant on a given issue, "one must take into
account not simply what Proto-Isaiah meant but how his work was modified through the additions of Deutero-Isaiah and Trito-Isaiah. A commentator must never fail to give attention to the sense a passage has in a
book taken as a whole."[6] Luis Alonso Schökel also argues that biblical diversity and the diverse origins of the scriptural texts themselves do not di-
minish the canonical status of the entire Bible. As Alonso Schökel writes,
"We are acquainted with many inspired writers, men moved by the Spirit
(2 Pet 1:21); some we know only through their books, others by name
as well; and we must admit that the language they speak is thoroughly
human, at times intensely so. Yet at the same time we believe that their
words are literally words of God, '*qui locutus est per prophetas.*'"[7] Even
though these are the words of God in human words the Bible is inerrant.

"Since Scripture is inspired by God, it follows that it cannot assert any falsehood: otherwise God himself would be commending falsehood to us in his own authority." Alonso Schökel goes on to say that the inerrancy of Scripture has been taught by tradition and must be associated with its positive correlation, truth. "Truth is a doctrine, a revelation, a light to our eyes: of the inspired word of God, too, we must say: 'In thy light we see light' (Ps 36:10)."[8]

The notion of biblical inerrancy could on the one hand be used to support some sort of fundamentalism, a situation where the biblical text is employed uncritically to advance or to support a position, whether moral or doctrinal, which had been arrived at on other grounds. In this regard, Richard Gula argues that Gerald Kelly's use of the story of Onan in his 1950s book *Medico-Morals* offers an instance of precritical use of Scriptures in Catholic moral theology before Vatican II. Kelly developed the theory for Catholic opposition to contraceptives first on the basis of natural law, then appealing to papal teaching on the matter. "Only after these forms of argument have been used does he then turn uncritically to the evidence of scripture in Onan's story of Genesis 38:8–10 to give biblical warrants for prohibition."[9] On the other hand, belief in biblical inerrancy and in canonical unity does not have to lead to fundamentalism or to proof-texting. The three authors mentioned above, Childs, Brown, and Alonso Schökel, insist on the necessity of a thorough hermeneutical reading of biblical texts in order to determine what it meant when it was first written and what it could mean now. As I pointed out in chapter 3 it has been a general characteristic of Catholic biblical scholarship at least since *Divino Afflante Spiritu* to insist on a thorough hermeneutical approach to the biblical text even when the author in question espouses the unity of the canon as inspired word. This is to say that even though such scholars believe in the entire Bible as the word of God, they also are generally aware that it is also human word, with all the limitations that this entails. Consequently, they are usually aware that not only does divine word need decoding, so to speak, but also that human words spoken in time and in different idioms and on cultural occasions need to be carefully interpreted in order to recover the truths therein buried under the layers of history and culture.

There is as well a counterapproach to the stance taken by scholars like Childs, Brown, and Alonso Schökel over scriptural authority and the unity of the canon. This method considers futile the efforts to retain canonical integrity by arguing for the unity of the Bible. Consequently it embarks on a selective reading by distinguishing levels of authority of the Bible usually with criteria which are extrabiblical. Jack Sanders, for example, recommends the continued use of the Bible through a selection of those concepts which "modern man" can accept.[10] The result of this approach to biblical authority is the creation of a canon within the canon. In post–Vatican II Catholic scholarship, this approach is perhaps most clearly illustrated in the work of Elisabeth Schüssler Fiorenza. Since Fiorenza's work has been extremely influential since the 1980s in identifying the problems and shaping the answers on the authority of the Bible for Christian life and praxis, it warrants considerable attention in order to bring out clearly what the issues are and what solutions she has suggested to the problems.

The Feminist Ethics of Elisabeth Schüssler Fiorenza

To understand the feminist ethics of Elisabeth Schüssler Fiorenza, I believe it is important to start with a discussion on the idea of patriarchy in feminist thought. The basic feminist complaint against much of the prevailing social order in Western society is that men have subjected and subjugated women to an inferior and secondary position, played down women's contributions to and role in history, and use maleness as *the* criterion for defining humanness.[11] Men define and evaluate women only in their relationship to men and only in their roles as wives, mothers, and lovers. Feminists have defined such a situation as patriarchal oppression, "a socio-political system and social structure of graded subjugation and oppressions" which defines women as "the other" and regards peoples and races as "the other" to be subjugated and dominated. According to Fiorenza, patriarchy conceives of society as analogous to the patriarchal household which was sustained by slave labor and defines women not only as the other of men but also as subordinated to men in power.[12] She argues that although we should be careful not to speak of patriarchy in terms of "male oppressors and female oppressed," as if it were a question of "all men over against all women,"[13] patriarchy affects every individual woman in some way and is the basic structure of women's oppression, especially in the Third World. Says Fiorenza, "In a patriarchal society or religion, all women are bound into a system of male privilege and domination." But it is the impoverished women of the Third World who constitute "the bottom of the oppressive patriarchal pyramid."[14]

    If Western society has been patriarchal to the core, so have the Bible and biblical religion. Fiorenza charges that biblical religion "ignores women's experience, speaks of the godhead in male terms, legitimizes women's subordinate positions of powerlessness, and promotes male dominance and violence against women."[15] The Bible is a male book, which not only bears male authorial and interpretive stamps, but also reflects "a dualistic ideology or androcentric world construction in language" and the marks of male religious experience, interests, and leadership.[16] Although Fiorenza admits that the Bible has provided support for many worthy causes—opposition to slavery, poverty, and sexism, to name just a few— she claims it has also been used as a patriarchal male instrument of oppression and subjugation. She writes, "Whenever women protest against political discrimination, economic exploitation, sexual violence, our secondary status in biblical religion, the Bible is invoked against us."[17]

In the face of what they perceive to be patriarchal oppression in the Bible, and the continued use of the Bible against women's interests, many feminists grapple with the question of whether a feminist can without contradiction be a Christian or whether there is a way to keep both in creative tension so that "being a feminist enhances and deepens (one's) commitment to live as a Christian."[18] Although postbiblical feminists have given up on the Bible and on biblical religion as irreformable and irretrievable, and a continued source of oppression for women, others like Fiorenza argue that to reject all biblical authority and to give up on biblical religion is to concede too quickly that women have no authentic history within biblical religion. This strategy, she says, "too easily relinquishes women's feminist biblical heritage" and strengthens the powers of oppression. And not only can it not command the allegiance of all women, it does not respect the positive "self identity and vision that women still derive from biblical religion."[19] Fiorenza therefore argues that since not all women who find meaning in Scripture can be written off as unliberated and unfeminist, something has to be done "to detect the antipatriarchal elements and functions of biblical texts, which are obscured and made invisible by androcentric language and concepts." This becomes even more urgent when we remember that "not all biblical stories, traditions, and texts reflect the experience of men in power or were written in order to legitimate the patriarchal status quo."[20]

Therefore, Elisabeth Schüssler Fiorenza has as her goal the reclamation of early Christian history as women's own past, the subjection of Christian history to feminist analysis with a view to revealing patriarchal history for what it is, and the reconstruction of women's history in the early Church as a challenge to and critique of patriarchy. This feminist reconstruction of Christian origins has both a theoretical and a practical goal: "It aims at both cultural-religious critique and at reconstruction of women's history as women's story within Christianity. It seeks not just to undermine the legitimization of patriarchal religious structures but also to empower women in their struggle against such oppressive structures. In other words, a feminist reconstruction of early Christian beginnings seeks to recover the Christian heritage of women, in the belief that for women, 'our heritage is our power.'"[21] Therefore, feminist reconstruction of Christian origins, for Fiorenza, proceeds on the assumption that the Christian past was also "women's past" and not just "a male past in which women participated only on the fringes or were not active at all." The road to this past lies in providing a new hermeneutical key, that is, in reading the Bible from a feminist perspective

The goal of Fiorenza's feminist critical hermeneutics is to analyze the biblical texts in order "to arrive at the lived ethos of early Christians that developed in interaction with its patriarchal cultural contexts," and to evaluate critically and determine the impact of this ethos on "the continuing structures of alienation and liberation."[22] Fiorenza's feminist hermeneutics therefore seeks to go beyond merely establishing the androcentric character of biblical texts and interpretations and beyond the questions of theological rejection and legitimation of the Bible. It seeks, moreover, to bring into focus "the history of women as participants in patriarchal history, society and religions," to set free "the liberating impulses of biblical traditions," and to bring women into focus as "historical agents and victims."[23] To carry out these tasks effectively, Fiorenza contends, feminist biblical hermeneutics must share in the critical impulses and methods of historical criticism and in the theological goals of liberation theologies.[24]

Fiorenza's model of feminist biblical criticism is built on five pillars: suspicion, critical correlation, proclamation, remembrance, and creative actualization through ritual and celebration.[25] A hermeneutics of suspicion assumes that biblical texts "are formulated in androcentric language and reflect patriarchal social structures." And like the woman who lit her lamp to search for her lost coin, it critically analyzes both contemporary scholarly tendencies and the traditioning process in the Bible itself to try to unearth "a feminist coin." A hermeneutic of suspicion assumes that all biblical texts are speaking about men and women unless the contrary is proved to be the case. It critically assesses and evaluates the patriarchal oppressive or "generic liberating dynamics of individual texts," and works against linguistic sexism in the original text as well as in contemporary translations of the Bible.[26] In short, not only does a feminist hermeneutics of suspicion place a label on all biblical texts, "Caution! Could be dangerous to your health and survival," it also tries "to detect the anti-patriarchal elements and functions of biblical texts which are obscured and made invisible by androcentric language and concepts."[27]

Although in earlier works Fiorenza moved from the hermeneutics of suspicion to the hermeneutics of proclamation, in her later writings she has inserted an intermediate stage between the two. She calls this a stage of critical correlation. The aim is to distinguish between "the unchanging content of the Christian message and the changing forms of cultural expression." It can achieve this distinction by on the one hand separating "the socio-critical prophetic-messianic principle or dynamics" of a biblical text or tradition, and on the other formalizing feminist experience and analysis "in such a way that it becomes a critical principle of affirmation and promotion of the full humanity of women." This principle ultimately functions as a basis for sorting through particular texts and by testing these texts in a process of critical analysis and evaluation to determine "how much of their content and function perpetrates and legitimates patriarchal structures, not only in their original contexts but also in our contemporary situation."[28] From the feminist principle of critical correlation she then moves to the hermeneutics of proclamation. This latter aspect of the feminist model of biblical interpretation tries to undercut the claim of patriarchal texts to scriptural authority. "Feminist theology must first of all denounce all texts and traditions that perpetuate and legitimate oppressive patriarchal structures and ideologies. We no longer should proclaim them as the 'word of God' for contemporary communities and people if we do not want to turn God into a God of oppression."[29] Only texts which affirm or articulate a liberating vision of human freedom, wholeness, and equality should be allowed a place in the Church's lectionary. And to determine whether a text truly fits this mold one must carefully assess its "political context and psychological function." For even texts which are apparently neutral or even positive in regard to women can sometimes in fact be oppressive toward them.

Next, to balance the feminist hermeneutics of proclamation is the feminist critical hermeneutics of remembrance. Its role is the recovery and reconstruction of all biblical stories from a feminist perspective.[30] With the help of historical critical analysis it tries to move beyond androcentric texts and patriarchal traditions to the history of women in biblical religion. And through the subversive power of remembrance it tries to reclaim the struggles and sufferings of women in "our patriarchal Christian past." By keeping alive the hope and sufferings of biblical women, feminist critical hermeneutics allows for "a universal solidarity among women of the past, present, and future."[31] "To reconstruct women's participation in biblical history, we therefore have to read the 'women's passages' as indicators and clues that women were at the center of biblical life. In other words, if we take the conventional ideological character of androcentric language seriously, we can claim that women were leaders and full members in biblical religion until proven otherwise."[32]

Next, in Fiorenza's approach, there is need for a hermeneutics of creative actualization. This aspect of feminist hermeneutics expresses "the active engagement of women in the ongoing biblical story of liberation" and allows them "to enter the biblical story with the help of historical imagination, artistic recreation and liturgical ritualization," as well as to celebrate the founding mothers and sisters of the Christian faith. Says Fiorenza, "Women not only rewrite biblical stories but also reformulate patriarchal prayers and create feminist rituals for celebrating our foremothers. We rediscover in story and poetry, in drama and dance, in song and liturgy our biblical foresisters' sufferings and victories. In ever-new images and symbols, feminist liturgies seek to rename the God of the Bible and biblical vision."[33]

It is clear then that for Fiorenza the integrity of the canon of the Scriptures as it now stands and the authority of the Bible as word of God cannot be accepted without qualification. To qualify to be considered Scripture, and therefore revelation, a biblical text or tradition "must articulate the liberating experiences and visions of the people of God." That is, "only those traditions and texts that critically break through patriarchal culture and plausibility structures have the authority of revelation." On the other hand, any texts or traditions which eradicate women "from historical-theological consciousness" perpetrate violence and alienation, or preach patriarchal subjugation "cannot claim the authority of revelation."[34] The Bible, Fiorenza argues, must not be understood as "unchanging archetype" but as "historical prototype." For whereas an archetype is an unchanging, timeless pattern, a prototype is "critically open to the possibility of its own transformation," and when applied as a hermeneutic to the Bible acknowledges positively "the dynamic process of biblical adaptation, challenge, or renewal of social-ecclesial and conceptual structures under the unchanging conditions of the Church's social-historical situations." In short, to regard the Bible as prototype would help the biblical community "to respond to new social needs and theological insights."[35]

In addition, an adequate feminist hermeneutics of the Bible is a critical theology of liberation. It adopts the advocacy stance of liberation theologies and shares in their basic insights and methodological starting point which is that "all theology knowingly or not is by definition always engaged for or against the oppressed." Like other liberation theologies it argues that it is impossible to be intellectually neutral in an exploitative world. Like these other theologies too, it believes that theology "cannot talk about human existence in general, or about biblical theology in particular, without identifying whose human existence is meant and whose God is found in biblical symbols and texts."[36] The experience of liberation, for women and all other oppressed peoples, thus becomes for Fiorenza the canon and norm for evaluating biblical traditions and texts. Feminist critical hermeneutics must articulate this experience of women and the oppressed in the Bible as locus for revelation and basis of and for biblical authority. In the end, the primary task for feminist biblical interpretation, in the view of Elisabeth Schüssler Fiorenza, is to try to keep alive the *memoria passionis* and the *memoria ductis* of early Christian women "who spoke and acted in the power of the Spirit" as reminder, inspiration, and guide for everyone in the contemporary Church.

In her effort to reconstruct Christian origins and with the aid of the feminist model of biblical interpretation, Elisabeth Schüssler Fiorenza arrives at the fundamental conclusion that the community which was originally called into being by the gospel and ministry of Jesus was "a discipleship of equals." In other words, the Jesus movement in its origin and intention was egalitarian and thus countercultural because of the position and place it gave to women and to slaves. Fiorenza argues that the passages which enjoin the submission or the subordination of women "do not simply reflect taken-for-granted religious behavior in the early Christian communities but witness to historical struggles in which two different social and symbolic forms were competing—the egalitarianism of the early Christian movement and the patriarchal codes that eventually triumphed in Christianity. Such passages are prescriptive not descriptive."[37]

The methodological presuppositions behind Fiorenza's work are very interesting in that they amount to a paradigm shift with regard to the way Catholic scholars usually approach the Bible. Using a feminist critical hermeneutics which shares in both the critical sociological approach and the historical critical method she tries to show that religion must be treated as a function of a coherent socioeconomic structure, a function that impacts upon and is itself affected by the surrounding milieu. This is not necessarily new. What is more important for our purposes here is that she has dealt with the canon in a very unusual way by mounting a critique of the canon using external criteria. For her the test of the scriptural status of the text is whether it enshrines and promotes the equal dignity of women with men or whether it is damaging to that aspiration. The canon and norm for evaluation of biblical traditions and their subsequent inter-pretations can be derived neither from the Bible nor from "the biblical process of learning within and through ideologies." Indeed the Bible or biblical faith cannot be regarded as *norma normans non normata*. Such a canon or norm "can only be formulated within and through the struggle for the liberation of women and all oppressed people."[38] This canon of lib-eration is the basis of feminist ethics which is committed to the liberation struggles of all women and the transformation of all patriarchal institu-tional structures of oppression. Fiorenza is open about her liberationist/advocacy stance. And her stated intention is the release of the liberating impulse in Christian origins as a guide for action in the contemporary world. And she convincingly shows also that biblical interpretation, as well as every other form of interpretation, cannot be a value-free ex-ercise.

Other Feminist Theologians

Fiorenza's position on the revelatory significance or quality of those bibli-cal texts abounding with materials which can be considered morally rep-rehensible to women or indeed to anyone else is not acceptable to all feminist theologians. Sandra M. Schneiders objects to eliminating all such texts from the Bible. She believes that the hermeneutical task in such a situation is to find a way to repudiate the morally unacceptable subject matter of the text without repudiating the text itself and its truth claim.[39] The text possesses a semantic autonomy which frees it from the con-straints of its compositional situation and makes it open to other possible interpretations in other places and at other times. Also, with time, a text generates its own history, which qualifies and transforms its meaning. Thus, "a text can actually come to mean something different from what it was originally intended or understood to mean, that is, it can 'develop.'" Schneiders uses the text of the American Declaration of Independence as an example of this kind of development. The central affirmation of this document, that "all men are created equal," referred in its original eighteenth-century application to white, property-owning males. This text is today understood to refer to all people.

The development of the text of the Declaration of Independence is an example of the interaction of effective history and surplus meaning. The text "all men are created equal" generated an historical experience in the new nation that gradually revealed to Americans the humanity and therefore the equal rights of all people, including women, children, people of color, immigrants, poor people, and handicapped people, as well as adult, white, male property owners. The text was susceptible of reinterpretation, without verbal change, because the word "men" as it occurs in a semantically autonomous text is not limited to the meaning intended by its eighteenth-century users.[40]

Texts therefore have a surplus of meaning, says Schneiders. This surplus of meaning interacts with the historical consciousness of the people to draw the text out of its very limited past into an expanded present. The biblical text must therefore develop in much the same way as the American Declaration of Independence. "The meaning of the New Testament is not limited to the meaning intended by its authors. Nor are Christian believers of the twentieth century faith clones of their first century forebears." Christian expanded consciousness, which is in large measure a result of its formation in the gospel, has come to see the moral unacceptability of slavery, anti-Semitism, and patriarchy and has led to the questioning of the text on these and other similar matters. Thus, if we discount the authority of Scripture, as Fiorenza and others do, due to the biases of the biblical authors, we might be rejecting the very resources which might transform the present. The presence of immoral or untrue material in Scripture is not sufficient ground for repudiating Scripture as revelatory text. To do so would be to fail to see the text as a "human (albeit a divinely inspired) text mediating the revelatory encounter with God." Also, it would be to fail to see the ongoing corrective which is possible as a result of never-ending dialogue between the faith community for whom this text is a mediation of transformative divine revelation and the historical consciousness of the believing community.[41]

Some other Catholic feminist scholars have also addressed the issue of the hermeneutical problem associated with the use of Scripture in ethics. In seeking to return to Scripture as a source of moral theology, feminist moral theologians, especially, have noted some of the inherent limitations of Scripture itself. One lesson learned from the biblical renewal in this regard, Lisa Sowle Cahill argues, for example, is that emphasis on the historical and cultural factors in the Bible has shown that the Bible cannot be treated as "a direct source of timeless moral rules." The Bible, as a diverse collection of works by different authors, spanning centuries, and written in many historical settings for different immediate purposes, is replete with gaps, repetitions, changes, inconsistencies, and even immoralities.[42] The internal pluralism in the Bible thus can limit its effectiveness or use in moral theology. Cahill maintains that since "biblical authors were interested in the virtues or conduct that would best express fidelity to God for their own communities," what they say in regard to particular moral questions must be applied with discernment, for "our circumstances may be different and may demand different responses." For example, "general biblical directives like the ten commandments ("Thou shalt not kill"), or Jesus' instruction to love our neighbors and enemies, are of perennial relevance, but they must be applied anew in every age."[43] Like Fiorenza, Cahill argues that a consequence of the Bible's internal pluralism and historical development might be that "some teachings, themes, or even texts cannot be re-appropriated constructively, in any form by the believing community today," but must be rejected as "non-revelatory, non-authoritative, and even destructive of an authentic relationship to God or to Jesus' fundamental message."[44] Cahill names the biblical teaching on violence, wars, genocide, slavery, and the patriarchal organization of family, society, and Church as examples of biblical moral teachings which are "offensive to the Christian view of a compassionate, redeeming God."

Cahill's position here contrasts with her earlier views on the nature and authority of the scriptural canon. In *Between the Sexes,* published in 1985, Cahill stated that the decision to use Scripture as authority was a faith decision which entailed a commitment to the reliability of scriptural authority. Such a commitment, she said, is grounded in the believer's experience within the community shaped by Scripture. "The authority of Scripture," Cahill wrote, "does not rest on any empirical or logical demonstration that Scripture, in its several parts or as a whole, can support *only* the sort of theology or religious faith that is 'authentic,' 'liberating,' or 'healing,' that is, congruent with one's experience of God, and with the understanding of God coherent with extra-biblical insights."[45]

Therefore, I believe it does not help to suggest expunging offensive texts and themes from the Bible. Sandra M. Schneiders's position on the surplus of meaning which the biblical texts contain must be taken seriously. Texts in their past limitations can be drawn into the present through dialogue with the believing community. This dialogue can result in a conscious effort by the present community to transcend the limitations of the text while leaving it intact for succeeding generations to engage in dialogue with and to learn from. If we were to excise every text and every theme we feel uncomfortable with today, how is what is left to be considered Scripture? For Scripture, like the incarnation, retains its efficacy precisely because it shows us the power of God to transcend human limitations, or rather to work with human limitations, in order to save us.

Further Questions on Scriptural Authority

Cahill's insight that biblical history and development and the varied nature of the Bible itself has shown the limitations of attempting to draw timeless moral norms from the Bible is valid to a point. One of the lessons which the biblical renewal has taught us is that it is hard to pinpoint a biblical theology of war, or of the organization of the family, for example. As Cahill herself has indeed shown in her many other writings, there is hardly a single point of view on any issue in the Bible. It is on this ground that Roland Murphy has argued that the very notion of scriptural unity should be abandoned on account of the divergences within the Bible. What he says about the attempt to construct a biblical theology of covenant, promise-fulfillment, among other themes and categories, can be applied to our discussion here. "In every case the rubric of unity turns out to be incomplete, whether it be covenant, *Heilsgeschicte,* or promise-fulfillment. Every such category, while it has a value in itself, is simply too limited to deal with the variety offered by the biblical material."[46]

One must be careful, however, not to infer from this that there is total inconsistency or fragmentation in the Bible. The truth the Bible teaches must be deciphered from a total reading of the biblical text. The idea that the Bible cannot be treated as a source of "timeless moral rules" must not be exaggerated. No serious Catholic theologian would doubt the need to get beyond the cultural and authorial limitations of the biblical text in order to get to the truth of what the Bible says or what the biblical text can mean for us today. However, I think it is too much to say that the historical and cultural factors in the Bible show that we cannot treat the Bible as a direct source of timeless moral rules. The Bible is indeed not just a rule book. But it does contain rules which are perennially valid for ordering human life and human society for all times and in all places. The Bible does indeed carry some heavy cultural and historical baggage which obscures the truth it contains. However, it does still function for the Christian faithful and others as a source of guidance and moral regulation, among other

things. Christian and other readers of the Bible can and do draw the conclusion based on the Bible and as part of the teaching of the Bible that certain things are right and some are wrong, always and everywhere. As we
saw in the discussion on the distinctiveness of Christian ethics, these affirmations do not necessarily lead to the conclusion that the Bible alone is
the source of all these moral truths. However, it is one thing to say this
and another to assert that the Bible cannot be regarded as a direct source
of timeless moral truths. The implication of this kind of assertion for
Catholic ethics is that it leaves room for a type of moral relativism in
which biblically inspired moral teachings become open to revision because they are considered to be merely products of a particular time and
place and must be overcome in light of so-called new experiences.

The question of scriptural authority in ethics has been taken up by
nonfeminist writers as well. Edouard Hamel, for example, insists that to
use Scripture rightly one must remember that Scripture as a voice from
the past needs to be decoded before it can be used today: "The word of
God in Scripture is transmitted to us under the wrapper of history in
forms that are necessarily dependent upon culture."[47] In order to make
the text speak to men and women of today, all possible means must be
used to interpret it. But in this exercise "we must allow ourselves to be
guided by its contents without trying to project into our own patterns
of thought." The biblical text is both history and history of salvation. Although written for a specific audience and with a particular aim, it is intended to offer to the world a permanent and immutable gift. The aim of
biblical interpretation is therefore "to establish a point of contact between
sacred texts of earlier origin and our contemporary era which approaches
it with our own questions, our own mentality and our own problems" in
order to unearth the permanent and immutable gifts contained therein.
Consider the question of human sexuality, for example. It is possible, says
Hamel, to study this problem in the Bible strictly from a historical, sociological, or archaeological perspective in order to understand what the Hebrews taught about it or what responses Paul gave to the questions put to
him by some of his contemporaries. However, to consider the issue only
from the point of view of history or sociology or archaeology would not
reveal its full meaning in the Bible and leaves the Bible practically unable
to say anything on this issue to the modern reader. The full import of the
biblical teaching on this issue can only be discovered if the Bible is considered to contain a permanent message of salvation for all of humankind.
Only then can we draw "from the biblical view of sexuality, a message that

can enlighten humankind today and tell it what God thinks of human sexuality, a light that can serve as the basis for, that can monitor, correct if necessary, and above all integrate into a more integral framework, its own concept of sexuality."[48] The goal is to set up a dialogue between the reader and the text on the issue of human sexuality in order to find a common perspective. In this dialogue, the text has a position of superiority as the word of God. Thus, it is not for the reader to call the word to account but for the text to challenge the reader. The reader would have to make an effort to penetrate the sacred text until that point is reached "where the wall separating the time of the biblical text and one's own time has finally disappeared, until a 'merging of perspectives' takes place"—that is, until the dialogue between the text and the reader is established at that transcendental level "where the latter finally grasps the message that God is addressing to the reader, where the word of God tells the reader something."[49] Hamel insists that what is taking place here is no different from what goes on in a situation where two people from disparate backgrounds enter into dialogue until they establish a common perspective, or when one studies a classical text to find a universal human experience. The only difference here is that the text in question is not just history, but also history of salvation. Thus, the human universal attained through hermeneutic effort in this case "is the human universal as God sees it, and tells it to us; it is a permanent message of salvation."[50]

Hamel states that the Bible does not necessarily provide answers at the level of concrete rules. Rather, it provides an integral vision that will help us to find more concrete answers with greater clarity. Scripture is meant to be read in faith. This is the only way the reader can grasp the truth of salvation that it contains. Hamel suggests a twofold exegesis of the Bible. The first step is a scientific and philosophical type of exegesis, consisting of a rigorous analysis of the text with the intention of discovering as accurately as possible the original sense as intended by the author. This first type of exegesis must be complemented and completed by an updating exegesis which is "based on the model of interpretation given by the sacred writers themselves," as when the words of Jesus are "applied" by Paul and John to the new community. Updating exegesis breathes life into the letters of the Bible and enables it to have something to say to the world of today. Otherwise, the Bible remains at best a history that is ineffectual, sans the ability to challenge and the power to mediate salvation to humankind. The aim of updating exegesis is to move beyond the categorical level to reach the permanent message of salvation which is contained in the Bible and whose value is eminently current. In regard to the moral message of the Bible, "the moral theologian knows that this truth of salvation that is found thanks to the hermeneutic effort made must of necessity be at the same time a permanent requirement of reason and of human dignity. The paths of revelation come together. God wants what is good for humankind. But what God wants is also what is good for humankind."[51]

Hamel is basically right when he stresses the necessity of faith in the Bible as word of God as a starting point for the appropriation of the message contained therein. Such a starting point helps to put the limitations of the text and the various uses to which the text has been put in Christian history in perspective. Better still, it helps us transcend the limitations in the biblical text to appropriate the life-giving message it contains, that life-giving message which the Second Vatican Council insists is the essence of the revealed word. As the Council says, "Seeing that all that the inspired writers affirm should be regarded as affirmed by the Holy Spirit, we must acknowledge that the books of scripture, firmly, faithfully and without error, teach that truth which God for the sake of our salvation, wished to see confided to the sacred scriptures."[52] Without faith in the essentially unerring quality of the Bible the discussion on scriptural authority is basically meaningless because it is carried out from a radically different and incommensurable starting point.

From Authority to Authorization

Beyond the question of the authority of Scripture itself, the next problem in the discussion on Scripture and ethics in recent times pertains to what Scripture authorizes as ethical judgments or stances. The issue has to do with whether, how, and to what extent the Bible can be used in part or as a whole to justify particular moral judgments, stances, or attitudes. The Catholic community, for example, claims scriptural authority with regard to its teaching on the indissolubility of validly contracted marriages. It also asserts the authority of Scripture against homosexual relationships and the taking of innocent life. It is easy to see how Scripture can be used in these areas. Whether one accepts scriptural authority on these matters or prefers to call up other nonscriptural authority, such as common human experience, is another matter. On many other issues, the scriptural warrant is often circumstantial or ambiguous. Consider, for example, the question of the use of violence in liberation struggles. What does Scripture say about the use of violence as means either for individual defense or for the liberation of peoples under oppression?

The use of the Book of Exodus as preferred text among liberation theologians is very well known and will therefore not detain us here. What I intend to do here is rather to show how a particular sociological reading of biblical history has tried to uphold a liberationist ethic which sometimes justified the use of violence to achieve its end. Although it builds on the story of Israelite origins, it reinterprets this story quite radically along Marxist sociological lines. I am here refering to the liberationist stance taken, or at least supported, by the Marxist sociological reading of Israelite origins in the work of Norman Gottwald and the school of biblical interpretation which has arisen from his work. I must make two points here. The first is that although Gottwald's work is a liberation theology, his conclusions with regard to the implications of his version of the story of Israelite origins for contemporary liberation theology, especially in Latin America, is not reflected in the work of mainstream theologians such as Gustavo Gutiérrez and Jon Sobrino and others whose works have defined this school of theology. Second, what follows is somewhat lengthy. Although much of the material is familiar to the experts in the field, it is necessary to reconstruct the views of this school of thought in order to bring out more clearly the issues at stake and to show why Gottwald and his supporters arrive at the conclusions they do.

The Revolt or Social Revolution Model of the Reconstruction of Israel's Origin

Scholars have employed three basic models to date in their attempt to reconstruct Israel's origin: the conquest theory,[53] the immigration theory,[54] and the revolt or social revolution theory. Two of the main proponents of the immigration theory, Martin Noth[55] and Albrecht Alt,[56] arrive at their positions from different starting points. We are interested here in the revolt or social revolution theory associated with the work of George Mendenhall and Norman Gottwald. Although Norman Gottwald has become the spokesman for this model, it was first put forward by George Mendenhall. Mendenhall had conceived of the origins of Israel in Palestine as a simple process with unlikely beginnings.

A group of slave labour captives succeed in escaping an intolerable situation in Egypt. Without any other community upon which they could rely for protection and support they established a relationship with a deity, Yahweh . . . Common loyalty to a single overlord, and obligation to a common and simple group of norms created the community, a solidarity which was attractive to all persons suffering under the burden of subjection to a monopoly of power which they had no hand in creating, and from which they received virtually nothing but tax collectors. Consequently, entire groups having a clan or "tribal" organisation joined the newly formed community, identified themselves with the oppressed in Egypt, and received deliverance from bondage.[57]

Although radically different, the revolt theory which Mendenhall put forward shares some basic assumptions with both the conquest and the immigration models. With the former it recognizes that the impetus to Israelite settlement in Palestine was created outside Palestine. With the immigration theory it shares the notion of an absence of "sharp distinction between Canaanite and Israelite" and the view that Israel was made up of "a collection of peoples with diverse ethnic backgrounds and histories which they later deposited into the common pool of Israelite traditions."[58] On the other hand, the revolt model is a categorical rejection of the main components of the conquest model. Says Mendenhall, "There was no statistically important invasion of Palestine at the beginning of the twelve tribe system of Israel. There was no radical displacement of population. There was no genocide, there was no large scale driving out of population, only of royal administrators (of necessity). In summary there was no real conquest of Palestine in the sense that has been usually understood."[59]

Norman Gottwald is in basic agreement with Mendenhall's theory that early Israel was an "inside" story, made up mainly of dissatisfied Canaanites, a revolt of "Canaanite peasants" against "the political economy in which they were exploited participants."[60] As Allen Myers points out in his review of Gottwald's book, Gottwald's position is that the way Israel came to be is closely related to the nature of the system which emerged.

> The resultant society was an alliance through various modes and degrees of affiliation by an eclectic assortment of underclass and outlaw elements of Canaanite society (feudalized peasants, 'apiru mercenaries and adventurers, transhumant pastoralists, tribally organized farmers and pastoral nomads, and probably also itinerant craftsmen and disaffected priests) who subordinated their intrinsic differences in a unified strike against the source of their common misery, the Canaanite ruling class.[61]

What social or political factors created such a large pool of marginalized persons? Revolt theorists in response trace this situation to the development of city-states in Canaan and to the feudal structure which the so-called Hyksos introduced to the region.[62] In his book *Essays on Old Testament History and Religion,* Albrecht Alt also traces to the Hyksos period in Palestine the formation of the Canaanite city-states. Prior to the arrival of the Hyksos in Palestine, says Alt, all available Egyptian records refer to Palestine as one large entity. At the close of the Hyksos period in that region, these records begin to refer to smaller territorial entities in the region. Alt concludes that this new political system "does not give the impression of having been created by the Egyptians, so presumably we must see it as a product of Hyksos domination."[63] The Hyksos are also credited with the introduction of the horse and chariot as instruments of war into Palestine. The impact of this on the social and political structure of Palestine was enormous. For one thing, a professional soldier corps was created whose members were endowed with aristocratic rank and rewarded with land forcibly taken from the nonsoldier class. So as a new aristocratic minority class developed, so did a depressed subservient class who were in the majority. On these fell the burden of taxation to maintain the state, the ruler and the nobility, and the construction of public works. The heavier the taxes grew, the more people who were consigned to indebted serfdom. "Indebted peasants, deprived of independent means of subsistence, were recruited as cultivators of large estates and compelled to serve the onerous demands from [which] they had little prospect of escape."[64]

When Egypt finally drove out the Hyksos from Palestine-Syria and took control of the land again, it retained the territorial divisions created during the Hyksos period.[65] Princes and rulers were allowed to keep their positions as long as they agreed to be vassals to Egypt. This meant that the princes now collected taxes both for Egypt and for themselves. During this period also—that is, between the end of the fifteenth century and the first half of the fourteenth century B.C., a period in the history of Palestine otherwise known as the Amarna Age—there is evidence of fighting and quarreling among the city-states themselves. The burden of taxation on the peasants apparently became heavier as more taxes were levied for the war effort. The result was an even larger population of marginalized and discontented Canaanites. At precisely this period the term *'apiru* makes its appearance in the Amarna letters.

Many studies have been done on the Amarna letters and on the meaning of the word *'apiru,* which is extensively used in those letters. In an authoritative article on the Amarna letters, Edward F. Campbell, Jr., describes the ʿapiru as elements of society "existing outside of societal status, presumably lacking legal rights."[66] They included persons of various nationalities who sometimes found themselves employed as mercenaries under foreign kings and rulers. Says Norman Gottwald,

> The one trait that best comprehends all the ʿapiru appears to be that of the *outsider status* they occupy vis-à-vis the regnant social and political order. The term "outlaw" conveniently catches the double nuance of the ʿapiru as those who stand recognizably outside the prevailing order, both as "fugitives" or "refugees" who *flee from the dominant order* and as "robbers" or "rebels" who *prey upon or threaten the dominant order*. But "outlaw," except as broadly redefined, tends to miss the many grades and variations of adaptation of which the ʿapiru "outsiders" were capable vis-à-vis the dominant social order.[67]

In other words, although the ʿapiru stood outside societal control and limits, they depended on existing societies for their sustenance by hiring themselves out not only as mercenaries but as farmers, organized robbers and brigands, construction hands, and so forth.

People were not born ʿapiru. They only become ʿapiru when they could no longer tolerate the conditions in the societies in which they were born. One became ʿapiru by choice through an act of defiance of the crown. A citizen could say, "I hate my king and my city," and by this statement renounce every obligation to his city and his king and deprive himself of any protection these could offer.[68] ʿApiru and *Hebrew* are thought to be semantically related.[69] If so, just as no one could be born ʿapiru no one could be born Hebrew. The Hebrew "entered the service of a citizen in some other political community as a slave," or "he banded together with other persons in a similar predicament to form a gang of freebooters like King David, or the group individually as a unit entered the service of a foreign king also like David in the service of Achish king of Gath."[70]

Another important element in the formation of early Israel was the pastoral nomads. Gottwald defines pastoral nomadism as "a socio-economic mode of life based on intensive domestication of livestock which requires a regular movement of the animals and their breeders (a movement which is neither aimless nor boundless) in a seasonal cycle dictated by the need for pasturage and water."[71] In the Palestine of the period under discussion, the transhumant life of the pastoral nomads came in conflict with the settled agricultural interests of rural farming communities. These conflicts,

Gottwald argues, were not conflicts of invaders versus defenders of the land. Instead, "they were conflicts over social organization and the appropriation of economic production between different segments of the population in Canaan, conflicts which arose intrasystematically." Thus by sheer reason of shared economic marginalization, the *ʿapiru* and the pastoral nomads were united broadly "by a 'tribal' form of social organization in opposition to the structurally dominant 'statist' form of social organization." Says Norman Gottwald,

> *ʿApiru* and pastoral nomads were themselves members of the Canaanite social world who opposed not all Canaanites, but Canaanite rulers and aristocrats and necessarily all those supporting the rulers and aristocrats. *ʿApiru* and tribal pastoralists, although unquestionably different in many details, were joined in an egalitarian conception of autonomous economic and political life which sought wherever possible to ameliorate or to overthrow the domination of "statism" and its specific oppression through taxation in kind, draft labour, and forced military service.[72]

Also caught up in the struggle for economic justice and survival were the peasants in the Canaanite city-states. Gottwald establishes therefore that the Palestine of this period was very much in turmoil owing to the ever increasing struggles of the various segments of the Canaanite underclass—the *ʿapiru,* the *shosu* (pastoral nomads), the *hupshu* (peasants)—against the overlords and sometimes among themselves. And although all these elements—rebellious serfs, pastoral nomads, and *ʿapiru*—ganged up together to remove their overlords, they did not share much sense of unity in struggle before the emergence of the Israelite entity. It was only in Israel that the divergent lines and tendencies met, transcended previous fragmentation, and ruptured the system from within. What emerged from this eclectic coalition over time, Gottwald argues, was "a conscious, organized, broad-scale egalitarian movement." From then on, a very interesting development occurred which transformed negative sentiments into positive ideology. "In Israel, antifeudal sentiment and protest has become antifeudal and pro-egalitarian ideology and social organization. Not only does Israel challenge Egyptian imperialism, it rejects city-state feudalism as well, and does so by linking up exploited peoples across the boundaries of the old city-state divisions. A class *in* itself, hitherto a congeries of separately struggling segments of the populace, has become a class *for* itself."[73]

In George Mendenhall's version of the social revolution theory, the center of and the impetus to Israelite unity was Yahweh as a God who liberates. In Mendenhall's theory, the disaffected peasantry of Canaan were attracted by stories told by a set of runaway ex-slaves from Egypt. The community solidarity which these ex-slaves had formed through common loyalty to Yahweh as the one who saved them from bondage was "attractive to all persons suffering under the burden of subjection to a monopoly of power which they had no part in creating" and provided further incentives for rebellion. "Consequently, entire groups . . . joined the newly formed community, identified themselves with the oppressed in Egypt, and received deliverance from bondage." And thus was born the nation of Israel.[74]

Norman Gottwald takes issue with Mendenhall's position on the role of Yahweh in the formation of Israel. He charges that Mendenhall's presentation of the issue gives the impression that "the religious ideas create the people." Gottwald's argument is that "the religious ideas take place within a social formation that is in the process of coming into being. The social, economic, political, cultural and religious factors all belong together."[75] In other words, although the religion of Yahweh was central to the formation and cohesion of early Israel, the method employed by Gottwald views it sociologically as a social phenomenon which was "related to all the other social phenomena within the system." Thus, contrary to previous scholarly positions, what made Israel unique and outstanding, in Gottwald's view, was not mono-Yahwism per se. Instead, "early Israel's uniqueness may be understood socially in terms of its success in bringing together the diverse underclass which the declining feudal-imperial system had until that time been able to keep separated." And although "Israel's vehement and tenacious identity as one people under one God has its indisputable axis around an anti-feudal egalitarian social commitment," Israel's unity—that is, the welding together of the eclectic mix of the Canaanite underclass—took a long time and cannot be accounted for "in terms of prior ethnic or cultural factors."[76]

Gottwald's version of the revolt theory thus minimizes the role of Yahweh and of the transcendent impulse in the foundation of Israel. As I said earlier, this sociological reading of the formation of Israel is intended to provide justification for the liberationist stance of some types of liberation theology which see the clash between the poor and the rich as a liberation struggle from the yoke of oppression. Among such liberation theologians this attitude to Scripture is used "to underwrite a commitment to the oppressed." In response to the moral question "What ought I to do?" they would respond, "Act to liberate the oppressed because God is committed to them."[77] Latin American liberation theologians in general believe that God continues to act in history as in biblical times to liberate the poor. In his book on liberation theology, Gustavo Gutiérrez understands the word "liberation" to be the meaning of Scripture. "The critical christological judgement here is that Christ is the complete savior, the total liberator."[78] Some other presuppositions underlying the position of the Latin American liberation theologians include a concern for the condition of underdevelopment and unjust dependence; a Christian interpretation of this situation as "a situation of sin"; and the imperative on the Christian conscience to work to remedy this situation.[79] The fundamental objective of liberation theology is therefore "to clarify the intrinsic relation there is in God's plan between sociopolitical, economic, and cultural liberation and the eschatological salvation by Jesus Christ."[80] The hermeneutic center of liberation theology is found in the generalization that liberation is the message of Scripture. This hermeneutic considers the exodus experience as paradigmatic both for what God intends to do and is indeed doing in the world, and for human participation in human liberation. The type of liberation theology inspired by the work of Gottwald would conclude that such participation can justifiably be violent, as was presumably the case with those of the Palestinian underclass in their struggle for liberation from their oppressive overlords.

At work in this type of liberation theology is the understanding of a particular type of biblical history as *historical prototypes* rather than as *mythical archetypes,* if one may borrow from Elisabeth Fiorenza. The meaning and possibility of life under an oppressive modern regime are seen within a particular form. First, wherever you live, you are probably living under one of the Canaanite oppressors. However, there is a more attractive world, a promised land, which has to be won. The way to this land is through a violent class struggle to topple all the regimes which stand in the way of the underclass on the way to possess the land. The Bible is thus used not only to show that this can be done but to prove that such an approach can be authorized by faith in God and by the example of what God himself has done in history. What is evident then in this case is that claims about scriptural significance are being used to reinforce ethical decisions which are derived from nonscriptural sources. But as Allen Verhey has indicated, to acknowledge the authority of Scripture is not to say "what moves are authorized in an argument from the Bible to the modern world."[81] Thus, even if the reconstruction of Israelite origins as presented by Gottwald and others who follow his lead is correct, it would still be hard to draw a unilateral conclusion on what the Bible authorizes with regard to the use of violence from this reading of Scripture or biblical history. There are also themes in the Bible which lend themselves to a pacifist approach, for example.

Other Approaches

Beyond the issue of authority, other questions relating to method have arisen in connection with the discussion on Scripture and ethics in the Catholic tradition since Vatican II. So far we have noted in some detail two of the more influential approaches to scriptural authority and to the use of Scripture to authorize certain behaviors and types of action. One important characteristic of these two approaches, the feminist and the liberationist, is that they, as William C. Spohn has pointed out, "appeal to Scripture in a pragmatic way as they search for 'a useable history' to inform their struggles."[82] Such an approach, no matter how useful, makes Scripture unacceptably ideological because it does not do justice to the totality of Scripture as word of God.

Many more attempts have been made to provide answers to the question of scriptural authority and authorization. William Spohn has provided a good summary of the various approaches of Catholic (and other) theologians to the issue. There is no need to duplicate his efforts here, and I will mention them only in passing. Spohn has noted that for some theologians the Bible contains the command of God which must be obeyed with precision at each moment. "In every moral decision, according to this approach, God is the commander and the believer is the one commanded. To the basic moral question 'What ought I to do?' there is a direct answer: You should listen to God's command and obey it without question."[83] For these theologians, Scripture furnishes us with summaries of God's commands, "*attitudes* that should inform our obedience, and *directions* of freedom inherent in the gift itself. It is not a collection of timeless divine rules."[84] Another approach to the use of the Scriptures in ethics is evident in the position of the autonomous ethics theologians which we have already seen. Charles Curran succinctly captures the essence of this approach:

> The Pastoral Constitution of the Church in the Modern World proposes a methodology of viewing reality in terms of the gospel and human

experience. Accepting this formulation, I would conclude that the gospel does not add a power or knowledge which *somehow or other* is not available in the consciousness of man called by God with regard to ethical consciousness and proximate dispositions, goals, and attitudes. The gospel does make explicit, and explicitly Christian, what can be implicit in the consciousness of all men who are called by God.[85]

Although Curran, like Fuchs, grants a role to Scripture in explicitly bringing the Christian to reflect on Christian identity, attitudes, goals, values, norms, and decisions, he insists that "in no sense can the Scriptures be used as a book of revealed morality." The hermeneutical obstacles are just too much to allow this role to Scripture. The Scriptures do furnish us, however, "with information about the self-understanding of the people who lived in covenant relationship with God and how this helped shape their lives and actions." The role of the Christian and the Christian ethicist today is to continue to reflect on this experience as recalled in the Scriptures, as well as on the experience of other persons as they try to determine "how they should live and respond to Jesus Christ in our times."[86]

What has become clear since the Council is that in spite of the agreement that Scripture is an authority, there are widespread disagreements about "the authorization for moving from Scripture to moral norms."[87] This hesitance has frustrated many moral theologians over the years who have looked up to Scripture and biblical scholars for guidance on specific moral problems and who had embraced the conciliar call for a more scripturally informed moral theology with great enthusiasm. Here is how the late Fr. Richard McCormick, S.J., expressed this frustration in an interview I had with him at his Notre Dame home in 1992:

I try to keep in dialogue with Scripture scholars. Some of them are very interested in moral problems from the New Testament point of view. However, I've found some Scripture scholars frustrating because you work out something like "Divorce and Remarriage: A Pastoral Approach" and you'll ask a Scripture scholar, "Is this compatible with Scripture?" and the answer will be "No no no no, you can't say that," and I'll say, "Well, why?" The answer is never clear. Then I'd come up with something else, and they'd say, "No no no no, you can't say that"; I'd say, "You know something you're not telling me!" It sometimes can be frustrating at the very practical pastoral level. Unfortunately we have occasionally to work out things for the gay phenomenon. What does Scripture say about this? I find the exegetes very unhelpful here. They don't cooperate very much. They're not telling us everything they know!

While one recognizes the perennial reluctance of most biblical scholars to move from textual and other critical studies of the Bible to doing theology—that is, moving from what the Bible meant to what it means today—the question here is really whether the Bible scholars themselves often know more than they are saying. Part of the difficulty here is also the question of how much one can stretch biblical meaning or stretch the Bible as a source of moral insight on any given question since the Bible could not obviously be said to have anticipated all our modern moral problems. This issue is real. The result is that some have all but given up on the Bible as a source of moral insight. Others have become fundamentalists in their uncritical use of the Bible. Yet others, as we have already shown, have embarked on a selective appropriation of biblical truth and insight to support previously and ideologically held positions. One thing is clear: All Christian ethics must in some way take account of the Bible as Scripture if it is to be taken seriously as a Christian enterprise.

Jesus and Ethics

In this section we are concerned with what Jesus has to do with ethics. In many ways, this question mirrors the one on Scripture and ethics, referring to the actual content of the teachings of Jesus on ethical matters and the authority such teachings have, as well as to the way such teachings can still be considered authoritative in modern society. I will not go into all those details here, nor will I discuss the particular contents of the ethical teachings of Jesus; this is not within the scope of this book. I will simply look at the way some recent Catholic moral theologians have seen the role of Jesus in ethics. This approach does not include the work of many scholars before and during this period under study; it is simply an attempt to discuss the way the normativity of Jesus has been considered in recent times in the Catholic tradition.

One Catholic scholar who has written extensively on the role of Jesus in ethics is William Spohn.[88] Spohn begins his discussion on Jesus and ethics by stating that the entire story of Jesus is normative for Christian ethics as "the concrete universal."[89] The story of Jesus, Spohn says, "is concrete because it has a particular shape in a definite time and place. It is universal because that shape and the moral dispositions engendered by the story are morally relevant in every situation in the Christian's life." The story of Jesus is not the only norm for the Christian. There are others. However, any other norms must be compatible with "the basic patterns inherent in the story of Jesus." Also, as concrete universal, Jesus may urge certain actions which other sources of ethical disposition may not emphasize, such as the forgiveness of enemies.

Jesus as concrete universal acts in three ways in Christian ethics: by affecting our perception, motivation, and identity. Jesus as norm of the moral life influences the believer's perception by indicating which features of the situation are religiously and morally significant. The Christian moral life is grounded in the person Jesus. Through certain spiritual practices mandated by the New Testament which have always drawn Christians into the life of Christ, such as the baptism, the Eucharist, intercessory prayer, biblical meditation and discernment, forgiveness, and solidarity with other human beings, especially the needy, Christians come in contact with Jesus Christ. Such contact makes Christians be in the mind of Christ, as Paul would say, and guides them to perceive which features of experience are significant.[90] To say that the Jesus of the gospels shapes our perceptions implies that we should be careful not to make him an icon. He leads us beyond himself to see other things the way he sees them. Thus, says Spohn, "Christians are called to follow Jesus, not to imitate him." Whereas the imitation of Jesus makes us concentrate on the person of Jesus, worshiping him like an icon, following Jesus makes it possible for us to become disciples of Jesus. To be a disciple of Jesus is first of all to accept the normativity of the life and teaching of Jesus. The life of Jesus "has a specific direction and definable shape, and an undeniable urgency that continues to make the fundamental moral claim on Christians of every generation."[91] To be a disciple of Jesus thus means taking seriously what Jesus took seriously. What Jesus took seriously, says Spohn, was not himself. What Jesus took seriously was God, and the affairs of God's kingdom such as the poor, the outcast, and the forgiveness of the sinner.[92] By following Jesus as concrete universal norm, the disciple is drawn to the type of concerns that Jesus had in his life and ministry.

Jesus as concrete universal also indicates how to act. Says Spohn, "Christians often dismiss Scripture as a moral resource because it does not address many of today's pressing problems. The lack of directly relevant prescriptive material is not such an obstacle, however, if scripture is seen to have its main moral effect on the imagination and dispositions." The story of Jesus indicates how the Christian should act, first by supplying the paradigms for action. Through analogical reflection these biblical paradigms are extended into new situations through dispositions which are configured into a pattern by the original events of the Bible or of Jesus' life in question. Thus, for example, "Exodus shapes the thirst for justice; the cross and resurrection structure hope and love of neighbor." These do not indicate what to do; rather, they frame perception and encourage certain dispositions and virtues.[93] "Dispositions shaped by biblical paradigms can tutor the imagination, enabling it to discern an appropriate response with ease and joy. When we know *how* to act, *what* to do may become clearer."[94]

Finally, Jesus as concrete universal bestows identity on the believer. The story of Jesus is at the core of the believer's identity because it synthesizes the believer's moments of experience into a coherent whole.

> Christian identity is relational rather than individualist. The relevant question is no longer *who* am I? but *whose* am I? . . . Becoming a disciple of Jesus changes the individual at the very core of her being. The New Testament's central images speak of this radically altered identity: people are born again, leave all behind to embark on a mysterious journey, pass from death to life, leave the old person behind to be part of the new humanity of Christ. Their individual identity is now bound up with the Master whom they follow as disciples.[95]

Spohn argues that the story of Jesus is normative for who Christians are called to become. Since Christian identity comes from commitment to the Master, the disciples of Jesus are also committed to the persons and causes to which the Master is committed which is the reconciliation and healing reality of God. Thus, belonging to the Lord Jesus helps liberate the Christian from self-centered existence and to focus her on the interests of Christ. "Every social role, personal accomplishment, career, or group membership must conform to the way of Jesus."[96]

The question of the role of Jesus in Christian ethics has been answered in recent Catholic theology by other Catholic authors along similar lines. For example, in his widely used moral theology textbook, Richard Gula asserts that Jesus is normative for Christian moral life "not on the basis of any explicit teaching he may have given, but on the basis of who he is and was." Gula acknowledges Jesus as "God's full revelation of the invitation of Divine love to us . . . the fullest human response to God." Jesus,

Gula continues, sums up the divine invitation and the human response "in a way which makes him the new covenant, the fullness of what the Christian moral life ought to be." Jesus is the model of what sort of persons we ought to become and the sort of actions we ought to perform as a full response of faith.[97]

The work of Catholic scholars like Spohn and Gula attest to the many good things about Catholic moral theology since the Council. Their work, like that of the others we have studied in this chapter, reflects serious scholarly efforts to understand Jesus and the Scriptures as central to the Christian moral life—an approach that was not always well pronounced in the manualist theology of the pre–Vatican II era. These scholars also manifest another trait of recent moral theology: the spirit of ecumenical dialogue and influence. In this regard, the influence of James Gustafson, and through him a long line of Protestant ethicists such as Albert Schweitzer, Rudolf Bultmann, C. H. Dodd, Reinhold Niebuhr, and many others, on the discussion of the role of Jesus in the moral life is unmistakable. This influence has opened Catholic scholars to some of the problematic issues as well, especially in the work of James Gustafson. One such issue is the reluctance to grant normativity to Jesus *also* on the basis of "any explicit teaching he may have given."

Like Gustafson, our authors discuss extensively the way faith in Jesus affects our perspectives, intentions, and motivation. I think they are right in what they say. My contention is that left at this point, the discussion would be incomplete. Does Jesus have any specific moral teachings which are peculiar to him? It is true that he has come to reveal God and God's salvific intention toward humanity. Does his mission also carry with it any significant moral insights as to how to organize life in this world? Spohn here improves on Gustafson when he states that solidarity with the poor and unconditional forgiveness of those who wrong us are essential elements in the teaching of Christ. But even this is still a partial picture. A fuller picture of the role of Jesus in morality would have to admit on the basis of Spohn's previous work,[98] for example, that Jesus as moral teacher is normative both by the explicit content of his teaching and by the way his life and his teaching combine, as Spohn has shown, to shape our characters and our lives.

Is Scripture alone normative? The Catholic answer to this question both before and after the Council, the greater attention to Scripture notwithstanding, is a resounding "no." It is clear that despite the renewed interest in Scripture as a source of moral reasoning since the Council, the

nat. law prior to acceptance of SS

Catholic Church both in its official teaching authority and in its theology has not abandoned the use of natural law in morality. Indeed, as Bruno Schüller has repeatedly argued, natural law is indispensable to Catholic moral reasoning. According to Schüller, the decisive reason for the indispensability of natural law to Catholic morality does not lie in the fact that Scripture has nothing to say to anyone making moral judgments about politics or economics, for example. The reason is that, in his words, "a faithful grasp of Christ's moral message is possible only to those who already experience the logically prior claim of natural law." As he puts it elsewhere, before being addressed in revelation, the human being is already an ethical being. The role of moral theology then is to "render explicit the understanding of the natural law contained in faith's law of Christ."[99] To all intents and purposes, faith (Scripture) appears necessary here only as an explication and confirmation of what is already knowable and known by natural law. As we have seen so far, the tension between this type of reasoning and the push for a Scripture-based moral theology is quite obvious. This tension will be explored further in the next chapter.

L

Natural Law in the Catholic Moral Tradition

Natural law has been a constant element of the Catholic moral tradition for a very long time. Catholic social teaching has especially been noted for basing itself upon "natural law," that is, upon "every nature or quality of the human person and upon the social relationships which flow from the essence of 'whatness.'"[1] For example, Pope Leo XIII based his doctrine of the individual's right to private property on the right which everyone "has by nature to possess private property. This is one of the chief points of distinction between man and animal creation."[2] The right to marriage is a "natural and primitive" right, and it is "a most sacred law of nature that a father must provide food and all necessaries for those whom he has begotten."[3] In *Pacem in Terris*, Pope John XXIII presents a catalogue of rights and a human rights doctrine based on natural law. "By the natural law" every human being has the right to life,[4] to respect for his person,[5] to the benefits of culture,[6] to worship God freely according to the dictates of conscience,[7] to choose freely the state of life which he prefers,[8] to work,[9] to associate and assemble with others,[10] to take part in public affairs,[11] and to juridical protection of his rights,[12] and so forth.[13] To these natural rights, there are also corresponding natural duties. According to the pope, "The natural rights with which we have been dealing are, however, inseparably connected, in the very person who is their subject, with just as many respective duties; and rights as well as duties *find their source, their sustenance and their inviolability in the natural law which grants or enjoins them.*"[14]

The Second Vatican Council also uses the language of natural law. In speaking against acts of savagery in warfare, for example, the Council insists that such acts are condemnable as criminal by the "permanent binding force of universal natural law and its all-embracing principles." The human conscience, it says, "gives ever more emphatic voice to these principles." Therefore, "actions which deliberately conflict with these same principles, as well as orders commanding such actions, are criminal."[15]

The use of natural law by the magisterium as the basis for morality in regard to human sexuality is also very well known. Jean Porter writes in this regard that "while it would be unfair to characterize [the natural law] as a sexual ethic only, its norms for sexual behavior comprise its most distinctive feature."[16] Porter seems to me to have overstated the point a little here. Natural law in the Catholic tradition is not primarily about sex ethics. Sex is only one normative area in which natural law has been applied in the Catholic tradition. Political philosophy is another, as evidenced by the use the popes have made of natural law in their arguments for the way society should be structured. Indeed, at the most basic and general level, natural law is not a normative theory but metaethics—a claim about the nature of moral knowledge and its principles rather than their content. However, Porter's point about the preponderance of natural law especially in recent Catholic theology of human sexuality and the controversial nature of the use of that theory in recent Church documents is noteworthy. For example, Pope Pius XI forbade contraception because it was against nature. "Since, therefore, the conjugal act is destined primarily by nature for the begetting of children, those who in exercising it deliberately frustrate its natural power and purpose sin against nature and commit a deed which is shameful and intrinsically vicious."[17] Pope Pius XII also declared direct sterilization and artificial insemination wrong and unacceptable because they both contravened the natural law.[18] Pope Paul VI reiterated this teaching in the encyclical *Humanae Vitae*. Here he stated that "the Church, nevertheless in urging men to the observance of the precepts of the natural law, which it interprets by its constant doctrine, teaches that each and every marital act must of necessity retain its intrinsic relationship to the procreation of human life."[19] Paul VI further asserted that the marriage act, while it unites man and woman in the closest intimacy, also brings into operation "laws written into the actual nature of

NL often cited in sexual eth.

man and of woman for the generation of new life."[20] The pope went on to defend the competence of the Church's magisterium to speak authoritatively on matters pertaining to natural law.

> No believer will wish to deny that the teaching authority of the Church is competent to interpret even the natural moral law. It is in fact, indisputable . . . that Jesus Christ, when communicating to Peter and the Apostles His divine authority and sending them to teach all nations His commandments, constituted them as guardians and authentic interpreters of all the moral law, not only, that is, of the gospel, but also of the natural law, which is also an expression of the will of God, the faithful fulfillment of which is equally necessary for salvation.[21]

The intention here is not to be exhaustive in the references to the use of the natural law in the official teachings of the Church. Rather, it is important at the starting point of our discussion in this chapter on natural law in moral theology to remind the reader of its pervasive use in the Catholic moral tradition. There are a few things to note about this preponderance of the natural law. First is that although the concept is ancient, it has come into more frequent use in recent years. Josef Fuchs attributes this to the fact that the primitive documents were far less concerned with issues of morality than we are today. Moreover, the Church in the modern world is dealing with a secularized world which calls fundamental natural institutions into question and is at the same time unsympathetic to the Church's doctrine of God or revelation. In such a situation the only way out might be to appeal to "the nature of things" and to people's goodwill.[22] Second, it has been noted that the use of the natural law by the magisterium in recent times in the area of sexuality and reproduction has grown more and more negative. The concept has been used more and more, especially in the area of human reproduction and sexuality, "to set limits on human action in the form of prohibitions against acts that violate the natural teleologies of biological processes."[23] Porter argues in her book on natural and divine law that the Scholastic use of the natural law was different because it was formulated "with a view to affirming the goodness of creation and drawing out the social implications of that affirmation, in response to those such as the Cathars who denied the goodness of the material world."[24]

It is clear then that natural law has been applied in various ways by different groups in the history of the Catholic tradition. However, it is also

magis—
NL as (−) LIMIT, not (+) affirmatn.

clear that within the Catholic tradition there is some continuity in the meaning of the concept even when it is used in different contexts by different thinkers. This continuity has been made possible in part by the fact that "teachers within the Church self-consciously link their use of natural law with the theological tradition and with Aquinas' work in particular."[25] Therefore every serious discussion of the concept of natural law in the Catholic tradition must begin with that concept as defined by St. Thomas Aquinas since all natural law theorists try either to build on his work, refute him, or improve on him. Consequently, I will begin the discussion on natural law in recent Catholic moral theology with an exposition of the important elements in the Thomistic doctrine on natural law which have been central to current discussions on the matter. Although this exposition may seem unnecessary to those who are learned in these matters, I believe it is important as a way to lay down for the general reader the basis of much of the other discussion on the subject, as well as on the issue of moral norms, which will be taken up in chapter 8. So, we will next engage in a somewhat lengthy exposition of the basic elements of Aquinas's teaching on natural law.

St. Thomas Aquinas on Natural Law

Although the origins of the natural law theory predate St. Thomas Aquinas, his classical formulation continues to provide the benchmark for the understanding of that concept in Catholic theology. Aquinas's treatment of the issue is located within his treatment of law in general. He defines law as "an ordinance of reason for the common good, made by him who has care of the community, and promulgated."[26] He also notes the different categories of laws such as canon law, criminal/customary law, and commercial law. Aquinas provides a rather lengthy exposition of natural law, human law, and the divine law given in the Old and New Testaments. He also mentions the *Jus Gentium,* which was originally a category of Roman law and was interpreted by Thomas as part of the natural law because it commends social decencies on specific matters. Aquinas also considers it to be part of positive law in that most people have chosen to enforce it.[27] Natural law arises from the existence of human beings as rational, political, and social animals. Human laws arise out of the human need to demarcate the lines and measures required for functioning within the human community, and the divine law is God's free self-disclosure and intervention in human history.

According to Aquinas, every law, properly so called, is a manifestation of the eternal law. "The Eternal Law is the plan of government in the Chief Governor; all the plans of government must be derived from Eternal Law. Therefore all laws in so far as they partake of reason, are derived from the Eternal Law."[28] First within this scheme is the natural law which Aquinas defines as the rational creature's participation in the eternal law.[29] Natural law is founded on human nature which is shared by all human beings. It regards primarily those things which pertain to human nature: the preservation of the being that is possessed, the preservation of the species, the inclination of the good which is possessed by the human person in accordance with reason.[30]

[handwritten margin note: not a habit but precepts of prac reason]

In question 94, article 1, of the *Summa Theologiae,* Aquinas asks whether the natural law is a habit. He responds that although it is held habitually, natural law is not a habit. Natural law consists of precepts of practical reason which are analogues to the precepts of speculative reason. "The precepts of natural law are to human conduct what the first principles of thought are to demonstration. There are several first principles of thought, and so, also, several precepts of natural law . . . Both are kinds of self-evident beginnings."[31] What Aquinas says of these first principles is noteworthy. There is more than one of them. They are also indemonstrable axioms either of thought (speculative reason) or of action (practical reason). They are also both self-evident.

The notion of self-evidence, as Aquinas himself shows, is important in understanding the primary precepts. These precepts can be self-evident in two ways: in themselves, and in our minds. A proposition can be self-evident to us if the predicate is contained in the subject. In the example Aquinas himself gives, "the whole is greater than its parts," we have an example of an analytic proposition where once we understand the meaning of the terms involved, we cannot but grasp, without reflection, the truth it contains. That is to say that if we know what "whole" means and the meaning of "parts," the truth of this proposition becomes clear. The truth of propositions which are self-evident in themselves is more difficult to discern, especially by the uninformed. In this regard, Aquinas notes that although anyone who says "man" says "rational being," the truth that man is a rational animal may not be self-evident to everyone. Many people do not possess an adequate understanding of the human person to be able immediately to make the connection between the terms "man" and "rationality."[32]

In the *Commentary on the Sentences of Peter Lombard,* Aquinas argues that just as everything which undergoes a change must proceed from something immovable and unchangeable, so does every process of reasoning proceed from unchanging principles from the deposit of knowledge. This knowledge is not the type which is arrived at through discursive investigation. Rather it is given or offered to the intellect.[33] This is the knowledge that makes all other knowledge possible, the basis on which it is built. In speculative matters this knowledge is found in the *habitus* of self-evident principles which Aquinas refers to as *intellectus principiorum*.[34] "In practical matters there is also a *habitus* involved whereby we are able to know self-evident principles, and this *habitus* is called *synderesis*."[35] Our knowledge of these self-evident general principles is not innate in us but rather depends on sensation and memory.[36] In another place, Aquinas states that these self-evident general principles of practical reason are the primary precepts of natural law.[37]

Applying the insight from this discussion on self-evident principles, Aquinas states that in the realm of theoretic reason, we apprehend before all else the *real*, the concept of being: "That which before anything else, falls under apprehension is *being*, the notion which is included in all things whatsoever a man apprehends." Thus, insofar as we apprehend being or the real, we are able to grasp the first principle of speculative knowledge which is that "the same thing cannot be affirmed and denied at the same time and in the same respect."[38] Commenting on this principle, Germain Grisez states that "the objective dimension of the reality of beings that we know in knowing this principle is simply the definiteness that is involved in their very objectivity, a definiteness that makes a demand on the intellect knowing them, the very least demand—to think consistently of them."[39]

As being is the first notion to fall under the apprehension of theoretic reason, so is *good* the first notion to be apprehended by practical reason. Aquinas asserts that every agent acts for an end, an end which is pursued as "the good." Consequently, the first principle of practical reason is founded on the notion of good, namely that good which all things seek after. Hence, this is the first principle of natural law: that good is to be done and pursued and evil is to be avoided. This, says Aquinas, is the very basis of every other precept of the natural law. For "whatever the practical reason naturally apprehends as man's good (or evil) belongs to the precepts of natural law as something to be done or avoided."[40] Good, here, is thus to be understood as that "toward which each thing tends by its own principle of orientation,"[41] or, as Aquinas himself puts it so often in the *Summa*, as that to which the human person has natural inclination. Practical reason presupposes the good and in its role as active principle thinks in terms of what can be an "object of tendency."[42] For Aquinas, as we have already seen, there are objects (goods) toward which the human person has a natural tendency, inclination, or orientation. These are: self-preservation, self-perpetuation through birth and education of offspring, and the orientation to act in accord with reason.

One question which arises in connection with Aquinas's teaching on the human orientation to ends is whether the ends toward which the human person tends are always natural and within human reach. Thomas answers that the human person has two ends: the natural and the supernatural which is the beatific vision or life with God. Thus, says Grisez, we should not understand this human tendency toward the good in merely moral categories. However, the good which is the object of practical reason is the human good. Natural law "does not direct man to his supernatural end; in fact, it is precisely because it is inadequate to do so that divine law is needed as supplement."[43] The good here referred to includes the moral good but is not exhausted by it. Or, as Grisez states, "the act which preserves life is not the life preserved." Both are goods. But they are so distinct "that it is possible for the act which preserves life to be morally bad while the life preserved is a human good . . . The pursuit of the good which is the end is primary, the doing of the good which is the means is subordinate."[44]

If "good is to be done and pursued and evil is to be avoided" is the first principle of practical reason, and if, as we have seen, there is more than one good to be sought, the question then arises concerning the nature of this first principle of practical reason and whether it is also a primary precept of natural law, and the only one. That good is to be done is surely a self-evident principle. Every normal person has a conscious feeling that certain actions are more befitting and more worthy of the nature of the human person than others, and that certain human goods are more in keeping with that nature than others. "This capacity we have, whereby it is possible to discern the value of different actions, makes the principle 'good is to be done and ensured . . .' more than merely analytic by giving it an ontological foundation, in the very nature of man."[45] A further question which arises concerning the first principle of practical reason is whether it is a law. Although Grisez considers it to be another of the primary precepts of natural law and hence a law,[46] opinions differ greatly. For Jacques Maritain this principle is not the law itself but only a preamble to natural law.[47] Eric D'Arcy regards it as a logical principle and governor of all moral reasoning.[48] Frederick Copleston also considers it a directive principle. He does not think that Aquinas believed, for example, that we could deduce the wrongness of extramarital sexual intercourse from the precept that good is to be done and evil avoided "simply by contemplating, as it were, this latter precept. We can no more do this than we can deduce from the principle of non-contradiction the proposition that a thing which is white all over cannot be red all over."[49]

Aquinas speaks in various places of the principle of practical reason as being coextensive with the primary precepts of natural law. However, he never gave the number of these precepts. This has given rise to plenty of speculation on this matter. Ross Armstrong, for example, places considerable importance on the Thomistic teaching on natural inclinations as a way to arrive at a possible list of the primary precepts. He argues in this regard that "corresponding to each category there exists a principle of a very general kind, the truth of which is able to be grasped by all normal people." He lists these principles as follows: "One ought to respect and preserve not only human life, but where possible, all life"; "the sexual relationship requires some form of regulation"; "the family group ought to comply with some fixed pattern"; and "we ought to live together in obedience to certain rules and regulations."[50]

Whatever list one arrives at, it seems clear to me that natural law as Aquinas understood it is not merely regulatory. It is dynamic, directing human activity and quest in the moral and nonmoral spheres to what it means to be human. For example, to be rational is not to be translated merely as to live in obedience to rules and regulations. Human rationality implies much more than that in Thomistic natural law teaching. Whatever list one arrives at concerning the number of the precepts of natural law, however, depends on whether one accepts or rejects Aquinas's concept of human nature. More importantly, it depends to a large extent on how one understands the concept of human nature in the teaching of Aquinas. Some have accused Thomas of promoting a static concept of human nature. John Macquarrie[51] and Thomas Gilby,[52] among many others, deny this charge. Gilby points out that there are present in Aquinas's work two concepts of nature, one Roman, the other Greek. Like the Greeks, and thus in line with Aristotle, Aquinas uses nature to mean "the principle of a thing's motion by its own spontaneity from within as opposed to a motion suffered or imposed from without by the action of some particular cause." The Roman understanding of human nature is evident in Aquinas's understanding of it in terms of essence, a typological notion which considers

motion (inclination to perfection)
vs essence

human nature in its more settled characteristics. These two views of nature are not at war; rather, they complement each other. The tendency among many contemporary commentators on the natural law has been to create a dichotomy between these two understandings of the notion of natural law in the work of Thomas Aquinas. The outcome is often a one-sided legislation or appraisal that does not do justice to Aquinas's thought or to the human person in all his or her ramifications: historical, ontological, biological, spiritual, social, and so forth. It is a fact that the human person, as St. Thomas understood him, has some basic inclinations which characterize him. It is also a fact that the *humanum* is continually unfolding, and thus the search for it is a continuing quest. It is also a fact, however, that the above facts notwithstanding, there continues to be a human essence, the basis on which I, a black man living in the early years of the twenty-first century, can consider myself equally human, like all other human beings of all places and times.

NL has ontol.

There is thus an ontological foundation to natural law. This means that *foundation* the being, the very essence or nature of the human person as composed of body and spirit, is seen as the norm of moral behavior. As Jacques Maritain puts it, "There is by the very virtue of human nature, an order or a disposition which human reason can discover and according to which the human will must act in order to attune itself to the essential ends of the human being. The unwritten law, or natural law, is nothing more than that."[53] There is "a divine thought at the root of all created things."[54] And it is the task of the human person to discover and respect the divine intention. In its ontological aspect, natural law is an ideal order relating to human actions, a divide between what is suitable and what is not, and between what is proper or not. What is proper or improper, or suitable or unsuitable, thus "depends on human nature or essence and the unchangeable necessities rooted in it."[55]

Bruno Schüller has argued that there is both a positive and a negative connotation to the idea of human nature as the objective ground of knowing the natural law. Negatively, it can be inferred from this that "the natural law cannot receive its existence and specificity through the free decision of *nature* the human beings whom it concerns."[56] Nature is in this case considered *as* fixed and not open to historical differentiation or considerations. This *fixed* metaphysical notion of human nature as the basis of natural law can in turn lead to a notion of natural law as absolutely unchanging and unchangeable. This, as I have indicated above, would amount to a wrong and *not* even ideological use of the thought of St. Thomas and indeed of the whole *TA's account* authentic natural law tradition of Catholic theology. There is, however, a positive way of looking at nature as the ground of moral knowledge. This implies that "human beings grasp the natural law insofar as they grasp their givenness as their task, the existence bestowed on them through no effort of their own as their unconditional obligation." Schüller, like most Catholic theologians in recent times, insists that in grounding moral knowledge in human nature it has to be understood that by "nature" is meant both the sheer humanness of human beings and the givenness of the material world. "The objective basis of knowledge of the natural law is the simple humanness of human beings, and indeed, insofar as this is given over to the free decision of human beings, as that from which it proceeds."[57] Theologians have spoken of the human givenness which Schüller talks of in this passage not just in terms of biological facticity, but also in terms of a natural inclination in the human person to become what he or she is destined to be in nature. From these inclinations, certain imperatives emerge which are recognized by reason as in conformity with human nature. These imperatives "are formed by reason into dictates that present themselves as demanding obedience. Appearing, as they do, in consequence of an inclination that reason recognizes as authentically human, they are 'natural' law."[58]

There is, as well, a gnosiological foundation to natural law. A general assertion which the natural law theory makes about moral knowledge in general is that it is knowable. In *Gaudium et Spes,* the Second Vatican Council expresses this understanding of the natural law in the discussion of conscience: "Deep within their consciences men and women discover a law which they have not laid upon themselves and which they must obey. Its voice, ever calling them to love and to do what is good and to avoid evil, tells them inwardly at the right moment: do this, shun that. For they have in their hearts a law inscribed by God."[59] Although the Council does not explicitly refer to this as natural law, there is no doubt as to the reference here.

Natural law as it is understood in the Catholic tradition therefore implies a strong commitment to moral universalism. Since moral norms are grounded in human nature, which is the same everywhere, they can be known by all reasonable men and women without the help of divine revelation. The Church affirms that the wounds of original sin notwithstanding, the human person can know the general principles of the natural law. In the words of Joseph Boyle, the above quotation from *Gaudium et Spes* expresses the core of the natural law doctrine as understood in the

Catholic tradition, "that within the foundations of the consciences of all human beings there are nonconventional, nonarbitrary moral standards which make possible genuine moral self-criticism, and so true moral knowledge even for those who have not received the moral instruction of divine revelation."[60] As Bruno Schüller sees it, prior to being addressed in revelation, the human person grasps and expresses himself as an ethical being—that is, a being capable of knowing what is right and what is wrong.[61] This affirmation of the ability of the human person to know right and wrong is affirmed in spite of the wounds which are believed by the tradition to be inflicted on the human person by original sin. In Thomas Aquinas it forms part of the larger discussion on the relationship between faith (revelation) and reason.

Aquinas's views are cast against the background of the theory of "double truth" attributed to Averroës. This theory states that "faith and reason are two totally different wellsprings of knowledge which have absolutely nothing in common, and which therefore can never contradict one another, be equal, or integrate and help each other."[62] Aquinas asserts the distinctness of faith and philosophy (reason) as forms of knowledge. He states that there are two kinds of sciences: "There are some which proceed from principles known by the natural light of the intellect, such as arithmetic and geometry and the like. There are also some which proceed from principles known by the light of a higher science." This higher science is based on "the principles revealed by God."[63] Speaking in particular about the knowledge of God, Aquinas maintains that we can come to knowledge of the existence of God through creatures since creatures "lead us back to the knowledge of God, as effects do their cause." However, by natural reason we can know of God "only that which of necessity belongs to Him as the cause [*principium*] of all things." In this regard we are dealing with the creative power of God "which is common to the whole Trinity." The creative power of God belongs to the unity of essence of the Godhead. By light of natural reason, we can know what belongs to the unity of essence but not what belongs to the distinction of persons in the Trinity. This knowledge can only be had through revelation (faith).[64] Faith is necessary for human salvation; because "man is directed to God as to an end that surpasses the grasp of his reason." It is also to humans' benefit that certain things which are beyond the grasp of reason be made known to man by divine revelation.[65]

Like Clement of Alexandria before him, Aquinas maintained that reason and faith cannot contradict one another because they have God as

[marginal handwritten note: fides et ratio]

their common author. Philosophical truth can thus not be in conflict with revealed truth since truth can never contradict truth. "When some contrast arises, this is a sign that it is not truth that is being spoken of but instead false or unnecessary conclusions."[66] And in fact, not only is there no conflict between faith and philosophy, "there exists between them a certain affinity because in things known by means of natural reason, there are encountered similarities with those communicated through faith." When philosophers reach conclusions which contrast with faith, "this cannot be accredited as much to philosophy as to the abuse of philosophy" which is a consequence of "some weakness of the reason."[67] Also, faith serves to guide reason to the complete truth of certain things. Thus, for example, "even if reason were autonomous and sufficient in knowledge of the fundamental truths of the natural order," it would still be incapable of penetrating the mystery of God, which is its ultimate good. However, "from the moment faith communicates to reason where truth lies, the philosopher knows in which direction to turn his research. Now his task becomes to render intrinsically evident that which, with the guidance of faith, he already knows to be true."[68]

In regard to the natural law, therefore, there are two points to note. The first is that human reason, though weakened by sin, is still capable of coming to knowledge of the general principles of natural law. Reason, as it were, reads the natural law in the nature of things, especially in the nature of the human person. Second, although natural law is knowledge in logical independence of divine revelation, it does not follow that natural law exists independently of revelation. "On the contrary, the natural law is grounded in God's wisdom as creator, and sanctioned by God's authority as supreme lawgiver."[69] However, the relationship between reason and faith becomes problematic on these grounds as well. The question would be that even though it is easy to see what revelation adds to our understanding of the mystery of God, for example, it is not always easy to understand what and whether revelation adds to the moral truth we are capable of knowing through reason from natural law. It is, as we saw in our discussion on the distinctiveness of Christian ethics, precisely on this ground that the question of the nature of Christian ethics has been debated since Vatican II.

The only theoretical reference to natural law in the documents of the Second Vatican Council occurs at the start of the decree on religious liberty. This means that only in this document do we get an explanation of what the natural law is, of all the conciliar documents, as distinct from its invocation as justification for various norms. Reference has already been made to the decree of the Second Vatican Council on religious liberty in the first chapter of this book; and there is thus no need to repeat what has already been said. However, it is important to note again in this context of the discussion on natural law the extent to which the Council in this document justifies the right of every human being to seek truth on natural law terms. Seeking the truth is a tendency which is inherent in human persons by their nature (*DH*, 2). The Council opines that the highest norm of life is God's law which is true and unchanging precisely because it is founded in the nature of God whose conception of things is eternal and unchanging. Since it is God who has given the human person the power to participate in his eternal and unchanging law in order to know the truth more deeply, no human power can remove the duty to exercise this right from people. In other words, the obligations and rights which accrue to or are due to individuals are matters which can become clear only through the effort of inquiry or reasoning. As Joseph Boyle puts it, the special point of the Council's teaching on the human obligation to seek the truth "seems to be that people's knowledge of moral truth can develop and deepen, and that consequently they have a duty, and so a right, to undertake to deepen it for the sake of forming prudent and sincere judgments of conscience." Thus, by emphasizing the grounding of all moral knowledge in God's transcendental providential plan, the Council underlines the objectivity and universality of the immanent principles of conscience.[70]

Natural Law and Revisionist Theologians since Vatican II

One notable criticism of the natural law theory assumes, from the work of David Hume and G. E. Moore, the impossibility of deriving moral "ought" from a "natural" "is." This same criticism of the so-called naturalistic fallacy has also found an echo in the work of some theologians who have argued, especially since the Second Vatican Council, that the Church's position on natural law sometimes amounts to what Charles E. Curran and Hans Küng have referred to as physicalism. Among these theologians physicalism connotes both a moral theory and an anthropology.

In the physicalist paradigm, the moral norm is derived directly from certain structures of nature, in particular, the structure of faculties or acts. The structures indicate an inherent goal-directedness, purpose or "finality" in the faculties or acts. Since these purposes are thought to manifest the will of God who created them, they provide a direct indication of the moral law. Thus the structures provide the material content of the norm, while the obligation deriving from the will of God, which is expressed in the structures, provides the formal content. The relevant structures of the faculties or acts, in this way of arguing, are considered in abstraction from the person. Further, they were sometimes, if not always, identified as the biological structures of faculties or acts, or "the biological laws" which could be discovered in such faculties or acts. Again, in certain particular contexts, these structures were taken to be those which pertained to that dimension which human beings had in common with animals. This latter feature was particularly important in the traditional analysis of sexuality.[71]

The use of natural law in Catholic moral discourse has become a matter for much debate since the publication of *Humanae Vitae*. The drafters of the Washington Declaration, we must recall, argued that the encyclical's conclusions concerning natural law were based on "an inadequate concept of natural law." Several revisionist theologians have persistently taken up the charge of inadequacy with regard to the use of natural law in official Church teachings since the Council. Here I will highlight the views of a few who have made these charges more clearly and loudly. There are three or four elements which make the use of natural law in these documents unsatisfying according to these theologians. First, according to Curran, is that the current use of natural law in official Catholic teaching seems to pay only lip service to the importance of other sources of ethical wisdom. In an essay appearing soon after the publication of *Humanae Vitae,* Curran states that the natural law theory "as applied to the encyclical has the merit of recognizing a source of ethical wisdom for the Christian apart from the explicit revelation of God in Jesus Christ." However, the difficult question for Christian theology, he says, centers on the relationship between the natural law and the distinctively Christian element in the understanding of the moral life of the Christian.[72] Curran argues that *Humanae Vitae* both in its methodology and argumentation seems to accept a view of the natural law as a self-contained entity to which the law of the gospel or revelation is added. He insists that it is wrong to absolutize the realm of the natural law as something completely self-contained and unaffected by any relationships to the evangelical or the supernatural law. An authentic Christian view of reality, on the other hand, is more encompass-

ing and would consider reality in light of "the total horizons of the Chris- *chr *total**ity
tian faith-commitment—creation, sin, incarnation, redemption, and the
parousia." He believes that the doctrine of the natural law in *Humanae*
Vitae does not seem to take into account these realities of the Christian
faith, especially sin. Instead, the encyclical presupposes a natural law concept that fails to indicate "the relative and provisional character of nature
in the total Christian perspective." It rather chooses to absolutize "what
the full Christian view sees as relative and provisional in the light of the
entire salvation history."[73]

Second, Curran finds the use of natural law in the encyclical unsatis- ~2
factory because he believes that it vacillates between the two aspects of the
natural law pertaining to the order of nature and to that of reason. He
notes that Thomistic natural law theory is influenced predominantly by
two traditions, one Roman, the other Greek, and argues that following the
influence of the Roman jurist Ulpian,[74] there is sometimes a tendency in
the natural law doctrine of St. Thomas to identify "nature" and "natural" as
well as human action with mere animal or biological processes. Ulpian's
notion of nature, says Curran, "easily leads to a morality based on the finality of a faculty independent of any considerations of the total human
person or the total human community." Although one must also avoid the
opposite danger of paying no attention to the physical structure of the act
or to external actions in themselves, that is not a danger with official
Catholic approaches to natural law. On the contrary, Catholic theology in
its natural law approach has suffered from an oversimple identification of
the human action with an animal process or finality.[75] In particular, Curran
insists that *Humanae Vitae* employs a physicalist methodology which tends
to "identify the moral action with the physical and biological structure of
the act."[76] In Curran's view, this overidentification of the human action
with an animal process or finality is also evident in more recent teachings
on human sexuality[77] and is an indication that there has been little change
from the moral theology of the manuals which used to differentiate between "sins against nature" and "sins according to (i.e., in accordance
with) nature." The former are "acts in which the animal or biological
process is not observed—pollution, sodomy, bestiality and contraception."
In the latter, although "the proper biological process" is observed, something is still lacking which is proper to rational beings. The sins in this
class are fornication, adultery, incest, rape, and sacrilege.[78] Karl Rahner
argues that this view of nature fails to recognize the shift in contemporary
consciousness of human nature as the lofty viceroy of God, to human

nature and nature in general as a material in which man experiences himself as a free creator who builds his own world according to his laws and
who puts nature at his service rather than serve it.[79]

Richard McCormick also argues that Ulpian's interpretation of nature,
which Thomas Aquinas incorporated into his theory of natural law, creates a definite danger of identifying the human action with a mere animal
or biological process and of judging the morality of human acts merely on
the correspondence of action with the exigencies of physical nature. Like
Curran he argues that this danger is evident especially in the Church's
teaching on sexuality, as he believes is evident from the following quotation from the encyclical *Casti Connubii:*

> But no reason, however, may be put forward by which anything in-
> trinsically against nature may become conformable to nature and
> morally good. Since therefore, the conjugal act is destined primarily
> by nature for the begetting of children, those who in exercising it de-
> liberately frustrate its natural power and purpose sin against nature
> and commit a deed which is shamefully and intrinsically vicious.[80]

Therefore to go against nature would be to go against God. Also, the order
of nature is superior to the order of reason. In fact, the role of reason is to
discover what is properly the action of man and to "ascertain within what
limits an action is permissible and when it is strictly forbidden."[81] The
problem with *Casti Connubii,* as McCormick sees it, is that it succumbs to
dualism. That is, it "confirmed past points of view and did not surpass the
dualism of those views (that the sexual act is an act of nature while other
relations are specifically human)."[82] It did nothing either to show that the
modifications to the notion of an "act of nature" elaborated over the centuries in Scholastic theology had somewhat undermined this notion.[83]
McCormick traces the development of the "physicalist" view of human nature even further back to Augustine of Hippo through several stages of the
Church's history up until *Humanae Vitae* and after. He has also highlighted
the controversies which have always surrounded it.[84]

McCormick insists that the foundation for natural law, as Thomas
Aquinas states, is not found in human biological nature alone but in human
rationality as well. The balance between these two tendencies in the
Thomistic natural law tradition must be maintained if we are to do justice
to the proper moral quality of human acts. McCormick claims inspiration
for his position from the Second Vatican Council's stand that "the moral

aspect of any procedure must be determined by objective standards which are based on the nature of the person and the person's acts."[85] For him "such integral personalism was a conciliar achievement" which "did not reflect the way decisive thinkers in the Catholic tradition proceeded." The regret for McCormick is that "official teaching, notwithstanding the deliverances of the Vatican II, still reproduces the basic anthropological assumptions of these decisive thinkers . . . That means that in some areas of practical moral instruction, the person is not really decisive."[86]

Third, the revisionist theologians argue that the teaching of the Church on sexuality since *Humanae Vitae* has tended to exhibit a classicist worldview instead of a historical consciousness by emphasizing nature and natural faculties rather than the good of the entire person as grounds for determining the rightness or wrongness of human acts and by insisting on a law model rather than a "responsibility model" as a moral methodology.[87]

Many scholars, following Bernard Lonergan, have in recent times spoken of a classicist worldview and a historical consciousness in theology and in the Church. The classicist worldview is described as perceiving the Church as essentially static and unchanging, an institution which by divine decree is immune to process. Although the Church moves through history, it is not affected by history in any meaningful way. Change is always cosmetic, or rather semantic. Historical consciousness, on the other hand, approaches history as a field of human and divine activity and interaction in which events are a result of human passions, decisions, and actions. "And just as each person is different from the other, so is each event and each culture. But not only are the 'events' of history contingent. So, too, are the *interpretations* of these events."[88] With reference to morality, these scholars describe classicism as conceiving of the Christian moral life as "that which conforms to certain pre-existing norms, natural law, ecclesiastical law. Its emphasis, therefore, is always on law, authority, *magisterium*, precedent." Classicism in the moral life is therefore deductive as opposed to being inductive in its approach. It deals with moral norms in abstract and pays little attention to circumstances and situations. Historical consciousness in morals, on the other hand, "conceives the moral life of the Christian as one of personal responsibility within changing historical conditions." Here, norms reflect the historical circumstances in which they were initially formulated and subsequently interpreted.[89] Richard McBrien insists that the classicist and historical worldviews are not antithetical. He believes that a balanced moral theology "cannot prescind from principles, precedent, and ultimate purpose, and so it must to some extent be deductive, deontological, and teleological. On the other hand, a balanced moral theology must attend to the person and the situation. Thus, it must be both historical and inductive."[90] For Charles Curran, this balance has often been missing in pronouncements from the Holy See since the publication of the encyclical on birth control. For example, he sees in the following passage from the "Declaration on Sexual Ethics" (1975), a clear indication of the classicist worldview at work in post–Vatican II moral theology:

> Therefore there can be no true promotion of human dignity unless the essential order of human nature is respected. Of course, in the history of civilization many of the concrete conditions and needs of human life have changed and will continue to change. But all evolution of morals and every type of life must be kept within the limits imposed by the immutable principles based upon every human person's constitutive elements and essential relations—elements and relations which transcend historical contingencies. These fundamental principles which can be grasped by reason are contained in "the divine law—eternal, objective, and universal—whereby God orders, directs, and governs the entire universe and all the ways of human community by a plan conceived in wisdom and love. Human beings have been made by God to participate in this law with the result that under the gentle disposition of divine providence they can come to perceive ever increasingly the unchanging truth." This divine law is accessible to our minds. (n. 3)[91]

Also, when it is stated in this text that the sexual teaching of the Church is based "on the finality of the sexual act" and that the principal criterion of its moral goodness of the sexual act is based on "respect for its finality," Curran believes that this indicates a classicist mentality, which has little or no regard for the person as the ultimate moral criterion in matters of sexual morality. What is paramount here is the sexual faculty and the sexual act. This according to Curran is indicative of the physicalism that has dominated official Catholic teaching and the teaching of the moral manuals for quite some time.[92]

The Magisterium and Natural Law

A second aspect to the debate on natural law in recent Catholic theology is concerned with the involvement of the magisterium in matters pertaining to natural law. Here, there are three discernible approaches to the issue. The first is of course the one defended in *Humanae Vitae,* as quoted above, to the effect that the magisterium has absolute competence to teach and legislate on issues pertaining to natural law. Such a view represents an understanding of natural law which sees it either as included in revelation or a development of revelation. In his famous manual *Moral and Pastoral Theology,* volume 1, Henry Davis states, "The revelation that has, in fact, been given to man, is the revelation of a supernatural destiny, and this includes all that natural law commands."[93] If natural law is included in revelation, then the magisterium of the Church, which has a direct mandate from Christ to teach the truth contained in revelation, has also the mandate to teach matters which are more explicitly known from natural law. This is the reasoning that is behind the position that the magisterium has competence over natural law. Germain Grisez, for example, argues that "the magisterium has authority—not in the sense of choosing but in the sense of judging—what belongs to revelation."[94] Grisez believes that "all natural law is implicitly revealed." Therefore the moral norms which the magisterium teaches "to be definitively held" are revealed, "if only implicitly" and "having been proposed with one voice by the Catholic Bishops as a requirement for salvation, the whole body of the moral teaching concerning acts which constitute grave matter meets the requirements articulated by Vatican II for teaching proposed infallibly by the ordinary magisterium."[95] Thus, not only does the magisterium have the competence to teach natural law, but also certain magisterial teachings which are derived from natural law, such as the teaching on contraception, are also infallibly taught because they have been constantly taught by the magisterium of the Church as necessary for salvation.

A second position on the question of the competence of the magisterium is one which, while not completely denying that the magisterium can teach natural law, tries to limit the extent of this competence. This second approach argues that closer attention has to be paid to the distinction between the so-called general principles of natural law and their application. As we have already seen, Thomas Aquinas makes this distinction, which has become an essential part of natural law discourse in the Catholic ethical tradition. Richard McCormick argues in this regard that a lot of confusion arises when the distinction between the general principles of natural law and the particular applications of these principles is ignored. For he believes that while the magisterium has competence in issues pertaining to the general principles, the same cannot be said with regard to the particular applications. Consider, for instance, the presumption in Catholic tradition against taking human life. This, says McCormick, represents the general principle. However, what this principle enjoins in the concrete is another matter. This is difficult to define "due to the broad sense in which the very understanding of the principle shifts or is modified" or to new insights arising from the "assessment of contingent facts in relation to the principle's term of reference."[96] The point here is that since applications can change in the very understanding of the principles themselves or in the assessment of the contingent data which are relevant to the case, there is no way the magisterium can have the competence to determine a priori the rightness or wrongness of matters at this level. We will see more of this argument when we discuss moral norms.

Finally, there are those who rule out the magisterium in any issues pertaining to natural law. Frank Mobbs states, for example, that the natural law lies outside the object of the authority of the magisterium and that the "magisterium has acted *ultra vires* in teaching on it as if it had divine authority to bind to belief." This being the case, "the teachings of the magisterium on natural law do not count as teachings of the Catholic Church."[97] Mobbs bases his position on what he considers to be the position of the theologians and the teaching authority of the Church that without such authority to teach natural law, human beings cannot be saved. The presumption here is that "only someone who knows moral right and wrong can be saved." That leaves out infants and "idiots" and a whole host of humanity "who are not likely to hear anything the magisterium has to say." Natural law is not a condition for salvation. "The magisterium cannot repeatedly, and emphatically, exalt revelation as the highest form of knowledge—both because of its certitude and also because of its value for salvation—the form it is divinely charged with propagating, and at the same time tack on the teaching of non-revealed matter, as if the boundary of the object of its authority had been adjusted only slightly."[98]

Some Remarks

One thing evident in the above discussion on the use of natural law in recent Catholic theology is not just a general reluctance, as Jean Porter has noted in her book on natural and divine law, on the part of many contemporary Catholic theologians to talk about the moral significance of human nature. What is even clearer is the reluctance of many theologians to grant moral significance to natural human faculties. Porter points out that even the so-called traditionalists like Germain Grisez and John Finnis have in their widely acclaimed natural law theory refrained from deriving moral conclusions from human nature.[99] In his treatment of natural law, Grisez states that the purpose of the first principle of natural law is to direct thinking toward "the fulfillment which is to be realized in and through human action." The principle points out the relationship between human goods and the actions appropriate for realizing them. Although he holds that the natural human tendencies or inclinations which Aquinas speaks of each correspond to a basic precept of natural law, Grisez maintains that these basic precepts of natural law are general determinations of the first principle of practical reason which states categorically that basic human goods are to be protected, pursued, or promoted.[100] And even though the principle of practical reason directs thinking to each basic good as something to be promoted, protected, and pursued, there is still the question of what these goods are and how they can be known. Although we will examine Grisez's position on the basic goods in a subsequent chapter, it is pertinent to point out here that none of the basic goods is derived from the finality of natural ends but from other criteria.

Veritatis Splendor reacts strongly to those who deny that human nature has moral significance. The encyclical's reaction is given against the backdrop of what it considers a misunderstanding of the idea of human freedom. This misunderstood freedom claims to be absolute and tends to treat the human body as "a raw datum, devoid of any meaning and moral values until freedom has shaped it in accordance with its design." Thus, in this case, human nature is only a presupposition or preamble, which is "materially necessary, for freedom to make its choice," but which is nonetheless "extrinsic to the person, the subject, and the human act." The moral theories which deny moral significance to human nature and, in the pope's view, absolutize freedom, do not correspond to the truth about the human person and about freedom. They are contrary to Scripture and tradition because they contradict the Church's teachings on the unity of the human person, "whose rational soul is *per se et essentialiter* the form of his body. The spiritual and immortal soul is the principle of unity of the human being, whereby it exists as a whole—*corpore et anima unus*—as a person."[101] Thus, such teachings which dissociate "the moral act from the bodily dimensions of its existence, revive in new forms, certain ancient errors which have always been opposed by the Church, inasmuch as they reduce the human person to a 'spiritual' and purely formal freedom." Such a reduction, the pope insists, misunderstands the "moral meaning of the body and of kinds of behavior involving it."[102] The pope points to the Christian teaching that the body will also share in the glory of the resurrection. Further, he points to the intrinsic link between reason and free will which are linked with the bodily and sense faculties:

> The person, including the body, is completely entrusted to himself, and it is in the unity of the body and soul that the person is the subject of his own moral acts. The person, by light of reason and the support of virtue, discovers in the body the anticipatory signs, the expression and the promise of the gift of self, in conformity with the wise plan of the Creator.[103]

Natural law, properly understood then, refers to "man's proper and primordial nature, 'the nature of the human person.'" It expresses and lays down "the purposes, rights and duties which are based upon the bodily and spiritual nature of the human person." This law can therefore not be considered simply a set of norms on the biological level. It must rather be seen as "the rational order whereby man is called by the Creator to direct and regulate his life and actions and in particular to make use of his own body."[104]

The issue of deriving moral meaning from natural human faculties is basically an issue of how to arrive at moral truth and how to recognize and protect permanent and enduring values which are necessary for human flourishing. It is also about the way to remain faithful to the will of God or, even more importantly, to understand what the will of God is. God speaks in different ways, including through nature. The problem is how to understand divine speech and how to harmonize the word of God spoken across various ages and cultures. There is a particularly Catholic way of sensing the divine intention through things, biology included. Although this type of reasoning has come under considerable assault in recent times from all sorts of angles, and sometimes for very valid reasons, it still seems to me that this is a line of thinking we cannot afford to forgo entirely.

Pluralism, global interdependence, and cultural diversity are a fact of life today. As we have already seen in this work, not only does Vatican II welcome these phenomena, it enjoins us to welcome them and to try to decipher through them the signs of the times. However, pluralism, globalization, and cultural diversity raise questions about truth which we cannot ignore. For example, does the fact that polygamy is practiced in some parts of Africa and Asia mean that this practice is good? Does the fact that homosexuality is becoming an acceptable mode of being together for many people in different Western societies mean that it is the right thing to do? In other words, is there still a difference between truth and error, or between what are merely differences in various perspectives and what is simply erroneous, the proponents of such views notwithstanding? And how can such a distinction be made? These are no easy questions. The proponents of natural law think that it is still possible to determine what is right from what is wrong with the help of natural law. In the discussion on norms in subsequent chapters we will see that the more complete argument of the revisionists is not that natural human faculties have no moral meaning. Rather, they argue that their moral significance cannot be determined in isolation from some other human factors.

[margin note: what revisionists really say]

The interlocutors in the debate on natural law in the Catholic tradition all assume that the natural law, according to Thomas, is a form of human participation in the mind of God, or as Joseph Boyle puts it, "a participation by human beings in God's providential plan." This participation is a special kind of knowledge about human beings, their possibilities, and their perfection.[105] Even so, natural law is not a divine command theory. "The obligatory force of moral norms can be appreciated by natural reason without the recognition of those norms as divine commands." Even so, "when moral norms are fully recognized for what they ultimately are, they are seen as expressions of God's will that humans should live in accord with his wise and loving plan."[106] In the search for truth, it seems to me that recognition of the nature component in the natural law theory is absolutely essential if we must not sink into unredeemable relativism. This does not mean that we must take biological facticity as a given about which nothing can be said. It simply means that in making moral decisions we must take such facticity into account where necessary and reasonably.

[margin note: not a command]

Also, if natural law is a form of participation in God's providential plan for humanity, it means that natural law is also about human salvation. It is an important element of the Christian faith that God's plan for humanity is to save humanity. It is the whole human person which is embraced in the salvific intent of God. Thus, I think the Church has a right and a duty to speak authoritatively about natural law in all its aspects—pastoral and doctrinal—because its teaching has to do with what is essential for human salvation. However, this does not imply an uncritical acceptance of the concept of nature which is implied in every ecclesial teaching on the matter of natural law. The ecclesial formulators of such

[margin note: salvation]

teachings must be careful to avoid identifying nature with the order of creation, especially in an essentialist manner. Curran has rightly pointed out passages in recent official pronouncements which contain such essentialist attitudes. The problem with such texts is that they do not allow for the rational element which must accompany the effort to determine whether a particular action or actions are contrary to nature and thus wrong or otherwise.

Magisterium and Morality

We have seen how *Humanae Vitae* raised a host of issues about sexual ethics and marriage. Many of these issues have broader implications for moral analysis, the question of acts versus whole life orientations, for example. However, there are other questions which have become more prominent since or as a result of *Humanae Vitae*—questions about who should have the final say on moral matters, questions of authority, and responsibility for moral teaching and moral judgments. Therefore, the most profound impact of *Humanae Vitae* did not necessarily relate to its teaching on sexuality—that teaching really contained nothing new in the final analysis, for all it did in this regard, to a large extent, was to restate the teaching of *Casti Connubii* on the matter. And even if Joseph Selling is correct in the assertion that the encyclical represented a departure from *traditional* teaching, such disjuncture, even by Selling's own admission, lies basically in the meaning which is attributed by the encyclical to marital sexual activity and thus to the justification which the encyclical tried to propose for an old teaching. The real revolution which took place as a result of the publication of *Humanae Vitae* occurred in connection with the rethinking of the role of the magisterial authority of the Church in moral matters.

Until the publication of *Humanae Vitae* most Catholics viewed morality almost entirely in an extrinsic way. They had been taught to listen to and obey their parents, their teachers, and their priests. The Church was

189

the sole authority for proclaiming the will of God. There was little effort to distinguish either the level of authority or the grade of teaching involved in that authority. All authority was vested in the pope as sovereign pontiff. As we have already seen in chapter 2, some authors have described this type of authority structure as pyramidal. Richard McCormick maintains that this manner of exercising authority was fostered and maintained by a number of factors, including the self-definition of the Church wherein "Church" almost always referred to a small few in authority; the state of information technology, which meant that information moved very slowly throughout the world, thus making it possible for people to form opinions without the rich contributions of the various distinct cultures and traditions in the Church; and the complex nature of the issues, which were often incomprehensible to many in the Church who had little or no theological training. Other issues had to do with the manner in which authority was exercised during that period, which was secretive and highly centralized; and the educational style of the day, wherein the master "handed down" wisdom to the pupil. These and other such factors, according to McCormick, generated a notion of magisterium in the Church with the following three characteristics:

(1) An undue distinction between the teaching and learning function in the Church, with a subsequent unique emphasis on the right to teach—and relatively little on the duty to learn and the sources of learning in the Church; (2) an undue identification of the teaching function with a single group in the Church, the hierarchy; (3) an undue isolation of a single aspect of teaching, the judgemental, the decisive, the "final word." Thus it was taken for granted by many that on any moral problem, however complex, *Roma locuta causa finita.* The term "magisterium" came to mean the hierarchical issuance of authoritative decrees.[1]

Humanae Vitae itself contributed enormously to creating the debate over the relationship between the magisterium and the individual conscience. The encyclical stated: "The Church is competent in her magisterium to interpret the natural moral law" (*HV,* no. 4). In another passage the encyclical asserts as well that "a right conscience is the true interpreter of the objective moral order" (*HV,* no. 10). These assertions "inevitably raised the question of the relationship between the individual's conscience and the hierarchical magisterium of the Church. It was not simply a speculative question but one which, as events have increasingly shown, has been an actual and agonizing one for many." This problem is often expressed in terms of "a voluntarist confrontation between the freedom of the individual and the binding force of the Church's ordinary non-infallible magisterium."[2] It can be seen in the discussion on the nature of the magisterium of the Church and the extent—that is, the competence—of this magisterium, as well as in the problem of dissent.

The Nature of the Magisterium

The Second Vatican Council uses the term "magisterium" to refer to the pastoral teaching office and to those who constitute it. The authentic magisterium of the Church owes its authority to the founding intention of Christ who "set up in his Church a variety of offices which aim at the good of the whole body"—the attainment of salvation (*Lumen Gentium [LG]*, 18).[3] Bishops are successors of the apostles by virtue of an unbroken succession which goes back to the beginning, and by divine will have "taken the place of the apostles as pastors of the Church." Therefore, "whoever listens to them is listening to Christ and whoever despises them despises Christ and Him who sent Christ" (*LG*, 20). In number 25 of the same document the Council declares that bishops are "authentic" teachers, "that is teachers endowed with the authority of Christ." When they teach in communion with the Roman pontiff they should be revered by all the faithful as "witnesses of divine and Catholic truth." The faithful, for their part, "are obliged to submit to their bishops' decision, made in the name of Christ in matters of faith and morals, and adhere to it with a ready and respectful allegiance of mind." This respectful submission of mind and will must be shown in a special way to the teaching authority of the pope even when he is not speaking *ex cathedra,* and in such a manner that "his supreme authority be acknowledged with respect and that one sincerely adhere to decisions made by him, conformably with his manifest mind and intention, which is made principally either by the character of the documents in question, or by the frequency with which a certain doctrine is proposed, or by the manner in which it is formulated."[4] Later in the same passage the Council states that individual bishops also enjoy the privilege of infallibility— that is, they proclaim the doctrine of Christ infallibly when they "preserve among themselves and with Peter's successor the bond of communion, in their authoritative teaching concerning matters of faith and morals" which should be held definitively and absolutely. And when they are assembled together with their head (the pope) in an ecumenical council they also constitute infallible teachers of and judges in matters of faith and morals "whose decisions must be adhered to with the loyal and obedient assent of faith." The document on divine revelation also had this to say about the hierarchical magisterium:

> The task of giving an authentic interpretation of the Word of God, whether in its written form or in the form of Tradition has been entrusted to the Living Teaching Office of the Church alone. Its authority in this matter is exercised in the name of Jesus Christ. Yet this magisterium is not superior to the Word of God, but is its servant. It teaches only what has been handed on to it. At the divine command and with the help of the Holy Spirit, it listens to this devotedly, guards it with dedication and expands it faithfully.[5]

Who constitutes the living teaching office which the Council speaks about in this passage? What or where are the loci of the Holy Spirit? The people of God? The pastoral office? Some charismatic persons in the ecclesial community? Did this passage or any other conciliar passage move beyond the manualist identification of authority in the Church with the authority of the pope and the bishops, or beyond the tendency "to reduce every other kind of theological authority to this one font"?[6] These questions have become especially urgent in the context of the debate over *Humanae Vitae* and its teaching. Consider again, for example, the rejection of that encyclical by the drafters of the Washington Declaration on the ground that it betrays "a narrow and positivistic notion of authority, as illustrated by the rejection of the majority view presented by the commission established to consider the question, as well as the rejection of the conclusions of a large part of the international Catholic community." Since the publication of *Humanae Vitae* questions have therefore been raised not only with regard to the constitution of the magisterium, but also concerning the loci of the Holy Spirit in the Church and what the presence of the Holy Spirit implies for the exercise of authority in the Church.

In the passage above, the term "magisterium" denotes both the teaching office of the Church and the bearers of its teaching function. Both aspects are said to belong to the hierarchy of the Church who as bearers of the teaching function of the Church possess the authority to teach authoritatively in matters of faith and morals including "everything which is divinely revealed" (*DV,* 10). It has been argued by some theologians that the merging of the two aspects of the term "magisterium" in *Lumen Gentium* is recent and rather restrictive in comparison to earlier uses and understanding of the notion in the Church.[7] Yves Congar, the French Dominican ecclesiologist, states in this regard that the teaching ministry in the Church has been connected either with *charismata* or with an authority endowed with charisma.[8] The word "magisterium" itself has at different times in the history of the Church been used to denote various forms of leadership in the Church. The current meaning of the word as referring to the body of priests with authority to teach first appeared in the nineteenth century, although the reality it denotes existed before this period.[9] Teaching in the Church has assumed several forms. In the primitive Church there were doctors, *didaskaloi,* who were more catechists than speculative theologians, as well as bishops.[10] From the second century, the bishop was characterized by the *cathedra,* the chair. This referred to "the episcopal function, its continuity, succession, *doctrina.*" The chair or *cathedra* of Peter was the one on which Christ built his Church "for Peter is the first to confess Christ." Peter is still in Rome in the person of his successors. *Cathedra,* says Congar, is the equivalent of what we call the magisterium. And the magisterium as the guarantor of apostolic succession was considered "not as a juridical authority possessing as such a power to compel, but as a function through which the Church receives the faith inherited from the apostles."[11]

Although there was opposition by pastors and councils to erroneous speculation by doctors, there was no statutory separation between them. Instead what obtained between doctors and pastors in this period before the Council of Chalcedon was mutual cooperation for the sake of dogmatic clarification. "Non-pastors, such as Tertullian, cooperated in this with Theodore of Mopsuestia and the Cappadocians. Since authority rests on truth and tradition, a non-bishop is listened to: Athanasius participates at Nicaea as a simple deacon, St. Augustine asserts his rights to invoke Jerome against Pelagius, Vincent of Lérins calls 'Patres' non-bishops."[12]

The Scholastics in the Middle Ages were the ones who formulated a distinction between doctrinal-Scholarly teaching and the pastoral teaching function in the Church. For example, St. Thomas Aquinas distinguished between the *magisterium cathedra pastoralis* or *pontificialis* (magisterium of the pastoral or the pontifical chair) and the *magisterium cathedra magistralis* (the magisterium of a master's chair). While one refers to power, par excellence, the other "is personal competence recognized publicly." It follows then, Congar argues, that the magisterium of a theologian can in fact be recognized as a public office in the Church whose substance comes from the theologian's scholarly competence. On the other hand, "the pastoral magisterium is linked to the public office of *praelatio*, that is, superiority or authority, to which belongs jurisdiction."[13]

Congar credits the apparent unilateral view of teaching and of teaching authority in the pre–Vatican II Church to several philosophical, social, and theological currents which existed between the Council of Trent and Vatican II. These include the suppression of faculties of theology in France during the French Revolution and at the time of Napoleon, as well as in Germany; and the sharp distinction between *ecclesia docens* (teaching Church) and *ecclesia credens* or *discens* (the believing or learning Church), which arose within the Jansenist controversy and was to become common in the nineteenth century. Other factors were the distinction of the ordinary from the extraordinary magisterium, the introduction of the notion of the universal magisterium, and the definition of papal infallibility, all of which were introduced by the First Vatican Council. These movements, Congar argues, introduced a unilateralism which came to a high point in the encyclical *Humani Generis* when Pius XII insisted on total obedience for the ordinary magisterium of the pope, and stated that once the pope had expressed his *sententia* on a hitherto controversial point there could no longer be any question of free theological discussion on the issue by theologians.[14] He reduced the theologian's task to finding theological justification for the teaching of the magisterium.[15] Is Pius XII's position in conformity with what nineteen centuries of the life of the Church tell us about the function of the *didaskaloi* or doctors in the Church? "No, not exactly," says Congar.

In response, Germain Grisez argues that nothing Congar says in these two articles shows "that theologians enjoy any teaching authority in the Church—that is, authority to which the faithful as such ought to submit their personal judgment."[16] Grisez then summarizes the debate on the nature of the magisterium in the following words: "In recent years some have argued that authority is of two sorts: some authorities are qualified (to determine what is true) by their experience or scholarly competence, while other authorities are qualified (to decide what will be done) by their social status. The former must be respected because they are in a position to know better; the latter must be obeyed because of their official power to decide." He maintains that it was never the intention of Jesus to divide his authority in two. Thus, Congar's division is inadequate. "It leaves out of account the authority enjoyed by one who communicates personal truth to be accepted with personal faith. The teaching authority of the bishops derives from that of Jesus, and belongs to the same category as his authority."[17] Grisez also believes that Congar set out to find reasons why the faithful should submit their personal judgment to the authority of theologians.

I do not believe that this is an adequate representation of Congar's position. Instead, it seems to me that he wants to demonstrate that it has been the tradition in the Church for the teaching authority to acknowledge theological expertise and to take it into account in the formulation of doctrine to which the faithful should "submit their personal judgment." It is doubtful that any serious scholar would regard "social status" as the basis of magisterial function of the bishops and the pope. Who would claim that theologians "know better" than the bishops? McCormick captures the truth which most Catholic theologians support when he says that only the pope with the bishops constitute authentic teachers—that is "teachers endowed with the authority of Christ."[18] The bishops constitute the authentic magisterium of the Church which speaks with genuine authority. Even though Congar is right to say that the teaching function of various elements in the Church became more diversified in the history of the Church as the offices of bishops and theologians developed further, and even though theologians have in the history of the Church had an ecclesial office which is in practice authoritative, just like that of the parish priests, it does not mean that bishops and the pope do not have a special role in settling disputed questions. The question is simply about the extent of this competence.

As Bruno Schüller points out, the magisterium speaks with genuine authority because "it speaks with the special assistance of the Holy Spirit God has guaranteed." As a consequence of the special gift of the Holy Spirit the magisterium speaks from "a superior insight" into the gospel and law of Christ. This insight "protects it in a special way from error." Thus the magisterium can vouch for the truth of its teaching and proclamations and deserves to be trusted. The magisterium is not an end in itself but is only a means to an end. Therefore one is obliged to it only to the extent that one needs help in finding the truth.[19]

Schüller argues that since the magisterium in its merely authentic teaching is not infallible, that means that it can occasionally err. Fallibility is an unavoidable human characteristic. "Thus all authority, in so far as it is exercised by humans, is *eo ipso* fallible authority." Fallible authority proves itself by what it does "as a rule" (*per se*). Also, it shows its fallibility by its failures "in exceptional cases" (*per accidens*). Since the authentic magisterium has the guaranteed assistance of the Holy Spirit, it can claim that "as a rule" its judgment and actions in matters of faith are infallible, although it can be wrong in "occasional cases." Two conclusions emerge from this. The first is that when the magisterium calls the faithful to trust in its leadership it correctly assumes that as a result of the unique gift of the Holy Spirit which offers it superior insight into the gospel and law of Christ "it is better protected against error than are the faithful." Second, the magisterium in the exercise of its merely authentic authority is not certain in any absolute way that it is empowered to decide infallibly. Nor can it guarantee to the faithful any absolutely dependable help in their search for truth. What it can say in any given circumstance is that the help it gives to the faithful in their quest for truth is the most dependable. Correspondingly, it offers the faithful this prospect: in the trust they give to it, they will "as a rule" find support and only "in exceptional cases" be disappointed.[20]

Obviously no Catholic scholar wants the abrogation of the teaching office of the Church. No one can do so and be considered a Catholic. For, as has been stated repeatedly so far, it is an important element of Catholic faith that God gave his apostles direct authority to lead the rest of the Church. Christ promised the Holy Spirit to the apostles. It is the belief of the Church that the bishops are successors of the apostles and that to them is also given all the gifts which the Lord Jesus had promised the apostles for the sake of the Church. While the magisterium needs the reflection of theologians and other intellectuals in the Church as well as the experience of the laity in general to fulfill its mission, this mission does not necessarily depend on the approval of the theologians or anyone else because the magisterium is the only official teaching body in the Church. As Richard Gula has pointed out, "While others can repeat the official teaching of the Church, no one else can designate a certain teaching of the Church as 'official' teaching." The pope and the bishops alone speak for the Church. Thus, they alone can "designate certain interpretations of the apostolic faith as the official interpretations of the Catholic Church which are to guide pastoral practice."[21] There is general consensus on this even when there is a general feeling among some in the Church since the publication of the encyclical on birth control that the special ministry of the teaching office of the Church needs improvement in many ways. Some of the new questions relating to the way this ministry is exercised pertain to the proper role of the bishop in his diocese in relation to the Roman Curia, the understanding and role of the local and universal Churches, and the place of episcopal conferences in the teaching office of the magisterium, among many others. Since these are matters for ecclesiologists, they will not delay us here. However, one of the more urgent questions which has arisen since the publication of *Humanae Vitae* pertains to the role of the magisterium vis-à-vis the conscience of the individual in the Church.

Authority and Conscience

The tension between authority and conscience arises in many areas of life: political, between the citizen and political authority; academic, between scholars and academic authority; ecclesial, between the believer and the institutional Church; and so forth. In other words, this problem is likely to arise "anywhere that authority asserts itself and is thought to impose an obligation to assent or obey."[22] This problem is more acute in the Catholic tradition, however, for two other reasons: the understanding of conscience in the Catholic tradition, and the nature of the Church.

The Supremacy of Conscience

Catholic moral tradition distinguishes between an objective norm and a subjective norm of morality. Right reason is considered the objective norm in that it apprehends the order of things including the will of God as manifested through nature and revelation. Conscience is the subjective norm of morality in that it is the faculty by which the individual appropriates for himself or herself the objective norm as it is made manifest in revelation and in nature. In other words, the individual possesses an ethical faculty by means of which he can make ethical determinations concerning what is the will of God, what is good, beautiful, and perfect (Rom 12:12). In other words, it is Catholic teaching that the human person recognizes the demands of the divine law through her conscience.

Thomas Aquinas propounded a most comprehensive treatment of the notion of conscience in the Catholic moral tradition by bringing together two ideas: synderesis and *conscientia,* which had been in use in the tradition before him. In Aquinas's work, synderesis refers to a natural disposition which is concerned with the basic principles of behavior. It refers to the intellect's grasp of the first principle of practical reason. *Conscientia,* on

Moral Theology in an Age of Renewal

the other hand, is concerned with concrete moral judgments—that is, with the application of general moral principles to concrete situations. Synderesis is infallible, since it points out in general that good is to be done and evil avoided. *Conscientia* is not infallible, since it is involved in the application of general principles to particular cases. The reason for this fallibility is obvious—poor logic, limited knowledge, sin, biases of one kind or another, and so forth—all of which can enter into the process of moral judgment in particular cases. Often, in the tradition, when people speak of conscience they mean *conscientia*, that ability we have to make practical decisions regarding what is right or wrong about a particular issue.

The Catholic tradition also speaks of different classifications of conscience. First, there is conscience that is formed in accord with higher norms (*conscientia recta*). Conscience can also be formed by norms that are objectively true (*conscientia vera*). Both types of conscience can reside in a person and be truly a good conscience. There can also be an outlaw conscience, *conscientia exlex,* which recognizes no norms higher than its own subjective imperatives; therefore it possesses neither rectitude nor truth. Finally, there is the case of the sincere but erroneous conscience. This type of conscience is formed in accord with higher norms that approve themselves to it, but these norms are not subjectively true, at least not with the fullness of truth (*conscientia recta sed non vera*).

In the Catholic tradition it has been generally held that a person's conscience may be out of place with what is objectively right, yet he is required to follow it. To do otherwise—that is, to go against one's conscience—is to sin. The manuals used the terms "virtual" or "hypothetical voluntary action" to describe a situation where a conscience goes against its own dictates. A virtual voluntary action is "an action which is willed not for itself but because it is known as a side effect, a circumstance, an inferior of the object actually and expressly willed."[23] Thus, for example, I may be certain here and now that it is wrong to eat meat; if I go ahead and eat meat, my will has made a choice and the object is chosen as precisely known—that is, as probably an illicit act. "This probable illiceity, since it is presented as a modification of the object of choice, vitiates the choice. The choice, it is true is to eat meat; but it must be remembered that the act is chosen as I know it, sc., as probably illicit."[24] To go against one's conscience in this way is to sin. However, to say that the individual has a duty to follow his or her conscience does not necessarily imply that every conscience is correct in its assertions and claims. The individual has a duty to form his or her conscience. Thus conscience is not autonomous. And conscience cannot speak clearly unless it has been properly formed. In the state, for example, the public authority has a duty to defend its citizens against those who would injure them while claiming to follow their conscience, by using force to restrain criminals or deter criminal actions no matter how well intentioned. But having said that, it is the Church's teaching that the conscience is sacred and must not be violated.

Magisterium and Individual Conscience

The second aspect which must be taken into account in discussing the problematic of the individual conscience versus authority in the Church is that the Church is in some very important ways different from either the state or an academic institution. As Avery Dulles points out, neither the state nor the university, for example, is committed to "any substantive sets of beliefs about the ultimate nature of reality." The Church, on the other hand, is a community of witnesses and continues to exist only to the extent that it adheres to a specific vision of the world which is centered around Jesus Christ as Lord and Savior. Unlike any secular reality, the Church has a deposit of faith which it must maintain intact and transmit to new members. The Church is different in its origins from any other human entity. It is established by the action of God in Jesus Christ. As such, it has definite structures, purposes, beliefs, and forms of worship which cannot be changed even by the highest officeholders in the Church. Finally, the Church has a way of discharging its mission which is different from that of any other organization such as the state or the university.[25]

The magisterium of the Church has a duty to teach, or to condemn false teaching which is contrary to the truth of the gospel. In carrying out its duty of condemning false teaching, the magisterium has sometimes in history erred either on the side of excessive permissiveness or excessive rigidity. Consider in this regard the reactions of the magisterium to Trinitarian controversies in the first half of the Middle Ages, the Galileo case, and the new developments in physical and historical sciences. In some of these instances the magisterium acted sometimes too hastily and without sufficient deliberation and has had to correct itself later or even issue apologies for the way it treated some of the persons involved in the incidents.[26] The point here is that "there can be such a thing in the Church as mutable or reformable teaching." The mutability of doctrine stems from the fact that such teaching "seeks to mediate between the abiding truth of the gospel and the sociocultural situations of a given time and place." The condemnation of usury in the Middle Ages, although based upon valid moral principles, was linked to a precapitalist economy. "Once the shift to capitalism had been made, the moral teaching had to be modified." The same goes for doctrinal changes which were linked to new astronomical discoveries (such as the overthrow of the Ptolemaic system), new methods in historical criticism, new biological theories (such as evolutionism), and new developments in politics. Such changes "have led to important shifts in Catholic doctrine, even within recent memory."[27]

As we have seen already, many of those who disagree with the teaching of *Humanae Vitae* insist that its conclusions against contraception are based on what they regard to be an obsolete biology. The new discoveries in the biological sciences signal a need for change. These assertions mean then that for the opponents of *Humanae Vitae* the teaching on contraception is a reformable one and therefore nonbinding. This stance raises another host of questions. Of importance to us here now is the question of what a person could do who considers that the teaching of the magisterium is in error. This issue is the core of the problem in the Church since Vatican II, the question of the role of the magisterium and that of the individual conscience.

Consider this case. Mr. and Mrs. Okafor live in the slums of Ajegunle, in Lagos, Nigeria. They are good Catholics in their midthirties who have had nine children. They know that it is wrong to use artificial birth control. Mrs. Okafor has just had her ninth child through a difficult labor and delivery. She has recently developed a heart problem and other complications due to many frequent deliveries. She has been told by the doctors that she risks death if she gets pregnant again. For the Okafors, natural family planning is out of the question because for some reason the method has failed them twice in the last three years. The question here is what they should do to obey the teachings of the Church and remain alive to look after the very young children they have. Stories like this are at the heart of the struggle between the individual and authority in the Catholic Church today. If the Okafors should come to the conclusion that given their financial and other resources they cannot cope with the birth of another child, are they sinning by using contraceptives? Are they really going against the teaching of the Church? What are the options open to them as good Catholics? If they were to go ahead and engage in contraceptive intercourse, they would be saying by their action that the teaching of the Church on this matter or some aspect of that teaching is in error. This was the position of the drafters of the Washington Declaration, as we already have seen. What should they do?

Dissent

Theologians agree that the answer to this question depends on a host of issues. The first concerns the kind of teaching involved. Infallible teachings command total assent. Refusal to give assent or the outright denial of a recognized dogma implies a renunciation of the Catholic faith and a rupture of communion. The issue gets a bit more complicated in the sphere of noninfallible teaching, which is reformable. "Such a teaching is not proposed as the word of God, nor does the Church ask its members to submit with the assent of faith. Rather, the Church asks for what is called in official documents *obsequium animi religiosum*."[28] The interpretations of this term are many. The kind of response it suggests depends also on a number of factors, such as the context of the teaching, the constancy of that teaching, the person or office from which this teaching appears, the kind of document in which it appears, and so on. As a general rule, most theologians would agree with Avery Dulles that the proper response to noninfallible teaching of the magisterium is certainly "more than a respectful hearing and something less than a full commitment of faith."

Richard McCormick lists essential aspects of the response due a noninfallible teaching. The first is respect for the person and the office of the teacher including an external respect that fosters respect for the magisterium. Second, one has to be open to what the teacher has to say. Third, there must be a readiness to evaluate critically one's own position on the issue in question in light of this teaching, with the intention of finding whether it can be supported on grounds other than those presented. Fourth, one must be very reluctant to conclude that the moral teaching of the magisterium is erroneous, even when one is clearly convinced of the inadequacy of the evidence and analyses which led to it. It would be better in such circumstances to conclude that the teaching was positively doubtful rather than erroneous.[29] One who follows these steps has responded to authoritative teaching in a proper way. Says McCormick, "Such a procedural respect will genuinely lead to assent, but assent is not the immediate proportionate response. And if dissent occurs, one would suspect that it would occur as a general rule, only after the passage of time, since time is needed for the arduous reflections suggested here."[30]

Bruno Schüller believes that the magisterium of the Church has only a subsidiary responsibility in determining what is right and wrong in the life of the individual. Such responsibility comes from the relative superiority of the moral insight of the magisterium. This insight is superior only because it is better protected from error than is the individual believer.

However, this is relative because "it does not have the only insight into the will of God. Each believer possesses that." Therefore, in situations of conflict one may not *always* say that the magisterium is right and thus must be right in this particular case. It can only be said in such situations that "as a rule" the magisterium is right, although it can be wrong "in exceptional cases." It may happen that the believer and not the magisterium is right. How then can we determine in any given case whether we have an exception to the rule? Schüller's response is that since the authentic magisterium is superior in moral insight it has to be regarded as *likely* to be issuing a correct teaching. That means that there has to be a presumption of truth on the side of the magisterium. Thus, the individual believer who takes a position contrary to the teaching of the magisterium has the burden of proof on him or her to show why and how the position he or she has taken is the correct one.[31]

As Avery Dulles points out, there are two possible errors to avoid in regard to the response due to the noninfallible magisterium. One is the temptation to treat the teaching as infallible. Such an excessive emphasis "could overtax the individual's capacity to assent and could lead to a real crisis of faith in the event of a later change in doctrine." The other error to avoid is treating noninfallible magisterial teaching as though it were simply a matter of theological opinion. The error here is that such a stance seems to suggest that the magisterium is a group of theorists, "and not a body of pastors who are sacramentally ordained and commissioned to teach the truth."[32]

Toward the close of *Humanae Vitae* Pope Paul VI told priests that it was their duty to show sincere obedience to the teaching of the magisterium because the "pastors of the Church enjoy a special light of the Holy Spirit in teaching the truth." It was this special gift of the Holy Spirit, he said, *"rather than the arguments they put forward* [which is the reason] *why you are bound to such obedience"* (no. 28). One of the problems *Humanae Vitae* raises in this regard is precisely the extent to which a papal teaching must appear "reasonable" or be "persuasive" to be acceptable. What does it mean to say that a doctrine is reasonable or persuasive? What are the standards of rationality to be employed in these cases? And if these teachings do not meet these criteria, what does a theologian do? The other issue is that of determining when a theologian or an individual has really shown sufficient obedience to the noninfallible authentic teaching authority of the magisterium.

The "Instruction on the Ecclesial Vocation of the Theologian," issued in 1990 by the Congregation for the Doctrine of the Faith, acknowledges that a theologian, or anyone for that matter, could for any number of reasons have difficulties with a particular teaching of the magisterium. Here is what it advises if the doubt persists:

> If, despite a loyal effort on the theologian's part, the difficulties persist, the theologian has a duty to make known to the Magisterial authorities the problems raised by the teaching in itself, in the arguments proposed to justify it, or even in the manner in which it is presented. He should do this in an evangelical spirit and with a profound desire to resolve the difficulties. His objections could then contribute to real progress and provide a stimulus to the Magisterium to propose the teaching of the Church in greater depth and with a clearer presentation of the arguments. In cases like these, the theologian should avoid turning to the "mass media," but have recourse to responsible authority, for it is not by seeking to exert pressure on public opinion that one contributes to the clarification of doctrinal issues and renders service to the truth.[33]

If, despite all attempts to give assent to the particular teaching, the theologian cannot in conscience bring himself to do so because "the arguments to the contrary seem more persuasive," the theologian still has the duty "to remain open to a deeper examination of the question." The document acknowledges that for one who deeply loves the Church such a situation can indeed be a difficult one. Nonetheless it asks the theologian to see the situation as possibly a call "to suffer in silence for the truth" with the assurance that "if the truth really is at stake, it will ultimately prevail."[34] No one would doubt that truth is worth suffering and even dying for. The problem since *Humanae Vitae* has been how to determine that truth. Sometimes it seems that punishment is inflicted on people too quickly and too severely even when the matter of the truth of some teaching is still ongoing. There is enough in our history as a community of faith to warn us against sacrificing people too quickly "for the truth."

good point

∗   ∗   ∗

In this chapter as in the previous one we have discussed the controversy over certain aspects of the life of the Church which arose as a result of the publication of the encyclical on birth control. The Washington Declaration introduced an era of organized dissent in the Church. The speed with which that document was issued created more problems than it set out to solve. First of all, it gave the impression of theology as a trade union, and theologians as the group which alone can speak for theology. However, as Karl Rahner said, "Joint declarations by theologians on a given issue can be a dubious approach, unless there is sufficient justification." Theologians "must not rush out and flood the world with declarations that seek to free them from the authority of the magisterium."[35] Such organized dissent hardens positions and makes dialogue difficult, if not impossible sometimes. The losers in such situations are truth, individuals, and of course the Church itself.

There is no doubt that there can be times when one can in conscience refuse to agree to a particular formulation of a doctrine or when one may believe that the Church's position on a particular issue does not represent the mind of Christ on the matter. John Noonan, Jr., has shown, for example, how much the theologians were instrumental to getting the magisterium of the Church to change its previous positions on usury, slavery, and certain issues pertaining to marriage.[36] The theologian achieves much more in such situations through patient and persistent work. We have the example of John Courtney Murray and many others in this regard. Moreover, organized dissent dissipates precious pastoral energy to no avail. And in this day and age, all of us could use those energies to make the gospel more effective in the world.

Apart from the question of dissent, the lessons from the *Humanae Vitae* debate are many. First, as I will show in the last chapter of this book, the controversy over *Humanae Vitae* paradoxically demonstrates that our agreements over doctrinal and moral matters are many. These agreements are so profoundly shared that they constitute as well the basis for our disagreements. For example, when Yves Congar speaks about the various configurations of the teaching office, he presupposes that all of us in the Catholic tradition believe in and accept the centrality of such an office for being a particular community of faith. When theologians discuss whether contraception belongs to the infallible magisterium, they presuppose already that the magisterium can teach infallibly on certain issues. When there is discussion on the relationship between the individual and Church authority, it is presupposed, among other things, that the magisterium of the Church has a role in determining how individuals should order their lives. The list goes on.

Just as the debate over birth control and other issues since the Council has shown that we have real and basic agreements, it has also shown that our disagreements are real and sometimes intractable. The question of authority in the Church is seriously divisive today. We have discussed only certain aspects which fall within the scope of this book. The place of *women* women in the authority structure of the Church is another issue which has emerged since the Council and on which there does not yet appear to be any answer due to deep disagreements which are genuinely held on all sides of the question. It could also be shown that even this issue illustrates how much we all hold together. For example, the priesthood must be important enough for both men and women in the Church to constitute a point of such great controversy.

My point here is simply that the Catholic tradition is alive and well. The debates we have been discussing attest to this fact. These debates and the entire moral discourse in the Catholic Church since the Council make more sense if they are understood as indicative of a tradition which is trying to update itself and expand its horizon.

good pts re: naming + listing what we hold in common + can presume

part three

Norms, Contexts, and Method

chapter eight

The Debate on Moral Norms

This chapter examines the debate on moral norms which has been going on within the Catholic community as part of the debate on birth control since the Second Vatican Council. Moral norms are important ways communities capture and preserve in a concise manner some of the values they consider important for human flourishing. From experience and from many authoritative sources, communities come to some appreciation of these values. Through statements of prohibition or inspiration they try to teach and preserve these important insights. Because norms are a human articulation of values, they may sometimes be incomplete in their expression of the value or values in question.[1] Richard Gula describes norms as "the criteria for judging the sort of person we ought to be and the sorts of actions we ought to perform in faithful response to God's call to be loving. As such, norms are more or less adequate expressions of moral truth."[2]

Thus, the debate over norms has been concerned with the meaning and limits of moral norms, the objectivity of human action, and the place of the magisterium of the Church, or any other authority for that matter, in determining what are right and wrong actions in this world. Like the debate on birth control, the debate on norms in general has understandably generated much acrimony within the Catholic community because it touches many important issues pertaining to right and wrong and how human beings ought to live their lives in faithful response to God's call to be loving. In order to appreciate properly the intensity and nuances of this debate we must start from the discussion on the attempts to reformulate a key moral principle, the principle of double effect, in recent Catholic theology.

The Principle of Double Effect → proportionalism

Since the second half of the twentieth century, the principle of double effect (PDE) has become the subject of intense debate with regard to its origin,[3] meaning/importance,[4] and scope.[5] Joseph Mangan traces the origin of the principle of double effect to St. Thomas Aquinas. "Before the time of Thomas," he says, there was no indication of a definitely formulated principle of double effect. Beginning with Thomas, "the development of this important principle kept pace, more or less, with the growth of the study of moral theology itself."[6] The *locus classicus* often adduced by scholars as Aquinas's own treatment of the principle of double effect is Aquinas's position on the lawfulness of killing another person in self-defense which is found in the *Summa Theologiae,* II-II, q.64, 7c. In answering the question whether it is lawful to kill another in self-defense, Aquinas answers:

II-II .64 self-defense

> There is nothing to prevent one act from having two effects, of which the agent intends one and the other is outside of the agent's intention. Now, moral acts take their character from what is intended, not from what is beyond intention, since the latter is accidental, as has been stated. Therefore, from the act of a person defending himself a double effect can follow: one is the preservation of his own life, the other is the killing of the attacker. An act of this kind, insofar as it is intended for the preservation of one's own life, is not illicit, since it is natural for every being to preserve its life as far as possible. Nevertheless, an act, which proceeds from a good intention, may be rendered illicit, if it is not proportioned to the end intended. Hence, if one uses greater violence than is necessary in defending his own life, his act will be illicit; for according to law one may repel violence with violence, if he observes the moderation of a blameless self-defense.[7]

The principle of double effect has come to be formulated variously over the years[8] and is meant to guide human action in situations of ambiguity— those situations where good and evil occur as a result of a moral decision and subsequent action. The question in such situations is whether a person may lawfully perform an action which is foreseen to bring both good and evil effects. Traditionally, the answer would be affirmative, provided *condᵢᵗᵢₒₙₛ* "1) that the action is itself from the very object good or at least indifferent; *ₜₒ fᵤₗfᵢₗₗ:* 2) that the good effect and not the evil effect be intended; 3) that the good effect be not produced by means of the evil effect; 4) that there be proportionately grave reason for permitting the evil effects."[9] In much of the current literature, the principle is rendered slightly differently and more or less in the following words: (1) the act *directly* performed is in itself good or at least indifferent; (2) the good accomplished is at least as immediate as the evil; (3) the intention of the agent is good; (4) there is proportionate reason for causing the evil.[10]

An important point in the debate on the principle of double effect was reached in 1965 when Peter Knauer, then a Jesuit doctoral student, concluded that prior to the manualist tradition in Catholic moral theology, the principle of double effect was interpreted not on the basis of the physical relationship between good and evil, but on the proportionality between the evil allowed or caused and the good achieved. He claimed that the question for Thomas, to whom he ascribed the origin of PDE, was not the separability or the immediacy of good and evil effect of an act, but the proportionality between the evil caused and the good achieved. In other words, the meaning of an act is not derived simply from its external effect. Rather, moral evil consists in permitting or causing physical evil without commensurate (proportionate) reason. Knauer thus reduced the various elements of the principle into one and made proportionate reason the sole determining factor of the morality of an act.

In what follows, I will provide an overview of the discussion occasioned by Knauer's thesis and fueled subsequently by the publication of *Humanae Vitae* in 1968. We will look at the proportionalist (or revisionist) views on the debate on the principle of double effect by examining mainly the works of some of the principal protagonists of the position that has come to be known as proportionalism in Catholic moral theology since the Second Vatican Council. In the first part of this chapter, I will provide a general picture of the proportionalist position. In the second part, I will attempt a reconstruction of the debate between McCormick and Schüller over certain aspects of the principle of double effect. I will also describe the positions of Germain Grisez, Joseph Boyle, and John Finnis, who have developed an approach on norms which is counter to the views held by the revisionist theologians.

Understanding the Principle of Double Effect

basic
points
PDE

The principle of double effect in its various forms (*a*) assumes that some actions are evil, *ex objecto* or intrinsically—that is, in spite of all other considerations—and (*b*) is silent on what is to count as proportionately grave reason.[11] An important distinction between the two versions of the principle given above is the insertion of the notion of *directness* into the second and more common version. Joseph Selling argues that what has come to be known as the direct/indirect distinction does not have to be

"direct/ indirect"

part of the principle of double effect, although it constantly creeps in and influences the way we speak of norms. For example, within the Catholic moral tradition, we often speak of direct and indirect sterilization, direct and indirect abortion, direct and indirect bombing of civilian populations in warfare, and so on. One problem then concerning the principle of double effect is to determine precisely what this distinction means and whether we can speak of direct and indirect actions in an unambiguous way. Does directness refer to much more than "that, which is done," the external act or concrete omission, for example? Would "indirect" therefore refer only to "the effects or consequences of what is done or the result of setting into motion a series of events," as Joseph Selling suggests? Selling

J. Selling def.

claims that "direct signifies the preference of an external act; indirect signifies anything which flows from that act (or the results of setting a series of events into motion)."[12] The problem with this understanding of the terms "direct" and "indirect" is that it seems to allow for a rather easy justification of actions for which one should be held accountable merely on the

→

grounds that it was only a side and therefore indirect effect of a morally justifiable act. The manuals justified the termination of pregnancies which threatened the life of the woman with little or no regard for the life of the fetus, whose death was often seen as merely the side effect of a good action. They seemed to forget that the same action that saved the woman also killed the child. The problem here, as Knauer and McCormick pointed out,[13] was that direct and indirect were tied too closely with physical causation.

In an initial response to Knauer, Richard A. McCormick argued that Knauer had given no meaning to "psychological intent" or indicated the "limits of intention in determining the meaning of concrete human actions."[14] Furthermore, because Knauer made proportionate reason constitutive of the object of an act in a manner that neither respected causality nor the moral significance of the external act, he had also made it "theo-

McC

can too quickly devolve into ends-justify-means

retically possible to assume into an act as indirect and licit any means, providing it is necessary to a value or an end envisaged."[15] Later on, in a lecture at Marquette University, McCormick came to accept "the substance" of Knauer's thesis that moral evil consists in permitting or causing physical evil without proportionate reason. Moreover, the meaning of an act is not determined solely from its external effect. Rather, using direct sterilization and contraceptive interventions as examples, he tried to show that what is morally wrong "can only be determined after we have examined the reason for the procedure." McCormick still had difficulty accepting Knauer's use of the terms "direct" and "indirect." He maintained that these notions were so closely tied to commensurate reason in Knauer's work that they have ceased to function at all or have any psychological intent. As we will see later, McCormick himself makes this same mistake when he tries to extend the applicability of proportionate reasoning to the issue of the bombing of civilian populations in war. In this case I will contend that he has so subsumed the notion of direct/indirect to that of proportionate reason that it has ceased to function at all.

Another scholar taking issue with Peter Knauer's project was Germain Grisez. The first of his many reactions to proportionalism can be found in his book on abortion, which was published in 1970.[16] In this book, Grisez reports Knauer as saying that the good effect in an action where the agent is faced with the possibility of bringing about an evil in the process of doing good, may depend objectively upon the evil effect. Such evil may be psychologically intended as a means provided the act has a commensurate reason. When this is the case, the evil, from a moral viewpoint, is only intended indirectly and cannot be intrinsically evil, no matter what means are employed. Grisez wonders what Knauer meant by "commensurate reason." He argues that Knauer employs this expression neither as implying "any serious reason whatever," nor to mean "proportionate reason" as traditionally understood in connection with the principle of double effect. Instead, by "commensurate reason" Grisez understood Knauer to mean "a value that is achieved by the act as effectively as possible." An act is therefore evil "if it is motivated by desire that unintelligently settles for a short-run, partial, or more limited realization of a value that could more effectively be attained by more rationally ordered action."[17] He argues that Knauer could not be accused of utilitarianism since "he correctly appreciates the impossibility of weighing and comparing incomparable values." Grisez finds Knauer's attempt to broaden the principle of double effect without falling into utilitarianism "interesting." Knauer was right, he says, to point out that "effects" in Aquinas's teaching on self-defense are actually not consequent upon that act but are rather distinct aspects of the act and to insist on the inseparability of the meaningful behavior which divides the human act into a purely mental meaning and a purely physical behavior. He also believes that a realistic theory of value was implicit in Knauer's position.

Grisez faults Knauer's article on several grounds, however. First of all, he believes that Knauer ignores the obligation that we not turn against the good in making our moral choices. His omission here makes it possible for him to redefine direct intentionality in a radically new way which bears no resemblance to the meaning of this term in the tradition and to dissociate moral intent completely from psychological intent. "The inadequacy of Knauer's position appears most clearly if we consider that it cannot exclude a fanatical dedication to any particular genuine value. A mad scientist would find support in Knauer's theory, so long as he was an intelligent and efficient investigator, for he could defend any sort of human experimentation, no matter how horrible its effects on the subjects, provided the experimental plan promoted the attainment of truth—on the whole and in the long run—in the most effective way." Grisez maintains that if Knauer were to reject the application of his theory in this way, on the grounds, say, that this would change the course of scientific inquiry by giving it a bad name, then he would be inconsistent. Second, Grisez notes that whereas Knauer would seem to approve some abortions in some cases which are not permitted by the usual application of the principle of double effect, and would allow contraception in those circumstances in which its use "deepens" and "preserves" marital love, he hesitates to accept that a woman faced with the choice of committing adultery in order to rescue her children from a concentration camp should do so. Third, by justifying capital punishment on the grounds that the death of the criminal in such a case is indirectly intended because there is no better way to protect the common good, Knauer clearly goes beyond Aquinas's understanding of unintended effect "according to which the psychological meaning of intention was not made into a separate entity over and against an arbitrary definition of 'intention' for moral purposes." Grisez believed that Knauer was "carrying through a revolution in principle while pretending only a clarification of traditional ideas."[18]

In response to Grisez's assertions, McCormick insists that Knauer's was a justified revolution, if revolution it is. He disagreed with Grisez that a mad scientist could put Knauer's ideas to some negative uses. "[Knauer] could answer (as Grisez acknowledges) that the fanatical investigator would really damage the cause of truth 'in general and in the long run' in the very means used. And if that were the case, Knauer would say that the action is morally evil, and indeed 'in itself.'" McCormick argued that the basic difference between Grisez's view and the position of Knauer was epistemological. The question is how we can know that certain actions are counterproductive—that is, wrong. Is this a type of knowledge we come to from experience through trial and error or is it something we intuit? Sometimes we know from experience that certain actions are wrong. Sometimes we come to such knowledge by intuition. There are also certain actions we know very little about and so must proceed to a normative position by trial and error and with a great deal of trepidation. "This would be true of our moral statements about DNA recombinant research, and on many technological matters where dangers and/or abuses are possible but where no experiential history is available to instruct us."[19] In short, it does not follow, says McCormick, that Knauer "would defend any sort of human experimentation, no matter how horrible its effects on the subjects, provided the experimental plan promoted the attainment of truth—on the whole and on the long run," as Grisez asserts.[20]

We must keep in mind some of the broader issues involved in these exchanges which would continue to be central to the discussion on norms in the Catholic tradition after the Second Vatican Council. These are: the question of moral absolutes—whether there are some human actions which can be considered wrong at all places and times and in spite of any other considerations; the role of human intention in determining moral rightness and wrongness of human action; the importance of inherited or perceived human values and how to preserve these in situations of moral conflict; and how and whether we can enter into weighing human values in moral conflict without slipping into utilitarian calculation.

Moreover, the debate over the principle of double effect must be seen, in its initial phase, as an attempt to find a way out of the impasse to which the Church had come on the question of contraception in the 1960s. Between the publication of Peter Knauer's article in 1965 and the end of the last century, several other factors also contributed to keep this debate alive. Some of these include homologous artificial insemination, organ transplantation and other medical quandaries which had developed through continued advances in medicine and technology, masturbation, and premarital sexual relationships. As James J. Walter points out, the "revolution" which Knauer started, and many others joined, "was a revision not only of the doctrine of double effect and all its implications about intrinsic evil but also of the very foundation and formulation of prescriptive behavioral norms" regarding these and many such issues.[21]

Anyone familiar with the debate under review here will understand how untidy the discussions on it can be. Walter has persistently advocated a three-step approach to the discussion on the principle of double effect to help anyone interested in the debate understand what the fundamental issues are and how to approach them: (1) the definition of terms, (2) establishing the criteria that indicate the presence or absence of proportionate reason, and (3) looking at the epistemic ways in which it can be known whether the criteria have or have not been met. The values in this three-step approach are many. Although I do not intend to adhere strictly to Walter's approach in what follows, I will keep it in mind as a compass for navigating through the confusing landscape of the debate on the principle of double effect.

Proportionalist Revisionism

The debate on norms has been carried on between those who support the revision of norms entailed in Knauer's rethinking of the meaning of the principle of double effect and those who oppose such a revision. For purposes of clarity, the former shall be referred to throughout this work either as proportionalists or as revisionists. These terms will be used interchangeably to mean the same thing.

It is important to begin this section with a discussion of the proportionalist position on moral norms. The proportionalist position argues that certain disvalues in our conduct (sometimes also referred to as ontic, nonmoral, or premoral evils) do not ipso facto make the action morally wrong. Louis Janssens speaks of ontic evil in these words: "We call ontic evil any lack of a perfection at which we aim, any lack of fulfillment which frustrates our natural urges and makes us suffer. It is essentially the natural consequence of our limitation." In themselves, our limitations are not evil. But "because we are thinking, willing, feeling and acting beings, we can be painfully hampered by the limits of our possibilities in a plurality of realities that are both aids and handicaps (ambiguity)."[22] Proportionalists have maintained that there is always ontic evil present in all our actions. As McCormick puts it, the good we achieve "is rarely untainted by hurt, deprivation (and) imperfection." Thus, "we must kill to preserve life and freedom; we protect one through the pain of another; our education must at times be primitive; our health is preserved at times by pain and disfiguring mutilation; we protect our secrets by misstatements and our marriages and population by contraception and sterilization."[23] Nonmoral/premoral or ontic evil is not really neutral and of no importance. Rather, it is something to be avoided in general, if one can do so. Proportionalists note that although nonmoral or ontic evil may be caused for a good reason, it should never be the end of the inner act of the will, "if by this is meant that which definitively and in the full sense of the word puts an end to the activity of the subject." To put the matter another way, it can be right, Janssens says, to intend an ontic evil as an end of one's inner act of the will, "if that end is not willed as a final end, but only as a *finis medius et proximus* to a higher end."[24] Thus, an action would be morally wrong when, all things considered, there is no proportionate reason for causing or permitting the premoral evil.

[handwritten margin note: proportionate reason]

The ultimate question for revisionist theologians then is to specify what accounts for proportionate reason. When proportionalists speak of proportionate reason they refer to "a proper relation (*debita proportio*) that must exist between the premoral disvalue(s) contained in or caused by the means and the end (*ratio*) or between the end and the premoral disvalue(s) contained in the further ends (consequences) of the act taken as a whole."[25] Louis Janssens, a leading proportionalist, states that an act must be in proportion to the end to which it is directed. An act is so proportionate "when there is no contradiction of means and the end within the totality of the act."[26] Thus, for example, violence which goes beyond what is necessary to safeguard one's life is morally wrong because it exceeds the bound of due proportion. The excess is not a means anymore. It has become part of the intention and is therefore morally reprehensible.[27] What then are the criteria that guide and establish proportionate reason? How does one determine when there is due proportion between an end and the means to it?

Richard McCormick, perhaps more than anyone else, has contributed a great deal to providing clear criteria for determining when proportionate reason has or has not been reached. For McCormick, proportionate reason implies that a value at least equal to that sacrificed is at stake; that "there is no less harmful way of protecting the value here and now"; and that "the manner of its protection will not undermine it in the long run." Or, put negatively, an action is disproportionate "if a lesser value is preferred to a more important one; if evil is unnecessarily caused in the protection of a greater good; if, in the circumstances the manner of protecting the good will undermine it in the long run."[28] It is often difficult in a situation of moral conflict to come to a proportionate judgment. What is proportionate, however, has to do with what in the circumstances best serves the values in the tragic situation of conflict. Therefore, an adequate account of circumstances must consider how much qualitative good can be salvaged in situations of conflict. It must weigh the social implications and the aftereffects of the action, it must apply the rule of generalizability and consider the cultural climate of the place—the biases, the reactions it is likely to generate and the biases it is likely to run up against. An adequate consideration of circumstances must pay attention to the context and draw as much as possible from the wisdom and experience of the past, particularly as embodied in the rules peoples of the past have found a useful guide in difficult times. It will draw from other mature, experienced, detached, and distant reflections whose ideas will serve as counterbalance to the often short-sighted and self-interested tendencies we experience when we are proximate to and closely involved in a case. Also, "it will take full force of one's own religious faith and its intentionalities to interpret the meaning and enlighten the options of the situation."[29] Thus it is never left to the individual whim alone to discover what constitutes proportionate reason. Rather "the individual will depend on community discernment" to a large extent.[30] Proportionate reason is not reducible to a simple utilitarian calculus. Instead, its criterion is governed by the *ordo bonorum* "viewed in Christian perspective."[31]

Like other leading proportionalists, Janssens insists that the requirements of proportionate reason must be established not just in consideration of personal goals and interests, but especially in the interest of society, culture, and humanity at large. The search for what is to count for proportionate reason is to be conducted based on the order of charity and on the hierarchy of values. These can help to clarify ambiguous moral situations. The order of charity awakens the agent to an equal regard for every human person as a free, conscious, and responsible subject made in the image and likeness of God, redeemed by Christ, called to be God's child and to participate in the eschatological kingdom. This love shows no partiality or preference relative "to idiosyncratic qualities and attainments."[32] The *ordo bonorum* or hierarchy of values forces us to recognize that the moral goodness of every person is an absolute value. Thus in our relationship with others we should never impel them to go against their consciences. Instead, every person should be treated as a moral agent who is "a conscious, free, and therefore responsible subject. His intrinsic value as moral subject must be respected in an absolute way."[33]

A number of points should be made quickly here. First, the need to measure or indicate proportionality has led to charges of utilitarianism and consequentialism against proportionalists. Second, it has led many of the opponents of this approach to morality to conclude that proportionalism is nothing but a way to avoid acknowledging the existence of moral absolutes. These criticisms are evident in *Veritatis Splendor,* Pope John Paul II's encyclical on moral theology.

Veritatis Splendor and Proportionalism

To understand what *Veritatis Splendor* has to say about proportionalism one must begin with the position of the encyclical on human acts. For *Veritatis Splendor,* there is an intrinsic relationship between the agent and his or her acts. "Human acts are moral acts because they express and determine the goodness or evil of the individual who performs them." The moral character of the human act is defined "by the relationship of man's freedom with the authentic good" (*VS,* 72). Thus a person is said to act in a morally good way when the choices made in freedom are in conformity with true human good and indicative of the person's true ordering toward her ultimate end which is God himself. Thus, morality is constituted by the "rational ordering of the human act to the good in its truth and the voluntary pursuit of that good known by reason." The morality of a human act cannot be determined either on the basis of the good intention of the agent or simply because the act is a means for attaining another goal. The moral life is therefore teleological but not in the sense that this term is used among revisionists. Its teleological character stems from the fact that it consists in "the deliberate ordering of human acts to God, the supreme good and ultimate end (*telos*) of man" (*VS,* 73). Some teleological ethical theories, says *Veritatis Splendor,* "claim to be concerned for the conformity of human acts with the ends pursued by the agent and with the values intended by him." The criteria for evaluating the moral rightness of an action "are drawn from the *weighing of the non-moral or pre-moral goods* to be gained and the corresponding non-moral or pre-moral values to be respected." For some, concrete behavior would be right or wrong depending on whether it is capable of conducting a better state of affairs for all concerned. Right conduct would be the one capable of "maximizing" goods and "minimizing" evils (*VS,* 74). Such theories are wrong and contrary to the teaching of the Church because they believe they can justify, as morally good, "deliberate choices of kinds of behavior contrary to the commandments of the divine and natural law." *Veritatis Splendor* asserts instead:

morality based directly on OBJECT, not on weighing of goods

> The morality of the human act depends primarily and fundamentally on the "object" rationally chosen by the deliberate will, as is borne out by the insightful analysis, still valid today, made by Saint Thomas . . . By the object of a given moral act, then, one cannot mean a process or an event of the merely physical order, to be assessed on the basis of its ability to bring about a given state of affairs in the outside world. Rather, that object is the proximate end of a deliberate decision, which determines the act of willing on the part of the acting person. Consequently, as the *Catechism of the Catholic Church* teaches, "there are certain specific kinds of behavior that are always wrong to choose, because choosing them involves a disorder of the will, that is, a moral evil." (n. 78)

object of act

There are a few important points to note here. One involves the nature of morality itself. Another has to do with the notion of moral object. A third has to do with the issue of intrinsic evil. A fourth has to do with the papal characterization of the work of the so-called revisionist moral theologians.

1. 2. 3. 4.

Veritatis Splendor maintains that the object of an act qualifies the will. In other words, what one chooses determines one's moral character. What the encyclical means, as Jean Porter puts it, is that "the objects of some actions, that is, those which are wrong by virtue of their object, are characterized by their intrinsic inconsistency with the good of the human person." The question of course is to specify which actions indeed are inconsistent with this good, "especially since the Catholic moral tradition has traditionally acknowledged that there are some kinds of actions which involve inflicting harm, and are yet morally justified."[34] Proportionalists have very little difficulty with the encyclical when it states that the morality of an act depends primarily upon the object rationally chosen. Disagreements begin when they consider what goes into the object. Is the choice to kill a person or to speak falsehood a sufficient description of the object of a moral act or must the reason for this choice be included in the notion of object? They answer that the *ratio* for an act is what makes the action a certain type of action. McCormick points out in this regard that "most people would not view the removal of a kidney from a living donor as an act separate from its transfer to the ill patient. They would view the whole process as an *act of organ transplantation*. Contrarily, they would judge aborting fe-

impt ⟹ OBJ is connected to WILL

harms sometimes justifiable

⟶ here, removal intrinsically tied to donation

tuses for population control, killing for world peace, etc., as fully constituted acts (therefore with their own intentional objects) aimed by ulterior
intent to a further end."[35] *⟶ here, killing is means to another,
entirely separate end*

Moral Objectivity

negative precepts of decalogue are

As we will see later, a central element in *Veritatis Splendor* is the teaching *always*
on the universal validity of the so-called negative precepts of natural law. *binding*
These precepts, says the encyclical, oblige each and every individual, always and in every circumstance. "It is a matter of prohibitions which forbid a given action *semper et pro semper,* without exception, because the
choice of this kind of behavior is in no case compatible with the goodness
of the will of the acting person, with his vocation to life with God and to
communion with his neighbor." The example the encyclical gives comes
from Jesus' reaffirmation of the Decalogue in Matthew 19: "If you wish to
enter into life, keep the commandments . . . You shall not murder, You
shall not commit adultery, You shall not bear false witness."[36] Alasdair
MacIntyre states that this and other similar passages in the encyclical tell
us that we cannot adequately characterize "that good towards the achieve- *judge the
good by
ment of which we are directed by our natures and by providence, except designating
what is
in terms which already presuppose the binding character of the excep- evil*
tionless negative precepts of the natural law." The same goes for that
which in our natures alone "makes us apt for and directed towards the
achievement of that good except in the same terms."[37]

Veritatis Splendor charges that proportionalists do not accept the notion of intrinsic evil and that they reduce morality to the weighing of the
goods with a view to discovering "the greater good" or "lesser evil" in a
given situation. *charges prop. w/ merely weighing greater +
lesser evils + goods — not putting boundaries
on evil*

The teleological theories (proportionalism, consequentialism), while
acknowledging that moral values are indicated by reason and by Revelation, maintain that it is never possible to formulate an absolute prohibition of particular kinds of behavior which would be in conflict in
every circumstance and in every culture, with those values. The acting
subject would indeed be responsible for attaining the values pursued,
but in two ways: the values or goods in a human act would be, from
one viewpoint, *of the pre-moral order,* which some term non-moral,
physical or ontic (in relation to the advantages and disadvantages accruing both to the agent and to all other persons possibly involved,

such as, for example, health or its endangerment, physical integrity, life, death, loss of material goods, etc.). (*VS, 75*)

Proportionalists have always protested the charge that "they maintain that it is *never possible* [italics added] to formulate an absolute prohibition of particular kinds of behavior." They have traditionally countered such charges by arguing that

prop. counter : evil/good depends on how you describe the act

individual actions independent of their morally significant circumstances (e.g., killing, contraception, speaking falsehood, sterilization, masturbation) cannot be said to be intrinsically evil as this term is used by tradition and the recent magisterium. Why? Because such concepts describe an action too narrowly in terms of its *materia circa quam* without morally relevant circumstances. The issue is confused by using value terms to describe the actions and then attributing this to "proportionalists" as if they are trying to justify adultery, stealing, lying, etc.[38]

Lisa Cahill accuses the encyclical of obfuscating the concept of intrinsic evil by giving examples on disparate levels "which are for the most part not under dispute by the so-called 'proportionalists.'" According to her, "Murder, adultery, stealing, genocide, torture, prostitution, slavery, 'subhuman living conditions,' 'arbitrary imprisonment' and 'degrading conditions of work,' have few if any defenders among Catholic theologians." She argues that these terms, as used in the encyclical, define acts in the abstract. Rather, the morality of acts like intercourse or homicide must be determined together with the conditions or circumstances which surround them. "Such acts are indeed wrong, because immoral circumstances have already been specified in the examples given. A single term like 'murder' or 'genocide' makes it clear that what might have been a justifiable 'act in itself' (homicide) was done in wrong circumstances; or a phrase like 'killing an innocent person,' which spells out exactly what circumstances of the homicide meant, results in an absolute norm. About this there is little disagreement."[39] Josef Fuchs, another leading proportionalist, puts the matter this way: "1) An action cannot be judged morally in its materiality (killing, wounding, going to the moon), without reference to the intention of the agent; without this, we are not dealing with a human action, and only with respect to a human action may one say in a true sense whether it is morally good or bad. 2) The evil (in a premoral

e.g. "murder"
"murder" def
by involves
great evil

sense) effected by a human agent must not be intended as such, and must be justified in terms of the totality of the action by appropriate reason."[40]

In one of his many reactions as author of the "Moral Notes" for *Theological Studies* to the charge that proportionalists have little regard for the existence of intrinsic evil, Richard McCormick has argued for a more nuanced discussion on the matter. He claims that although the notion of intrinsic evil has a variety of understandings, many contemporary discussions seem concerned with the term *"as it has been used in recent theological and magisterial literature."*[41] In this literature, he says, certain kinds of actions such as "directly killing an innocent person and direct sterilization have been proscribed as wrong, the circumstances notwithstanding." What the theologians who see the notion this way are doing is discoursing with their own tradition and arguing that it is not possible to isolate the object of an act, declaring that it is wrong in all imaginable circumstances. "One can, of course, begin to add a variety of circumstances to the description of an object so that such an action is always wrong. For instance: abortion of a fetus in order to avoid a medical (delivery) bill. That is always wrong— and, if one wishes, intrinsically wrong (scil., *praeceptum quia malum,* not *malum quia praeceptum*)."[42] According to McCormick there are many other actions which fit this label but not as it is *"used in recent theological and magisterial literature."* The position of the revisionist theologians, he says, is that actions which are always morally wrong are so neither as a result of the unnaturalness of the actions in question nor owing to a defect of right. Rather they are wrong because "when *taken as a whole,* the nonmoral evil outweighs the moral good, and therefore the action is disproportionate." McCormick believes that although one could refer to such an action as intrinsically evil, it would be too confusing to do so, given the way he believes the term has been used in recent tradition wherein actions are so described without circumstances "as morally wrong *because unnatural* (contraception) or *because of lack of right* (direct killing of an innocent person)." In this usage, "the term is tied to a kind of deontological understanding of moral norms that (a) has been persuasively argued to be invalid, and (b) has been shown to be inconsistent with the teleological grounding of norms in every other area of Catholic tradition."[43]

It could be argued that the response of Lisa Cahill and Richard McCormick and other proportionalists generally on these issues seems designed to confuse the issue. It seems clear that proportionalists, whatever the precedents in the tradition, are really in disagreement with the pope and the entire Catholic moral tradition here because the norms they say are nonabsolute are held by the tradition to be absolute. For example, when McCormick and others say that there are no moral absolutes prior to an all-things-considered judgment about the action, they deny the dictum the manualists took from Aquinas: *Bonum ex integra causa; malum ex quocumque defectu.* This rule, the opponents say, obviously allows decisive moral evaluation prior to an all-round evaluation. Similarly, the nature of the all-round moral evaluation can be construed in any number of ways. Indeed, some theologians who fault some aspects of the proportionalist position would emphasize the role of prudence or some other virtue, and therefore would not necessarily interpret all-round moral evaluation as the proportionalists do. The idea that proportion in this context has to mean something like the greater good or lesser evil is not self-evident, even though it appears to be the preferred proportionalist interpretation.

The problem P.O. sees is that prop. rests on a "weighing" process

Moral Norms

The difference between the pope's and other opponents' perception of what proportionalists are doing and what proportionalists themselves say they are doing lies in the understanding of the meaning of moral norms. Revisionist theologians maintain that the discussion on norms needs more nuancing than is often the case. There are two types of norms: one refers to the sort of persons we ought to be; the other, to the sort of actions we ought to perform. One indicates "what should always be present in every moral act."[44] One prescribes right conduct, the other plays an interpretive function, helping the moral agent to understand what is right or wrong in a particular situation and what course of action to take in such situations.[45] The first are called *formal norms,* the latter *material norms.* Formal norms constitute "fixed points to divine revelation and what is universal to human kind." They are permanent and enduring,[46] and they transcend all cultures since they owe their origin "to the knowledge of divine law and human nature."[47]

Formal norms are grouped into two categories: those which enjoin certain actions (be chaste, be kind, respect life, and so on) and those which forbid certain actions (do not commit murder, do not steal, do not commit adultery, and so forth). This second group of norms is expressed in synthetic terms—that is, in terms which refer to the material content of any action as well as formulate a moral judgment.[48] Synthetic terms are compact value terms whose purpose is not to convey information about the exact content of what is prohibited. These norms presuppose that we

formal norms presume we know the meaning of those things prohibited

Keenan
person (striving) vs action (objectively) (obj/wrong) right/wrong vs formal vs material

(paranetic) Formal

encouraging prohibit

know this already. Their purpose is "to remind one of what he is presumed to know and to exhort him to do (or avoid) it." Thus, formal norms, according to Richard McCormick, fall into the category of para- *evaluative* netic discourse.[49] This does not mean that formal norms are useless. Rather, it means that their purpose is different in that they are meant to challenge the agent into allowing the moral insights of the norms to touch him personally and lead him "to act as he knows he ought to act."[50] Since *formal* formal norms are context-invariant and constitute a judgment about the *norms* moral rightness or wrongness of an act, their infringement obviously con- *DO NOT* stitutes a sinful act. Thus actions so qualified as "murder," "theft," and *change* "adultery," for example, can never be justified. "Such formal norms are ab- *w/* solute and have no exceptions. However, they do not determine the con- *context* crete content of our actions, i.e., they do not specify the concrete actions one must do in order to be just, chaste, etc., nor do they specify the concrete actions one must avoid in order not to be unjust, unchaste, etc."[51]

If formal norms seek to motivate, invite, and judge, material norms *Material* behave differently. They relate to the sort of actions we ought to perform and try to give us a clue to moral dilemmas in situations of conflict. Unlike formal norms, material norms try to grapple with the concreteness of *concrete* the situations by calling the attention of the moral agent to the values that must be taken into consideration in making a moral decision. "Concrete material norms have both a descriptive and a normative function." And, unlike formal norms which employ evaluative language (for example, to *"descrip-* murder), concrete material norms employ descriptive language (e.g., to *tive"* kill). However, these norms also embody a normative judgment according to the way the actions thus described involve or cause premoral judgment. According to Janssens, an action admitting or causing a premoral disvalue is morally right when it serves a higher premoral value or safeguards the priority given to a lesser premoral disvalue. "In other words, we can have a proportionate reason to depart from the norm. Consequently concrete material norms are relative in the sense of being conditioned. They are not binding, if there is a proportionate reason why the case at issue is not governed by them."[52] This is also what McCormick implies when, in response to *Veritatis Splendor,* he states that proportionalists consider it necessary to look at all morally relevant dimensions (circumstances) of an action "before we know what the action is and whether it should be said to be contrary to the demands of the divine and natural law."[53] He insists that the weighing of all the morally relevant detail in an act before arriving at a moral evaluation of the act cannot be bypassed. This view is a staple of the revisionist position on the formulation of moral norms. Consider his elaboration on this point in an interview he granted me in his home at the University of Notre Dame in 1992:

> I deal with priests all the time in continuing education situations. I say, "Let me test you on this." I'd say, "A just killed B. Is that morally right or morally wrong?" They would all say, "We don't know." I'd say, "Why don't you know?" "Well, we don't know the circumstances." I'd say, "All right, another example. A just deceived B in speech. Is that morally right or morally wrong?" "We don't know whether that is a lie in that value sense or not, because we don't know why he did it or what the circumstances might have been. It could have been protection of confessional secrets or whatever." Another example: "A just took the property of B. Morally right or wrong?" "We don't know yet, our tradition allows for certain cases of exceptions in dire circumstances." I'd say," All right, watch the next step. A and B just had contracepted intercourse. Morally right or morally wrong?" And they would all say, "We don't know yet." I'd say, "Oh yes, you do! The Church has taught you clearly that, no matter the circumstances, that act, as defined, is intrinsically evil. If you are saying all along, in all these other areas, that there are morally relevant circumstances that tell you whether the action is morally right or wrong, then why are we saying this about a physiologically defined action? There is no answer to that that is satisfactory, that I have seen."

Proportionalism and the Catholic Moral Tradition

Proportionalists claim that theirs is not a new theory or "revolution" as is often suggested. They maintain that all they are trying to do is apply a general mode of moral reasoning that had been used in all other areas for centuries, to certain areas, which have been excluded up to now.[54] As Jean Porter points out, they further argue that their position on the need for consideration of circumstances in the determination of norms is similar to that of Thomas Aquinas.[55] In this section we will undertake an examination of the notion of the primary precepts in the natural law theory of St. Thomas with a view to ascertaining the basis of the proportionalists' claim, and to see whether it is a misreading of Aquinas or a legitimate but necessary extension or development of the thought of St. Thomas. It will indeed become clear, if my reading of Thomas is correct, that proportionalists can rightly claim that their position on norms is Thomistic in some way. Whether that makes their thesis right or wrong is another matter altogether.

As we have already seen in the discussion on the Thomistic teaching on natural law, Aquinas teaches that the natural law consists of precepts of practical reason which are analogous to the precepts of speculative reason: "Good is to be done and evil is to be avoided is the first principle of practical reason." Thomas states that there are several objects to which the human agent is inclined. These are self-preservation, self-perpetuation through birth and education of offspring, and the orientation to act in accord with reason (Ia-IIae, q.94, a.2). The question arises about the nature of the first principle of practical reason. Is it also a primary precept of natural law? The only one? In *De Veritate,* Thomas states that the general principles of practical reason are the primary precepts of natural law (q.16, a.1, 2, 3). If this is the case, the question arises whether the principle that good is to be pursued and evil to be avoided is a law. I have also shown in the chapter on natural law (chapter 6) how some writers place considerable importance on Thomas's teaching on the natural inclinations as a way to arrive at a list of the primary precepts. Ross Armstrong argues, for example, that to each of these inclinations there is a corresponding principle of a very general kind, which can be grasped by normal people. He lists these principles as follows: "'One ought to respect and preserve not only human life but all life,' 'The sexual relationship requires some form of regulation,' 'The family group ought to comply with some fixed pattern,' and 'We ought to live together in obedience to certain rules and regulations.'"[56] Whatever the number and composition of the primary precepts of natural law, Aquinas does not seem to consider them as constituting the entire natural law. In the *Supplement to the Summa* he states the existence of the secondary precepts of natural law, infringement of which equally constitutes an infringement of natural law.

> If an action be improportionate to the end, through altogether hindering the principal end directly, it is forbidden by the first precepts of natural law, which hold the same place in practical matters, as the general concepts of the mind in speculative matters. If, however, it be in any way improportionate to the secondary end, or again to the principal end, as rendering its attainment difficult or less satisfactory, it is forbidden, not indeed by the first precepts of the natural law, but by the second which are derived from the first even as conclusions in

speculative matters receive our assent by virtue of self-evident principles; and thus the act in question is said to be against the law of
nature.[57]

The distinction which Aquinas makes in this passage between principal and secondary ends of actions is noteworthy. Primary precepts are
infringed by actions, which hinder the principal end directly. Let us illustrate. Aquinas restates in this passage the traditional teaching on the ends
of marriage. Marriage, according to this teaching, has several ends the
principal of which is the begetting and education of children. The secondary ends of marriage in this view are the allaying of concupiscence, and
the formation of a community of conjugal life and love through the sacrament. Following from this, anything that hinders the begetting and rearing
of children is considered a direct attack on the principal end of marriage
and therefore an infringement of the primary precepts and thus an offense
against natural law. It is on this ground then that the Church considers the
use of contraceptives immoral. It is said to constitute a direct attack on a
principal end of marriage, which is the begetting and rearing of offspring.
Actions which, on the other hand, make the attainment of the principal or
secondary ends difficult attack the secondary precepts. They constitute an
infringement against the secondary precepts and thus against natural law.
Aquinas uses polygamy to illustrate his point:

> Accordingly plurality of wives neither wholly destroys nor in any way
> hinders the first end of marriage, since one man is sufficient to get
> children for several wives, and to rear the children born of them. But
> though it does not wholly destroy the second end, it hinders it con-
> siderably: for there cannot easily be peace in a family where several
> wives are joined to one husband, since the husband cannot suffice to
> satisfy the requisitions of several wives, and again the sharing of sev-
> eral in one occupation is the cause of strife: thus the potters quarrel
> with one another, and in like manner several wives of one husband.
> The third end it removes altogether, because as Christ is one, so also
> is the Church one.

This consequentialist argument is of course utterly inadequate against
polygamy. Many polygamous families have managed to work out a *modus
vivendi* which ensures peace and harmony among all parties to the marriage,
and in some cases puts monogamous marriages to shame. The point, how-

ever, is that St. Thomas believes that actions which hinder or make it difficult to attain either the primary or secondary ends are against natural law.

Human reason, says Aquinas, proceeds from the general to the particular, and the secondary precepts are like "particular conclusions drawn
from the primary precepts."[58] The latter are prior to the former as our
knowledge of the general is prior to our knowledge of the particular.
Thus, for example, it is first in our practical reason as self-evident principle that murder is contrary to natural law before we can even determine
in particular circumstances what actions in fact constitute murder. In
other words, while primary precepts are more abstract formulations, secondary precepts "are more deeply involved in the varying circumstances
and details which surround every moral action."[59] Secondary precepts follow or are proximately derived from the primary precepts. Aquinas distinguishes further between those secondary precepts the truth of which can
be established after *multa consideratio diversorum circumstantiarum*,[60] and
those secondary precepts which need only *modica consideratio*. In short,
the concrete applications of the natural law can only be made "by the exercise of human intelligence, reflecting on human experience,"[61] or, in the
words of Aquinas himself, "by reasoned effort,"[62] bearing in mind that the
more we descend to detail "the more it appears how the general rule ad-
mits of exceptions."[63]

Proportionalist revisionists also claim to find support for their position on the role of ends in moral determination in the work of St. Thomas.
In a celebrated article published in 1982, Louis Janssens maintained that
for Aquinas, moral actions are essentially voluntary and hence specified by
the end.[64] The will is the principle of moral action and the end is the
proper object of the will. Although he holds, as does the inherited tradition, that evil is a privation of the good, Aquinas adds that mere privation
is not the source of the essential difference between good and evil action.
This difference is located in the inner act of the will. Thomas writes, "In
the object of the will two elements are to be considered: a quasi material
element, scil. the willed object, and a quasi-formal element, scil. the reason why the object is willed and this reason is the end."[65] The interior act
of the will receives its species from the end, which is its proper object.
"But that which proceeds from the will is related as the formal element to
that which the exterior act effects, because the will uses members as instruments and the exterior actions are only moral acts insofar as they are
voluntary. Consequently, the moral species of the human action results
formally from the end and materially from the object of the exterior

action. Therefore Aristotle (*Ethic.*, 1.V, c.2) says that a man who steals in order to commit adultery is properly speaking more an adulterer than a thief."[66]

The chief end and final principle of the moral life is the final end, according to St. Thomas. For it is from the final end that reason orders all actions. Janssens maintains that Aquinas's position is based on human experience:

> Our actions are ours, insofar as we are their authors, insofar as they are voluntary, i.e., insofar as we have a notion of an end and of the proportion of our exterior action, what we do (*id quod est ad finem*), to this end. Our interior act of the will with the end, its proper object, is the principle and source of what we do. It is this that Thomas means when he says that the end is the formal and the exterior action the material element. In other words, what we do has to be proportioned to the end in the sense that it must be able to be really *id quod est ad finem*, an effective means to the end. This proportion has to be established by reason illuminated by faith. Therefore, reason has to determine whether the end we pursue is a due end and whether in truth our external action is really a *materia debita modo disposita* to the end.[67]

Aquinas and contemporary revisionist moral theologians share some important things: the necessity of moral rules, with a corresponding understanding that rules have their limits and can sometimes admit of exceptions; the admission of a hierarchy in our value system and the general belief in the exceptionlessness of some moral norms, provided that these have been arrived at after careful consideration of circumstances— those things which are outside an act and yet touch the act. In short, the Thomistic foundation of some of the proportionalist claims is not in doubt. However, whether the entire theory represents a misreading of Aquinas[68] or an attempt to correct Thomas in parts[69] is still open to question. One thing is certain here. The above illustrates the point William Frankena made long ago that what we have in these debates is a "family party."[70] My contention in this book is that this "party," if I may continue with the metaphor, has been made possible because the menu is composed of foods the whole family knows about, foods on which every member of the family has grown and which in some ways continue to define their culinary interests. In other words, the debate on norms, as well as the other debates in Catholic moral theology, is made possible because

[handwritten: presuppositions]

[handwritten: the shared foundation behind it all]

of shared assumptions and shared texts. Part of the problem is how to continue to understand both the texts and the common presuppositions which are deeply held by all in light of contemporary human reality.

The Direct/Indirect Distinction

[handwritten: — recent — often causes confusion creeps into magisterial statements]

As I indicated at the start of this chapter, a close look at the various versions of the principle of double effect shows some interesting differences in the way the principle is presented by various authors. The earliest versions of the principle present the four conditions of the principle in more or less the same language, as we have already demonstrated. These earlier versions are silent about the term "direct/indirect" in the principle.[71] As Joseph Selling points out, this term is of rather recent origin. Moreover, it "does not have to appear in the principle of double effect but it often creeps in and has had an impact even upon the way we speak of norms."[72] The distinction has increasingly been used in documents of the official magisterium of the Church. Pius XI employed the term when he tried to show the wrongness of deliberately taking the life of the unborn. He asks, "What could ever be a sufficient reason for excusing in any way the direct murder of the innocent?"[73] Pius XII applied the distinction in several of his teachings on sterilization:

[handwritten: therapeutic use of pill]

> If the wife takes her medication not with a view to preventing conception, but solely on the advice of a physician, as a necessary remedy by reason of a malady of the uterus or of the organism, she is causing indirect sterilization which remains permissible according to the general principle concerning actions having a double effect. But one causes a direct sterilization and therefore an illicit one, whenever one stops ovulation in order to preserve the uterus and the organism from the consequences of a pregnancy which they are not able to stand.[74]

[handwritten: "indirect sterilization"]

In an address to the Congress of Hematologists in 1958, Pope Pius XII further stated: "When about ten years ago, sterilization began to be more widely applied, it became necessary for the Holy See to declare expressly and publicly that direct sterilization, permanent or temporary, of a man or woman is illicit by virtue of natural law . . . By direct sterilization we mean an act whose aim is to make procreation impossible."[75] Pope Paul VI employed the term in *Humanae Vitae* to re-emphasize the teaching of his predecessors on sterilization and other forms of artificial birth control:

> Therefore we base our words on the first principles of human and Christian doctrine of marriage when we are obliged once more to declare that the direct interruption of the generative process already begun and, above all, direct abortion, even for therapeutic reasons, are to be absolutely excluded as lawful means of controlling the birth of children. Equally to be condemned, as the magisterium of the Church has affirmed on various occasions, is direct sterilization, whether of the man or of the woman, whether permanent or temporary.[76]

Recent magisterial documents have continued to employ the term "direct/indirect." Pope John Paul II teaches in *Evangelium Vitae,* for example, that direct abortion is wrong. "I declare," he says, "that direct abortion, that is abortion willed as an end or as a means, always constitutes a grave moral disorder, since it is the deliberate killing of an innocent human being."[77]

Even though it has a relatively shorter history as part of the elements making up the principle of double effect, the direct/indirect distinction so permeates the principle that the latter is not understandable today without it. The term is traditionally used in three or four areas: sterilization, scandal, abortion, and cooperation. The problem in recent times, especially since the beginning of the proportionalist debate, is to ascertain what this term means and how it is relevant to morality. The disagreement over the meaning of the term is evident even among the revisionists themselves, as we will see in the following review of the discussion between two Jesuit ethicists, Richard McCormick and Bruno Schüller, on two issues: the difference between a permitting and an intending will, and the moral relevance of the direct/indirect distinction in the reinterpretation of the principle of double effect. I will also argue that the discussion of these two men in this area, especially as the distinction between direct/indirect actions pertains to the morality of targeting civilian populations in war, represents an unfinished item on the proportionalists' agenda.

In a 1972 article Bruno Schüller expressed doubts that traditional theology had been correct in attributing to the direct/indirect distinction the overwhelming significance that it has for ethical norms.[78] He argued instead that the key to understanding the direct/indirect distinction lies in understanding the notion of intending and permitting will. Intending as a means and permitting reveal the same moral disposition. Therefore, the doctor who is faced with aborting a fetus to save a woman's life says, "I would not be prepared to do this unless it were necessary to save the life of the woman." This attitude manifests a basic disposition toward and acceptance of the abortion only under certain conditions. Thus, whether the doctor permits or intends the abortion as a means to save the woman, both of these arise from the same mentality. On the other hand, intending as an end reveals a different moral disposition altogether. One can intend the evil that is done. This attitude reveals approval. If one intends evil as an end, and that is what direct scandal is, he is intending the wrongdoing of another.

The distinction between an intending will and a merely permitting will is therefore necessary when one is faced with the issue of moral evil. Moral evil, as we have already seen, refers to "any lack of a perfection at which we aim, any lack of fulfillment which frustrates our natural urges and makes us suffer."[79] Nonmoral evils or disvalues such as pain, sickness, error, death, and so on, should only be caused conditionally—that is, if there is proportionate reason.[80] Whereas traditional theology establishes the intrinsically evil nature of cooperating in another's sin and leading others into sin on teleological grounds, the norms forbidding suicide and contraception are established on deontological grounds and their infringement is seen as morally evil in itself. This is also why the direct/indirect distinction has been traditionally applied to these cases. Schüller argues, however, that this distinction can be valid only if the death of a person (i.e., the killing of another) and contraception are absolute disvalues—that is, moral evils. The killing of another is always the destruction of a fundamental value. But it is not always a moral evil since even the tradition itself accepts the moral legitimacy of some forms of killing, especially in self-defense. Since the death of another is not an absolute evil in the sense of moral evil, it is not necessary to appeal to the notion of permission to establish its moral licitness. The moral rightness of such a case can only be established teleologically, not deontologically, using proportionate reasoning.[81]

McCormick, like Schüller, believes that in situations where two or more values conflict, the choice as to what values to preserve would have to be made on teleological grounds. He insists that proportionate reasoning has in fact been the decisive factor even in traditional theology, which viewed a nonmoral evil as justified because it was indirect, or as immoral because of direct intentionality. Psychological indirectness was not radically decisive at all: "What was decisive is the proportionate reason for acting."[82]

The question arises about the fate of the exceptionless norms of traditional morality if psychological or physical causality is not solely determinative of the morality of human acts. McCormick, Schüller, and other revisionist theologians make two interesting claims. First, they say that there cannot be exceptionless norms, though there can be norms which are held to be "virtually exceptionless." Such norms are so because they cannot as yet foresee any circumstances which can excuse their infringement. Second, what had always been regarded as exceptionless norms have in fact been considered such on teleological grounds. Take sterilization, for example. Traditional Catholic morality would usually allow it for relief of the pain of a patient who is suffering after many vaginal deliveries, which have resulted in lacerations, infections, and erosions in the *cervix uteri*. What is at work here, McCormick insists, is straightforward proportionate reasoning. That this procedure is considered morally right in this instance means that although sterility is not chosen as a means there is still a recognition that to sacrifice a value (fertility) would not subvert but rather enhance the overall well-being of the woman and her family.

The position of the revisionist theologians on direct/indirect intentionality raises problems in a number of areas. Consider the issue of the indiscriminate bombing of civilians in warfare, for example. The Catholic moral tradition upholds the principle of noncombatant immunity. All the revisionist theologians seem to agree that that is an exceptionless norm. The principle, McCormick says, derives its absolute nature also on teleological grounds—that is, from the consideration of the long-term consequences that can arise as a result of the totalization of war, regardless of the short-term gains from such a policy. The teleological considerations notwithstanding, the direct/indirect distinction also comes into play in the moral evaluation of the violation of the principle of noncombatant immunity. The difference between the indiscriminate bombing of innocent civilian populations and the incidental death of innocents in the attempt to repel the enemy's war machine lies in intentionality. In the one case the action is chosen and intended as means. In the other it is merely permitted. The former is more closely associated with evil and bespeaks a greater willingness that it occur, a willingness that McCormick says "is morally acceptable only to the extent that such an intention represents a choice of what is the lesser of two evils." On further insistence from Schüller, McCormick dropped this emphasis on the importance of the direct/indirect distinction with regard to the morality of targeting civilian populations in war. Schüller had insisted that killing noncombatants as a means to weaken the enemy is condemnable not because it is a direct action but because "it violates the principle of *moderamen inculpatae tutelae* (the moderation of a justified defense)." This means, as he puts it, "in any course of defending others or yourself against an unjust aggression, you are not permitted to do more harm than necessary to repel the aggressor effectively."[83]

It must be recalled that in an earlier response to Schüller's initial article on direct/indirect killing, McCormick had written that although he thought, as did Schüller, that direct (descriptively speaking) killing must be judged teleologically, it did not follow that the same proportionate reason which justifies an indirect action (speaking descriptively) would always justify what is direct. "In other words, there may be a proportionate reason for doing something in one way which is not proportionate to doing it another way."[84] McCormick then went on to argue that the terms "direct" and "indirect" were not totally superfluous in all matters regarding the relation of the will to evil since how the evil happens "not only can tell us what kind of action we are performing, but can have enormously different and long-term implications, and therefore generate a quite different calculus of proportion."[85] In further reaction to a later critique of his position by Schüller, McCormick withdrew his insistence on the ethical relevance of the direct/indirect distinction even on the issue of noncombatant immunity. Here is how he puts the matter:

> I think Schüller is correct in his basic assertion that a killing of a human being is not morally wrongful because it is direct . . . Furthermore, I believe the general lines of his analysis of intending/permitting are very illuminating. In this vein, his challenge to my analysis is successful. I had attempted to show a difference in direct and indirect killing through appeal to deleterious consequences and to assert that these consequences are due precisely to the *directness* of the killing. I then concluded to the practical absoluteness of norms prohibiting direct killing of non-combatants in warfare on the basis of these teleological considerations. I believe this is unsatisfactory . . . In short, such killing is disproportionate to the good being sought because it undermines through the association of basic human goods the very good of life. Briefly, all things considered, it cannot be said to be necessary.[86]

There are some problems with McCormick's capitulation to Schüller on the moral relevance of the direct/indirect distinction in regard to the violation of noncombatant immunity on two grounds. First, his argument on this issue seems rather utilitarian. Second, I believe that the direct/indirect distinction still has moral significance in this matter. In other words, there is a very definite descriptive and therefore moral difference between collateral (indirect) damage and direct killing of innocents. Killing noncombatants is wrong because it is unnecessary and unjustifiable on any grounds. There is certainly both a descriptive and a prescriptive difference between an intentional and deliberate dropping of bombs on a crowded market in Sarajevo and the targeting of a military weapons factory which happens to be situated close to a market, even if one knows that there is the possibility that the bomb could drop on the market and cause collateral damage. Proportionate reasoning can never explain the first, though it can make the second case understandable. The first is wrong because it is a deliberate and unjustifiably intended destruction of a basic good to achieve an end. This is what it means to do evil to achieve good. This is at least one case where one must understand directness in the sense both of physical causation and of the lack of proportionate reason. It is also where one cannot prove the wrongness of an act with unassailable logic. The only ground on which to rely for condemning the direct targeting of civilian populations would be our moral instinct.

One charge which continues to dog the revisionist effort is that of consequentialism. Consequentialism is the belief that morality is determined only by weighing the consequences of an act. One of the most pungent attacks on proportionalism in this regard has come from John R. Connery. In a 1973 article Connery accused some prominent proportionalists of discarding the "deontological response of Catholic morality" in favor of "a teleological approach." According to this latter approach, said Connery, "what one ought or ought not do depends entirely on the consequences of the act. If the consequences on the whole are undesirable, the act ought not to be done; if they are desirable, it ought to, or at least may, be done."[87] Connery does an exposé and critique of act-utilitarianism and rule-utilitarianism—two prevailing forms of consequentialism. He associates Peter Knauer, Josef Fuchs, and Bruno Schüller with rule-utilitarianism because all rules "are subject in one way or another to the principle of consequences." Knauer is presenting a morality of consequences because he puts the whole moral burden on consequences. What is clear in Knauer's work, according to Connery, is that "a commensurate good will justify any evil connected with the act. If this good is lacking, the act will be morally bad, since the evil will be directly intended."[88] Fuchs as well "demands a *proportionate* reason and Schüller a *greater good* to justify any evil involved in a human act." Connery argues that these positions are vulnerable to allowing acts which go against commonly held convictions, especially those pertaining to justice.

In reaction to Connery, Schüller agreed that utilitarianism was unattainable as a moral principle.[89] He insisted, however, that it was wrong to equate proportionalism with utilitarianism. Teleological grounding of norms does not amount to espousal of utilitarianism. Furthermore, he objects to forcing the discussion on norms into the neat division of teleology and deontology, as these terms are defined by C. D. Broad. Schüller objects to the way Connery appears to have forced all teleological tendencies to conform to Broad's model of teleology in order to label them all as consequentialist. Proportionalism cannot be regarded as a form of consequentialism. He refutes Connery's charge in this regard using the example of the sheriff in a Southern town in the United States. In this well-known example, a judge faces a dilemma as a mob demands that he condemn a black man for rape and murder, which the judge knows the man did not commit. Would he give in to the mob and condemn an innocent man, or would he risk the ire of the mob, which was prepared to burn the whole place down in their rage? "The immediate indictment and conviction of the suspect would save many lives, as well as prevent other bad consequences, so it would be the best thing to do from the viewpoint of consequences," Connery wrote. The act-utilitarian, with whom Connery locates the proportionalists, would, according to him, seem to be committed to this consequentialist alternative, "in spite of the fact that it goes against the traditional norms of justice."[90] Schüller maintains that it would be presumptuous to think that a teleological theory would be necessarily forced to draw this conclusion. He argues that Connery completely overlooks the fact that not only does the life of one person versus that of many others hang in the balance, but that also the entire institution of criminal law is at stake. The judge in this case would only be justified in condemning the innocent person if somehow his action could be raised to a universally acknowledged and practical rule which would actually promote the common good. This is impossible in this case. Therefore condemning the innocent black man to satisfy an angry white mob is contrary to the common good and unjust. There is thus nothing in the proportionalist theory to suggest that the protagonists of this theory would support such a conclusion.

In reacting to Connery's article, McCormick argues that it is incorrect to describe proportionalism as "a morality based *solely* on consequences," if by "consequence" is meant "intended consequences." This is not what revisionist theologians are saying, nor should they be forced to say so, according to McCormick. All would admit, for example, an inherent value in keeping secrets and an inherent disvalue in revealing them. So, the question is not that it is morally wrong to reveal secrets because of bad consequences. "It is rather: when is it legitimate to bring about the admitted disvalue of breaking secrecy, and why. Schüller, Fuchs, Knauer and Janssens insist that we are talking about an *evil* (nonmoral, premoral, ontic) where revelation of a secret is concerned. Therefore, as soon as the action involved is seen as containing such evil, it is no longer a matter of 'consequences alone,' revelation of secrets would have to be seen as neutral in itself, not as an ontic evil."[91] Elsewhere, McCormick makes the point that revisionists do not hold that human acts are of themselves meaningless. What they are saying instead is that the inherent goodness (and therefore meaning) of a promise, for example, "is a *limited goodness* and may concur with a more urgent value demanding value preference." In other words, "if a promise need not be kept, that conclusion does not deny, nor can it be logically forced to deny, the inherent meaning and value of promise-making. It denies only that this inherent good and meaning is an *absolute* value."[92]

Closely related to the charge of consequentialism is the charge that "proportionalism" is simply another word for "utilitarianism." Grisez presents proportionalism as a theory which holds that "a moral judgment is a comparative evaluation of the possibilities available for choice." Each of the options is examined "to see what benefit and harm are likely to come about if it is chosen and the choice is carried out. Suppose one possibility promises considerably more benefit than harm, while another promises less benefit than harm; one ought to choose the first possibility, according to proportionalists, because it gives a better proportion of good to bad." Although he acknowledges that some people would take issue with his definition of proportionalism, he still maintains that the very notion of proportion which is central to proportionalism requires some method of weighing harms and benefits in order to determine which promises the most attractive proportion.[93] It is clear therefore that for Grisez, proportionalism is just another name for utilitarianism. The essential problem with proportionalism, as in most other forms of utilitarianism, is the comparative evaluation of benefits and harms promised by available possibilities. "Even if proportionalism is used only to judge whether to act in a certain way, a comprehensive evaluation must be made of the benefits and harms expected in either case."[94]

[margin handwritten note: Grisez: prop. as utilitarianism]

The response of proportionalists to this charge has already been given above. Simply put, they argue that although there is some weighing of goods in the situation this does not amount to ascertaining the cost and benefits in a given situation so as to arrive at the option which guarantees the most benefit. They would insist that proportionalism is involved in the weighing of options in situations of conflict where one has to choose from two evils. Even so, the choice is not necessarily determined on the grounds of utility but on the grounds of the option which serves the cause of good in such situations of tragedy. Recall that McCormick praises Maxmillian Kolbe's choice at Auschwitz and that he also never considered that Mrs. Bergemeir was right to choose to commit adultery to save even the life of her husband. Sometimes some things are just too high and too precious to weigh on a scale, or, as Grisez would say, some things are simply incommensurable.

The Moral Methodology of Germain Grisez, John Finnis, and Joseph Boyle

Germain Grisez has not only provided a persistent challenge to the proportionalist position, he has over the years, together with Joseph Boyle of the University of Toronto and John Finnis of Oxford University and the University of Notre Dame, produced a well-known moral theory which in many ways may be considered an alternative to the revisionist moral methodology since the Council. I believe it is important to present their moral theory as well in order to give a more complete picture of the debate on moral norms in the Catholic tradition since Vatican II.

The moral theory of Grisez and his collaborators starts with Thomas Aquinas's first principle of practical reason that "good is to be done and pursued and evil is to be avoided."[95] Grisez states that the purpose of the first principle of natural law is to direct thinking toward "the fulfillment which is to be realized in and through human action." The principle points out the relationship between human goods and the actions appropriate for realizing them. Aquinas also states that human beings grasp as good all the fulfillments toward which they are inclined. "Since being good has the meaning of being an end, while being evil has the contrary meaning, it follows that reason of its nature apprehends the things towards which man has a natural tendency as good objectives, and therefore to be actively pursued, whereas it apprehends their contraries as bad, and therefore to be shunned."[96] Although Grisez holds that the natural human tendencies or inclinations which Aquinas speaks of correspond each to a basic precept of natural law, he maintains that these basic precepts of natural law are general determinations of the first principle of practical reason which states categorically that basic human goods are to be protected, pursued, or promoted.[97] One of the persistent charges Grisez and his colleagues level against proportionalism is that it does not provide an adequate account of human goods. These goods which are compared by that theory exist for proportionalists only in concrete instances of their realization and not in the choices and commitments which people make. On the contrary, Grisez insists that "it is precisely in choices and commitments that existential human goods, such as marital friendship, have their primary and proper reality."[98] Thus, central to Grisez's dissatisfaction with proportionalism is what he believes to be its inadequacy with regard to the basic human goods. He maintains that proportionalists are measuring the incommensurable when they try to determine proportionality in human choice in conflict situations. Grisez's position, on the other hand, is that options for choice are incommensurable and any attempt to commensurate between several options leads to lack of choice.

Basic goods are basic in the sense that they "are appealing and can be sought on their own account" unlike some other goods which are only means to some more fundamental goods.[99] Although the principle of practical reason directs thinking to each basic good as something to be promoted, protected, and preserved, there is still the question of what these goods are and how they can be known. For Grisez, the basic human goods include life, play, aesthetic experience, speculative knowledge, integrity, practical reasonableness, friendship, religion, and marriage. These goods are basic because "one can act for their sake alone."[100] They are human because they are goods of the person "which create the field within which self-determination is possible." With regard to how these goods can be known, Grisez says they are known either through sense experience, through natural curiosity, or intuitively. To know the basic goods and even to be disposed toward them is not in itself a moral act. Morality can only be found in human choices, "in acts consequent upon choices, and in forms of voluntariness somehow conditioned by choices or by the failure to make them when one should make them."[101]

The notion of free choice is another important component of the moral theory of Germain Grisez and his colleagues. They define choices as "actuations of the will, guided by moral norms, by which we determine

free choice impt

ourselves with respect to human goods."[102] Choice is about the agent's intention to act in a certain way, or, as Grisez and his colleagues put it, choice signifies "a volition bearing on an action to be done."[103] Human choice always involves at least one of the basic goods, in some ways. "As ideals to be realized, the basic goods clarify possibilities of choice but do not determine the moral quality of human choice. What determines this is the attitude with which the choice is made. To make a morally right choice one has to choose with a realistic attitude, that is one would have to choose a particular good 'with an appreciation of its genuine but limited possibility and its objectively human character.'"[104]

with right ATTITUDE

In response to the question of how we know what specific choices to make in concrete situations, Grisez states that to be able to move from the understanding of the basic human goods "as fields of practical possibility" and from being disposed to them by "simple willing" to having and articulating specific wants, we need another principle. Such a principle must refer to the many basic goods and should be formulated so as to serve as a standard for practical judgment. Such a principle is the "first principle of morality." Grisez formulates it as follows: "In voluntarily acting for human goods and avoiding what is opposed to them, one ought to choose and otherwise will those and only those possibilities whose willing is compatible with a will toward integral human fulfillment."[105] Grisez argues that this principle both adds the element of choice to the first principle and envisages the basic goods not just as diverse possible fields of action "but as together comprising the stuff of integral human fulfillment." Integral human fulfillment refers to "the realization of all human goods in the whole human community." It does not refer to individualistic satisfaction or to "a definite goal to be pursued as concrete objectives of cooperative human effort."[106]

1st prin. of morality

integral fulfillment

Grisez realizes, however, that the first principle of morality is still too general to provide practical guidance. Thus, it needs further specificity to bring about more clearly the relationship between the choices and integral human fulfillment. This further specification is achieved by what Grisez calls "modes of responsibility." Modes of responsibility are "intermediate principles which stand between the first principle and the completely specific norms which direct choices . . . [They] pin down the primary moral principle by excluding as immoral actions which involve willing in certain specific ways inconsistent with a will toward integral human fulfillment."[107] Thus, whereas the primary principle of morality seeks to point out what is meant by "right reason," the modes of responsibility "exclude

modes of responsibility relate choice to fulfillment

specific ways of acting unreasonably." As Grisez puts it, they protect commitments "in line with integral fulfillment" and against the tendency to partial goal setting and inadequate fulfillment.[108]

Modes of responsibility are thus more definite than the basic principles of morality but are still more general than norms "regarding specific kinds of acts to which they lead." Here are the eight modes of responsibility as Grisez outlines them.

1. One should not be deterred by felt inertia from acting for intelligible goods. 2. One should not be pressed by enthusiasm or impatience to act individualistically for intelligible goods. 3. One should not choose to satisfy an emotional desire except as part of one's pursuit and/or attainment of an intelligible good other than the satisfaction of the desire itself. 4. One should not choose to act out of an emotional aversion except as part of one's avoidance of some intelligible evil other than the inner tension experienced in enduring that aversion. 5. One should not, in response to different feelings towards different persons, willingly proceed with a preference for anyone unless the preference is required by intelligible goods themselves. 6. One should not choose on the basis of emotions which bear upon empirical aspects of intelligible goods (or bads) in a way which interferes with a more perfect sharing in the good or avoidance of the bad. 7. One should not be moved by hostility to freely accept or choose the destruction, damaging, or impeding of any intelligible human good. 8. One should not be moved by a stronger desire for one instance of an intelligible good to act for it by choosing to destroy, damage, or impede some other instance of an intelligible good.[109]

These modes of responsibility taken all together are meant to guide human action toward integral human development. Any action which violates any of them is therefore morally wrong. However, the first and last of the modes of responsibility are particularly important, especially in light of Grisez's opposition to proportionalism. As Jean Porter points out, these two modes of responsibility, taken together with the seventh, lead Grisez "to the view that some kinds of actions are never morally justified, or as the Catholic tradition expresses it, are intrinsically evil. That is, if the description of an action indicates that it necessarily involves 'destroy[ing], damag[ing], or imped[ing]' some instances of a basic good, then the act is ipso facto morally wrong."[110]

Although the modes of responsibility and their corresponding virtues are normative principles which incline and direct people to live morally good lives, they are not specific enough to serve as norms. Thus the question still remains whether we can draw a specific norm from a mode of responsibility and how this can be done. In answering this question, Grisez says, it is best to begin with the conclusion to be reached—a specific moral norm. According to Grisez, a norm is a proposition about a kind of action; the predicate characterizes the kind of action normatively as wrong, good, obligatory, or permissible. In other words, specific moral norms refer to kinds of actions and apply moral determinants to them. This being the case, one needs a middle term by which one can draw a specific norm from a mode of responsibility, something common to kinds of action and to moral principles. "What is common to both are relationships of the will to basic human goods. The modes of responsibility indicate the moral exclusion of certain relationships, and various kinds of action are morally significant insofar as they involve such relationships."

Grisez states that there are two types of moral norms: the negative moral norms and the positive ones. Grisez articulates two steps in the process of the formulation of a negative moral norm. The first step considers the will in a certain kind of action—for example, whether one is acting out of hostility, malice, destructiveness, and so forth, toward a basic human good. The next step would be to consider the moral determination which the modes of responsibility indicate between voluntariness and the basic human goods in this particular action. For instance, "beating a man to teach him a lesson, with a definite risk to life, is a kind of act which involves a will hostile to the good of life. 'To teach a lesson' in the sense intended here brings this kind of act under the seventh mode of responsibility, for one is acting out of hostility and accepts the destruction of a basic human good. Therefore, this kind of action is wrong."[111] As for specific affirmative moral norms, these, according to Grisez, depend on the affirmative first principle of morality which "directs those and only those possibilities whose willing is compatible with a will toward integral human fulfillment. Thus a certain kind of action is morally good if it offers a way of voluntarily serving a human good and involves no voluntariness excluded by any of the modes of responsibility."[112]

Grisez's positions have elicited many reactions over the years. McCormick's disputations with Grisez, for example, are too well known to need complete recounting here. McCormick believes that Grisez is correct to insist on the indivisibility of action or behavioral process. In other words, the good and bad effects in a situation of moral conflict where an action is likely to produce an evil effect as well as a good one have to be immediate. The evil effect in such a case is neither a means, morally speaking, to the good effect, nor the object of an intending will. However, McCormick finds Grisez's claim that one cannot turn against a basic good when the evil occurs as a means, and is the object of an intending will, to be problematic. The problem, as he sees it, has to do with Grisez's refusal to admit the viability of the notion of proportionate reasoning. He argues that a more receptive attitude to this notion could have led Grisez to understand that whether the will is intending or permitting in moral choice in conflict situations is not the decisive factor in such a situation. Rather, what is important is whether the reason in either situation is proportionate. Grisez's disdain for proportionate reasoning in conflict situations leads him instead to focus narrowly on the posture of the will in the discussion on unavoidable evil in human action. Grisez's position on this issue, as we have already seen, is informed by his deep repugnance toward anything remotely resembling utilitarianism. We have also noted that proportionalism for him is just another word for utilitarianism because he believes it is based on commensuration and calculation of values to determine the rightness or wrongness of particular moral acts. McCormick points out that Grisez himself does not escape commensuration and the calculation he accuses proportionalists of engaging in. Grisez grants, argues McCormick, that although the human good is not calculable, he would certainly not hesitate to make a calculation in a situation where, for example, one is faced with the possibility of either having an operation which saves the mother but kills the child, or one that saves the child but kills the mother. In both situations the good and the evil effects would occur in an indivisible process.[113]

*   *   *

I have tried in this chapter to present an overview of the debate on moral norms which has characterized Catholic moral theology since the Second Vatican Council, and especially in the wake of the debate over birth control which intensified with the publication of *Humanae Vitae*. We considered the position of the so-called proportionalists as well as that of their major opponents on some of the key issues involved in the discussion. I have also tried to show that the proportionalists are right to claim to be Thomistic in some ways. Perhaps too they have gone beyond Thomas in some other ways. I next traced the discussion between McCormick and Schüller on the continued relevance of the direct/indirect distinction in the assessment of the moral rightness or wrongness of human acts. Finally, we noted briefly the continuing relevance of this distinction at least in some cases such as that of the deliberate targeting of civilian populations in war. A section of the chapter also surveyed the positions of Grisez, Boyle, and Finnis on moral norms. The positions taken by these two groups have left a lasting imprint on the understanding of moral methodology in Catholic ethics.

In the course of this discussion on proportionalism, I have pointed out a few areas of disagreement between the revisionist theologians and the wider academic and ecclesial communities. As anyone who is familiar with the literature knows, the debate on some of these issues has been vigorous and long-lasting; the numerous articles and books published on this debate attest to this fact.[114] I have highlighted some of the contentious issues occupying the interlocutors in this debate, including the question of moral objectivity, as well as that of the continuing relevance of the direct/indirect distinction, and the charge that the revisionists espouse a consequentialist and utilitarian position, among others. Although we could not examine every one of these issues, since they have been so thoroughly discussed in the literature, it was necessary to discuss a number of them in order to show how theologians have sought to clarify their positions through dialogue with their opponents since the Council.

I have contended all along that these dialogues make sense when seen in the light of a tradition which is seeking to expand its knowledge of the goods which characterize it. Thus, the debate on norms, like the one on birth control, is uniquely a Catholic affair in many ways. That is not to say that the issue of the absoluteness of norms or how to determine right from wrong is only a Catholic affair. It is to say that the way this debate has been going on in the Catholic tradition since the Council can better be appreciated if one understands that the interlocutors share very basic assumptions from the fact of their being Catholic. Consider, for example, some of the terms on which the debate has been pursued. All the interlocutors position themselves as authentic perfecters of the tradition by appealing to some of the benchmarks of the tradition, such as the work of St. Thomas Aquinas or the best of the moral manuals. Consider also some of the concrete questions which are used as important test cases for the validation of the various viewpoints, such as contraception, certain aspects of the conduct of war, modern medical technological advances relative to life and death, and reproductive technologies. Although we were not always explicit in showing the way these examples are related to the discussion, anyone who is familiar with the debate on norms knows that it is conducted with these particular issues in mind. Consider finally that all parties to the discussion on norms insist that they uphold the existence of moral absolutes, even when they disagree on how these are to be determined or what particular norms are to be so regarded. In other words, they all want to show that they are in line with the tradition at its best, and properly understood.

chapter nine

Two Alternative Approaches: Virtue Ethics and Casuistry

The prolonged bickering between revisionist theologians and their opponents has left many scholars in the Catholic tradition unhappy over the question of method. The frustration stems mainly from a feeling that the discussion on moral norms has gone nowhere. This lack of progress is a result of what many of these theologians consider a major flaw in the work of proportionalists and their adversaries: too much attention on moral action and none or too little on the moral agent. At issue here is that the interlocutors on the norms debate seem to have forgotten, as Richard Gula puts it, that "there is more to us, and more to life, than what we do. Our interior life affects our external behavior."[1] To complete the discussion on norms and method in current Catholic theology we will take a very cursory look at the renewed interest in virtue. In the second section, we will take a brief look at what one might refer to as the new casuistry.

Virtue Ethics

Here is how James Keenan, one of the proponents of this new movement in the discussion on norms in Catholic moral discourse, explains this new interest in what is often referred to as virtue ethics:

Renewed interest in virtue ethics arises from a dissatisfaction with the way we do ethics today. Most discussions about ethics today consider major controversial action: abortion, gay marriages, nuclear war, gene therapy, and so forth. These discussions basically dominate contemporary ethics. Many writers . . . belong to a variety of different schools of thought that measure whether a controversial human action is right or wrong. Virtue ethicists are different. We are not primarily interested in particular actions. We do not ask "Is this action right?" "What are the circumstances around an action?" or "What are the consequences of an action?" We are simply interested in persons. We believe that the real discussion of ethics is not the question "What should I do?" but "Who should I become?"[2]

The proponents of virtue ethics maintain that the emphasis on virtue is meant to complement and not supplant completely the stress on norms. Here again is Richard Gula:

Virtue, duty, and principles are complementary aspects of the same morality. Virtues express those habits, affections, attitudes, and convictions that lead to genuine human fulfillment, that is, to being with God and so with one another and with the environment. With virtue, we carry out religious devotions or do our moral duty not because someone is commanding us to do them or is keeping a watchful eye over us to assure that we do them. Rather, with virtue, we act out of an internal, self-directing commitment to the values at stake. Virtue ethics stresses that who we are overflows into what we do. Virtues link us to action by providing a sensitivity to what is right and a motivation to do what human well-being demands. Whether an obligation is prescribed by duties or principles, and whether or not anyone is watching, virtue makes us alert and responsive to the claims of the situations, often with little attention to rationalizing, calculating, or counting the cost. With virtue, we act naturally. We do not ponder, argue, or fuss. We simply move.[3]

The discussions on virtue ethics have certain characteristics. Some of these are: the increasing attention which is paid to the tradition as the context of moral inquiry, the importance of narrative in ethics, the teleological basis of moral justification, the focus on moral action as manifestation of the values and commitment which are central to the character of the moral agent, a moral psychology concerning the way virtues and vices develop, and "a theory of human fulfillment which describes the goal towards which virtues lead and/or in which the virtues are components."[4] These indices refer as well to the work of all virtue ethicists, including non-Catholic theologians and philosophers. The interest here is in the turn this discussion has taken among Catholic ethicists in recent years. Even more specifically we are interested in those theologians whose work on the virtues is based on the retrieval of the theory of virtues in the work of St. Thomas Aquinas—notably Jean Porter and James Keenan.

The Retrieval of Aristotle and St. Thomas Aquinas

Any discussion on the importance of virtue in recent Christian ethical discourse must acknowledge the contribution of Alasdair MacIntyre, whose work since the late 1970s and early 1980s has given impetus to and helped to sustain the interest of many theologians and philosophers in this area. MacIntyre clearly elaborates his moral theory in contradistinction to the work of Enlightenment moral philosophers and their followers, who concentrated on specific acts which are justified by consequences or rules to the neglect of virtues, character, and tradition in ethics. This reality, which MacIntyre refers to as the "Enlightenment Project," is essentially characterized by the quest for universal standards by which to justify particular courses of action in everyday life. Even though "the Enlightenment thinkers manifestly did not agree as to exactly *which* principles might be acceptable to rational persons . . . they nevertheless collectively propagated the doctrine that such principles must exist, and that moral conduct must be subject to intelligible vindication or criticism."[5] Thus, at the heart of the "Enlightenment Project" is this search for "a rational vindication of morality."[6] A central claim in MacIntyre's work is that this quest resulted in failure and subsequently in the lack of any public, shared rationale or justification for moral discourse.[7] Hence, the disjointed moral speech which MacIntyre sees as characteristic of modernity. MacIntyre contends that "any rational method for resolving the moral disagreements requires a shared tradition that embodies assumptions about the nature of man and our true end," in contradistinction to the assumption of liberal society that a just society can be arrived at by freeing individuals from all tradition.[8]

As has been indicated above, MacIntyre maintains that the failure of the Enlightenment Project stems from the detachment of ethical theory and practice from the presuppositions of what he refers to as the "classical tradition" in ethics. This tradition is Aristotelian in that it is inspired in some way by the discussion on the role of the virtues in the ethical writings of Aristotle. However, Aristotle stands in this tradition not necessarily as its originator but as one who has attempted to inherit and sum up a good deal of what had gone before him and as a source of stimulus for later thought.

The basic structure of the Aristotelian classical tradition is contained in the *Nicomachean Ethics*. Within the teleological scheme contained in *Nicomachean Ethics,* which is the historical ancestor of the morality of the Enlightenment philosophers like Kant, Hume, and Diderot, writes MacIntyre, "there is a fundamental contrast between man-as-he-happens-to-be and man-as-he-could-be-if-he-realized-his-essential-nature." It is understood as the task of ethics in this scheme to help the human person understand how to make the transition from the former state to the latter. "Ethics therefore in this view presupposes some account of potentiality and act, some account of the essence of man as a rational animal and above all some account of the human *telos.* The *precepts* which enjoin the various virtues and prohibit the vices which are their counterparts instruct us how to move from potentiality to act, how to realize our true nature and to reach our true ends. To defy them will be to be frustrated and incomplete, to fail to achieve that good of rational happiness which it is peculiarly ours as a species to pursue."[9] We may therefore summarize the contrasting characteristics of the "classical" Aristotelian tradition and the central doctrine of modern liberalism as follows. For one, the rules of morality and law cannot be derived from or justified on the basis of some more fundamental conception of the good of the human person. Since the question about the *good life for man* is regarded, at least from the public standpoint, as systematically unsettleable, all that matters in regard to the moral life are rules. "Qualities of character then generally come to be prized only because they will lead us to follow the right set of rules."[10] For the other—that is, the classical Aristotelian tradition—any rational method for resolving moral disagreements can be found only in a tradition of shared assumptions about the nature of the human person and of his true end. In fact, the whole point of MacIntyre's position on tradition is centered on the claim that the rules of morality are derived from and justified in terms of some more fundamental conception of the human good. Such a conception can be provided only by tradition. Indeed, such a conception is best provided by the Aristotelian tradition in its widest sense. MacIntyre describes this tradition as "philosophically the most powerful of pre-modern modes of moral thought."[11] Thomas Aquinas stands within this Aristotelian classical tradition as its perfecter. MacIntyre himself argues that the Thomistic synthesis was superior within the history of this tradition within which it stood. This synthesis was itself a result of Aquinas's accommodation of both the Augustinian claims and the Aristotelian theorizing in a single dialectically constructed enterprise.[12] At the heart of this enterprise stands a single set of assumptions (the virtues) about moral actions, the reason for acting, and the goal of human moral activity, and about the moral agent.

Contrary to the position of positivism and liberalism, which tends to see the individual as detached from the entanglements of history, society, and his or her own past, MacIntyre argues that the human subject is both a story-telling animal and a being with a story and a past. The individual can arrive at self-conscious selfhood only because he both has a story and is capable of telling stories. Consequently, human actions should not be seen as isolated bits of behavior independent of the agent's setting, beliefs, and intention.[13] Thus, the self finds its identity, moral or otherwise, through membership in a family, city, neighborhood, and so forth. These bestow moral particularity on the agent. Although the self does not have to accept all the limitations which this particularity entails, it cannot be itself without it.

MacIntyre notes that the individual as part of a community with a past, is a bearer of tradition. Traditions themselves are shaped by, transmitted, and borne through practices which themselves have histories. These practices, on the other hand, are also shaped, borne, and transmitted through particular traditions. Traditions as worlds of meaning define, or at least try to set the parameters for defining, what are the relevant goods for man. However, these goods are not defined once and for all. Thus for MacIntyre, a living tradition, as opposed to one which is dead, is one in which this search for the goods is not settled and sealed. Rather, "a living tradition . . . is an historically extended, socially embodied argument, an argument precisely about the goods which constitute that tradition." It is within traditions that the individual generally conducts his or her search for the goods.[14] This search is made possible in the first place because there exists a shared set of assumptions (virtues) about right and wrong, provided by the tradition in question.

Following Alasdair MacIntyre, some scholars for various reasons have delved deeply into the works of St. Thomas to try to unearth the theory of virtue contained therein and to try to suggest ways this approach to morality could help us out of the impasse that Christian ethics has faced following the recent debates on norms.

Jean Porter on the Thomistic Theory of Moral Virtues

Jean Porter, currently John A. O'Brien Professor of Christian Ethics at the University of Notre Dame, provides a highly developed view of the teaching of St. Thomas on the virtues. Porter is interesting because she represents a new group of younger Catholic moral theologians who have consciously tried to distance themselves from the classical norms debate in recent Catholic theology by returning to the work of St. Thomas on the virtues as an alternative to the issue of moral methodology. In a 1990 book, Porter stated her intention "to reconstruct the moral theory of Thomas Aquinas' *Summa Theologiae* in light of the problematics of contemporary Christian ethics."[15] The problematic in question is basically the debate on norms in recent times in Christian ethics. Porter argues that at the root of the fragmentation of Christian ethics is a problem similar to the one MacIntyre had identified as the cause of much of the malaise in recent moral philosophy. "Like their secular counterparts," says Porter, "today's Christian ethicists have seized on the fragments of what was once a *unified moral tradition* as a basis for their interpretation of Christian ethics." These theologians have tried to construct a moral theory based on accounts of the human goods and their relation to human choice out of these fragments from a once unified tradition. "Unfortunately, while those fragments once fitted together and made sense as part of one unified theory of morality, none of them on its own seems to be adequate as a basis for a convincing contemporary theory of morality."[16] Porter has spent considerable energy trying to find a way "to restore a basis for common conversation in the field of Christian ethics."[17] She identifies this common ground in the work of Thomas Aquinas, whom she believes provides a unified moral theory which holds together the different motifs found in the works of various contemporary Christian ethics. Porter contends that although our starting points may be different from Aquinas's there is a lot we can learn from him for moral discourse in our own day.

An important lesson Aquinas teaches is the interconnectedness of the various motifs which ground Christian moral theory. In the *Prima Secundae* and in the *Secunda Secundae* of his *Summa Theologiae*, Aquinas provides a theory of human good grounded in a general theory of goodness that rests upon a particular theory of nature. The point of this theory is that the human person is considered the active agent of his own actions. Aquinas considers the human person to be the origin of his own action, and he, unlike the animals, acts on the basis of an intellectual apprehension that the object of his action is in some way good. As Porter points out, every creature, according to Aquinas, "seeks the good, that is, every creature is oriented toward its own goodness." This means that every creature is oriented toward the fullness of its own being, in accordance with the ideal of its species. However, this orientation to an end must not be seen in too narrow a manner which benefits either the individual or a particular species of creatures alone. The universe for Aquinas "is a web of creatures bound together by relationship of mutual benefit, in which each is oriented to the good of some others, and all together, in their ordered relationships, are ordered to the good of the whole."[18] *human end;*

The human person has both a natural and a supernatural end. Porter *nat +*
points out that Aquinas's moral theory presupposes his position that natu- *supernat*
rally attainable specific perfection of the human person is the proximate
norm of morality. Even though the ultimate perfection of the human person is not natural but supernatural, still "the natural end of human life, that is, the attainment of specific perfection as human beings, is not rendered otiose or irrelevant by the fact that we are actually directed towards a supernatural end."[19] The question to ask then is what the specific ideal of humanity is according to Aquinas, and what sorts of actions and habits would promote the attainment of that ideal and which would be inconsistent with it. The answer to these questions, according to Porter, partly lies in Aquinas's theory of virtue.

Porter on Aquinas

Aquinas, like Augustine before him, defines virtue as "a good quality of the mind, by which we live righteously, of which no one can make bad use; which God works in us, without us."[20] Aquinas states that the last clause in this definition applies to infused virtues, which he describes as those virtues which God bestows on us without action on our part. Thus, Aquinas makes a distinction between infused and acquired virtues. The *←*
human person, it must be remembered, has both a natural and a supernatural end. Acquired virtues are those enduring traits of character which a human person has insofar as he is human and a member of human society, and which he acquires by his own natural powers, from his own acts.[21] Infused virtues, on the other hand, are given to us by God to direct us to a supernatural end. God is the efficient cause of infused virtues. However, although infused virtues are caused by God without any action on our part, they are not caused without our consent.[22]

Aquinas also classifies the virtues into intellectual and moral virtues. Virtues of the speculative intellect are those which perfect the speculative intellect for the consideration of truth. These virtues, which include wisdom and knowledge, for example, are morally neutral. Moral virtues are those which shape the passion and the intellect insofar as it is oriented to action. They are natural or quasi-natural inclinations to particular actions. They are particular habits which make us choose well by directing our intentions to a due end.[23] To each distinct faculty of the soul there is a corresponding virtue. Prudence enables the moral agent to choose in accordance with what is good for the agent's entire life. Says Aquinas:

> Prudence is a virtue most necessary for human life. For a good life consists in good deeds. Now in order to do good deeds, it matters not only what a man does, but how he does it, in other words, it matters that he do it from right choice and not merely from impulse or passion. Now since choice is about means to end, rectitude of choice requires two things, namely the due end, and that which is suitably ordained to that due end. Now man is suitably directed to his due end by a virtue which perfects the soul in the appetitive part, the object of which is the good and the end. But to that which is suitably ordained to the due end, man needs to be rightly disposed by a habit of his in his reason, because counsel and choice, which are about man's ordained end, are acts of reason. Consequently an intellectual virtue is needed in the reason, to protect the reason and make it suitably affected towards means ordained to the end; and this virtue is prudence. Consequently, prudence is a virtue necessary for a good life.[24]

Justice is a virtue which orients the will toward giving the other what is his due. There are two aspects to this virtue. In one aspect, justice refers to the virtue which inclines the moral agent to give to each and every one what is his due. In a wider sense, justice inclines the will toward the common good. "Justice, properly so called, is one virtue whose object is the perfect due, which can be paid in the equivalent. But the name justice is extended also to all cases in which something due is rendered . . . That justice which seeks the common good is another virtue from that which is directed to the private good of the individual; and so public law differs from private law . . ."[25] Temperance is the virtue which shapes the passions of desire and directs the moral agent to choose only those things which are truly good and in the overall good of the agent. Fortitude "shapes the irascible passions in such a way as to resist obstacles to attaining what is truly good."

For Aquinas, these virtues are cardinal virtues because it can be said in some sense that "all other virtues are contained under them." For example, "any virtue that causes good in reason's act of consideration may be called prudence; every virtue that causes the good of rectitude and the due in operations, be called justice; every virtue that curbs and represses the passions, be called temperance; and every virtue that strengthens the soul against any passions whatever, be called fortitude."[26] Thus for Aquinas, "anyone who possesses any true virtue must necessarily possess all of them."[27] However, the virtue of justice occupies a special place among the cardinal virtues. According to Thomas, all moral virtues which are about operations bear in some way the character of justice. Justice is a special virtue which orients the will toward the pursuit of the good of others.[28] It is the greatest of the virtues properly so called.[29] "It is because justice orients the will, and thereby the whole person, to the wider goods of other persons and the shared life of the community, that it serves to set the norms by which true temperance and fortitude can be distinguished from incomplete or counterfeit forms of these virtues."[30] In his theory of morality, and based on his anthropology, which, like Aristotle's, stresses that the human person is a social being who can exist and flourish only in a community context, Aquinas gives prominence to the common good. It is justice which sees to the proper coordination and balance among the various components of the community.

Like MacIntyre, Porter points out as well the role of the community in Thomas as providing the resources which make all knowledge—epistemologically and morally speaking—possible. Says Porter,

> Although Aquinas does not say so explicitly, it is clear that his theories of knowledge and language imply that some sort of social life is necessary to the exercise of the rational capacities that are distinctive to the human creature (cf. 1.84–88). Because we come to knowledge through a process of discursive reasoning (unlike the angels [1.79.1]), our mental processes presuppose a language and a shared body of knowledge, both of which are cultural artifacts. Moreover, the whole superstructure of human thought and actions—language, culture, shared traditions and their informing histories—constitutes a good in itself that transcends the good of any individual who participates in and contributes to it.[31]

Porter considers Aquinas's account of the virtues to be fundamentally sound in that it depends centrally on a prior account of goodness in action "according to which fully human actions are both perfective of the powers and capacities of the agent, and good in their correspondence to the norms of reason, analogically understood in the context of the kind of act that is in question." This insight, she says, enables Aquinas to offer a cogent explanation of the traditional doctrine of the cardinal virtues, to show how the cardinal virtues are connected, and to bring about a plausible synthesis of diverse accounts of the human virtues.[32] Aquinas's account of the virtues ultimately depends on his theological and philosophical account of goodness in general and in regard to the human person and his acts.

However, Porter believes that despite its basic soundness, Aquinas's account of the human virtues needs some reformulation. Such a reformulation should make it easier to see how the virtuous person as envisaged by Aquinas would be capable "of rational self-criticism and transformation of her individual and cultural ideals." It would extend our understanding of a prudent person as well as indicate that "Aquinas's account of moral judgment, comprehensively construed to include the practice of the virtues, includes an account of rationality which is strong enough to generate principled social criticism, as well as individual self-reflectiveness."[33] Porter believes that Aquinas's account of how the virtues are acquired needs reformulation as well to take into account the fact that "the mental processes of the human agent presuppose, and are deeply conditioned by, the complex interactions between the individual and the wider community, as it is mediated to her by the caretakers, peers, and the institutions of her society."[34] This view implies that one's awareness of oneself as a human being and of one's individuality depends on a capacity for empathic identification with others and takes a long process of teaching by immersion in a culture and tradition to develop. The aim of such a cultural immersion is to lead the agent through the complicated process of growing up through childhood, adolescence, and adulthood to the point where the agent comes to a sense of him- or herself "as a unified center of activity, who occupies a variety of roles and situations within her/his community, but cannot be reduced to any one of them or to their heterogeneous sum." Porter tries to show how this psychological process can work. First, she seems to accept Aquinas's notion of the cardinal virtues as near-synonyms. She argues with regard to the virtues of fortitude and temperance, for example, that they both refer to what might be described as "ubiquitous standing temptations of human life, which are built into the organism, so to speak." In other words, these two virtues find their context "in recurring forms of desire or aversion that easily could, and often do, deflect individuals from pursuing wider aims through ongoing activity, and which often lead them moreover, to act at variance with their standing commitments." Therefore, some degree of temperance and some degree of fortitude are necessary if the human agent must function as a member of society and as a self-determining agent.[35]

Although the road to acquiring the virtues starts with imitation, the individual can become proficient in the virtues only when she or he is able to make the transition from imitation "to a reasoned grasp of the point of the paradigms of virtuous action that she has learned."[36] Such a reasoned grasp of the virtues is arrived at within particular human cultures and in dialogue/tension with the socially mediated experience which cultures offer. This means, according to Porter, that although there is "a grain of truth" in the classical claim that "human nature sets parameters around the appropriate expressions of our desires and aversions," yet "we cannot sustain the claim that human nature perspicuously grounds a set of moral prescriptions." Nor can we claim that "it is possible to arrive at any determinate account of human nature at all, prior to, and apart from, the conception of our capacities and limits that emerges after many generations of socially mediated experience of ourselves as creatures acting in the world." All conceptions of human nature are only provisional social constructs. And while it is possible to ground moral norms on such constructs, "we cannot therefore say that norms are grounded immediately in human nature, seen as standing over against culture and providing an independent basis for its critique."[37] What we can say of human exigencies is that they do have an impact on the formation, specification, and revision of moral norms by providing grounds on which individuals can call particular destructive norms in question.

Third, Porter also faults Aquinas for considering fortitude and temperance as self-regarding whereas he sees justice as being wholly other-regarding. She argues that this division, although useful in some ways, creates difficulties for Aquinas when he tries to deal with virtues such as mercy and mildness and vices such as anger which are certainly other-regarding but have strong passional components. The problem here is that Aquinas considers justice as a virtue of the will, which is a more comprehensive faculty than the passions of desire and aversion. Since the will is directed naturally to the individual's good, "it must be informed by the other-regarding virtue of justice if the individual is to desire and act in accordance with the good of others and of the community of which he is a member."[38] The removal of the passional element from the character and nature of other-regarding virtues creates a difficulty. According to Porter, it makes Aquinas treat the virtue of chastity, for example, as if it were primarily a capacity to moderate one's desire and enjoyment of physical pleasure "rather than seeing it as a capacity for appropriate feeling and action with regard to other *people*."[39] This same faulty psychology is also evident in Aquinas's treatment of such virtues as mercy and mildness, which he finds difficult to classify because they appear "to straddle a double line between will and passions, and between what concerns another, and what concerns oneself."[40] Porter notes that for Aquinas it is not important for the agent's pursuit of his or her aim in society that he or she has the capacity for care and responsiveness for others. Rather, what is important for the agent's well-being and functioning in society is the fundamental capacity for desire and aversion. These two are enough for the agent to be able to choose the correct other-regarding action to perform. Porter insists instead that it is impossible to separate the other-regarding capacities for empathy, care, and concern for others from the virtues of self-restraint and courage, or from a commitment to justice. Some degree of empathy is necessary for understanding the basic moral notions.

Thus, although it does not follow that an agent must necessarily acquire a concern or empathy for others to be capable of action, nonetheless these virtues are both desirable and beneficial to the agent, and to those around him as well. Therefore, if it is true that the virtues of caring are internally connected to the good of the agent himself, "one consequence is that we cannot draw a sharp distinction between self-regarding and other-regarding virtues." Even if there is some merit to this distinction, it must not be carried too far. For "even the most basic virtues, without which no one can function at all, are practically inseparable from other-regarding concerns . . . Similarly, the other-regarding virtues have a self-regarding dimension."[41] The trick is to find a way to balance the competing claims of mercy, caring, justice, conscientiousness, and other such virtues. Porter believes that this balance can be attained only through the process of intelligent actions in situations of conflict and diverse ideals. "The person who is able consistently to achieve a felicitous balance between the demands of caring and the demands of conscientiousness will necessarily be a prudent person, whose wisdom is grounded in a sound and reflective conception of the human good."[42]

Porter concludes that Aquinas is basically correct, however, in his claim that the traditional cardinal virtues are such because they represent the characteristic perfection of the human action per se. He is also correct to assert that the cardinal virtues are connected in such a way that "intellectual judgement and passion or sensibility are inseparably linked." However, she believes that a reformulation of Aquinas's doctrine of the virtues in light of contemporary understanding of the human person and of human psychology is necessary as a basis for social critique and reform and for individual self-criticism. Aquinas's connection of the virtues with the notion of goodness in action limits what anyone can ascribe to any particular virtue and the forms of social life which are consistent with justice broadly understood. In other words, "The constraints set by the virtues on particular conceptions of the human good also set constraints on what can count as just social institutions, in that they help to determine what the institutions of society must look like, if individuals and communities are to be able to pursue and sustain lives of real goodness." These constraints are somehow obvious, says Porter.

> If a society is to be sustainable, it must encourage its members to develop those same qualities of self restraint, minimal courage, care and conscientiousness that are necessary for action at the individual level; or, if that proves too formidable a task, it must at least refrain from undermining these qualities. There are two further constraints that a society must respect, if its members are to pursue and live out sustainable conceptions of the human good. First of all, it must allow for what have been described as intermediate institutions, localized communities, since it is only within the parameters of such communities that more fully developed conceptions of the human good can emerge and be sustained. Secondly, it must sustain the conditions for open enquiry that are necessary for the ongoing pursuit of truth and goodness in all their forms.[43]

James Keenan on the Thomistic Theory of Virtue

Another advocate of virtue ethics is James Keenan, a Jesuit who teaches at Weston Jesuit School of Theology. James Keenan is one of those theologians who advocate not only greater attention to virtue ethics but a retrieval of the Thomistic tradition on the issue as well. Keenan speaks for many others when he states that for virtue ethicists the starting point of

Keenan

ethics is not the question "What should I do?" but rather "Who should I become?" In fact, he says, virtue ethicists expand that question into three related questions: "Who am I?" "Who ought I to become?" "How am I to get there?"[44] According to Keenan, virtue ethicists believe that "the fundamental task of the moral life is to develop a vision and to strive to show how to attain it." And inasmuch as that vision is who we ought to become, then, the key insight is that we should always aim to grow, becoming more and more the persons we ought to be.

Although Keenan anchors his position on the role of the virtues in the moral life in the teaching of St. Thomas Aquinas, he does not do so uncritically. There is no need to go into a full discussion of Keenan's understanding of the virtue theory of Aquinas. I will attend only to those aspects of his understanding of Aquinas which are necessary to indicate his contribution to this discussion.

TA's list of cardinal virtues inadequate

Like Aquinas, Keenan holds that the cardinal virtues—prudence, justice, temperance, and fortitude—are essential to helping the moral agent become the kind of person he ought to be. Keenan argues, however, that the classical Thomistic list of cardinal virtues essential for the moral life is inadequate for the moral life in the modern world. There is thus need for a fresh determination of the list of what may be regarded as cardinal virtues for today. Keenan points out that for Aquinas temperance and fortitude are auxiliary virtues which exist to make a person become just. So also the virtue of courage. Keenan believes that the picture of the just person which emerges from the work of St. Thomas is insufficient and needs to be revised to accommodate the various demands on the acting person today from family, friends, community, and many other relationships which insist that one act in particular ways toward each of these people,

virtues can oppose each other

and thus provide particular nuances to the definition of justice. Keenan maintains that the virtues are "distinct and sometimes opposing strands," contrary to what Aquinas thought when he taught that justice is supported by fortitude and temperance and that none contradicts, opposes, or challenges the claims of justice. Keenan points out that there is a widely held opinion among virtue ethicists today that "the moral person cannot only be just; the demands to care for a loved one may conflict with the call to be fair to everyone."[45] Also, Keenan insists that rather than regard the virtues as perfecting a particular disposition in the moral agent, as Thomas believed, it would be more accurate to think of the virtues not just as perfecting individual powers but rather as perfecting the way we relate to one another. If it is true then that the virtues make us capable of relationships

perfecting relationships, not individ power

with one another, Keenan believes therefore that a new list of virtues is needed. Such a list would include justice, fidelity, self-care, and prudence. While justice urges us to treat all persons equally, fidelity is the virtue that "nurtures and sustains the bonds of those special relationships that we enjoy whether by blood, marriage, love or sacrament. Fidelity requires that we treat with special care those who are closer to us. If justice rests on impartiality and universality, fidelity rests on particularity." However, as relational beings we are called not only to treat all people fairly or to sustain the specific relationships that characterize our lives, "we are also called to self-care that no one else can provide." Prudence is necessary therefore as a virtue which determines what constitutes justice, fidelity, and self-care for any individual. Furthermore, it has the role of negotiating how the cardinal virtues should interact and which of them should be given preference in any given situation.[46]

I have presented here the views of two contemporary authors on the virtues especially from the point of view of St. Thomas's work. The point that must be emphasized here is that although the virtues may dispose the moral agent toward being good and choosing to do good, they may not necessarily always inform the agent what options are right in a particular situation of moral conflict. There is need for analyses and for reflection. I think Gula is wrong when he says that "with virtue, we act naturally. We do not ponder, argue, or fuss. We simply move." I think he overstates the matter here. I believe the virtues make our pondering easier and our arguing more selfless and our fussing disinterested. Being virtuous does not remove the pain of having to make hard decisions in this life. Ethical ambiguity is not always a result of sin or lack of virtue. It is sometimes a consequence of our creaturehood. Sometimes the facts are very complicated and bewildering, and the relevant ethical norms are both difficult to find and tricky to apply because they often "offer conflicting counsel."[47] Moral dilemmas are a fact of human existence. The sources of moral ambiguity stem from human creaturehood and finitude. As created and finite we do not know everything. We are limited in our vision and choice and must, as McCormick puts it, only grow progressively in knowledge and understanding.[48] In these circumstances, then, good and evil are very closely intertwined; the good we achieve is "rarely untainted by hurt, deprivation (and) imperfection."[49] Thus: "We must kill to preserve life and freedom; we protect one through the pain of another; our education must at times be punitive; our health is preserved at times by pain and disfiguring mutilation; we protect our secrets by misstatements . . . ."[50] Therefore *every*

virtue: conflict remains, but inclination to do right more pronounced

choice is a sacrifice, and could bring about an omission, which is mixed and ambiguous. The point the virtue ethicists are making is that a virtuous character would always be inclined to do what is right in every situation. This makes choosing a bit less of a burden than would be the case for someone else who is less virtuous. However, there is no dispensing completely with analyses or with attention to moral action, as Jean Porter has also shown from the work of St. Thomas. Moral analyses, character, and action come together especially in particular situations of conflict.

In recent years, scholars have tried to complement the discussion on norms and on the moral agent with a discussion on casuistry. The aim in the next section is to discuss briefly the revival of casuistry in recent Catholic ethics.

Casuistry

Defining Casuistry

In a very broad sense, casuistry is "the method that applies the principles of a science to particular facts."[51] In Christian ethics, casuistry "signifies that part of moral theology that treats of the application of moral principles to singular cases"[52] with a view to determining the morality of these particular cases.

In the course of its history, casuistry has sometimes acquired a negative connotation. For some, it has meant a system which niggles in codification to the point of absurdity, invites the reasoning "which makes a thing legally right when it is patently wrong from an ethical standpoint," and substitutes an externally legislated ethics for an ethics of responsibility. It represents a surrender of the individual to the skilled expert who can interpret and manipulate the law.[53]

Although there has been plenty of abuse of casuistry in the history of the Church, casuistry need not be seen this way. The aberrations which occur in the history of the concept's development, like all aberrations in other spheres of human endeavor, need not determine the nature or the fate of the method. In casuistry we are dealing not with the abolition of rules, but with the application of these rules and principles to particular cases and to individual circumstances. We are dealing with a way or ways to make rules take on responsive and responsible existence, a way to bridge the gap between concrete action and abstract norm. Thus, casuistry has two functions: to illustrate principles and to study moral problems of concrete life.

We can thus speak of *case* and *practical* casuistry. In case casuistry, confessors and counselors learn to handle moral principles and are "initiated into the prudent and judicious solutions of cases of conscience."[54] Practical casuistry applies Christian principles to contemporary life and tries to make real the Christian ideals in the various spheres of life—individual, family, social, and professional. A further distinction can be made between casuistry as applied to completed action and casuistry as applied to an act not yet performed. The former, sometimes known as merciful casuistry, is a casuistry of the confessional. It takes its inspiration from Jesus' words to the woman caught in adultery: "Neither will I condemn thee" (Jn 8:11). As Edouard Hamel says, this form of "casuistry is designed especially for the confessor who must make an objective yet merciful judgement of his penitent, and even hold him innocent, if possible, in doubtful cases."[55]

Casuistry is "morality in detail."[56] In other words, whenever or wherever reasoned answers are presented or attempted with regard to the determination of the moral rightness or wrongness or the appropriateness of an action, we are dealing with some form of casuistry. As Aristotle points out, there are different kinds of knowledge: scientific knowledge, practical wisdom, and intelligence, among others.[57] Objects of scientific knowledge exist of necessity and are eternal, indemonstrable first principles, from which conclusions can be drawn as in a syllogism. Theoretical wisdom encompasses scientific knowledge and intelligence, and thus also deals with indemonstrable first principles which are of no practical relevance to humans. Practical wisdom, on the other hand, is concerned with human affairs, with particular human action. Aristotle states that the whole of ethics belongs to this sphere which he says is also deliberative and calculative.[58] And, says the philosopher, the most important characteristic of the person of practical wisdom is to deliberate well. And to "deliberate well about human action" one must "have experience."[59] The aim of casuistry is therefore to make ethics a practical exercise which caters to concrete persons in concrete situations, and which tries to resolve ethical difficulties in people's lives through careful deliberations undertaken by people "who have experience." Good casuistry is neither a legalistic scheme nor a reckless antinomianism, as some charge. Instead, it is prudence in action, a prudence which seeks through careful thought to preserve and protect basic human goods as much as is possible within the

often tragic and ambiguous situations in which human beings find themselves.

The Return of Casuistry

In 1988 Albert R. Jonsen and Stephen Toulmin published a seminal work
on the history of casuistry in which they argued that a return to casuistry
or the case method approach to moral reasoning was needed if progress is
to be made on some of the very divisive moral questions of the day.[60] A
few books and a lot of articles have appeared since then on casuistry.[61] The
net effect of these efforts has been an increasing respect for the case method
approach to ethics. It would be wrong, however, to attribute this increased
interest in the case method approach to ethical reasoning solely to these
works. Even before the appearance of these books and articles, the return
to casuistry was already evident, especially in the Catholic tradition, from
about the middle of the last century. As has already been noted, "casuistry
emerges as a method of moral reasoning whenever extraordinary new
issues materialize."[62] At such moments, casuistry becomes a preferred way
by which communities sort out the practical implications of their ethical
beliefs in the face of these new realities.[63]

The return of casuistry in the years after the Council can be attributed
to a number of factors, such as scientific developments, especially in the
areas of health and medical technology; issues pertaining to war and
peace, especially on the international scene; and the intractable debate on
moral norms which has characterized Catholic moral theology in this period. Here is what Richard McCormick wrote in 1981 about some of the
moral quandaries which advances in medicine and medical technology
have given rise to:

> We live at a time when nearly every morning newspapers bring us an-
> other biomedical breakthrough—and problems. Some of the recent
> ones include the following: surgery on the fetus *in utero* to correct
> bladder pathology; laparoscopic introduction of relief valves into the
> fetal cranium to prevent hydrocephalus and the subsequent retarda-
> tion associated with neural tube defects; the transitional use of totally
> artificial hearts; *in vitro* fertilization procedures to overcome tubal oc-
> clusion.[64]

While the breakthroughs in biomedical technology enable medicine to
prolong life, cure diseases, and provide therapy to people who are suffer-

ing, they also sometimes raise a host of questions about what might or might not promote or protect the *humanum*. Sometimes the questions have to do with the criteria employed for making particular choices in situations of conflict and with who decides what to do in such situations.

The challenges medicine has posed to theology in recent times have been grouped into four broad categories by Richard McCormick: (1) those relating to the sanctity of life; (2) those pertaining to the meaning of sexuality and family; (3) those pertaining to the value of the relationship between patients as persons and the physician; and (4) those issues which concern the individual and social justice in health care delivery.[65] The first of these categories covers cases relating to life-sustaining and resuscitative devices. What is at issue in those circumstances is not just physical life but the quality of life as well. Says McCormick, "The sanctity of life as embracing also its quality is at the heart of the following problems: keeping alive, allowing to die, hastening death, abortion, radical surgery, definition of death, allocation of scarce medical resources, treatment of retardation, drug use and abuse, alcoholism, and care of the elderly."[66]

Sanctity of life cases have sometimes arisen when a person is diagnosed as being in a persistent vegetative state and is therefore dependent on artificial life support systems to carry out the normal human functions such as breathing and feeding. Such cases have also arisen when a person was in a condition of irreversible physical and mental impairment and dependent on a nasogastric tube for feeding. Sometimes in such cases the question has been whether to continue to keep the patient on life-support machines or whether to keep feeding the patient, even when that is the only intervention meant to sustain her and keep her alive. Here is an example proposed by McCormick concerning the decision whether a person should be allowed to die or not:

> It is the instance of spina bifida with a meningomyeloecele. This is a birth defect involving an opening along the spinal column with protrusion of the spinal sac. It is often associated with paralysis from the site of the lesion down, with hydrocephalus, mental retardation, permanent incontinence, etc. Prior to the 1950s, few babies born with this defect survived for very long. Hence the moral problem was not seen as terribly urgent. Now, however, advances in medical knowledge and technology make it possible through surgery to prevent further contamination of the spinal fluid and lethal infection. If surgery is not performed, the infant will probably contract meningitis due to bacterial invasion of the open sac of spinal fluid and die. However, the

surgical prognosis is highly variable. Sometimes it is quite poor. At other times, it is good, but even with a fairly good prognosis, these children can end up severely impaired and in a constantly deteriorating condition that represents a tremendous burden to the child and the family.

The question here is whether this operation should be performed or omitted with only supportive care provided. Ultimately, the issue is whether such a life should be saved. As McCormick points out, although to operate may save this child—but for a crippled, painful, retarded existence—to refuse to operate is to imply that the quality of this infant's life is not worth it. This latter decision raises a host of other questions such as who has the right to say what quality of life is tolerable and what is not; what are the criteria involved in such a determination; and why it is preferable to let the child die rather than hasten the process of his death by active intervention. "This list of questions expands to an even larger list of more general questions: what is the moral difference between active euthanasia and forgoing extraordinary means? Is the 'sanctity of life' crucially dependent on a concept of God as Creator and ultimate destiny of life? Is there a right to die? What is the value of terminal suffering?"[67]

The casuistic approach to sanctity of life cases has tended to pay attention to the individual variables in each case. This has sometimes yielded different conclusions to similar cases or among various ethicists. A few criteria seem, however, to guide the deliberations of many Catholic ethicists in their deliberation on issues in this area. The first of these criteria is that life is a gift from God. This implies the very notion of stewardship of life. Like every gift, life is meant to be looked after and protected. Catholic theologians involved in deliberations over sanctity of life cases have generally taken the human stewardship of life into account. An extension of this notion implies as well that there is an ontological aspect to human existence which does not lend it to whimsical manipulation by human beings. A second principle evident in the treatment of sanctity of life cases is that although life is a basic good, it is not an absolute value. The understanding here is that there are other values which can sometimes be given precedence over physical life. Thus for the good of eternal life someone may decide to face death rather than sin against God or go against the dictates of conscience. In deciding what remedies to apply or not to apply, ethicists have often invoked the principle of ordinary and extraordinary treatment. The thinking is that there are times when it is the right thing to do to let a life go rather than continue to save it. What I have just outlined are simply some of the general principles which are evidently in operation in the casuistry of many modern Catholic theologians who have been faced with sanctity of life quandaries which have arisen in recent times in bioethics.

Another set of quandaries arises from two recent biological achievements which challenge the meaning of sexuality and family. These are birth control means and devices which separate sexual expression from procreation and the achievement of procreation apart from sexual expression. Some of the biomedical advances in this regard are contraception, sterilization, in vitro fertilization, artificial insemination with donated sperm (AID), artificial insemination using the husband's sperm (AIH), and possibly cloning. As we have seen throughout this book, some of the most contentious issues in Catholic moral theology in recent years come from this area. Thus, there seems to be very little room for the application of casuistic principles to these issues. Contraception is considered to be absolutely wrong. Artificial insemination in any sense is also thought to be inadmissible on the grounds that it sunders the unitive and procreative aspects of procreation, and in some instances, such as when donor sperm is used, represents a third-party intrusion in the marriage. The one area which has been open to casuistic reasoning here is sterilization. Although the tradition, as we have already seen, considers direct sterilization to be immoral, it considers indirect sterilization to be permissible. The role for casuistry in this regard is to determine when sterilization is indirect and thus permissible. This is one of the tasks with which the principle of double effect was originally concerned.

The issue of the physician-patient relationship is bound up with the following problem areas: confidentiality, the patient's right to be informed, malpractice problems, the role of the physician as counselor, medical treatment of minors, and so on.[68] Another issue of interest to casuistry in the Catholic tradition is HIV/AIDS. HIV/AIDS is raising many questions for all ethical traditions everywhere. Elsewhere, I have tried to show what challenges the pandemic is raising in regard to confidentiality, the patient-physician relationship, the distribution of scarce medical resources, experimentation with certain types of drugs, individual privacy and the right to control information about oneself, and certain practices pertaining to human sexuality, marriage, and the family.[69] It is the role of casuistry, as moral morality in detail, to show how as Christians struggling with this entirely new phenomenon, we can both do what is right and preserve the

Casuistry as morality in detail

moral values which are necessary for our flourishing as individuals and as a community with a distinct heritage.

The two approaches to doing ethics which we have discussed here are not new in any way in the Catholic tradition. What seems new here is, first, the renewed realization that, as Riccoeur would say, no one speaks from nowhere. Thus, the moral traditions we inhabit have tremendous influence on the way we make moral judgments since they provide both the resources for approaching the issues and the grounds for determining what solutions can be considered satisfactory. Second, who we are is important in helping determine what we do in situations of moral conflict. In such situations, the saying is usually true that as a tree tends, so does it fall. No one can guarantee that all our actions will always be right. The life of virtue, however, guarantees that they will, at least normally, be actions that come from a good heart.

part four

A Living Tradition

chapter ten

Catholic Moral Tradition in an Age of Renewal

We have so far examined in some detail the discussions on a number of key issues in the area of fundamental moral theology since the Second Vatican Council. These discussions show how diverse and pluralistic the Catholic moral theological landscape has become. In the first chapter, we considered the various elements from the Second Vatican Council that have helped to shape theological thinking in the Church in the years subsequent to the Council. Some of these elements are theological and pastoral, while some pertain to anthropology. The influence of the Council has been both substantive and inspirational, thus making the Council itself the overall point of reference for the effort to renew moral theology. Another very influential element in Catholic moral theology since the Second Vatican Council is the encyclical on the regulation of birth, *Humanae Vitae,* which was published by Pope Paul VI in 1968. In the second chapter I tried to show how this encyclical affected discussions on human sexuality and became a lightning rod for debates on issues in many other areas, such as the nature and competence of the magisterium, the relationship between the individual and authority, and the right of the individual believer to dissent from authoritative teaching of the magisterium; this encyclical thus set much of the agenda in post–Vatican II moral theology. The third chapter discussed some theological questions, notably the movement for biblical renewal and Karl Rahner's contribution to the discussion on non-Christian religions, and fundamental freedom—issues which have also had tremendous impact on moral theology since Vatican II.

Part of the gain to moral theology from the biblical renewal is the realization that since scriptural revelation was conditioned by its historical circumstances, the moral teaching of the Bible was itself also conditioned by those circumstances. I pointed out the way biblical scholars advise caution in the way we rush to conclusion concerning what the New Testament taught concerning morality, first of all by paying close attention to the historical and cultural circumstances within which the biblical text arose.¹ Scholars like Eugene LaVerdiere, for example, insist on a general principle of biblical scholarship which recognizes the importance of a historical critical approach to the study of the Bible. With specific reference to the study of the teaching of the Bible on human sexuality, with a view to developing a contemporary ethic of sexuality, LaVerdiere suggests a two-tier approach. The first step would be an exegetical investigation which tries to reach the meaning of the text in its ancient context. The second stage of the investigation would confront the ancient text with our modern situation in order to translate it into contemporary theology. LaVerdiere shows how the teaching of the New Testament on human sexuality was influenced by the various stages of ecclesial development in the New Testament and shows how the sexual ethics of the New Testament in particular emerged in relation to the various contexts of the New Testament formation. The point is that any hermeneutical interpretation of New Testament teaching on morality must respect the nature of the various documents of the New Testament and their histories. Our task, he says, "is to discern the position of the Church today in relation to that which underlies the various letters and Gospels which we accept as challenging and normative for Christian living." The significance of New Testament ethical teaching for modern life should emerge in light of this relationship.² Since the study of the New Testament has shown that ethical issues often emerge in a particular historical context in response to definite historical situations, neither the teachings of Jesus nor those of the early Christian community can be understood apart from their "social and political contexts and the challenges these periods posed."³ As we saw in chapter 5, this particular insight has led to several debates on the import of using the Bible as warrant for teaching in particular areas in ways which are at variance with the "experience" of several peoples or groups in the contemporary world. For, as Allen Verhey points out, "To say scripture is an authority is not yet to say

[handwritten: ✓ very impt]

what moves are authorized in an argument 'from the Bible to the modern World.'" Therefore, an important first step toward methodological clarity in this regard would be to distinguish between "authority and authorization." Thus, we saw that for many theologians "the question of *whether* (and within the believing communities, the agreement that) Scripture is a source and canon for moral discernment and judgment must be distinguished from the questions of *what* this source provides or *how* this canon functions as a norm." Thus, in spite of the agreement that Scripture is an authority, there is widespread disagreement about the authorization for moving from Scripture to moral norms.[4]

We have considered the contribution of the renewal of biblical studies to the study of moral theology in some detail in chapter 3. Even so, I believe it is important here to stress one issue which has already been mentioned elsewhere in the book. The most obvious contribution of Catholic biblical renewal to moral theology has been the realization implicit in the call of the Council fathers for the renewal of moral theology that the Bible has a lot to say about the way people live their lives and about how human society is to be constructed. Later on, the problem would arise as to how to use Scripture for these tasks. However, the encouragement, indeed the marching orders, to theologians on the use of Scripture in ethics would certainly not have happened had the biblical renewal not taken place. *[handwritten: – personal conduct; society]*

Chapters 4, 5, 6, and 7 were devoted to the study of the nature of Christian ethics in the Catholic tradition. Beyond the early controversies concerning the distinctiveness of Christian ethics (chapter 4) we discussed the debate on the place and use of Scripture in this moral tradition (chapter 5), the question of the place of natural law in Catholic moral discourse (chapter 6), and the debate on the role of the magisterium as moral teacher (chapter 7). Chapters 8 and 9 examined the question of method in post–Vatican II moral discourse in Catholic theology. While chapter 8 was devoted to the famous debate on norms, chapter 9 examined two emergent alternatives to the norms debate: virtue or character ethics, and casuistry. In the last chapter of this work, I will discuss the concerns of Pope John Paul II with regard to the direction taken by some moral theologians since the Council, as well as his views on the course moral theology should take to be faithful to its nature and mission.

There could be a temptation for someone who has gone through this book so far to write off Catholic moral discourse since the Council as relativistic, chaotic, and too fragmented. I think that to give in to such temptation would be to make a grave mistake and would be to fail to understand

[handwritten: chaos + fragmentation]

the dynamic which has been at play in this discipline since the Council. It
has been part of my contention, in line with Alasdair MacIntyre's position,
that one of the characteristics of a truly living tradition is vigorous argument. Only in this way can the goods which characterize the tradition in
question be preserved and expanded. A deliberate effort has been made
throughout this book, therefore, to show that postconciliar moral theology
in the Catholic Church, contrary to much of its recent past in the manualist tradition, has been characterized by vigorous debate; and that these debates are not necessarily signs of weakness in the Catholic moral tradition,
but rather are indicative of a tradition which is seeking to expand and develop by finding ways to grapple with new and hitherto unknown problems or situations—it is a tradition which is truly alive.

In the preface to his manual on moral theology which had been in use
before the Council, Henry Davis describes the task of moral theologian as
that of repeating and transmitting age-old moral insights from one generation to the other. In Davis's words, the matter with which moral theology is
concerned "is one that has been treated with the greatest acumen and
scholarship during well-nigh three centuries and there is no room for originality."[5] Here we have a partial explanation for the tempo, rhythm, and atmosphere of unanimity which prevailed in the moral theology of this
period, an atmosphere which resulted from a feeling that there was "nothing new under the sun." Our effort so far has shown that the spirit of
post–Vatican II moral theology was vastly different from that of its precon-
ciliar predecessor. The former seems to be marked more by disagreements,
daring, and innovative tendencies which suggested that there was still
room for some originality in its conclusions. Whether this originality of
thought did indeed happen is another thing. What is important to note at
the moment, however, is the sense of mission which motivated the work of
moral theologians in these two eras. While theologians in the pre–Vatican
II era saw themselves as merely repositories of a finished tradition, theologians in the post–Vatican II era have tended to look at their work as a continuing quest to expand the reach and meaning of the Catholic moral
tradition.

Two important factors, among many others, can help to explain the
difference in the mentality of the theologians of these two eras. One is the
different intellectual atmosphere in which the theologians did their work.
Vatican II and its aftermath coincided with the changed atmosphere following the 1960s as people everywhere tended to hold authority of any
sort in lesser regard than had been the case before. In the West, the various student uprisings, the Vietnam War, and the general spirit of discon-

tent which these events generated created an atmosphere of distrust of authority generally. The debate on birth control is in some ways indicative of this tendency as well. A moral theology built on the views of inherited authority was bound to come under closer scrutiny. Like many others at this time, some moral theologians could no longer accept the validity of an answer to a moral question simply because such a view had been considered correct by scholars for many centuries, or because it had been issued by an authority, even a religious one.

(2) widespread social changes

Second, the social, political, and economic situation everywhere in the 1960s and 1970s was raising new issues, and sometimes old ones in new ways. The wars fought in various parts of the world since 1939, for example, raised questions concerning the definition of a just war vis-à-vis the very lethal instruments of modern warfare. In a 1945 article John Ford wrestled with the issue of obliteration bombing and how this new phenomenon in the tactics of war could be regarded from the point of view of the teaching on just war. This article was one of the early signals that the certitude on many issues in moral theology could no longer be taken for granted. Consider as well the reality of decolonization in the late 1950s and early 1960s, as the various European colonial powers were forced or obliged to relinquish their claims to their colonies in many parts of the world. Think of the awakening of various peoples to the reality of their peoplehood and the social and political ferment which such realizations created.

As a consequence of all these changes, and many more, many of the inherited Catholic moral teachings were coming under pressure in a way and on a scale hitherto unknown. It is to the credit of the Catholic moral tradition that it tried hard to respond to these social, economic, and political developments through the teachings of the popes and the worldwide episcopacy on social questions. These teachings are beyond the scope of this book. However, the last fifty years or so were years of great ferment in all parts of the world which challenged the Catholic Church, as well as other Christian Churches, to find creative responses to the questions and challenges of the times. One of these areas of challenge was that of medical technology. We have already mentioned the debate around birth control and the contribution the development of the birth control pill made to the escalation of this debate. Medical technology has so affected moral theology that a whole subspeciality has arisen to address the issues in this area. The point here is that moral theology in the pre– and post–Vatican II era behaved differently as an intellectual discipline because it was reacting to vastly different stimuli.

med-tech

We must, however, question the assumption implicit so far in our discussion that Vatican II was a dividing line between two significantly different epochs in the discipline. The fact is that even before the Council,
cracks had begun to appear in the certitude which surrounded moral discourse, as in many other areas in the Catholic Church. The Council is
used as a reference because, as has been repeatedly shown in this book, it
tried to patch up the existing cracks and to indicate ways in which the
Church could function authentically. With particular reference to moral
theology, it has been my contention also that several features of the Council have combined to shape the discipline—with remarkable results.

My task in this chapter is to indicate some of those elements on which
there is fundamental agreement and which mark moral theology as a
unique form of moral discourse. I will first present these elements in summary form, and then elaborate on them. First, moral theology is God-talk.
Not only is God central here, moral theology has a particular understanding of God which characterizes and warrants the assertions it makes. Second, moral discourse in the Catholic tradition is characterized by the
understanding that there is continuity between common human morality
and revealed morality. Third, Catholic moral discourse since the Council
is person-centered. The particular understanding of the nature of the
human person in this tradition gives Catholic ethical discourse a particular slant which might in some ways be different from other traditions
of moral discourse. Fourth, there is respect for institutional objectives in
Catholic moral theology. In other words, moral discourse in this tradition
has an eminently pastoral goal: to help the individual attain his or her supernatural end. Finally, and as a consequence of all of the above, Catholic
moral theology is a tradition-based discourse which has its own canon of
rationality and justification of human action. It must be pointed out immediately that we are not speaking here of "discoveries" in the sense of
findings which no one had known of previously. Thus the areas of development of which I speak here are either insights which were perhaps
known before but neglected, or approaches which could be said to be la-
tent in the tradition but which became dominant in the discussions which
took place in post–Vatican II moral theology.

Catholic Moral Theology as God-talk

Catholic moral theology is God-talk. Although this may not always seem
obvious, given the emphasis on reason and natural law, moral theology

has always understood itself as theology. This means that even when it is
engaged in speculative reasoning which appears to have nothing specifically theological about it, moral theology has understood such an attempt
as an effort of faith seeking understanding, or more precisely, as an effort
of faith seeking rational grounds for human action. The manuals generally
stressed the theological nature of the discipline in their definition of moral
theology. In his manual, which had been in use before Vatican II, Eduard
Génicot defines moral theology as "that part of *theology* [emphasis added]
which considers the human act in regard to the supernatural happiness (of
the human person)." While the material object of moral theology is the
human act, its formal object is the capacity of the human act to lead the
human person to supernatural happiness.[6] Henry Davis defines moral theology also as that branch of *theology* which states and explains the laws of
human conduct in reference to the supernatural destiny of the human person, which is "the vision and fruition of God." Davis notes that moral theology assumes the existence of God, the fact of a supernatural human
destiny, the possibility of attaining such a destiny by human acts with the
help of divine grace, the freedom of the will, and the existence of a teaching infallible Church. Thus, according to Davis, there are three elements
which distinguish moral theology from all other forms of ethics. First,
moral theology assumes the fact of a divine mandate. Second, it is part of
an ecclesiastical tradition. Third, it presupposes a supernatural order.
Davis might also have added that it is an exercise of reason.

A closer look at Davis's attempt to differentiate moral theology from
other forms of moral discourse immediately reveals the tension which has
always dogged moral theology as theology; and moral theology as a human
rational attempt to supply answers to the questions of how to determine
right and wrong human conduct, and to determine the direction of human
action in this world. We have so far in this book spoken of this tension in
terms of the relationship between faith and ethics or in terms of the distinctiveness of Christian ethics. While noting that moral theology relies on
divine revelation for determining right and wrong, Davis also states that
philosophical ethics, on the other hand, relies on human reason and is
perfectly capable of arriving at the rightness or wrongness of human action based on human reason. The difference then is that reason in moral
theology operates within a milieu which acknowledges divine revelation
as a source of ethical insight.

As I have said already, Catholic theology assumes a close rapport between faith and reason as allies in the search for truth. In chapter 4, I
showed the roles played by Clement of Alexandria and subsequently by

Thomas Aquinas, among many others, in achieving the reconciliation of revelation and reason as partners in the Catholic theological tradition. This reconciliation is built on the understanding that rational nature is not destroyed by its supernatural elevation, but is rather perfected by it. Hence, Catholic moral theology has for a long time spoken of reason informed by faith. The reason that is meant here is reason which has been so transformed by faith that it operates out of what Karl Rahner used to refer to as a "moral instinct of faith." This reason "sees" with an eye of faith because it is part of the new creation which has been made so, according to Paul, by the death and resurrection of the Lord Jesus.

One of the important developments in moral theology since the Council, as we have already seen, is the recognition among theologians that for the Christian, the moral life is a life lived in response to God, who has revealed himself in Jesus Christ. The Christian faith teaches that God so loved the world that he sent his Son to save the world. The incarnation is, as it were, a statement of love and commitment from God toward the human race. Jesus' love—that is, the love of God—is very evident in his life and teaching but especially in his death. As St. Paul says, "God proves his love for us in that while we still were sinners Christ died for us" (Rom 5:8). Jesus thus reveals to us a new face of God and a new basis for understanding the world. The response of the Christian believer to God's revelation in Christ is total commitment of the whole person to God—that is faith. As Pope John Paul II has said, faith is first of all obedient response to God which implies that God is to be acknowledged as divine, transcendent, and supreme freedom. By faith, human beings give assent to God's testimony about himself. In other words, they acknowledge "fully and integrally the truth of what is revealed because it is God himself who is the guarantor of that truth."[7] As Joseph Sittler puts it, to be a Christian is to accept what God gives. What God gives is Jesus Christ as God's self-giving love. The faith response is itself *empowered* by the God who is himself the author of our redemption.[8] There are thus two fundamental issues in the Christian moral discourse. The first is the response in faith to God's self-disclosure in Christ, which we have already mentioned. The second aspect in the Christian moral discourse is that it is a call to discipleship. This not only implies that Christians look to Christ for guidance, inspiration, and challenge, but it means as well that Christians find the life and teaching of Jesus normative for the way they order their own lives.

We have also seen throughout this work that although Christians generally agree on the normativity of Jesus, they do not always agree on how

to understand his normativity in moral matters or even on what it means
to say that his teaching and life are normative. The problem is how a Jew
(or anyone else) who lived in mostly rural Palestine of the first century can
determine for the peoples of the twenty-first century the way to live and to
construct their world. A possible answer and one that is frequently heard as
the world becomes more and more secular is that Jesus is not normative for
today. His teaching and his life may have been inspirational in some sense
but that is all. The world today is and has to be organized on terms totally
different from his teaching. Such an answer misses what is obvious—that
millions of people today still live in ways which show that they find real
significance and meaning in the life and teaching of Jesus. These people
pattern their lives on his teaching and life and get directions from these for
the way they try to organize their lives and the world. A second answer to
the question of the normativity of Jesus would be to try to pattern one's
own life on an imitation of Jesus, in the sense that one would try to live as
if Jesus had already anticipated every moral quandary which would come
our way in the twenty-first century. Such an approach would amount to
fundamentalism because it ignores some of the real differences in time and
understanding of reality in general which mark the time of Jesus and our
own time.

Moral theology has in recent times tried to reconcile these two extremes. As God-talk, moral theology has shown itself to be the believer's
reasoned attempt to find in what ways the faith we bear as Christians in
the life, teaching, and mission of Christ can be brought to bear on how we
live our lives in this world. Moral theology is an effort of reason. But it is,
as I said above, an effort of reason informed by faith in Christ. This is
what makes moral theology distinct from all other forms of ethical discourse. This distinctness is sometimes evident in the issues with which
moral theology is concerned and in the presuppositions it brings to the
answers to commonly debated questions. Let us briefly consider the issue
of contraception.

The debate on contraception in the Catholic Church, especially since
the Second Vatican Council, has baffled many outsiders, who seem hard-
pressed to find justification for the amount of attention this issue has received and the level of acrimony it has generated within the Catholic
community. For many people outside the Church the use of artificial contraception is justified not only on personal grounds of privacy rights but
also on other grounds like population control, the rights of women to
choose, avoidance of unwanted pregnancy (especially for teenagers), the

need to stem the spread of diseases such as HIV and other sexually transmitted diseases, and so on. These considerations, in this view, render the
issue moot. The only worry is how to find ways to make the means of
birth control more effective and more readily available. Thus, the position
of the Catholic Church on contraception and abortion has been a serious
source of dispute even in international forums where reproductive issues
are discussed, as in the United Nations International Conference on Population in 1994. The Catholic Church is often accused of "intransigence,"
wanting to keep women under control and domination by men, insensitivity to the plight of those suffering from HIV/AIDS or other sexual diseases which could be alleviated or contained through the use of condoms,
insensitivity to the plight of poor families who could not continue to care
for their increasingly large families, and so forth. It is not necessary to address these charges directly here since other writers have already evaluated
them in a most admirable way.[9] What is important here is to point out that
such accusations often fail to understand the fundamental basis of these
positions.

The position of the Catholic Church on contraception is based on a
certain view of God and an understanding of the human person (including human sexuality) which flows from this theology. Whereas other persons outside the Catholic Church might see the issue of contraception
from other grounds, the issue is, for the Catholic Church, eminently a theological one. It is tied up with God's will and God's purposes in the world.
It is also connected then with the eternal destiny of the individual. Most of
the interlocutors in the debate on this issue in the Catholic Church share
these assumptions. This is why the issue is even considered important
enough to merit all the attention and time it has gotten and to be put at
the forefront of ethical discourse in the Catholic Church. What the interlocutors do not always share is agreement on the way God's will can be interpreted or read in the matter.

A careful look at the debate on contraception in recent Catholic moral
theological history will reveal basic assumptions about God, the Church
as mediator of God's will and presence in the world, and about the human
person, which sustain the interest on this issue which would otherwise be
considered marginal or as settled by the rest of society. I do not mean to
suggest that the particular points about nature and biological processes, or
about artificiality and physicality, or about the institutional Church and
the individual conscience are not important. All that is being suggested is
that the very discussion on contraception is important in the Catholic tra-

dition not just because it is a matter of human sexuality, but more fundamentally because it is a God-question. What is involved are particular understandings of God and of God's purposes in the world. It is this fact of
God which both sets the agenda for moral theological discourse in the
Catholic Church, especially since the Council, and even supplies many of
the terms on which many of the issues are debated. Therefore, when the
opponents of the teaching of the Church on contraception argue that the
Church cannot teach authoritatively on the issue, for whatever reason,
they are in effect saying that contraception must not be seen as a theological issue. Such a position cannot be sustained, given the particular understanding of God and the human person operative within the Catholic
tradition. We shall return to this issue later.

What has been said here about contraception as part of the theological
self-understanding of the Church is applicable also to many of the issues
which have been discussed in this book. The discussion on the nature of
the magisterium and the role of the magisterium in teaching morality presupposes a God-given teaching office of the pope and the bishops in the
Church. The use of natural law and the role of the human person as autonomous being in morality all imply in some way the understanding of
God as supreme legislator. As in the case of contraception, these presuppositions are not without problems. One such problem is how to understand the role of God as supreme legislator vis-à-vis the human person
who is autonomous and possesses free will. Another problem arises from
the discussion on the distinctiveness of Christian ethics and on the relationship between faith and ethics. The question in this regard concerns the
way in which the promise of eternal life is relevant to or related to human
action in this world. Josef Fuchs, among many others, has raised this
issue. Vatican II, to my mind, has given a cogent and compelling response
to the question. We will return to these questions shortly. What I am interested in here is to acknowledge what is very obvious but rather neglected about moral theology: that it is a reasoned discussion about the
implications of the self-disclosure of God in Jesus for the way we organize
life in this world.

Revelation and Reason in Catholic Moral Theology

Moral discourse in the Catholic tradition is also characterized by the understanding that there is continuity between the common human morality

and revealed morality. We have amply demonstrated this relationship in the main body of this work, especially in the chapters on natural law, Scripture, and the distinctiveness of Christian ethics. The basic assumption is that God has spoken and continues to speak. The Christian Scriptures represent a privileged articulation of God's will for the world. However, logically prior to God's revelation in Scripture God has also spoken through the created order. Thus, as Lisa Cahill says, the Catholic position on natural law implies an understanding that "moral values and obligations are grounded in a moral order known by human reason reflecting on experience."[10]

There is great emphasis on the nearness of God to his creation in the Catholic tradition. Andrew Greeley has shown in a recent book on the Catholic imagination how much Catholics believe that God's love is evident and sacramentally mediated by so many aspects of creation.

> The objects, events, and persons of ordinary existence hint at the nature of God and indeed make God in some fashion present to us. God is sufficiently like creation that creation not only tells us something about God but, by so doing, also makes God present among us. Everything in creation, from the exploding cosmos to the whirling, dancing and utterly mysterious quantum particles, discloses something about God and, in so doing, brings God among us. The love of God for us, in perhaps the boldest of all metaphors, . . . is like the passionate love between man and woman. God lurks in aroused human love and reveals Himself to us . . . through it.[11]

Like all living traditions, the Catholic tradition shapes the imagination in a distinct way through its ritual and other practices, belief systems, and linguistic utterances. The greatest symbol which affects most decisively the way the Christian regards life and construes moral obligation is God. Here is what Andrew Greeley says in his book about the Catholic imagination: "Catholics live in an enchanted world, a world of statues and holy water, stained glass and votive candles, saints and religious medals, rosary beads and holy pictures. But these Catholic paraphernalia are mere hints of a deeper and more pervasive religious sensibility which inclines Catholics to see the holy lurking in creation. As Catholics, we find houses and our world haunted by a sense that the objects, events, and persons of daily life are revelations of grace."[12] The deeper reality to which these paraphernalia point is the reality of God who is ever present to the human person to direct him or her to the truth of himself.

harmony of faith &
reason—

We have spoken in this book of the Catholic defense of the harmony
between faith and reason. The defense of this harmony must not be un- *defend*
derstood to imply the assimilation of reason by faith. One of the hall- *autonomy*
marks of Catholic theology since Clement of Alexandria has also been the *of both*
vigorous defense of the autonomy of both spheres—the sphere of faith
and the sphere of reason. The First Vatican Council taught that the truth
taught by reason and that taught by faith are neither mutually exclusive
nor identical. It means that each has its own sphere of interests and inquiry and yet each is related to the other. Pope John Paul II speaks of this
relationship between the knowledge of faith and the knowledge of reason
in this way:

> The world and all that happens in it, including history and the fate of
> peoples, are realities to be observed, analysed and assessed with all
> the resources of reason, but without faith ever being foreign to the
> process. Faith intervenes not to abolish reason's autonomy nor to re-
> duce its scope for action, but solely to bring the human being to un-
> derstand that in these events it is the God of Israel who acts. Thus the
> world and the events of history cannot be understood in depth with-
> out professing faith in God who is at work in them. Faith sharpens
> the inner eye, opening the mind to discover in the flux of events the
> workings of providence.[13]

Since the second half of the twentieth century, Catholic scholars have
moved beyond discussion of the harmony between faith and reason understood as philosophy to a discussion of the harmony between faith and
culture. Since culture includes all human achievement in all fields, the axiological, the ethical, the technological, and the symbolic, it has a wider
scope than simply science or philosophy. This expanded notion of reason
finds support in the work of the Second Vatican Council. The Council, as
we have seen, vigorously defends the autonomy of culture. Culture is so
essential to the makeup of the human person that it is part of the mission
of the Church to encourage "the human spirit to develop its faculties of
wonder, of understanding, of contemplation, of forming personal judgements and cultivating a religious, moral and social sense."[14] Culture as
human creation can also be contaminated with evil and thus is in need of
the salvific action of Christ.

The good news of Christ continually renews the life and culture of
fallen humanity; it combats and removes the error and evil which

flow from the ever present attraction of sin. It never ceases to purify
and elevate the morality of peoples. It takes the spiritual qualities and
endowments of every age and nation and enriches them with heavenly
resources, causes them to bear fruit, as it were, from within; it fortifies,
completes and restores them in Christ. In this way the Church carries
out its mission and in that very act it stimulates and advances human
and civil culture, as well as contributing by its activity, including liturgical activity, to humanity's interior freedom.[15]

The point being stressed here is that the Catholic tradition continues to
see the human sphere as also the sphere in which the divine is evident.
The incarnation reveals, as the title of the late Catherine Lacugna's book
states, a "God [who is] with us." The expanded interest in culture as a
locus of divine revelation is particularly evident in the renewed attempt at
inculturation in the post–Vatican II Church. Often when people speak of
inculturation they seem to assume that this is something dogmatic theologians and liturgists do. The fact is that moral theologians since the Council have been involved in trying to find ways the gospel can remain in
constant dialogue with modern cultures. Consider, for example, all the
efforts that have been made by theologians since the Council to address
public and social policy issues, ranging from abortion, euthanasia, cloning,
and stem cell research, to issues of poverty, debt relief for poorer countries, capital punishment, and racism. Many Catholic ethicists have
sought to articulate these issues from their particular points of view as
Catholics and to offer their reflections to the wider community in the understanding that what they think about these issues has also some measure of persuasiveness as do the ethical reflections of any other groups or
persons.

As was indicated in chapter 3, the Catholic position on the relationship between faith and reason reveals an incredibly optimistic strain in the
tradition with regard to God's action in the world of non-Christianity. Karl
Rahner's position on non-Christian religions was shown to be indicative of
such optimism. However, it also reveals some of the problems which have
always dogged the Catholic tradition on the matter. Even though, as
William Spohn points out, Rahner's theory of grace addresses the major
puzzles for many contemporary Christians, such as "how can some religiously indifferent people live exemplary, even heroic, moral lives?,"[16] it
has helped to raise an old question in a more acute way. The question
which has continued to be debated in the Catholic tradition with regard to

the relationship between revealed morality and natural law morality is whether revelation does indeed add anything new to human morality which is not known or cannot be known through the exercise of reason. We have noted the various responses to this question. We must recall that the discussion on the relationship between revealed morality and natural law arose in part from a moral theology which wanted to enter into critical dialogue with other intellectual systems of the day. Such an engagement was made possible by many factors which have already been discussed. However, it represented a new expression of the traditional Catholic belief in the basic goodness of the created order, as well as in the ability of the human mind and will to know and do what is right and good in spite of original sin—a belief that has also been fueled in recent times by the teaching of the Second Vatican Council on the goodness and autonomy of the created order.

Normally, one should expect a few pitfalls in a situation where there is assumed to be continuity between revealed morality and human morality. One of them would be the danger of a too-quick assumption that we can read the mind of God, even in those situations where this might not be too obvious. The dissenting voices in the birth control debate represent in part a contestation of this claim on the ground that there is a limit to what we can know about God's purposes through nature. The other perennial danger comes with a too-facile doctrine of sin. One Protestant writer has charged that the Catholic doctrine of sin "leaves too much confidence in human beings to know and do the right thing."[17] St. Thomas Aquinas himself was concerned that we may not always advert to the full effects of sin on our ability to know God's will. "Yet because human nature is not altogether corrupted by sin, namely, so as to be shorn of every good of nature, even in the state of corrupted nature it can, by virtue of its natural endowments, perform some particular good, such as build dwellings, plant vineyards, and the like; yet it cannot do all the good natural to it, so as to fall short in nothing."[18] The denial by some Catholic theologians that revelation contributed anything new to morality save in motivation was in some ways a refusal to accept the limits which sin imposes on moral knowing. Such denial therefore threatened to offset the delicate corrective which revelation had been thought to provide to moral knowing, even in Catholic ethical tradition. Proportionalism was sometimes also guilty of this disregard of the limitations of reason as a result of sin in its efforts to set standards for what could be regarded as proportionate reason for choosing to do evil in a particular situation of conflict. There was hardly any discussion of the effects of sin on the decision regarding what war was justified or not, for example. With regard to war, little attention was paid to the fact that every war is a triumph and incarnation of evil of one sort or another for which we should all feel remorseful, even if we had proportionate reason for justifying it. These problems notwithstanding, the Catholic moral theological discourse in the years after Vatican II has admirably held on to the understanding not only that God's will has been expressed in revelation but also that this will is knowable by all in whatever place and situation. This knowledge is available for the salvation of the world.

The Anthropological Bases of Catholic Moral Theology

All ethics is about human persons and their actions. One of the most important achievements of post–Vatican II moral theology has been the shift of focus from "human nature" to "the human person" as a methodological approach to moral reasoning. As Brian Johnstone points out, to describe the change as simply a move from nature to person would be misleading. Rather, what is taking place is "a transition from a methodology based on a particular interpretation of human reality or 'anthropology' and a particular account of moral reasoning, to another methodology, also including an account of human reality and an account of moral reasoning." This change, which is still ongoing in moral theology, has been described as a move from a "physicalist paradigm" to a "personalist paradigm."[19]

Although some European existentialists and phenomenologists had provided the foundation for the attention to the person in moral thinking and had thus "become fecund influences on Catholic thought" on this issue,[20] much of the impetus for the personalist thinking in Catholic moral theology in recent times comes from the Second Vatican Council. Equally important as well is the fact that much of the criteria—that is, the particular account on which post–Vatican II personalism was based—comes from the account of the human reality which is articulated in the documents of the Council and has become an architectonic idea in the work of many moralists after the Council.[21] One of the most prominent features of the moral theology of the Second Vatican Council is what it says concerning the way this personalism can function as a moral methodology. In the second part of *Gaudium et Spes,* which is essentially a development of the themes found in the social encyclicals, we find the beginnings indeed of a personalist methodology. Although what the Council had immediately in mind here is the regulation of birth, what it says here has been used in other areas since the Council: "When there is a question of harmonizing conjugal love with the responsible transmission of life, the moral aspect of any procedure does not depend solely on sincere intentions or on an evaluation of motives. It must be determined by objective standards. These, based on the nature of the human person and his acts, preserve the full sense of mutual self-giving and human procreation in the context of true love" (51). Two issues need to be discussed here. First is to ascertain in what ways the personalist emphasis of the Council has indeed influenced the work of theologians since the Second Vatican Council. The second is to show how a personalist methodology is indeed different from what went before in the Catholic moral tradition.

To answer the first question we must begin with the way contemporary moral theology has tried to provide an expanded and more inclusive index of the notion of the human person. Of course, this expanded list is not totally exclusive to Catholic theologians, nor does it owe all of its impetus to the Second Vatican Council. However, the imprint of the Council is clearly discernible as inspiration and with regard to content.

The notion of person and of what determines personhood is sometimes a hotly debated one in the general literature. There are two sides to the issue: the first has to do with what can be termed the indices of human personhood; the second concerns the qualities appropriate for human beings in their pursuit of their ends and goals. For some, personhood is the quality of being distinct from a thing. In this regard, every human being is a person, as opposed to a house, a tree, a mountain, a car, and so on, which are things. The distinguishing feature here is that whereas the value of things depends upon the degree and kind of service they may be to us in the execution of our aims, persons cannot, on the other hand, merely be used as means to someone's end; they are, as Kant would say, "end-in-themselves and sources of value in their own right."[22]

Much of the modern philosophical definition of the human person in Western consciousness flows from the definition given by Boethius toward the end of the fifth century A.D. of person as *naturae rationalis individua substantia* (an individual substance of a rational nature). Thus, for Kant, a person is a being conscious of its identity through time. For Leibniz a person is that which conserves "the *consciousness* or the reflective inward feeling of what it is." These definitions of personhood center on the ability of a being to be rational and to perform self-conscious acts. The same is true of the views of the theologian and ethicist Joseph Fletcher, who maintains that the following functional characteristics are determinants for the personhood of any being: minimal intelligence, self-awareness, self-control, a sense of the past, a sense of the future, a capacity to relate to others, concern for others, communication, control of one's existence, curiosity, change and changeability, balance of rationality and feeling, idiosyncrasy and neocortical function. The last mentioned is for Fletcher the hinge that holds all other qualities together.[23] There are also theories of human personhood which ascribe personhood to a being mostly on relational grounds. Here human personhood is characterized by man's relation to the world, by his having a nature, and by his living in community. Human beings live in interdependence, and through a common social life determine their nature and define their personhood.[24]

These theories and others on this issue are serious attempts to establish who are to be considered members of the human community. The outcome of this attempt has far-reaching consequences in such areas as abortion, euthanasia, and the treatment of persons with disabilities. In other words, whether a human being is treated as mere substance or part of a collective, or is taken seriously, depends on whether he or she is considered a human person like everyone else. Thus, the purely legal definition with its tendency to exclude segments of humanity from the concept of the person raises very troubling problems and prospects. So does the tendency to define persons in terms of rationality and the ability to perform conscious acts. This stress on rationality further raises the old issue of actuality and potentiality. Since the criterion of actual rationality cannot be applied to the unborn, for example, the question is whether we can apply to it the criterion of potential rationality, for after all, as Tertullian would say, "He is a man who will become a man." Joseph Fletcher's stress on neocortical function as the hinge and conclusive determinant of personhood clearly implies that the anencephalic infant, the severely mentally retarded, and the elderly suffering from the most severe stage of Alzheimer's disease or who is in a state of vegetation cannot be admitted into the community of persons. This would be wrong.

In line with the Christian tradition and echoing the Second Vatican Council, many moral theologians continue to insist to the contrary that all human beings are made by God in his image and likeness and are thus constituted into persons by the very act of creation. All persons are of equal worth and equally loved by God "even when it is obvious that not all persons possess an equal capacity for self-conscious activity." Thus, infants, "idiots," brain-damaged persons, and fetuses are all valued by God in this Christian perspective even though they are not capable of conscious activity and of all the neocortical activities with which "persons" are associated in the modern world.[25] Thus, "the value of the human individual does not depend on its physiology, as Fletcher believes, or merely on the fact that this physiology will eventually lead to functional differences which are morally relevant, as the classical position holds. Neither physiology nor potentiality alone, nor both of them together, constitutes the source for human personhood or gives the reason for respecting the human being. Each human being has an intrinsic dignity which is not subject to whims and calculations."[26] The greatest affirmation of this alien dignity "is of course, God's Word-become-flesh. As Christ is of God, and Christ is *the man,* so all persons are God's, his darlings, deriving their dignity from the value He is putting on them."[27] As Marjorie Reiley Maguire puts it, "In Christian theology, a person is a being who is so valued and loved by God that God would be willing to die for this being—symbolized by Jesus' death on the cross." Consequently, a person is a being who should be loved and valued the same way God loves and values persons, someone who should be treated as sacred by the human community. This is in itself the very foundation of all morality.[28]

One theologian who has tried to establish a complete theory of the human person in Catholic ethics since the Council is Louis Janssens, who taught for many years before and after the Council at the Catholic University of Louvain in Belgium. The influence Janssens's theory of the human person has had in the whole discussion on personalism in Catholic moral theology in the postconciliar years makes it deserving of some attention here.

Louis Janssens's personalism is built upon an understanding of the human person in all his or her aspects. Janssens lists these "aspects" as follows: the human person is an embodied and moral subject with a conscience and is called to act in freedom and responsibly; the human person is marked by corporeality and is therefore part of the material world; the human person is a relational being and directed to the other. Persons need to live in social groups with structures and institutions that are worthy of them. Human persons are open to transcendence. Hence they are called to know and worship God. The human person is a historical being with successive life stages and continuing new possibilities. Each human person is unique. However, all human persons are fundamentally equal.[29] Janssens has tried to formulate from the various dimensions of the human person a general criterion for determining right and wrong conduct . For Janssens, an act is morally right if it is beneficial to the human person in himself—that is, as a free, responsible, and embodied moral subject—and in his relations—that is, as a material, relational, social being.

Many theologians since the Council have consciously tried to identify themselves as personalists and to espouse the idea of personalism. This move has had enormous implications especially with regard to the understanding of moral norms. In this regard, moral norms as concrete actions which prescribe or proscribe an action are viewed according to whether they promote or attack a human value. Much of the debate on norms and moral methodology in post–Vatican II moral theology in the Catholic Church has been devoted to determining which actions meet these criteria and when they do so. Those actions which promote a particular value are thought to be prescribable, whereas the actions which generally attack a value are proscribed. However, whether an action promotes or attacks a value is determined according to its relation to the order of persons. The basic constant requirement, what one can therefore call the credo of personalist moral theology since the Council, is the promotion of the human person adequately considered—that is, in all his or her aspects. This has become the basis of moral obligation. The problem, however, is what criteria to use in determining when the interest of the human person has been adequately taken care of.

Brian Johnstone argues that three strands of personalism are evident in contemporary moral theology. The first is what he refers to as "ontological, complementary personalism," which tries to extend the account of human reality to include certain aspects of the person and by so doing enlarges the objective features which are available for consideration by reason as it makes moral judgments. Thus, where previously moral judgments would normally be made on the bases of mere biology, attention is also now paid to the ontological nature of the person as well. Johnstone writes, "In short where a norm was once defended because it derived from the structure of biology, the same norm is now upheld because it derives from the structures of the person." Johnstone cites *Donum Vitae*, the *Instruction on Respect for Human Life in Its Origin and on the Dignity of Procreation,* as an example of a document which promotes this type of personalism.[30] Johnstone also isolates a second brand of personalism which he refers to as "totalist, revisionist personalism." Like the first type, this brand of personalism goes beyond biology and takes into consideration all aspects of the human person. The basic difference here, according to Johnstone, is that the old

act-analyses approach to moral reasoning is replaced "with the discernment of proportionate reason, according to the 'proportionalist' method."
This method, according to Johnstone, may lead to a modification of some
previously accepted norms. A third form of personalism, "the personalism
of the dignity of conscience," while including a wider range of possibilities, — 3
"stresses such elements as freedom and conscience." This is the case, according to Johnstone, with *Gaudium et Spes.*

Johnstone notes the advantage of the first form of personalism especially in regard to the justification of organ donation. Whereas an earlier
act-centered methodology of the manualist tradition would argue that
such transplants were intrinsically immoral since, based on the argument
from finality, the organ was made to serve the body of its possessor and
not the body of the recipient, ontological personalism would justify such
an act on the basis of human interrelatedness.[31] Johnstone maintains that
although this type of personalism can make a successful case for modify-
ing an existing norm, it is a transitional stage in the change to the new
paradigm. In other words, it is not yet quite personalism. Johnstone also
faults the revisionist form of personalism on the grounds that it does not
quite explain what the various dimensions of the human person, such as
sociality, relationality, and so forth, may mean. "Is the list of dimensions
intended as a descriptive phenomenology, or an ontology or a hierarchical
list of values? It seems to be a catalogue of dimensions with no unifying
principle."

I believe that Johnstone's classifications may be somewhat misleading
if taken too far. First of all, all personalist approaches in recent Catholic
theology have gone out of their way to include the person in all his or her
aspects. This understanding is not bound to yield the same results. Thus,
for example, it is wrong to assume that Vatican documents like *Donum
Vitae* arrive at conclusions different from those of certain theologians on
issues pertaining to sexuality because they apply only limited personalist
criteria such as ontology and thus disregard the other aspects of the humanity of the person in their consideration of what is normative in sexual
matters. Second, it is also wrong to assert that there is no unifying element
in the anthropological dimensions which theologians like Janssens employ
in their work. These dimensions are only a way to describe what is in fact
an indivisible entity—that is, the human person. Any attempt to determine the needs of the human person adequately considered must keep all
these dimensions in dynamic tension. Even so, some dimensions could at
a particular point be considered more in need of attention than others.

This is the source of the ongoing tension and debate over norms and moral methodology in Catholic moral theology since the Council.

The proportionalist debate that has been discussed in this book is built around the need to determine what actions are beneficial to the needs of the human person *qua* human person. There is a general understating that it is not always easy to determine what particular procedures or forms of conduct are for the overall good of the person. The proportionalist argument is that the assessment of such actions or procedures must consider the various aspects of the action or procedure—exterior action, intention, circumstance, and consequences—before an adequate moral assessment can be made to determine whether an action is worthy of the human person or appropriate to him. One of the disturbing aspects of proportionalism is that some of the proponents seem to suggest sometimes that only when the above questions have been determined can an action, even one which is good *ex objecto,* be without blame. For example, in speaking of what he refers to as the Roman model of morality, Janssens uses the case of giving food to the hungry to differentiate between the so-called Roman model of morality and proportionalism. For him, the Roman model derives the morality in this instance primarily from the good of the object itself, while ignoring the motive of the giver of the food. For example, this action could be done out of a need to look good or from a genuine desire to help the poor. Although Janssens grants that the act of feeding the hungry by itself is good, he states, however, that the morality of the action in this case can be determined only by what the motive is for this action—that is, on whether the donor is acting out of egotism or from a true sense of altruism, whether, in other words, there is proportionate reason.

I believe that analyses like this again carry the idea of proportionality too far. First of all, this approach forgets that there can be nothing like complete altruism. Our actions are a mixture of a lot of tendencies of which we cannot always be fully aware. Second, feeding the hungry, as Janssens acknowledges, is always a good thing. It is not a bad thing no matter what the intentions are. Perhaps proportionalists should also acknowledge a class of morally good actions which cannot be bad whatever the circumstance, just as they acknowledge a class of bad actions which can be the right thing to do under certain circumstances. The point, in any case, is that, contrary to Johnstone's assertion that the reason for the different answers to the same issues between some Vatican documents and the position of some theologians is that the Vatican texts use limited personalist criteria while others employ a wider canvas, it would be more correct to say that even when the same personalist dimensions are taken into account, they are not stressed the same way by everyone, hence the differences in conclusions.

Personalism and Natural Law

One issue which has played a prominent role in what conclusions the various "personalisms" in Catholic moral discourse have reached on certain issues since the Council is natural law. In chapter 6 we examined the Thomistic teaching on natural law, as well as some of the debates over the way that teaching can be understood today. Important opposition to what I may call the classical Catholic position comes, again, from proportionalists. For these theologians, as Dolores L. Christie points out, "the autonomy and responsibility in freedom of the human person and the achievement of the human person rank above any so-called moral laws in nature."[32] In other words, we cannot derive a moral ought simply from a biological given. To do so would be to give in to physicalism, and is contrary to deriving the moral meaning of an action from the good of the person "adequately and integrally considered." Consider this quotation from Bernard Häring:

> A personalistic "natural law ethics" does not accept any taboo, since it does not adore created things. It is always a matter of understanding their final goal in view of the dignity of the persons and their relationship. Monotheism gives man a tremendous freedom toward the nonpersonal world, a responsible freedom which could never have become a common attitude under animism or pantheism. Man is called to shape the events, to transform the natural processes, and even to administrate his own biological and psychological heritage. The only moral limit is the dignity of every person and the building up of a brotherhood which as yet gives honor to the creator.[33]

What Häring says here raises a troubling question. It is difficult to see how "the only moral limit" to what natural law ethics can say about right and wrong conduct "is the dignity of every person and the building up of a brotherhood which . . . gives honor to the creator." An assertion like this comes perilously close to the famous situationism propounded by Joseph Fletcher in which the only thing required for an action to be morally right was for one to do "the loving thing." Häring is of course here addressing the situation in the past where an almost mechanical signifi-cance was attached to the so-called natural inclinations, and divine wis-dom was read into those natural inclinations from which norms were derived which were believed to be absolutely inviolable. As we have seen throughout the course of this work, many theologians since the Council have challenged this tendency on grounds that biological facticity alone is not sufficient as an indication of moral ought. While it may appear from the above passage that there are theologians who since the Council have held that the *biological givenness* of human sexuality *should not be considered* in determining what sexual acts are promotive or destructive of the good of the human person, it is important to realize that even among so-called revisionist theologians this view does not represent the position of most theologians on this matter. Here is a slightly different view from Richard McCormick, who I think captures more clearly the position of many Catholic theologians since the Council on this matter:

> Many contemporary theologians argue that the extent to which these "natural ends" must be respected in individual cases depends on whether they must deserve the preference when in relationship with concurring personal values. To decide that is the natural end of the power of human judgment. In other words, to say that procreation is the highest end served by sexual intercourse is not to say that such an end must always be served, or that its frustration is necessarily wrong.[34]

It seems to me that McCormick's stance here grants some importance to biological givenness even while it still holds that there must be more in the determination of what sexual practices do or do not promote the good of the human person, adequately considered. Let us return once more to the debate on human sexuality and marriage in the Catholic tradition to show how central the personalist criterion have become in the determina-tion of moral rightness or otherwise of human action.

The Personalist Criterion and the Catholic Teaching on Sex and Marriage

The Christian understanding of marriage implies that children are the greatest gift of the marriage relationship. As a gift, they are not the entitle-ment of anyone to be "acquired at all costs."[35] However, as Jean Porter points out, "they are a gift that should not be refused lightly."[36] Thus, there is widespread agreement among many Catholic theologians that "there is something problematic, from the Christian standpoint, in the deliberate choice to remain childless throughout a marriage." The Christian faith is deeply "profamily." Given its declared commitment to family and to procreation, we should, as Porter says, "expect the Christian community to discourage any use of contraceptives. We as a community cannot celebrate human procreation as a centrally important way of expressing our faith in the goodness of God's creation without also implying that the deliberate frustration of human fertility is at best regrettable."[37] As has been noted already, many of the interlocutors in this debate agree that every contraceptive choice is a regrettable one. For many, what is at issue in the debate is whether there are no moments when given the human situation such a choice cannot be a better option for a particular couple on a particular occasion. Many people have said that such judgments should be left to the individual couple. In any case, it seems to me too much to ask the Church not to say anything at all about this issue. The questions of human sexuality, marriage, procreation, and family are of such importance both to the Christian faith and to humanity in general that they must be part of the concerns of the gospel of Christ preached by the Church.

It is not my intention to revisit all aspects of the discussion on contraception. I have tried to do that in chapter 2. What I have tried to show here is that Catholic moral discourse since the Council has been decidedly carried out in personalistic terms. I have also argued that the debate on contraception also reflects this interest in seeking the good of the human person adequately considered, the various positions on the issue notwithstanding. I said above that these divergent opinions on contraception presuppose God in a certain way. In what follows, I will argue further that the debate on contraception since the Council masks some very important assumptions about the human person, especially human sexuality, and is indeed possible precisely because of these assumptions.

Some of the agreements behind the arguments on contraception in recent Catholic moral discourse can be stated as follows. First, there is a basic understanding among all the interlocutors in the debate on contraception that sex is a good gift from God. By sex here is meant the whole range of feelings and acts in which embodied persons engage in their process of relating to each other. This simple affirmation which has always been part of Christian teaching has become more evident today both in the teaching of the official Church and in the work of theologians and

others engaged in teaching and in discussion on this issue since Vatican II.
There is a new sense today that the incarnation of the Son of God is God's
affirmation of our sexuality and that therefore all Docetist tendencies are
contrary to the revealed word of God.[38] Thus all forms of Gnostic du-
alisms which ascribe sex and materiality to the evil one are wrong and
anti-Christian. The incarnation reaffirms the line from Genesis that God
considers all things he has made to be very good.[39] Second, it is understood here that human sexuality can also be sacramental—in the sense
that it can be a means through which God communicates himself and his
love through human beings to others. This is what the Second Vatican
Council meant when it referred to marriage as a community of conjugal
life and love. Third, it is understood that even though sex is a good gift
from God, it has been affected by sin as in all human situations. As a
result, human sexuality has had an ambiguous history and has been the
locus for very conflicting feelings and attitudes: love/anger, tenderness/
aggression, intimacy/adventure, romance/predatoriness, pleasure/pain,
empathy/power.[40] Thus, sex is not just a private affair. It is an issue of
communal concern as well which requires some regulation. Fourth, there
is agreement in recent Catholic theology that the aim of sexual morality is
to allow for the biological goals of reproduction as well as for the instinc-
tive need for pleasure, and to structure this fulfillment into a socially coherent scheme such as work and family where the individual can be
conscious of her or his social functions and personal creativity.

Finally, the Roman Catholic tradition has constantly offered one key
insight that, perhaps more that any other, has served to unify and give co-
herence to the many values pertinent to human sexuality. This key insight
is that genital sexual activity so deeply involves all the potentials of the
human person that it is best expressed in a stable and enduring union between a man and a woman. To put it in other words, the meaning of genital sexual activity is such that it calls for the personal union we know as
marriage. Only in the context of marital fidelity can genital sexual acts
have the possibility of accomplishing all the goodness for which the acts
are apt. Thus, in the Christian tradition sexuality is understood to be
meaningful within the framework of a stable and faithful union of man
and woman—that is, within a love relationship that is free, mature, creative, integrated.

These are only a few of the agreements which are assumed in the recent debate on contraception. None of them is a completely new discovery or insight; however, all of them have been brought into sharper focus
by several factors inside and outside the Church since the Second Vatican

Council and reflect the even more fundamental assumption within the Catholic community about the importance of human sexuality both for the continuation of the human race and for the fulfillment of other human needs.

The questions about the ways best to protect the human sexual and reproductive goods will go on as long as there are human beings in this world and in the Church. What impact should population and other considerations such as modern technologies have on the Church's views on human sexuality and reproduction? Is the homosexual lifestyle an acceptable and normative expression of our sexuality? As I stated above, the questions will continue as the community searches for ways to serve the good of the human person adequately considered. As Klaus Demmer has stated, the goal in this quest is "to find a middle ground between the extremes of a personalism that is forgetful of nature, on one hand, and a naturalism that is inattentive to the person, on the other."[41] Such a solution, while not suspending the biological dimension, would still certainly provide important hints in the formulation of moral judgment. For even though biological nature provides essential elements for the formulation of moral norms, the relevance of these elements for ethics may not always be apparent but must be carefully thought out.

Pastoral Goals

Moral theology in the Catholic Church has a basic institutional objective—that is, the salvation of the human race. If the aim of all theology is to help persons of faith to come to a better and more rational appropriation of their faith, moral theology as theological discourse is the attempt to work out the practical implications of the faith for daily living in obedience to the will of God. Everyone has the experience of being summoned by a moral claim and of being called to something greater than his or her whims and caprices, a moral claim which is absolute and uncompromising in its appeal. This call to moral truth is addressed to the person's total being and is the one chance we all have of living a worthwhile existence in this world. But beyond life in this world Christianity believes in an eternal existence to which all human beings are called. Thus, ethical discourse in the Catholic tradition has two essential aims: to help people and societies find ways of organizing a humane and livable world and to teach them what actions are conducive to being allowed to participate in the eternal life with God. Both of these aspects are interconnected and yet distinct.

We have seen throughout this book the teaching of the Second Vatican Council on the need to respect the autonomy of the earthly order. The Council warns against subordinating the earthly order to the supernatural order. This world is to be organized by human beings in ways that respect human dignity and freedom, out of human ingenuity and intelligence. However, while respecting the earthly order, the Council also reminds us that we, as human beings, "have no lasting city here." Thus, human action must be directed as well by our eternal destiny with God. The goal of moral discourse in the Catholic tradition is to keep these two ends in view in a way that respects their proper limits while keeping the tension alive. As the Council says, what we do in this world has important significance for our eternal destiny and salvation. This teaching has roots in the Christian Scriptures where it is taught that feeding the hungry or visiting the sick or working to comfort the afflicted in any way has eternal repercussions. In *Veritatis Splendor* Pope John Paul II was clear about the role of moral theology in evangelization. Evangelization, he wrote, "also involves the proclamation and presentation of morality."[42] Such a role implies, among other things, calling people to conversion and a life of holiness. And, it is the task and "vocation of the moral theologian" to be at "the service of the believing effort to understand the faith." This task can be carried out only, said the pope, by a theology which is in "profound and vital connection with the Church, her mystery, her life and her mission."[43]

One of the most intriguing developments in recent moral theology is the tendency by some theologians such as Josef Fuchs to disconnect the link between what we do here on earth and our salvation by speaking of moral rightness and moral goodness. Moral rightness, as Fuchs sees it, is concerned with how we organize our lives in this world. It has nothing to do with our salvation. Moral goodness, on the other hand, pertains to our eternal salvation. One can immediately see that this distinction arises out of the desire to respect the earthly order and autonomy of earthly things. However, stretched too far, this view misses the connection, which the Scriptures so eloquently speak about and which the Second Vatican Council so clearly taught about, between this world and the kingdom of God.

Specific Canons of Rationality

Another important characteristic of moral theology since the Council concerns the widespread agreement in the discipline on the importance of certain persons and events as benchmarks and reference points for what

history

can be regarded as acceptable bases for rational and authentic moral discourse in the Catholic tradition. I have mentioned already in the discussion on contraception that part of the problem in recent moral theology has to do with the way history is read in the Catholic Church today. Recent Catholic moral theology has enthroned some historical figures while ignoring others or relegating them to a lesser status. Consider the role of St. Augustine, especially in the area of marriage and sexuality. One consequence of the recent theology of marriage following the Second Vatican Council is the minimizing of Augustine's theology of marriage and human sexuality. *— citation?*

If Augustine's influence in certain aspects of recent moral theology has diminished somewhat, the influence of St. Thomas Aquinas has increased tremendously. Recall that Pope Leo XIII in *Aeterni Patris* had decreed a return to Thomas and the Scholastics as sources of theology. The result of the response of theologians to the pope's call has been quite obvious in *> Lottin ?* nearly all aspects of Catholic theology, except moral theology—until now. We know of the great efforts of people like Marachel, Rahner, Lonergan, and many other dogmatic (systematic) theologians who went to work on the theology of St. Thomas. We also know of the great centers of medieval studies in Toronto, Louvain, Notre Dame, and other places which have sprung up and flourished since *Aeterni Patris*. Many of these centers, theologians, and philosophers have devoted tremendous energy and resources to everything but moral theology. But much of that has changed since the Council. Although John Gallagher has written of the efforts the authors of the manuals made at the turn of the twentieth century to indicate their indebtedness to the work of Aquinas and the Scholastics, he also points out that such connection to the theology of St. Thomas was indeed very superficial.[44] Thus, for the first time since *Aeterni Patris*, the Thomistic revival which Leo XIII decreed has indeed reached moral theology.

Thomas Aquinas in Recent Moral Theology   *TA as canon*

The importance of the work of Thomas Aquinas in recent moral theology is evident in many ways. Aquinas has become canonical in Catholic moral discourse. To say that something has acquired canonical status is to say that the thing in question has become a norm for measuring other things. In recent Catholic moral theology, Aquinas's work has acquired canonical status as norm against which moral theological discourse is determined to be authentic, rigorous, and orthodox.

As I have tried to show already, Aquinas's natural law theory is the benchmark for understanding that theory today. Scholars have tried to develop other approaches to natural law in the wider tradition and in other traditions as well,[45] yet the Thomistic theory of natural law has remained for the Catholic moral theologian the normative basis for discussion. I am not implying that there is an uncritical appropriation of the teaching of St. Thomas on natural law in recent moral theology. What I am saying is that his work on this issue has increasingly in recent years become the prolegomenon to any discussion on the issue. Thus even when scholars like Grisez, McCormick, Curran, Fuchs, and Porter criticize some aspects of Thomas's theory or its interpretation in recent moral theology, their criticisms presuppose the basic importance and soundness of this theory.

The importance of Aquinas is also evident in the discussion on moral norms. Recall that virtually all attempts to reformulate moral norms in Catholic moral tradition in recent years have begun with a discussion on Thomas Aquinas on norms. This is the case from Joseph Mangan's initial discussion on the principle of double effect,[46] to the historic work of Peter Knauer on the reformulation of the principle,[47] to the various essays of Louis Janssens, Richard McCormick, Germain Grisez, and Lisa Cahill on the question of norms.[48] As I showed in chapter 8, the interlocutors in the debate on norms have tried to show that whatever position they hold is correct and Catholic because it represents in some ways either a true interpretation of the work of Aquinas or a legitimate offshoot of his position on norms. The revisionists go further to argue that they have Aquinas on their side when they hold that general moral principles are one thing, and the particular details and individual circumstances of the moral agent are another and must be taken into consideration when determining the agent's culpability or innocence. Finally, we saw the way some theologians, such as Jean Porter and James Keenan, have returned to Aquinas's theory of the virtues to try to discover alternative approaches to the norms debate. Even when these theologians criticize some aspects of the teaching of St. Thomas on the virtues, they do so against the basic assumption of the importance of this theory and its ability to provide the resources for proper evaluation of human action.

The importance of St. Thomas Aquinas in current moral theology is thus very great, and his work constitutes a very significant aspect of current moral theology. A look at the moral theology encyclicals of Pope John Paul II (of which we have written extensively in various parts of this book) also shows evidence that even the magisterium gives certain aspects of Aquinas's work near canonical stature. Moral theological discourse in recent Catholic history certainly relies on other thinkers and approaches as well. However, none of them approaches the importance of St. Thomas as guide and arbiter of authenticity, orthodoxy, and rigor in Catholic moral theology.

The Second Vatican Council   *V2 as canon*

Although I have spoken extensively about the Second Vatican Council throughout this work, a bit more must be said about the Council as canon for Catholic morality. A good deal of attention and energy in recent Catholic moral theology have been devoted to interpreting and furthering the thought of the Second Vatican Council. Whereas the Council of Trent was once the basis for determining the success and orthodoxy of theologians' work, the Second Vatican Council has now become the basis for such determination. As I tried to show in the first chapter, the Council's influence on moral theology is both inspirational and substantive. Many persons, including the hierarchy of the Church, have tried to show that they are the authentic heirs of the teaching of the Second Vatican Council on moral matters. The role of the magisterium in morality is usually debated on terms supplied by the Council, for example. There is contention among some whether recent teachings of the Church on contraception, moral norms, and the specificity of Christian ethics might in some ways constitute a betrayal of the moral teachings of the Second Vatican Council. No matter what side one is on in these debates the importance of the Second Vatican Council as canon and as reference point in recent Catholic theology is immense.

Catholic moral theology continues to advert to other important elements as sources of wisdom—the Scriptures, the Fathers, other writings and writers in the tradition, other academic disciplines such as philosophy, the social sciences, the behavioral sciences, the physical sciences, and so on. The above two elements—Aquinas and the Second Vatican Council—have been singled out because they have influenced Catholic moral thought in a way that is unique and particular to Catholic moral theology as Catholic and as theology.

*   *   *

What we have presented so far are only a few of the important elements which shape the Catholic moral tradition, thereby giving it its uniqueness. Some of these elements are shared by other Christian religious bodies, or even by other non-Christian communities to some extent. What makes them affect the Catholic moral tradition in a distinct way is the combination of all of them and the level of importance that the Catholic community attaches to them, singly and as a whole. These elements and many others taken together form the basis and the character of a moral tradition that is specifically Catholic. Therefore to be able to appreciate Catholic moral theology, its goals, its interests, and its contributions to general ethical discourse, one must take into account the fact that moral theology constitutes a tradition of moral discourse. This is to say, as has already been demonstrated, that moral theology begins with certain assumptions about the world and about the human person which are unique. These assumptions are part of the ethos of the Catholic Christian community which gives that community a certain identity. To understand that moral theology is a tradition-based discourse is to understand both the strengths and limitations of the discipline. Often one hears people complaining about certain tendencies in or demands on the discipline which want it to take up certain questions or concur with certain answers which have been arrived at by other forms of ethical discourse. The elements which I have highlighted in this chapter are meant as well to show why moral theology is different and why it is all right for moral theology to be different, just as it is all right for other forms of ethical discourse to be different in their assumptions and conclusions. All ethical discourses begin from some fundamental assumptions about the human person and the world, and hence are also tradition-based discourses in some way. Therefore the nature of moral theology does not make it or other forms of religious discourse an inferior or protected discourse, as some secular ethicists from the liberal academy have charged lately.

I have tried to show that Catholic moral theology *qua* Catholic moral theology derives its status from a narrative structure which is founded on belief in what Joseph Sittler refers to as "God's engendering deed" in Jesus Christ. This narrative structure provides a basis on which the believer is able to comprehend reality and to live in relation to that reality. It also provides the basis on which moral theology can be regarded as theology. The crisis of pre–Vatican II moral theology results precisely from its failure to remain attached to its Christian roots. Thus in the end what resulted was a "theology" which was rendered contextless and which ultimately turned into everything else but theology. One of the great strengths of contemporary moral theology has been the effort to stay in touch with its scriptural and ecclesial roots while remaining open to other traditions and approaches as well. This has also been one of the sources of the enduring problem of identity in the discipline: how to hold on to its valid insights about the human person and his or her actions in this world, and still manage to make sense to the outsider and be able to speak coherently and intelligibly even if not always persuasively to everyone about its conclusions.

Pope John Paul II
on Postconciliar Moral Theology:
An Epilogue and a Beginning

Nearly thirty years after the close of the Second Vatican Council and the publication of *Humanae Vitae*, Pope John Paul II issued an encyclical which in his own words was the first papal attempt to "set forth in detail the fundamental elements" of Christian moral teaching.[1] Although it had been in the making since 1987, when the pope promised on the feast of St. Alphonsus Liguori to write an encyclical which would treat "more fully and more deeply the issues regarding the very foundations of moral theology,"[2] the roots of the pope's letter go back even further to the directive from the Second Vatican Council for the renewal of moral theology and to the crises precipitated by *Humanae Vitae*. *Veritatis Splendor* is a papal assessment of the theological and pastoral responses to the Council's injunction and to some of the fallout from the various debates in the area of fundamental moral theology. This initial papal assessment of the developments in the area of fundamental moral theology was followed a few years later by another papal discourse on issues in the area of applied ethics in the encyclical *Evangelium Vitae*. What we have then, in *Veritatis Splendor* and *Evangelium Vitae*, and to some extent in *Fides et Ratio*, which followed a little later, is basically a papal report card on the outcome of the movement for renewal in moral theology since the Council. As report cards these papal texts take note of basic issues in fundamental moral theology and in the areas of applied or practical ethics. They cover issues relating to the nature of Christian morality, the sources of moral obligation, method, the questions relating to the moral agent, and the nature of moral agency and method, among others. Therefore these texts constitute a very important roadmap to the issues covered in moral theology since the Council. They are also important because of the weight of the authority behind them, which largely explains the widespread attention they have received.

I have decided to close this study of moral theology since Vatican II with the papal statement on moral theology in this period in order to ascertain the pope's position on issues central to the discipline. The chapter on *Humanae Vitae* and its aftermath examined the impact of a papal action on the development of moral theology since the Council. This chapter complements and completes that one as a study of the course another pope, John Paul II, believes the renewal could have taken and should indeed take. In a way, the works of Pope John Paul II under study here are part of a continuum of papal involvement in directing the course of Christian ethical discourse in the last century. In short, these two chapters show how moral theology has been influenced by the deliberate action of the magisterium of the Church.

This chapter has three main components. The first part is a reconstruction of the papal teaching in *Veritas Splendor* and *Evangelium Vitae*. The second looks at some of the critical reactions to the pope's project. In the third and final section, I offer some brief and tentative remarks of my own in which I will try to link the findings of the chapter with the discussion in the rest of the book.

The Pope on Postconciliar Moral Discourse

It would be safe to say that *Veritatis Splendor* might not have been issued if the pope had been satisfied with the fundamental emphasis of moral theology following Vatican II. In fact, aside from a passing reference to the work of theologians "who found support for their work in the Council's encouragement," there is little by way of appreciation for the massive efforts of so many people after the Council to renew moral theology. As we have seen, Catholic moral theology has been marked since the Council by a lot of disagreement. *Veritatis Splendor* points to the divisions even on crucial moral matters within and outside the Catholic community. Indeed the encyclical was born out of a sense of alarm at what the pope believed to be a growing trend toward relativism and individualism even within the Catholic community. Behind this trend, says the pope, is the growing influence of secular thought which has led some Catholics to "an overall and systematic calling into question of traditional moral doctrine on the basis of certain anthropological and ethical presuppositions," and even to "a denial of certain fundamental truths of Catholic moral doctrine."[3] In view of this, the pope is determined in the encyclical "to set forth, with regard to the problems being discussed, the principles of moral theology based upon Scripture and the Living Apostolic Tradition, and at the same time to shed light on the presuppositions and consequences of dissent which that teaching has met."[4] The pope pursues his stated intention in this encyclical in three chapters.

The first chapter, an extended meditation on the dialogue between Jesus and the rich young man in Matthew 19, provides a remarkable synthesis of the biblical basis of Christian morality. According to the pope, the young man's question "Teacher, what good must I do to have eternal life?" is the question every human person must ask who is serious about the human condition and the human situation. Thus, more than a mere pious reflection on an ideal, this section is indeed a serious invitation from the pope for all to consider the moral life on a much wider canvas than merely in terms of moral obligation. Oliver O'Donovan notes that the pope shows in his reflection in this first chapter that moral theology is a pastoral and evangelistic response "to the questions constantly thrown up by the human agent who needs to find a ground and an end of action. This response unfolds in a carefully ordered sequence of forms. It is teleological, it offers a conception of the good. It is deontological, proposing a code of moral commands. It is eschatological, arousing a hope of transcendent perfection."[5] The refection on the encounter between Jesus and the rich young man in *Veritatis Splendor* is therefore programmatic. It is intended to show that the ideal of moral perfection is meant to be "a normative standard for faithful Christian living" and vital to salvation. "It is not an optional ideal, but a basic requirement of Christian discipleship, not limited to an elite few but mandatory for all the faithful."[6] It is also intended as a critique of the understanding of morality which tended to border on a kind of brinkmanship, a carryover from the pre–Vatican II moral manuals. Many years after the Council, and in spite of so much debate, this brinkmanship still influences the concerns of the discipline as well as

pursuit of moral perfection

the ways most debates are carried out in regard to the moral good. Above all, the first chapter is a critique of the tendency among some theologians to dissociate faith completely from morals. The road to moral perfection passes by way of the cross and can sometimes lead to martyrdom. For most Christians, however, who will not have the privilege of dying a martyr's death, the call to moral perfection is a call to "a consistent witness which all Christians must daily make, even at the cost of suffering and grave sacrifice, even sometimes to a heroic degree."[7] As James Hanigan notes, the pursuit of and advance to the ideal of moral perfection is undertaken in a sinful world which makes the pursuit of such an ideal a most difficult and dangerous task. "This dangerous, conflict-laden situation highlights the urgency and the normativity of the ideal." It also shows that both the call to perfection and the ability to respond to that call are gifts of grace.[8]

In the second chapter, the pope surveys some currents in contemporary moral theology and finds many of them wanting and sometimes erroneous. These theories, according to him, distort moral truth by exalting freedom "to such an extent that it becomes an absolute, which would then be the source of moral values."[9] They advocate a complete sovereignty of reason in the domain of moral norms and turn conscience into an independent, ultimate, and infallible criterion for determining good and evil. The contrary, says the pope, is the truth. "The power to decide what is good and evil does not belong to man, but to God alone." Human freedom finds authentic and complete fulfillment in the acceptance of the moral law given by God who alone is omniscient and good, and by virtue of his love for humanity proposes what is good for humanity in the commandments.[10]

"truth"

In the third chapter the pope continues to paint a picture of a world in which the connection among freedom, truth, and goodness has been all but severed. Separated from the saving power of truth, freedom alone is left, by itself, to decide good and evil. Such relativism, he says, is tantamount to a denial of divine wisdom and of the fact that "when all is said and done, the law of God is always the one true good of man."[11] Behind the detachment of freedom from truth and goodness is a more serious disjunction of faith and morality, an attitude that denies any moral content to faith. Indeed, faith has a moral content, the encyclical says, and the final answer to morality lies in the crucified one alone. Faith in Christ calls for a life of commitment, "which is manifested and lived in the gift of self, even to the total gift of self in the supreme witness of martyrdom."[12]

The pope's main concerns in this encyclical can be summarized under three broad headings: the morally deplorable state of modern society, the responsibility of the Church for a moral renaissance of modern society, and the special tasks of bishops and theologians in the Church to aid human society.[13]

The State of Modern Society

Pope John Paul II has always been concerned with the state of modern culture. Earlier, in another context, he had for example spoken of a culture of consumerism in the modern world which can be damaging to the physical and spiritual well-being of the individual and society.[14] Although there is much to rejoice about in modern culture, with its technological progress, there is much cause for worry as well. According to the pope, one crucial cause for worry concerning modern societies is the phenomenon of growing secularism, a situation where more and more people "think and live 'as if God did not exist.'"[15] Secularism manifests itself in various ways. The first is by the denial of transcendent truth "in obedience to which man achieves his full identity."[16] In commenting on the collapse of Communism in the former Soviet Union and in Eastern Europe, Pope John Paul II argued that at the root of all totalitarianism is the denial of transcendent truth. When people refuse to acknowledge transcendent truth, then the force of power takes over, and each person tends to make full use of the means at his disposal in order to impose his own interests or his own opinion, with no regard for the rights of others. "The root of modern totalitarianism is to be found in the denial of the transcendent dignity of the human person who, as the visible image of the invisible God, is therefore by his very nature the subject of rights which no one may violate—no individual, group, class, nation or state."[17] Thus, in line with documents of Vatican II, especially the document on religious liberty, the pope argues vigorously that human beings are impelled by their nature and bound by moral obligation to seek truth.[18] Human beings have an inner duty to search for truth and to shape their lives by it through development of the intellect and formation of the conscience. This is an argument John Paul II would return to in his two other subsequent encyclicals on the issue of life and on the relationship between faith and reason. In the latter case, for example, he maintains that the Church has a specific responsibility, which is the *diakonia* of the truth. This mission of the Church makes the community of faith a partner with the rest of the world in the human quest for truth and obliges it to proclaim "the certitudes arrived at."[19] However, reason has its own specific field in which it can inquire and understand, "restricted by its finiteness before the infinite mystery of God."[20] Thus, it needs the light which comes from revelation and from faith to lead it beyond partial truth to the seminal plan of love which began with creation.[21]

A second indication of secularism in modern societies is the widespread individualism and exaggerated notion of individual autonomy which absolutizes freedom by detaching it from truth. This exaggerated sense of freedom is evident in the way many people regard conscience today and in a philosophical attitude which tends to deny human transcendence. The tendency in much of contemporary society, as the pope sees it, is that rather than consider conscience as the act of the person's intelligence charged with the task of applying here and now the universal knowledge of the good to specific situations with regard to the conduct to be chosen, "the individual conscience is accorded the status of a supreme tribunal of moral judgement which hands down categorical and infallible decisions about good and evil."[22] This is the kind of individualism that can lead to the denial of human nature. John Paul II insists that freedom is not an absolute which creates its own value. On the contrary, freedom establishes itself in the acceptance of truth contained and articulated in the moral law. As such, there is neither contradiction nor conflict between freedom, properly so called, and the moral law, for the moral law reflects the goodness of God, who alone knows what is perfectly good for the human person. Human freedom finds its fulfillment in the acceptance of the moral law given by God.[23] Indeed, without this ultimate reference human freedom cannot exist. Like the Second Vatican Council, the pope reaffirms the rightful autonomy due to every human person. However, this autonomy, rightly considered, means that there is a natural law to which created things must adhere. "Created things have their own laws and values which are to be gradually discovered and utilized and ordered by man." Human beings cannot be considered without reference to the creator, and autonomy itself cannot mean that human reason "itself creates values and moral norms"[24] or that "created things are not dependent on God and that man can use them without reference to their creator."[25]

Third, secularism is manifested today by the widespread denial of moral absolutes. There is, in the understanding of Pope John Paul II, a direct correlation between the denial of transcendence and the denial of moral absolutes. Thus "today's widespread tendencies towards subjectivism, utilitarianism and relativism appear not merely as pragmatic attitudes or patterns of behavior, but rather as approaches having a basis in theory and claiming full cultural and social legitimacy."[26] With the disappearance of moral absolutes there is nothing left but self-interest of various kinds to guide the relationship between people. The best that can be achieved in this situation is mere compromise in which any reference to common values is lost, giving way to complete relativism where "everything is negotiable, everything is open to bargaining: even the first of the fundamental rights, the right to life."[27] This relativism has so permeated the fabric of modern society and is now apparent in legal systems that justify certain laws based on majority whims and not on what is right. It is also evident in an understanding of democracy that considers relativism an essential condition of democracy, "in as much as it alone is held to guarantee tolerance, mutual respect between people and acceptance of the decisions of the majority, whereas moral norms considered to be objective and binding are held to be authoritarian and intolerant."[28] Pope John Paul II insists to the contrary that provisional and changeable majority opinion cannot be the basis for determining values in a democracy or in any other human society. It must be acknowledged that the objective moral law which, like the natural law, is written in the human heart is the obligatory point of reference for civil law itself. Thus, democracy cannot be idolized to the point where it is then substituted for morality or made a panacea for immorality. Democracy is not an end but only a means to an end. Its moral value is not automatic, "but depends on conformity to the moral law to which it, like every other form of human behavior, must be subject: in other words, its morality depends on the morality of the ends it pursues and the means which it employs." Thus the value of democracy stands or falls "with the values which it embodies and promotes."[29]

A central element in *Veritatis Splendor* is therefore the forceful *"reaffirmation of the universality and immutability of the moral commandments,* particularly those that prohibit always and without exception *intrinsically evil acts."*[30] These so-called negative precepts oblige everyone always and in every circumstance. They allow no exception, because the choice of such behavior is always incompatible with "the goodness of the will of the acting person." The example the pope gives of these types of precepts are from Jesus' reaffirmation of the Decalogue in Matthew 19:17–18: "You shall not murder, you shall not commit adultery, you shall not steal, you shall not bear false witness."[31] These precepts, the pope says, are "valid for all people of the present and the future, as for those of the past."

There is something in the human person that transcends particular cultures. "This 'something' is human nature." Thus one of the lessons from these negative precepts of the natural law is the acknowledgment of a permanent structural element characteristic of all persons in all times and circumstances which is the duty of the moral code to safeguard and protect. As Alasdair MacIntyre puts it, these binding precepts are meant to order our passions, habits, motives, intentions, and purposes. And thus, they help us to articulate clearly the good toward which we are directed by our nature, as well as to characterize adequately that in our nature "which alone makes us apt and directed towards the achievement of that good."[32] It is clear that the pope sees in these precepts at least a lower limit, without regard to cost or consequences. He raises an alarm in this encyclical that the bottom has fallen off this minimal container. The result is an unbridled moral relativism whose consequences are all apparent everywhere and especially in what he would later term "the culture of death." It is the mission of the Church, the pope says, to direct human society in the path of truth, the path which leads to God.[33]

The Culture of Death

The fourth and perhaps most insidious consequence of the loss of the sense of the transcendent in modern societies is the emergence of a culture of death, which the pope has characterized as a massive attack on life, an "endless series of wars" and conspiracy against innocent human life. The pope believes that this conspiracy against life is so widespread that it involves important segments of society, local and international, and so deep that it can best be described as a cultural pattern.[34] This is why the pope speaks of the problem in terms of culture. The conspiracy against life constitutes indeed a veritable structure of sin which "is characterized by the emergence of a culture which denies solidarity." There are a number of characteristics of this culture of death, according to Pope John Paul II. One is widespread abortion, which is supported with enormous sums of money meant to discover newer and more efficient means of killing the fetus in the womb without recourse to medical assistance.[35] Another is the perfection of techniques of artificial reproduction, which separates "procreation from the fully human context of the conjugal act," leading in turn to the production of so-called spare embryos which are destroyed or used for research under the pretext of scientific or medical progress. These procedures, in fact, do no more than reduce human life "to the level of simple biological material to be freely disposed of."[36] A third characteristic is infanticide, which denies basic care to babies born with serious handicaps or illnesses.[37] Fourth is a Promethean attitude "which leads people to think that they can control life and death by taking decisions about them in their own hands." This attitude is especially evident in the spread of euthanasia—disguised and surreptitious, or practiced openly and even legally. Euthanasia is often justified on utilitarian grounds that try to avoid costs "which bring no return and which weigh heavily on society." Thus euthanasia is proposed "to eliminate malformed babies, the severely handicapped, the disabled, the elderly, especially when they are not self-sufficient, and the terminally ill."[38] A fifth characteristic of the culture of death is evident in what the pope refers to as antibirth policies, which include contraception, sterilization, abortion, and other procedures, which are employed to force down the birthrate and stem the so-called population explosion. These policies, which have resulted in "a disturbing" decline or collapse of the birthrate in the developed world, are being "foisted on poor countries which have a high rate of population growth, difficult to sustain in the context of low economic and social development and even, sometimes, extreme underdevelopment."[39]

The sheer magnitude of this structure of sin in the twentieth century has marked that century as an era of massive attacks on life, "an endless series of wars and a continual taking of innocent human life," an era when false teachers and prophets had their greatest success.[40] For the pope, the phenomenon of the culture of death, this vast modern conspiracy against life, is intriguing considering that this is an age which loudly proclaims the inviolable rights of the person as well as the value of life. The pope laments that many people do not seem to see the contradiction between the solemn declarations for life and human dignity which have become the hallmark of the age and the denial of these same rights to the most vulnerable—the unborn, the elderly, and the infirm. Contradictory as the situation is, it is not surprising. For when the sense of God is lost, the sense of the human person is also threatened and poisoned.[41] The human person is reduced to being a thing, unable any longer to grasp the transcendent character of human existence or to appreciate that life is a gift of God, a sacred trust, meant to be looked after with loving care and veneration. Ultimately, life becomes a mere thing "which man claims as his exclusive property, completely subject to his control and manipulation."[42] This tendency is also extended to the distorted view of nature as a thing to be manipulated according to human whims and caprices, and in total disregard of the fact that "there is a truth of creation which must be acknowledged, or a plan of God for life which must be respected." Consequently, the eclipse of the sense of God and of man inevitably leads to a practical materialism, which breeds individualism, utilitarianism, and hedonism.

The Church and Modern Culture

Ecclesiology plays a large role in *Veritatis Splendor*. Pope John Paul II has always insisted that the Church has a duty to evangelize modern culture in order to help it serve better the cause of the human good.[43] The Church has not only faithfully preserved what the word of God teaches but has always reflected on it, and thus "senses more urgently the duty to offer its own discernment and teaching with a view to helping human beings in their journey towards truth and freedom." Maura Anne Ryan summarizes the role which *Veritatis Splendor* understands the Church to play in the relationship between Christ and the disciple:

1) The Church is the immediate locus for the divine-human encounter; it is the body, the extension of Christ wherein the believer meets the Teacher (n. 7, 21). It is the suite where the deepest questions of faith and morality are posed and answered (n. 117); and it is the witness to God's great deeds in history and "to the inviting splendor of that truth which is Jesus Christ himself" (n. 27, 83); 2) The Church, through the function of its magisterium, "receives and hands down the Scriptures," promoting and preserving both conditions for faith encounter and the community's understanding of the normative Christian life (n. 27). Taking the role of Jesus in the meeting between searching disciple and the God alone who is good (cf. Mk. 10:18; Mt. 19:17; Lk. 18:19), the Church faithfully expounds God's commandments, correctly interpreting divine law in whatever historical circumstances obtain (n. 25, 95); 3) The Church is the "pillar, the bulwark of the truth" (1 Tm. 3:15); its teaching magisterium not only promotes witness to the truth of Jesus Christ, but defends against error and division within the community (n. 26–27). In seeking out the most adequate expression of faith in a particular time or in the insights of individual believers—it "runs interference," so to speak—by way of its access to transcendental truths (n. 53); 4) Finally, the Church is an agent of hope in an increasingly (dangerously) dechristianized world (no. 97; 106–109). The path Jesus offers the rich young man is a universal invitation to true human fulfillment. By keeping the challenge

and the promise alive for itself, the community preserves an essential human legacy.[44]

Veritatis Splendor also insists that the Church has a crucial role to play in relation to human society as a whole. Moral theology, which is "the Church's moral reflection, always conducted in the light of Christ, the 'good teacher,'" has always, as it were, been the repository of the Church's wisdom and insight. However, in *Veritatis Splendor,* the pope surveys various currents of thought within recent Catholic moral theology itself and finds them mostly flawed. The moral theological landscape in the Church since the Council has been replete with doubts and objections with regard to the teaching of the Church. This reality is very troubling to the pope because it seriously undermines the Church's ability to teach truth and to provide a firm foundation on which modern society could be anchored. The problem is so wide and so deep and is "no longer a matter of limited and occasional dissent but of an overall and systematic calling into question of traditional moral doctrine" which manifests itself in various ways, including rejection of the traditional doctrine of natural law, the rejection of the permanence and universal validity of the precepts of natural law, the outright rejection of some of the Church's moral teaching, and the limiting of the authority of the magisterium in morality to "exhort conscience" and to "propose values" in light of which each individual will independently make her or his decisions and choices. To prove how deep and widespread the dissent from traditional Catholic doctrine has been since the Council, the pope provides a lengthy catalogue of what one might call "the un-Catholic" characteristics of many contemporary tendencies in Christian ethics in general, and especially in moral theology. From my reading of this encyclical there appear to be three broad areas of concern to the pope with regard to the work of Catholic moral theologians since Vatican II. These are the relationship of faith and morality, the question of method, including the question of moral objectivity, and the role of the magisterium in teaching morality.

Three Areas of Concern to the Pope

A fundamental position of the pope in *Veritatis Splendor* is that Christian morality is a revealed morality. "Christ is the Teacher . . . who opens up to the faithful the book of the Scriptures and, by fully revealing the Father's will, teaches the truth about moral action."[45] Moral theology itself, as understood by this encyclical, is the science which accepts and examines divine revelation while at the same time responding to the demands of human reason. It is theology insofar as "it acknowledges that the origin and end of moral action are found in the one who alone is good and who, by giving himself to man in Christ, offers him the happiness of divine life."[46] Although reason has an essential role to play in the human effort "to understand the full range of the moral demands of the Christian life," still reason "operates in the light of revelation and in service of faith, not as an independent and primarily independent critical agent."[47]

The charges the pope brings against dissident moral theologians are many. In the first place, the pope is very concerned that some Catholic theologians have, since the Council, denied any role to revelation in determining morality. These theologians, the pope says, question the capacity of the commandments of God to guide individuals and entire societies in the daily decisions which they have to make, and question whether it is possible to obey God and neighbor, without respecting these commandments in all circumstances. There are also questions regarding "the intrinsic and unbreakable bond between faith and morality," which suggest that issues of faith are those issues which pertain to membership in the Church and her internal unity, "while in the sphere of morality a pluralism of opinions and of kinds of behavior could be tolerated, these being left to the judgement and individual subjective conscience or to the diversity of social and cultural contexts."[48] Some theologians, he says, have even gone as far as positing a *complete sovereignty of reason* in the domain of moral norms regarding the right ordering of life in this world, thus disregarding the dependence of human reason on divine wisdom and the need, given the present state of fallen nature, for divine revelation as an effective means for knowing moral truths, even those of the natural order. Such norms would constitute the boundaries for a merely "human" morality, and "would be the expression of law which man in an autonomous manner lays down for himself and which has its source exclusively in human reason."[49] Also in this regard, some theologians have introduced a sharp distinction which, according to the pope, is contrary to Catholic doctrine, between an *ethical order* which would be human in origin and of value for this world alone, and an order *of salvation* for which only certain intentions and interior attitudes regarding God and neighbor would be significant. "This has led then to an actual denial that there exists, in Divine Revelation, a specific and determined moral content, universally valid and permanent. The word of God would be limited to proposing an exhortation, a generic paranesis . . ."[50]

[margin: sounds like / why are / dg... result / resemblar / determine]

There are two things to note concerning the pope's understanding of Christian ethics. First is that it is theonomous. In this regard, moral agents would act in accordance with certain norms especially because they perceive those norms to be the expression of the will of God. Second, it is Christocentric. For not only does faith have a moral content; the true and final answer to the problem of morality lies in Christ alone. Morality involves doing the will of God through a life of self-giving like Christ. Like Christ too, the Christian must be prepared to bear the supreme witness of martyrdom rather than disobey God. Thus, one could say that for the *[margin: ethics / as Chr. / life]* pope, Christian ethics refers to common assumptions within the community of Jesus' disciples about the normativity of Jesus Christ for our construal of self, the other, the world, and all reality. The Christian finds in Christ an uncompromising stance toward doing the will of God. Central to this stance is the cross which stands in eternal opposition to those who seek "to set freedom in opposition to the truth" and as a beacon to those who search for truth and authentic freedom.

Closely related to the issue of the nature of Christian ethics is the issue of the role of the magisterium, the Church's teaching authority in moral matters. Indeed, one of the problems *Veritatis Splendor* sets itself to counter *[margin: n.b. / for → / diss.]* is the view which denies that the magisterium has competence in moral matters or considers that the magisterium "is capable of intervening in matters of morality only in order to 'exhort consciences' and to 'propose values,' in light of which each individual will independently make his or her decisions and life choices."[51] *Veritatis Splendor* reaffirms the authority of the magisterium to intervene "not only in the sphere of faith, but also, and inseparably so, in the sphere of morals." There is a threefold aspect to the involvement of the magisterium in moral matters. First, the magisterium *[margin: 1 —]* has the task of discerning "by means of judgements normative for the consciences of believers, those acts which in themselves conform to the demands of faith and foster this expression in life and those which, on the contrary, because intrinsically evil, are incompatible with such demands." *[margin: 2 —]* Second, the magisterium "teaches the faithful specific particular precepts and requires that they consider them in conscience as morally binding." Third, the magisterium has also the task of staying vigilant and of warning *[margin: 3 —]* the faithful of the presence of possible error in certain opinions.[52] It is not, however, the duty or the intention of the magisterium as it carries out its *[margin: but NOT / to impose]* duty to impose any particular theological or philosophical system. However, in the course of its duty, it is also the task of the magisterium to point out any philosophical affirmations and theological thinking that are "incompatible with revealed truth."[53] This is what the pope has amply done in this encyclical in refuting the theories of "consequentialism" and "proportionalism."

We have already noted the importance of the question of moral objectivity in both *Veritatis Splendor* and *Evangelium Vitae*. For *Veritatis Splendor,* secularism has not left the Church unscathed. The influence of the de-Christianized and atheistic world on contemporary Christian ethical thinking, as with the rest of the world, is also evident in the rejection of the notion of an absolute and permanent evil. This rejection is most evident in the moral methodologies, consequentialism and proportionalism, which have become hallmarks of much of Catholic moral theology since the Council. According to the pope, these ethical theories hold that "it is never possible to formulate an absolute prohibition of particular kinds of behavior which would be in conflict, in every circumstance and in every culture, with those values."[54] The moral order, for these theories, consists of "the moral order" and of "the premoral order." The latter is also termed nonmoral, physical, or ontic "in relation to the advantages and disadvantages accruing both to the agent and to all other persons possibly involved, such as, for example, health or its endangerment, physical integrity, life, death, loss of material goods, etc." These theories judge the moral rightness or wrongness of an act on either the basis of the subject's intention in reference to the moral goods, or "on the basis of a consideration of its foreseeable effects or consequences and of their proportion." In such a situation, the will of the acting person is not factored into the determination of the moral rightness or wrongness of an act. It does not matter if this act contradicts a universal negative norm. All that these teleological theories are interested in is "the evaluation of the consequences of the action, based on the proportion between the act and its effects and between the effects themselves" with regard to the premoral order and insofar as the agent is faithful "to the values of charity and prudence, without this faithfulness being incompatible with choices contrary to certain particular moral precepts."[55]

The pope insists that these teleological theories are not faithful to the Church's teaching because "they believe they can justify, as morally good, deliberate choices of kinds of behavior contrary to the commandments of the divine and natural law." And their claim to being a legitimate offshoot of the Catholic moral theological tradition is baseless since that tradition, even in its casuistic practice, never called "the absolute validity of negative moral precepts, which oblige without exception," into question. On the

difference between casuistry and proportionalism

contrary, casuistry in the Catholic tradition has been concerned only with finding ways to achieve the good in certain concrete situations where the law was uncertain, and not with evading the moral absolutes.[56] Although there is need to take account of intention and consequences of human action, these are not sufficient for judging the moral quality of a concrete choice. These as part of the circumstances of an act, "while capable of lessening the gravity of an evil act, nonetheless cannot alter its moral species." Moreover, it is impossible to provide an exhaustive rational calculation of all the good and evil consequences and effects involved in one's acts, or to determine criteria for establishing adequate proportions on the basis of which to justify an absolute obligation.[57] The pope insists to the contrary in this encyclical that the morality of human acts depends primarily and fundamentally on the "object" rationally chosen by deliberative will.[58] The object of the act of willing is the cause of the goodness of the will to the extent that it is in conformity with the order of reason. If this object, this freely chosen kind of behavior, conforms to the order of reason, it perfects the acting person morally and disposes him or her "to recognize our ultimate end in the perfect good, primordial love." Thus, the object of the moral act cannot refer to a process or an event "of the merely physical order, to be assessed on the basis of its ability to bring about a given state of affairs in the outside world. Rather, that object is the proximate end of a deliberate decision which determines the act of willing on the part of the acting person."[59] Since the moral category of a human act depends on its object, good intention alone is not enough to make an act good. A correct choice of actions is necessary to determine whether or not the object "is capable or not of being ordered to God, to the one who alone is good." Objects which are by their nature incapable of being ordered to God are considered so because "they radically contradict the good of the person" made in God's image. "These are the acts which, in the Church's moral tradition, have been termed 'intrinsically evil' (*intrinsice malum*): they are such *always* and *per se,* in other words, on account of their very object, and quite apart from the ulterior intentions of the one acting and the circumstances."[60]

For Pope John Paul II, the question of the morality of human acts and of intrinsically human acts is a question about the human person, of his truth and of the moral consequences flowing from that truth. By insisting on the intrinsically evil nature of some human acts, "the Church remains faithful to the integral truth" about the human person thus respecting and promoting him in his dignity and vocation.[61] It is therefore clear, as has al-

m oral absolutes

ready been indicated, that the pope is very much concerned for the social and political implications which would arise from a denial of moral absolutes. For him, universal and unchanging norms are "the unshakable foundation and solid guarantee" of a just, peaceful, and democratic society built on the basis of the equality of all members who possess equal rights and duties.[62] These norms serve human freedom and prevent totalitarianism, which can arise as a result of people's failure to acknowledge transcendent truth. Only a morality which acknowledges certain norms as perennially valid and absolute can resist the force of power from taking *when the certain are powerful* over at all levels—personal, national, and international. Thus one important element in *Veritatis Splendor* is the concern about "an alliance between democracy and eternal relativism which would remove any sure moral reference from political and social life, and on a deeper level make the acknowledgement of truth impossible."[63] The human good cannot be discerned through the balancing of the goods in question. *Veritatis Splendor* has particularly harsh words for anyone who makes his or her weakness the criterion of truth about the good, so he or she can be self-justified, without even the need to have recourse to God and to God's mercy. Such an attitude, it says, "corrupts the morality of society as a whole, since it encourages doubt about the objectivity of the moral law in general and a rejection of the absoluteness of moral prohibitions recognizing specific human acts, and it ends up by confusing all judgements about values."[64] This attitude is also pharisaic because it seeks to eliminate awareness of one's limits and one's own sin.[65]

sum of critique against propor.

The charges against "consequentialism" and "proportionalism" can therefore be summarized thus: (1) that they do not accept the notion of intrinsic evil; (2) that they reduce morality to the weighing of goods in any given situation; (3) that they produce and foster a permissive view of morality; and (4) that they turn personal weaknesses into criteria for deciding right and wrong.

An Initial Summary

I have so far laid out some of the salient features of the two encyclicals the pope authored on moral matters in 1993 and 1995. One of these is the concern that secularism is gaining much ground and determining much of the direction of the culture of the modern world—with unacceptable consequences for the Christian conscience. Another salient feature is the assertion that much of the moral theology of the years after Vatican II has been co-opted by the secular world in the fight against truth and the gospel. This fact is especially sad because it blunts the efforts of the Church toward the new era of evangelization. A third important feature of the encyclicals is the effort the pope makes to show that there are practical consequences to the denial of absolute truth. He tries to show the connection therefore between the denial of absolute norms and abortion, different forms of infanticide, euthanasia, totalitarianism of all sorts, the prospect of an alliance between democratic civilization and moral relativism, with its inevitably tyrannous tendency, and so forth. Intimately linked to the problem of absolute norms is the issue of method—that is, the way of determining what is wrong and what is right.

Reception

Evident in the reactions of the theologians and other experts to the teaching of these encyclicals is both a narrow and a broad reading of the texts. Some among the older generation of moral theologians, whose outlook was shaped in many ways by the bruising postconciliar debate over contraception, have tended to read the papal letters as either a vindication of their theological cause or as an attempt to condemn their points of view. For example, Germain Grisez apparently sees the encyclicals as supporting his position in his longstanding debate against those he derisively usually refers to as "dissenters" on especially the question of intrinsic evil.[66] Grisez sets up a straw man by making his "dissenters" sound as if they condone adultery and murder as being right in some circumstances. Then he proceeds to use *Veritatis Splendor* as a tool to knock them on their heads. Finally, he declares, "Theologians who have been dissenting from the doctrine reaffirmed in this encyclical now have only three choices: to admit that they have been mistaken, to admit that they do not believe God's word, or to claim that the Pope is grossly misinterpreting the Bible. No doubt, many will make the third choice. In doing so, they will greatly escalate the conflict which has divided the Catholic Church during the past thirty years."[67]

Bernard Häring, on the other hand, reported that he felt strongly discouraged by the encyclical.[68] He believed the encyclical was part of a longstanding papal agenda which was intended simply to force total assent and submission to the teaching on sexual matters, particularly on the intrinsically evil nature of contraception. Other evidence of this agenda includes

Häring

papal utterances on the matter, the criminalization of dissent in the code of canon law of 1983, the complete control of nominations of all theologians teaching in Church-related institutions of higher learning, and the type of appointees to bishoprics and other positions of responsibility in the Church. In Häring's view, *Veritatis Splendor* is simply one more step in the direction of total control over thinking in the Church. He believes the authors of *Veritatis Splendor* do not have a proper picture of the state of moral theology; the insinuations in the encyclical are too grave and do not represent the work of any moral theologians of good repute in the Church. Finally, Häring finds the tone of the letter too harsh and lacking in the pastoral approach which should be an essential characteristic of the Petrine office.

> There is surely nothing whatsoever in this text that could be taken as relating to a task laid on Peter to teach his brothers about an absolute norm forbidding in every case any kind of contraception. Nor did Jesus tell Peter to teach a complete set of norms and laws to be followed by everyone, including negative laws constraining everyone. Was not Peter wavering about whether the new Christian converts should observe Jewish laws? Did not Paul have to confront him and set him right about this?[69]

McC

Like Häring, Richard McCormick maintains as well that the impulse toward *Veritatis Splendor* had been building up for some time.[70] Thus he thinks the text contained nothing new which had not been said before. Like Häring, McCormick believes that the encyclical had one unstated agenda: to uphold the teaching on contraception: "The pope will reject a priori any analytic adjustments in moral theology that do not support the moral wrongness of every contraceptive act. Proportionalism certainly does not give such support."[71] McCormick disputes the characterization of the work of revisionist theologians in the encyclical: "In brief, the encyclical repeatedly states of proportionalism that it attempts to justify morally wrong actions by a good intention. This, I regret to say, is a misrepresentation . . . No proportionalist I know would recognize himself or herself in that description."[72]

James Hanigan is one of the Catholic moralists who has provided a broader reading of *Veritatis Splendor*. Although he notes that the encyclical is very relevant to the Church's teaching on sexual ethics, he has tried to place his understanding of the document in the context of a larger papal program for the Church:

> My own reading of the encyclical has tried to place it in the context of a larger papal program for the Church, a program that emerges from a background of fierce struggle against Nazism, Communism, and western materialism and individualism, a struggle that continues today, despite the apparent defeat of Hitler and the collapse of the Soviet Union. My reading suggests that the world, and inevitably the Church which lives in the world, daily experiences an incredible number of human actions that betray human dignity, violate human rights, and deny, fundamentally and of their very nature, the truth of the human person as proclaimed in the Gospel.[73]

Speaking specifically as an American, Hanigan indicates agreement with the strict implications of the pope's teaching in the area of human sexuality:

> With specific regard to sexual ethics, both within and without the Church, it seems highly implausible that the most pressing need is for moral justification of greater sexual license, of more divorce and remarriage, or of single-parent families. It seems most unlikely that teenagers will be helped to grow in moral perfection by being told that masturbation is fine because everyone does it or that the avoidance of sexually transmitted diseases is the sole or even primary concern they should have about their sexual behaviors. There is little reason to think that married couples will find greater marital stability, unity and joy or the wisdom to be better parents by learning moral justifications for easier technological ways to avoid conception. . . . Certainly, there are obvious trends in American culture that point to the urgency and necessity of speaking the moral truth about human sexuality. The necessity and urgency of that truth is a major way in which *Veritatis Splendor* is relevant to sexual ethics.[74]

Lisa Sowle Cahill provides a nuanced feminist reading of *Veritatis Splendor*. She appreciates the warning issued by the encyclical against relativism and notes that the danger of relativism is also real in feminist thought with its emphasis on "women's experience":

> The problem that arises as a result of feminist theology's appeal to "experience" is the danger of replacing oppressive generalizations with

bottomless particularity. If women's experience alone is exalted as final moral standard, we run the danger of a feminist relativism which is ultimately unable to give any real reasons for preferring equality rather than hierarchy.[75]

Cahill hopes that *Veritatis Splendor* can provide the resources for everyone, feminists included, "to move back from particularity to the sense of shared human values which is co-central to natural law." By affirming a moral foundation by which it is possible to recognize and eradicate all forms of injustice, *Veritatis Splendor* may also serve as a resource for feminist theology. Cahill argues, however, that there is a definite male bias in *Veritatis Splendor,* as well as a strong tendency to resolve genuinely difficult questions by resort to authority. She believes that these tendencies obfuscate the message of the encyclical.

$$* \quad * \quad *$$

As can be seen from our discussion in this book, the issues the pope highlights in his moral encyclicals have deep roots in the recent moral tradition of the Church. We have already discussed the question of authority at some length in the previous chapter, and have considered many other issues, such as those pertaining to natural law and moral norms, elsewhere. I believe that the architectonic issue governing Pope John Paul II's assessment of how well the renewal of moral theology has gone since the Council is that of the relationship of faith and ethics. In our treatment of this issue we noted that some prominent ethicists in the post–Vatican II period denied any concrete normativity to Christianity with regard to ethics. Alfons Auer speaks for these theologians when he states that "neither the individual Christian nor the Church has any revelation about what is or is not the concrete expression of the moral demand."[76] It is obvious that *Veritatis Splendor* sets out deliberately to counter this position. Not only does faith have a moral content, but the true and final answer to the problem of morality lies in Christ alone. Morality involves doing the will of God through a life of self-giving like Christ. Like Christ too, the Christian must also be prepared to bear the supreme witness of martyrdom rather than disobey God.

The question here is whether the pope has, by these assertions, definitively answered the question of the relation of faith and ethics. At one level he has. Christian ethics refers to common assumptions within the community of Jesus' disciples (the Christian community) about the normativity of

Jesus Christ for our construal of self, the other, and the world, and all reality. The Christian finds in Christ an uncompromising stance toward doing God's will even to the point of the cross. On another level, the question of the nature of Christian ethics is still a very open one, as we have seen. What specific addition does faith make to what Richard McCormick refers to as essential morality? Is faith an arcane source of moral insights? For example, is it left only to the person of faith to discover that the unjust killing of the innocent is wrong, or that abortion is wrong, or that it is not morally right to take another's property against his or her reasonable will, or that unjust wages or forcing up prices by trading on the ignorance or hardship of people, and so forth, are all morally wrong? If all we can say is that faith grants us certain postures in relation to reality, and influences our intentions toward the self, the other, and the world,[77] are we not playing down the importance of particular prohibitions or injunctions? Is it correct to limit the role of faith in morality to that of a value-raiser rather than an answer-giver, as McCormick does? In other words, does Christian faith not do more than influence the determination of the good, the shaping of the moral agent, the formulation of moral judgment?

Closely related to the question of the relationship between faith and morals is the attitude of the encyclicals toward secular culture. The pope's insistence that modern culture (at least in the West) is widely "de-Christianized" and secular[78] serves two purposes. First, it highlights an attitude that has a wide impact on the way people make moral judgments and decisions. The Christian is therefore warned that he or she may not be immune from the forces which influence the criteria for moral decision making in such a world. Second, it identifies the reason why dialogue on some moral matters might be difficult between Christians and their secular compatriots.

The pope's reading of modern culture raises a host of questions as well. These questions pertain to the accuracy and comprehensiveness of his reading of modern cultures. Is this reading consonant with or discordant with the one Vatican II offered in *Gaudium et Spes*? What has changed between the time of the Council and 1993–95, when these encyclicals were issued? Does the papal reading of culture in the encyclicals under discussion take us back to *Testem Benevolentia* and *Pascendi*? In other words, does this reading display the long-standing suspicion of modern culture contained in these two texts, or is it a realistic assessment of the modern situation as it is today?

When as a seminary teacher in Nigeria I read these two encyclicals under discussion, I wondered how an African living at the beginning of the twenty-first century could read what the pope is saying in *Veritatis Splendor* and *Evangelium Vitae*. It struck me that at one level there is a temptation to dismiss the encyclicals as irrelevant to African circumstances. This may partly explain the scant attention the publication of these two encyclicals received in African theology institutes. For, after all, people in Africa can identify neither with the all-intrusive technological culture the encyclicals speak of, nor with the godless and de-Christianized world it warns us about. We still believe that wrong is wrong and right is right and that some are so absolutely. On a more profound level, however, these encyclicals are as relevant to the African context as to any other. The relationship of Christianity to contemporary culture, the specificity of the Christian contribution to moral discourse, the role of theologians and theology in the Church, the possibility of an alliance between totalitarian and relativistic forces—these are all burning issues in all human societies. So are questions relating to life and death, as well as issues of human rights and dignity.

Veritatis Splendor and *Evangelium Vitae* can provide a blueprint for Christians as they enter into dialogue with other segments of their various societies on how to recreate society. We must bring to this discussion a sensitivity to the importance of the individual—every individual, irrespective of religious or ethnic affiliation or socioeconomic standing—and the need to protect and nurture all life from conception to the grave. The encyclicals invite and also help us to take a more critical stance toward culture. Being a human creation, culture has its own share of sin. The moral theology encyclicals of Pope John Paul II provide Christians everywhere with some important standards for measuring to what extent a culture is truly human, and therefore a civilization of love, or demonic, and therefore a culture of death.

However one reads the present culture, there is much in it to critique. The pope is correct to insist that moral theology must play this role. Moral theology must be a critical theological enterprise. To be able to do this, it must particularly prize its origin as theology—that is, as an enterprise which ensues from the effort of faith to seek understanding.

notes

Other Texts

RMT1: *Readings in Moral Theology*, no. 1, *Moral Norms and Catholic Tradition*. Edited by Charles E. Curran and Richard A. McCormick. Mahwah, N.J.: Paulist Press, 1979.

RMT2: *Readings in Moral Theology*, no. 2, *The Distinctiveness of Christian Ethics*. Edited by Charles E. Curran and Richard A. McCormick. Mahwah, N.J.: Paulist Press, 1980.

RMT3: *Readings in Moral Theology*, no. 3, *The Magisterium and Morality*. Edited by Charles E. Curran and Richard A. McCormick. New York: Paulist Press, 1982.

RMT4: *Readings in Moral Theology*, no. 4, *The Use of Scripture in Moral Theology*. Edited by Charles E. Curran and Richard A. McCormick. New York: Paulist Press, 1984.

RMT5: *Readings in Moral Theology*, no. 5, *Official Catholic Social Teaching*. Edited by Charles E. Curran and Richard A. McCormick. New York: Paulist Press, 1986.

RMT6: *Readings in Moral Theology*, no. 6, *Dissent in the Church*. Edited by Charles E. Curran and Richard A. McCormick. New York: Paulist Press, 1988.

RMT7: *Readings in Moral Theology*, no. 7, *Natural Law and Theology*. Edited by Charles E. Curran and Richard A. McCormick. New York: Paulist Press, 1991.

RMT8: *Readings in Moral Theology*, no. 8, *Dialogue about Catholic Sexual Teaching*. Edited by Charles E. Curran and Richard A. McCormick. New York: Paulist Press, 1993.

RMT9: *Readings in Moral Theology*, no. 9, *Feminist Ethics and the Catholic Moral Tradition*. Edited by Charles E. Curran, Margaret A. Farley, and Richard A. McCormick. New York: Paulist Press, 1996.

RMT10: *Readings in Moral Theology*, no. 10, *John Paul II and Moral Theology*. Edited by Charles E. Curran and Richard A. McCormick. New York: Paulist Press, 1998.

RMT11: *Readings in Moral Theology*, no. 11, *The Historical Development of Fundamental Moral Theology in the United States*. Edited by Charles E. Curran and Richard A. McCormick. New York: Paulist Press, 1999.

AAS (*Acta Apostolicae Sedis*)

VS (*Veritatis Splendor*): Encyclical Letter of Pope John Paul II Regarding Certain Fundamental Questions of the Church's Moral Teaching. Boston: St. Paul Books and Media, 1993.

EV (*Evangelium Vitae*): The Gospel of Life

NMT1: *Notes on Moral Theology: 1965–1980*, by Richard A. McCormick. Lanham, Md.: University Press of America, 1980.

NMT 2: *Notes on Moral Theology: 1981–1984,* by Richard A. McCormick. Lanham, Md.: University Press of America, 1984.

Introduction

1. Josef Fuchs, "Moral Theology According to Vatican II," in his *Human Values and Christian Morality* (Dublin: Gill and Macmillan, 1979), p. 1.

2. Bouquillon reports the dissatisfaction expressed by Cardinal D'Annibale who observed that "what the old theologians considered broadly and at length we scarcely touch with our fingertips." An anonymous commentator in *Civita Cattolica,* the Jesuit weekly from Rome, added, in agreement with Cardinal D'Annibale's observation, that "with few exceptions, we have a mass of compendiums made and fashioned with a somnolency almost senile, without a trace of profound study or exact criticism. If one happens to find some proof of diligence, it has been used merely in collecting and copying the sayings of others." Bouquillon also quotes a Father Barthier who had referred to moral theology as "one of the plagues of theological science." Thomas J. Bouquillon, "Moral Theology at the End of the Nineteenth Century," in *RMT* 11, pp. 91–92. This article was first published in *Bulletin of the Catholic University of America* (April 1899).

3. Bouquillon, "Moral Theology at the End of the Nineteenth Century," pp. 92–93.

4. Ibid., p. 102.

5. Ibid., p. 104.

6. Ibid., p. 109.

7. Ibid., pp. 109–10.

8. Some of the manuals of moral theology produced in this period include *Lehrbuch der Moraltheologie,* first published in 1907 by Franz M. Schindler; *Moraltheologie,* first published in 1922 by Otto Schilling; and *Catholic Moral Theology and Its Adversaries,* issued for the first time in 1915 by Joseph Mausabach. Others are *Moral Theology,* published by Joseph A. McHugh and Charles J. Callan in 1928, as well as Marcellinus Zalba's *Theologiae Moralis Compendium,* which appeared in 1958 right on the eve of Vatican II. These and many other manuals written in this period or revised from older texts on the same basis as the newer ones were in use throughout much of the Catholic world prior to the Second Vatican Council.

9. In this letter, the pope called for a restoration of "the golden wisdom" of St. Thomas Aquinas and for the spreading of that wisdom everywhere "for the defense and beauty of the Catholic Faith." Pope Leo XIII, "Aeterni Patris," in *One Hundred Years of Thomism,* edited by Victor B. Breznik (Houston: Center for Thomistic Studies, 1981), p. 195.

10. John A. Gallagher, *Time Past, Time Future: A Historical Study of Catholic Moral Theology* (New York: Paulist Press, 1990), p. 37.

11. Ibid., p. 37.

12. Richard A. McCormick, *Corrective Vision: Explorations in Moral Theology* (Kansas City, Mo.: Sheed and Ward, 1994), p. 2.

13. Richard A. McCormick, "Moral Theology 1940–1989: An Overview," in *RMT* 11, p. 14. This article was originally published in *Theological Studies*. It has also appeared in other places. See for example, Richard A. McCormick, *Corrective Vision*, pp. 1–22.

14. Paulinus I. Odozor, *Richard A. McCormick and the Renewal of Moral Theology* (Notre Dame, Ind.: University of Notre Dame Press, 1995), p. 8.

15. Henry Davis, *Moral and Pastoral Theology* (London: Sheed and Ward, 1946), p. vii.

16. John Langan, "Catholic Moral Rationalism and the Philosophical Bases of Moral Theology," *Theological Studies* 50 (1989).

17. Germain Grisez, *The Way of the Lord Jesus;* vol. 1: *Christian Moral Principles* (Chicago: Franciscan Herald Press, 1983), p. 29.

18. John Mahoney, *The Making of Moral Theology: A Study of the Roman Catholic Tradition* (Oxford: Clarendon Press, 1987), p. 1.

19. See John Mahoney, *The Making of Moral Theology*, pp. 1–36.

20. Second Vatican Council, *Optatam Totius*, 16.

21. For example, I have tried in an earlier book to present a comprehensive study of the work of one of the most influential moral theologians of this period. See Paulinus I. Odozor, *Richard A. McCormick and the Renewal of Moral Theology*. See also the work of Éric Gaziaux on the works of Josef Fuchs and Phillipe Delhaye, *Morale de la foi et morale autonome: Confrontation entre P. Delhaye et J. Fuchs* (Leuven: Leuven University Press, 1995). There are many other works which study aspects of the significant theological figures who mark this period.

22. Mahoney, *The Making of Moral Theology*.

23. Gallagher, *Time Past, Time Future*.

24. Bernard Hoose, *Proportionalism: The American Debate and Its European Roots* (Washington, D.C.: Georgetown University Press, 1987).

25. Lucius Iwejuru Ugorji, *The Principle of Double Effect: A Critical Appraisal of Its Traditional Understanding and Its Modern Reinterpretation* (Frankfurt am Main and New York: P. Lang, 1985).

26. Odozor, *Richard A. McCormick and the Renewal of Moral Theology*.

27. Ibid., p. xiii.

28. Jeffrey Stout, *Ethics After Babel: The Languages of Morals and Their Discontents* (Boston: Beacon Press, 1988), p. 210.

29. John Mahoney, "The Challenge of Moral Distinctions," *Theological Studies* 53 (1992), p. 672.

30. Ibid., p. 671.

31. Ibid., Enda McDonagh, *The Making of Disciples: Tasks of Moral Theology* (Wilmington, Del.: Michael Glazier, 1982), p. 1.

32. See Odozor, *Richard A. McCormick and the Renewal of Moral Theology*, pp. 174–75.

33. Servais Pinckaers, *The Source of Christian Ethics* (Washington, D.C.: Catholic University of America Press, 1995), p. 304. Originally published in French as *Les sources de la morale Chrétienne* (Fribourg: University of Fribourg Press, 1985). This translation by Sr. Mary Thomas Noble, O.P., is from the third edition of the French original.

34. Pinckaers, *The Sources of Christian Ethics*, p. 305.

35. Richard A. McCormick, "Moral Theology from 1940 to 1989: An Overview," in *Corrective Vision: Explorations in Moral Theology* (Kansas City, Mo.: Sheed and Ward, 1994), p. 11.

chapter one
The Second Vatican Council and the Renewal of Moral Theology

1. Josef Fuchs, "A Harmonization of the Conciliar Statements on Moral Theology," in *Vatican II: Assessment and Perspectives: Twenty-five Years After (1962–1987)*, vol. 2, edited by René Latourelle (New York: Paulist Press, 1988), p. 479.

2. Phillipe Delhaye, "The Contribution of Vatican II to Moral Theology," *Concilium* 75 (1972), p. 66.

3. Second Vatican Council, *Gaudium et Spes (GS)*, no. 10.

4. *GS*, no. 30.

5. Delhaye, "The Contribution of Vatican II to Moral Theology," p. 66.

6. Antonio Moser and Bernadino Leers, *Moral Theology: Dead Ends and Alternatives* (Maryknoll, N.Y.: Orbis Books, 1990), p. 23.

7. Ibid., pp. 26–27.

8. See Richard A. McCormick, *Corrective Vision: Explorations in Moral Theology* (Kansas City, Mo.: Sheed and Ward, 1994), pp. 5–6.

9. Edward Schillebeeckx, *Church: The Human Story of God* (New York: Crossroad, 1991), p. 198.

10. Ibid.

11. Richard A. McCormick, *The Critical Calling: Reflections on Moral Dilemmas Since Vatican II* (Washington, D.C.: Georgetown University Press, 1989), p. 54.

12. See, for example, the article by Cardinal Walter Kasper on the Church. Walter Kasper, "On the Church," *America* 184 (April 23–30, 2001), pp. 8–17.

13. Richard A. McCormick, "The Moral Theology of Vatican II," in *The Future of Ethics and Moral Theology*, edited by Don Brezine and James V. McGlynn (Chicago: Argus Communications, 1968), p. 9.

14. Schillebeeckx, *Church*, p. 209.

15. "Justice in the World" (Synod of Bishops, 1971), in *Catholic Social Thought: The Documentary Heritage,* edited by David J. O'Brien and Thomas A. Shannon (Maryknoll, N.Y.: Orbis Books, 1998), p. 287.

16. Josef Fuchs, "A Harmonization of the Conciliar Statements on Moral Theology," in *Vatican II: Assessment and Perspectives,* edited by René Latourelle, p. 485.

17. J. Bryan Hehir, "The Social Role of the Church: Leo XIII, Vatican II and John Paul II," in *Catholic Social Thought and the New World Order: Building on One Hundred Years,* edited by Oliver F. Williams and John W. Houck (Notre Dame, Ind.: University of Notre Dame Press, 1993), p. 38.

18. Second Vatican Council, *Lumen Gentium* (referred to in this work as *LG*). The text I am using throughout this book, unless otherwise stated, is *The Basic Sixteen Texts: Vatican II: Constitutions, Decrees, Declarations: A Completely Revised Translation in Inclusive Language,* edited by Austin Flannery (New York: Costello Publishing Company; Dublin: Dominican Publications, 1996).

19. See Phillipe Delhaye, "Les Points Fort de la Morale à Vatican II," *Studia Moralia* 24 (1986), p. 21.

20. Mark O'Keefe, "Purity of Heart and the Christian Moral Life," in *Method and Catholic Moral Theology: The Ongoing Reconstruction,* edited by Todd A. Salzman (Omaha, Neb.: Creighton University Press, 1999), p. 72.

21. McCormick, *The Critical Calling,* p. 14.

22. Charles E. Curran, *History and Contemporary Issues: Studies in Moral Theology* (New York: Continuum, 1996), pp. 104–5.

23. Luigi M. Rulla, Franco Imoda, and Joyce Ridick, "Anthropology and the Christian Vocation: Conciliar and Postconciliar Aspects," in *Vatican II: Assessment and Perspectives,* edited by René Latourelle, pp. 411–12.

24. David J. O'Brien and Thomas A. Shannon, "*Gaudium et Spes:* Introduction," in *Catholic Social Thought: The Documentary Heritage* (Maryknoll, N.Y.: Orbis Books, 1998), p. 164.

25. Edouard Hamel, "The Foundations of Human Rights in Biblical Theology Following the Orientations of *Gaudium et Spes,*" in *Vatican II: Assessment and Perspectives,* edited by René Latourelle, p. 463.

26. Rulla, Imoda, and Ridick, "Anthropology and the Christian Vocation," p. 421.

27. The Council gives some examples of the way human beings must never be treated. "The varieties of crimes are numerous: all offenses against life itself, such as murder, genocide, abortion, euthanasia and willful suicide; all violations of the integrity of the human person, such as mutilation, physical and mental torture, undue psychological pressures; all offenses against human dignity, such as subhuman living conditions, arbitrary imprisonment, deportation, slavery, prostitution, the selling of women and children, degrading working conditions where people are treated as mere tools for profit rather than free and re-

sponsible persons: all these and the like are criminal: they poison civilization; and they debase the perpetrators more than the victims and militate against the honor of the creator" (*GS*, 27).

28. Gregory Baum, "Faith and Liberation: Development Since Vatican II," in *Vatican II: Open Questions and New Horizons,* edited by Gerald M. Fagin (Wilmington, Del.: Michael Glazier, 1984), pp. 75–104.

29. See Delhaye, "The Contribution of Vatican II to Moral Theology," p. 59.

30. Gérard Gilleman, *The Primacy of Charity in Moral Theology,* translated from the French edition by William F. Ryan, S.J., and André Vahon, S.J. (Westminster, Md.: Newman Press, 1959), p. xxi.

31. Theodore Mackin, *Divorce and Remarriage, Marriage in the Catholic Church Series* (New York: Paulist Press, 1984), pp. 505–45, esp. pp. 507–16.

32. Ibid., p. 508.

33. Ibid., p. 511.

34. Charles Rodgers and Drostan Maclaren, *The Social Teaching of Vatican II: Its Origin and Development* (Oxford: Plater Publications; San Francisco: Ignatius Press, 1982), p. 73.

35. Thomas Aquinas, *Summa Theologiae,* I-II, q. 91, a.2.

36. Rodgers and Maclaren, *The Social Teaching of Vatican II,* p. 73.

37. Ibid., p. 74.

38. Vatican II, *Dignitatis Humanae,* no. 3.

39. Joseph Boyle, "The Place of Religion in the Practical Reasoning of Individuals and Groups," *American Journal of Jurisprudence* 43 (1998), p. 22.

40. Josef Fuchs, "Moral Theology According to Vatican II," in *Human Values and Christian Morality* (Dublin: Gill and Macmillan, 1970), p. 26.

41. Ibid., p. 3.

42. Ibid., p. 8.

43. Ibid., p. 11.

44. Ibid., p. 15.

45. Ibid., p. 16.

46. Josef Fuchs, "The Christian Morality of Vatican II," in *Human Values and Christian Morality,* p. 56.

47. Fuchs, "Moral Theology According to Vatican II," p. 19.

48. Fuchs, "The Christian Morality of Vatican II," p. 58.

49. See Servais Pinckaers, *Morality: The Catholic View* (South Bend, Ind.: St. Augustine's Press, 2000), pp. 42–43.

50. Richard A. McCormick, *The Critical Calling,* pp. 9–22.

51. Andrew M. Greeley, "The Failures of Vatican II After Twenty Years," *America* 146 (Feb. 6, 1982), pp. 86–89; also, "Going Their Own Way," *New York Times Magazine* (Oct. 10, 1982), quoted in Timothy G. McCarthy, *The Catholic Tradition: The Church in the Twentieth Century,* revised and enlarged 2nd ed. (Chicago: Loyola University Press, 1998), p. 71.

52. Peter Hebblethwaite, *The Runaway Church: Postconciliar Growth or Decline?* (New York: Seabury Press, 1975), p. 13. Quoted in McCarthy, *The Catholic Tradition,* p. 70.

chapter two
Humanae Vitae and Its Aftermath

1. I am indebted in this section to John T. Noonan, Jr., *Contraception: A History of Its Treatment by the Catholic Theologians and Canonists,* enlarged ed. (Cambridge, Mass.: Harvard University Press, Belknap Press, 1986). See also Robert Blair Kaiser, *The Politics of Sex and Religion: A Case History in the Development of Doctrine* (Kansas City, Mo.: Leaven Press, 1985).

2. Noonan, *Contraception,* p. 481.

3. Ibid., p. 480.

4. Cf. Noonan, *Contraception,* pp. 480–89.

5. Pope Pius XI, "Casti Connubii," in *Seven Great Encyclicals* (Glen Rock, N.J.: Paulist Press, 1939), no. 71.

6. Ibid., no. 103. The question of the Church's competence in morality was taken up by Pope Pius XII also. In the allocution *Magnificate Dominum,* he stated more explicitly that the Church's competence exceeded the so-called matters religious and extended into the foundation, nature, interpretation, and application of natural law. And when the Church's magisterium made any rulings on matters concerning natural law, "the faithful must not invoke that saying (which is wont to be employed with respect to the opinions of individuals), 'the strength of the authority is no more than the strength of the arguments.'" The obligation to obey was still there whether the argument which accompanied the teaching in question was persuasive or not. Cf. Pius XII, "Magnificate Dominum," *AAS* 46 (Nov. 2, 1954), pp. 561–62.

7. Pope Pius XII, "Mystici Corporis," in *Encyclicals of Pius XII* (no author, publisher, or date of publication).

8. John T. Noonan, "Permitted and Disputed Means of Controlling Conception," *RMT*8, p. 104.

9. *AAS* 22, p. 5601.

10. *AAS* 43, pp. 845–46.

11. Louis Janssens, "Morale Conjugale et Progestogènes," *Ephemerides Theologicae Lovanienses* 39 (1963), pp. 787–826. Also see Jacques Ferin and Louis Janssens, "Progestogènes et Morale Conjugale," *Bibliotheca Ephemeridum Theologicarum Lovaniensium* 22 (Louvain: Publications Universitaires; Gembloux: Duculot, 1963), pp. 9–48. The quotation here is taken from Kaiser, *The Politics of Sex and Religion,* p. 30.

12. John Mahoney, *The Making of Moral Theology* (Oxford: Clarendon Press, 1989), p. 266.

13. John Gallagher, "Magisterial Teaching from 1918 to the Present," *RMT*8, p. 85.

14. Mahoney, *The Making of Moral Theology,* p. 267.

15. Pope Paul VI, "Encyclical Letter on the Regulation of Births" *(Humanae Vitae),* in Vatican Council II, vol. 2, *More Post Conciliar Documents,* edited by Austin Flannery (Northport, N.Y.: Costello, 1982).

16. *Humanae Vitae,* no. 3.

17. Ibid., no. 12.

18. Ibid., no. 15.

19. Ibid., no. 16.

20. Ibid., no. 11.

21. The full term in the official Latin text is usually given as *obsequium animi religiosum.* It is often translated as "religious submission of the mind" or as "respect for the religious authority of the magisterium." Other translations are possible and are often given, depending on one's inclination. It is therefore a very controverted term which has serious implications concerning the question of dissent, for example. I prefer to leave the phrase in Latin and allow the reader to decide what it actually means.

22. *Humanae Vitae,* no. 8.

23. See William H. Shannon, *The Lively Debate: Response to "Humanae Vitae"* (New York: Sheed and Ward, 1970), especially pp. 117–46.

24. *Our Sunday Visitor,* Aug. 18, 1968.

25. See John C. Ford and Germain Grisez, "Contraception and the Infallibility of the Ordinary Magisterium," *Theological Studies* 39 (1978), pp. 259–311.

26. Charles E. Curran, *Ongoing Revision in Moral Theology* (Notre Dame, Ind.: Fides, 1975), p. 268.

27. Ibid., p. 269.

28. Ibid., p. 271.

29. Ibid., p. 280.

30. "Text of the Statement by Theologians," *New York Times,* Aug. 31, 1968.

31. Charles E. Curran, *History and Contemporary Issues: Studies in Moral Theology* (New York: Continuum, 1996), p. 107.

32. Bernard Häring, "The Inseparability of the Unitive-Procreative Functions of the Marital Act," in *Contraception: Authority and Dissent,* edited by Charles E. Curran (New York: Herder and Herder, 1969), p. 176.

33. "Rhythm method" and "natural family planning method" (NFP) are used interchangeably in this text to describe the practice used by couples who abstain from sexual intercourse at certain times of the month, following the woman's menstrual cycle, when it is believed that conception is unlikely.

34. Häring, "The Inseparability of the Unitive-Procreative Functions of the Marital Act," pp. 179–80. Häring gives an example of the constant change in nature in these words: "We know, for example, that certain animals capable of

begetting offspring two or three times a year adjust rapidly when transferred from tropical or subtropical regions to the northern areas with a long winter. By a change in their biological laws and rhythm they adjust the process of begetting to once a year. Man's biological nature differs from that of the animals; it is slower in its changes. However, man survives precisely because he can make use of such artificial means as clothing, modern technology and most importantly, modern medicine in adjusting in a typically human way" (p. 182).

35. Ibid., p. 183.

36. Ibid.

37. Ibid., p. 185.

38. Ibid., p. 188.

39. Ibid., p. 190.

40. Dietrich von Hildebrand, "The Meaning of Marriage and the Principle of Superabundant Finality," in *RMT8*, pp. 116–17.

41. Ibid., p. 117.

42. Ibid., p. 124.

43. Ibid., p. 118.

44. Ibid., p. 119.

45. Germain Grisez, Joseph Boyle, John Finnis, and William E. May, "NFP: Not Contralife," *RMT8* (1993), p. 126.

46. Joseph Selling, "The 'Meanings' of Human Sexuality," *Louvain Studies* 23 (1998), p. 26.

47. Ibid., p. 27.

48. Ibid., p. 28.

49. Ibid., pp. 28–29.

50. Ibid., p. 31.

51. Ibid., p. 35.

52. Richard A. McCormick, *NMT1*, pp. 216–17. Also see Richard A. McCormick, "Conjugal Love and Conjugal Morality," *America* 110 (1964), pp. 38–42; and Richard A. McCormick, "Family Size, Rhythm, and the Pill," in *The Problem of Population* (Notre Dame, Ind.: University of Notre Dame Press, 1964), pp. 58–84.

53. Richard A. McCormick, *NMT1*, p. 218.

54. See Paulinus I. Odozor, *Richard A. McCormick and the Renewal of Moral Theology* (Notre Dame, Ind.: University of Notre Dame Press, 1995), pp. 48–49.

55. Richard A. McCormick, "Book Review," *America* 111 (Nov. 14, 1964), pp. 628–29.

56. CDF, "Instruction on Respect for Human Life in Its Origin and on the Dignity of Procreation," in Thomas A. Shannon and Lisa Sowle Cahill, eds., *Religion and Artificial Reproduction: An Inquiry into the Vatican: "Instruction on Respect for Human Life in Its Origin and on the Dignity of Human Reproduction"* (New York: Crossroad, 1988), p. 140.

57. Shannon and Cahill, *Religion and Artificial Reproduction*, p. 104.
58. Ibid., p. 161.

chapter three
Some Theological Supports for the Renewal of Moral Theology

1. Pope Pius XII, *Divino Afflante Spiritu,* in *The Papal Encyclicals 1939–1958,* edited by Claudia Carlen (Wilmington, N.C.: McGrath, 1981), p. 73.
2. Thomas Aquinas Collins and Raymond Brown, "Church Pronouncements," in *The Jerome Biblical Commentary* (Englewood Cliffs, N.J.: Prentice-Hall, 1968), p. 625.
3. Ibid.
4. Vincent MacNamara, *Faith and Ethics: Recent Roman Catholicism* (Washington, D.C.: Georgetown University Press, 1985), p. 17.
5. My debts to John R. Donahue's essay on this issue must be obvious to the reader. See John R. Donahue, "The Challenge of the Biblical Renewal to Moral Theology," in *Riding Time Like a River: The Catholic Moral Tradition Since Vatican II,* edited by William J. O'Brien (Washington, D.C.: Georgetown University Press, 1993).
6. Edward Schillebeeckx, *Jesus: An Experiment in Christology* (New York: Seabury Press, 1979), p. 48.
7. Ibid., p. 52.
8. Eugene LaVerdiere, "The Witness of the New Testament," in *Dimensions of Human Sexuality,* edited by Denis Doherty (Garden City, N.Y.: Doubleday, 1979), pp. 21–38.
9. Ibid., p. 31.
10. Donahue, "The Challenge of the Biblical Renewal to Moral Theology," pp. 75–76.
11. Allen Verhey, "The Use of Scripture in Ethics," *Religious Studies Review* 4:1 (Jan. 1978), p. 28.
12. See the following scriptural passages, for example: Gal 2:11–14; 1 Cor 8–10; Acts 10:1–34; Acts 15:19–20.
13. Donahue, "The Challenge of the Biblical Renewal to Moral Theology," p. 71.
14. Ibid., pp. 64–65.
15. Charles E. Curran, "The Role and Function of the Scriptures in Moral Theology," in *RMT4,* p. 181.
16. Richard M. Gula, *Reason Informed by Faith: Foundations of Catholic Morality* (New York: Paulist Press, 1989), p. 172.
17. Curran, "The Role and Function of the Scriptures in Moral Theology," p. 186.
18. Karl Rahner, "Anonymous Christians," in *Theological Investigations,* vol. 6 (London: Darton, Longman and Todd, 1969), p. 391.

19. Walter Kasper, "Absoluteness of Christianity," in *Sacramentum Mundi: An Encyclopedia of Theology*, vol. 1, edited by Karl Rahner (New York: Herder and Herder; London: Burns and Oates, 1969), p. 311.

20. Karl Rahner, "Christianity and Non-Christian Religions," in *Theological Investigations*, vol. 5 (London: Darton, Longman and Todd, 1966), p. 118.

21. Ibid., p. 119.

22. Ibid., p. 125.

23. Karl Rahner, "History of the World and Salvation-History," in *Theological Investigations*, vol. 5 (London: Darton, Longman and Todd, 1966), p. 98.

24. Rahner, "Christianity and Non-Christian Religions," p. 122.

25. Ibid., p. 123.

26. Ibid., p. 129.

27. Rahner, "Anonymous Christians," p. 391.

28. Ibid., pp. 391–92.

29. Karl Rahner, "Observations on the Problem of the Anonymous Christian," in *Theological Investigations*, vol. 14 (London: Darton, Longman and Todd, 1976), p. 283.

30. See Vatican II, *Lumen Gentium*, 14.

31. Vatican II, *Ad Gentes*, no. 7.

32. Vatican II, *Gaudium et Spes*, no. 22.

33. Karl Rahner, "Anonymous and Explicit Faith," in *Theological Investigations*, vol. 16 (London: Darton, Longman and Todd, 1979), p. 53.

34. Ibid., p. 55.

35. Ibid., p. 56.

36. Rahner, "Anonymous Christians," p. 393.

37. Rahner, "Anonymous and Explicit Faith," p. 57.

38. Ibid., p. 58.

39. Rahner, "Observations on the Problem of the Anonymous Christian," p. 292.

40. Rahner, "Anonymous and Explicit Faith," p. 58.

41. Rahner, "Christianity and Non-Christian Religions," p. 132.

42. Ibid., p. 133.

43. Rahner, "Anonymous and Explicit Faith," pp. 58–59.

44. John Mahoney, *The Making of Moral Theology: A Study of the Roman Catholic Tradition* (Oxford: Clarendon Press, 1989), p. 99.

45. John Macquarrie, *Thinking About God* (New York: Harper & Row, 1975), p. 95.

46. Mahoney, *The Making of Moral Theology*, p. 101.

47. Eugene Hillman, "Evangelism in a Wider Ecumenism: Theological Grounds for Dialogue with Other Religions," *Journal of Ecumenical Studies* 12 (Winter 1975), p. 4.

48. Justin Martyr, *Apologia*, 1.10, 46.

49. Walbert Bühlmann, *The Chosen Peoples* (Maryknoll, N.Y.: St. Paul Publications, 1982), p. 95.

50. Josef Fuchs, "Is There a Distinctively Christian Morality?" in *Personal Responsibility and Christian Morality* (Dublin: Gill and Macmillan; Washington, D.C.: Georgetown University Press, 1983), p. 53.

51. Ron Highfield, *Barth and Rahner in Dialogue: Toward an Ecumenical Understanding of Sin and Evil* (New York: Peter Lang, 1989), p. 50.

52. Karl Rahner, *Foundations of Christian Faith: An Introduction to the Idea of Christianity* (New York: Crossroad, 1984), p. 94.

53. Ronald Modras, "The Implications of Rahner's Anthropology for Fundamental Moral Theology," *Horizons* 12 (1985), p. 74.

54. Rahner, *Foundations of Christian Faith*, p. 97.

55. Ibid., p. 98.

56. Modras, "The Implications of Rahner's Anthropology," p. 74.

57. Bernard Häring, *Sin in a Secular Age* (Garden City, N.Y.: Doubleday, 1974), p. 185.

58. Ibid., p. 182.

59. Richard A. McCormick, *The Critical Calling: Reflections on Moral Dilemmas Since Vatican II* (Washington, D.C.: Georgetown University Press, 1989), p. 176.

60. Ibid., p. 177.

61. Ibid.

62. Germain Grisez, *The Way of the Lord Jesus*, vol. 1, *Christian Moral Principles* (Chicago: Franciscan Herald Press, 1983), p. 383.

63. Servais Pinckaers expresses his views on this theology in the following words: "On reproche également à la morale traditionelle d'être trop dépendante des catégories philosophiques païennes, spécialement aristotéliciennes." See Servais Pinckaers, *Le renouveau de la morale: Études pour une morale fidèle à ses sources et à sa mission présente* (Tournai: Casterman, 1964), p. 17.

64. Vincent MacNamara, *Faith and Ethics: Recent Roman Catholicism* (Dublin: Gill and Macmillan; Washington, D.C.: Georgetown University Press, 1985), p. 3.

65. Josef Fuchs, "Moral Theology According to Vatican II," p. 3.

66. MacNamara, *Faith and Ethics*, p. 15. See also Fuchs, "Moral Theology According to Vatican II," and Bernard Häring, *The Law of Christ*, vol. 1, pp. vii ff.

chapter four
The Distinctiveness of Christian Morality

1. Dionigi Tettamanzi, "Is There a Christian Ethics?" in *RMT* 2, p. 21.

2. Battista Mondin, "Faith and Reason in Roman Catholic Thought from Clement of Alexandria to Vatican II," *Dialogue and Alliance* 1:1 (Spring 1987), p. 20.

3. Ibid.

4. Anthony Giddens, *The Consequences of Modernity* (Stanford, Calif.: Stanford University Press, 1990), p. 64.

5. Malcolm Waters, *Globalization, Key Ideas* (London: Routledge, 1995), p. 1.

6. Roland Robertson, "Globalization, Modernity and Postmodernism: The Ambiguous Position of Religion," in *Religion and the Global Order: Religion and the Political Order,* vol. 4, edited by Roland Robertson and William R. Garret (New York: Paragon, 1991), p. 283.

7. Roland Robertson, *Globalization: Social Theory and Global Culture* (Thousand Oaks, Calif.: Sage, 1992), pp. 67–70.

8. Ibid., p. 141.

9. Peter L. Berger, *A Rumor of Angels: Modern Society and the Rediscovery of the Supernatural,* expanded ed., with new intro. (New York: Anchor Books, 1990).

10. E. Niermann, "Secularization," in *Encyclopedia of Theology: The Concise Sacramentum Mundi,* edited by Karl Rahner (New York: Crossroad, 1986), p. 1554. Also see Paulinus I. Odozor, "How Can the Gospel Be Heard in the Secular Culture of Africa's Cities?" in *The Gospel As Good News for African Cultures: A Symposium on the Dialogue Between Faith and Culture,* edited by Juvenalis Baitu (Nairobi: The Catholic University of Eastern Africa Publications, 1999), p. 63 ff.

11. Jean-Marie Aubert, "Debats autor de la morale fondamentale," *Studia Moralia* 20:2 (1982), pp. 198–99.

12. Anthony Thiselton, "Knowledge, Myth and Corporate Memory," in *Believing in the Church: The Corporate Nature of Faith: A Report by the Doctrine and Faith Commission of the Church of England* (Wilton, Conn.: Morehouse-Barlow; Toronto: Anglican Book Centre, 1982), p. 45 ff.

13. Tettamanzi, "Is There a Christian Ethics?" p. 22.

14. Charles E. Curran, "Is There a Catholic and/or Christian Ethic?" in *RMT* 2, pp. 60–61.

15. Jeffrey Stout, *Ethics After Babel: The Languages of Morals and Their Discontents* (Boston: Beacon Press, 1988), p. 109.

16. Germain Grisez, *The Way of the Lord Jesus,* vol. 1, *Christian Moral Principles* (Chicago: Franciscan Herald Press, 1983), p. 25.

17. See Alfons Auer, *Pastorale Konstitutionüber die Kirche in der Welt von Heute. Ester Hauptteill. Kommentat Zum III. Kapitel, in LTK. Das Zweite Vatikanische Konzil,* t.3, 1968, pp. 377–97. See also his *Autonome Morale und Christlicher Glaube* (Düsseldorf: Patmos, 1984).

18. "La 'réalité' *(wirklichkeit)* est le fondement de l'éthique (morale de l'être). 2) La morale consiste dans un 'oui' autonomie de l'homme aux requêtes de cette 'réalité.' 3) Ce 'oui' est autonome parce qu'il relève de la ca-

pacité effective de l'homme de penser son existence et son agir dans le monde ou parce qu'il ne relève pas d'une 'connaissance explicite de Dieu.' 4) Cependant, ce 'oui' de l'homme autonome au réel ne se produit pas, pour le chrétien, sans 'l'aide active de Dieu.' Cela signifie que ce 'oui' autonome existe comme tel dans des 'relations' au Transcendant, relations a) d'origine (protologie: Dieu-Logos) et b) de sens et de but (sotériologie/ecclesiologie— eschatologie: Dieu-Christos-Kyrios). C'est là l' 'horizon de sens' qui constitue le *'proprium'* chrétien. 5) Cet 'horizon de sens' propre à la foi chrétienne a un impact au niveau de la recherche autonome des normes morales (= fonctions d'intégration, de stimulation et de critique) et à celui de l'agir chrétien dans le monde (= courage invincible dans l'engagement). Remarquons bien cependant qu'il est sans influence sur la détermination matérielle, donc sur le contenu de l'agir moral, lequel ne dépend que de l'homme et de sa raison." Réal Tremblay, "Par dela la 'Morale Autonome' et l' 'Ethique de la Foi': À la recherche d'une 'via media,'" *Studia Moralia* vol. 20:2 (1982), p. 224. The translation in the text is my own.

19. Josef Fuchs, "Is There a Specifically Christian Morality?" *RMT2*, p. 4.

20. Ibid.

21. Josef Fuchs, *Human Values and Christian Morality* (Dublin: Gill and Macmillan, 1979), p. 114.

22. Fuchs, "Is There a Specifically Christian Morality?" p. 5.

23. Ibid.

24. Ibid., p. 6.

25. Ibid.

26. Richard A. McCormick, *Corrective Vision: Explorations in Moral Theology* (Kansas City, Mo.: Sheed and Ward, 1994), p. 59.

27. Fuchs, "Is There a Specifically Christian Morality?" p. 8.

28. Josef Fuchs, *Personal Responsibility and Christian Morality* (Dublin: Gill and Macmillan; Washington, D.C.: Georgetown University Press, 1983), pp. 73–74.

29. Ibid., p. 74. Fuchs takes this question from P. J. Weber, *Dissertatio Theologica inauguralis de genuina idea moralis christianae*, 1778.

30. Vincent MacNamara, *Faith and Ethics: Recent Roman Catholicism* (Dublin: Gill and Macmillan; Washington, D.C.: Georgetown University Press, 1985), p. 41.

31. Fuchs, "Is There a Specifically Christian Morality?" p. 9.

32. Says Fuchs, "It is, therefore, up to man to discover what kind of life is proper to him as one who is responsible to the Absolute and oriented towards his fellow human beings, responsible for human-worldly reality—so that his whole life may do justice to the nature and personal dignity of being-human. By so doing he does God's will. It is the will of God that man himself construct the 'blueprint' of genuinely human conduct, that he take into his own hands the

reality of man and his world, in order to lead it to its highest human potential, and turn himself and humanity toward a lofty, truly human history and future. If beyond this we speak of God's will and his commandments in the plural, we imply only that either revelation makes 'fallen' man, who is so selfish and so easily errs, conscious of a number of necessary ways of expressing the genuine 'Humanum'—which he could find also by himself—or that we ourselves, in society and church, believe we have found some essential values of the genuine 'Humanum' and formulate them accordingly." Fuchs, "Is There a Specifically Christian Morality?" p. 10.

33. It follows from this, says Fuchs, that "Christians and non-Christians face the same moral questions, and that both must seek this solution in genuinely human reflection and according to the same norms, e.g., whether adultery and premarital intercourse are morally right or can be so, whether the wealthy nations of the world must help the poor nations and to what extent, whether birth control is justified and should be provided, and what types of birth control are worthy of the dignity of human person. Such questions are questions for all humanity. If therefore, our Church and other human communities do not always reach the same conclusions, this is not due to the fact that there exists a different morality for Christians from that of non-Christians." Fuchs, "Is There a Specifically Christian Morality?" p. 11.

34. Fuchs, "Is There a Specifically Christian Morality?" p. 14.

35. "The examples of such Christian motivation may be taken from the letters of Paul. When Paul exhorts Christians to do and speak the truth, he does not base himself on the 'Inhumanum' of lying—this is presupposed—but on the negation of their shared existence in the one mystical Body of Christ that is the Church. When he warns the Christians of Corinth against prostitution, he presupposes the 'Inhumanum' of such conduct, explicitly reminding his hearers that their bodies belong to Christ, are holy as temples of the Holy Spirit, and that the body's goal is to be glorified with the risen Lord (1 Cor 6:12–20)." Fuchs, "Is There a Specifically Christian Morality?" p. 15.

36. Josef Fuchs, "A Harmonization of the Conciliar Statements on Moral Theology," in *Vatican II: Assessment and Perspectives: Twenty-five Years After (1962–1987)*, edited by René Latourelle (New York: Paulist Press, 1988), p. 482.

37. Josef Fuchs, "Moral Truths—Truths of Salvation?" in his *Christian Ethics in a Secular Arena* (Washington, D.C.: Georgetown University Press; Dublin: Gill and Macmillan, 1984), p. 50.

38. Ibid., p. 51.

39. Ibid., p. 52.

40. Ibid., p. 53.

41. Josef Fuchs, "The Christian Morality of Vatican II," in *Human Values and Christian Morality* (Dublin: Gill and Macmillan, 1979), p. 58.

42. Paulinus Ikechukwu Odozor, *Richard A. McCormick and the Renewal of Moral Theology* (Notre Dame, Ind.: University of Notre Dame Press, 1995), pp. 72–73.

43. Bruno Schüller, "Introduction," in his *Wholly Human: Essays on the Theory and Language of Morality,* trans. Peter Heinegg (Dublin: Gill and Macmillan; Washington, D.C.: Georgetown University Press, 1986), p. 2.

44. Ibid. See also Bruno Schüller, "Autonomous Ethics Revisited," in *Personalist Morals: Essays in Honor of Professor Louis Janssens,* edited by Joseph A. Selling (Leuven: University Press; Leuven: Uitgeverij Peeters, 1988), p. 62.

45. For example, he quotes from and extensively refers to the moral manuals and to the Scriptures to prove his point. From the work of Franz Hürth and Pedro Abellan he offers this reference: "All the moral precepts of the 'new law' are also precepts of the natural law. Christ did not add to the natural moral law even a single moral precept of a purely positive kind . . . This holds even for the commandment of love . . . The moral requirement of love for God and of love for man on account of God is a requirement of the natural law." Franz Hürth and Pedro Abellan, *De Principiis, de Virtutibus et Praeceptis* (Rome: Pont. Univ. Gregoriana, 1948), vol. 1, p. 43. See Bruno Schüller, "Autonomous Ethics Revisited," p. 61; and *Wholly Human,* pp. 2–3.

46. Bruno Schüller, "The Debate on the Specific Character of a Christian Ethics: Some Remarks," in *Wholly Human,* p. 20.

47. Ibid., p. 21.

48. Ibid., p. 25.

49. Ibid., p. 37.

50. Alasdair MacIntyre, *Whose Justice? Which Rationality?* (Notre Dame, Ind.: University of Notre Dame Press, 1988), p. 350.

51. Lisa S. Cahill, "On Richard McCormick: Reason and Faith in Post Vatican II Catholic Ethics," *Second Opinion* 9 (Nov. 1988), p. 111.

52. Richard A. McCormick, "Human Significance and Christian Significance," in *Norm and Context in Christian Ethics,* edited by Gene Outka and Paul Ramsey (New York: Scribner's, 1967), p. 235.

53. Ibid., p. 236.

54. Cahill, "On Richard McCormick," p. 117.

55. Richard A. McCormick, *NMT*1, p. 136.

56. Ibid., p. 129. In another place McCormick argues that refusing to accept this in fact amounts to a diminution of the Christian story. Cf. McCormick, *NMT*2, p. 27.

57. Richard A. McCormick, *The Critical Calling: Reflections on Moral Dilemmas Since Vatican II* (Washington, D.C.: Georgetown University Press, 1989).

58. *Documents of the Vatican II,* edited by Walter M. Abbott, S.J. (New York: America Press, 1966), p. 209.

59. McCormick, *The Critical Calling,* pp. 191–207. In other words, the Christian story is only a privileged articulation which tells us "the kind of people we ought to be, the goods we ought to pursue, the dangers we ought to avoid, the kind of world we ought to seek"; it does not articulate in every given situation of moral conflict what action we ought to take. That is the job of *recta ratio.* Cf. Richard A. McCormick, *Health and Medicine in the Catholic Tradition* (New York: Crossroad, 1984), p. 50.

60. Richard M. Gula, *What Are They Saying About Moral Norms?* (New York: Paulist Press, 1982), pp. 34–40.

61. Norbert Rigali, "On Christian Ethics," *Chicago Studies* 10 (1971), pp. 227–47.

62. Cf. McCormick, *The Critical Calling,* p. 195.

63. Ibid.

64. Ibid.

65. Ibid., p. 196.

66. Cahill, "On Richard McCormick," p. 114.

67. "Story" here refers to the foundational and originating event, the life, death, and resurrection—the entire mission of Christ.

68. McCormick, *Health and Medicine in the Catholic Tradition,* pp. 59–60.

69. Aubert, "Debats autor de la morale fondamentale," p. 199.

70. Eric Gaziaux, *Morale de la foi et morale autonome: Confrontation entre P. Delhaye et J. Fuchs* (Leuven: University Press; Leuven: Uitgeverij Peeters, 1995), p. 208.

71. Aubert, "Debats autour de la morale fondamentale," p. 200.

72. "L'autonomie humaine ne peut donc se comprendre que comme un don de Dieu. Cette communion à Dieu donne une valeur salvific à l'action profane du chrétien et fait de l'engagement éthique du chrétien une participation à l'action de Dieu dans l'histoire." Gaziaux, *Morale de la foi et morale autonome,* p. 208.

73. MacNamara, *Faith and Ethics,* p. 69.

74. Ibid., p. 70.

75. G. Emercke, "Christlichkeit und Geschichtlichkeit der Moraltheologie," in *Catholica* 26 (1972), pp. 193–211.

76. See B. Stöckle, *Wörterbuch der christlichen Ethik* (Freiburg: Herder, 1975). See also Gaziaux, *Morale de la foi et morale autonome,* p. 210.

77. Joseph Ratzinger, "Magisterium of the Church, Faith, Morality," *RMT2,* p. 177.

78. Ibid.

79. Ibid., p. 178.

80. Ibid.

81. Ibid., p. 179.

82. Ibid., p. 181.

83. Ibid., pp. 182–83.

84. Ibid., p. 184.

85. MacNamara, *Faith and Ethics*, p. 58.

86. Ratzinger, "Magisterium of the Church, Faith, Morality," p. 185.

87. Phillipe Delhaye, "Questioning the Specificity of Christian Morality," *RMT2*, p. 250.

88. Ibid., p. 251.

89. Ibid., pp. 251–52.

90. See Vatican II, *Dei Verbum*, 24, and *Optatam Totius*, 16.

91. See Rom 3:27.

92. See St. Augustine, *De Spiritu et Littera*, chap. 24; *Patrologia Latinae*, vol. 44, col. 225.

93. Aquinas writes, "Et ideo principaliter lex nova est ipsa gratia Spiritus Sancti quae datus Christi Fidelibus." *ST*, 1a-IIae, q.106, a.1.

94. See, for example, *Lumen Gentium*, no. 25.

95. Pope Paul VI, "La morale Chrétienne: Une manière de vivre selon la foi," in *Documentation Catholique* (1972), p. 752. Quoted in Delhaye, "Questioning the Specificity of Christian Morality," p. 253.

96. Delhaye, "Questioning the Specificity of Christian Morality," p. 254.

97. *Dei Verbum*, 6.

98. Pope Paul VI notes this fact well in this address delivered at the general audience he gave on July 26, 1972: "Some persons, frequently enough also those in the Christian world, would like behavior, especially in its public and exterior manifestation, to be secularized in an exclusive and absolute fashion. There are trends of thought and of action that propose to detach morality from theology; morality should concern itself exclusively with interpersonal relations and with the personal conscience of the individual; there should be no need for any religious dogma in the sphere of morality. Because it is legitimate to say that many expressions of human thought and of human action are ruled by criteria peculiar to them (the sciences, for example) and that a sound and reasonable secularity presides in the organization of the state, some people would like religion not only no longer to appear in public, but also no longer to exercise any influence for the purpose of inspiring or orienting civil legislation and practical conduct." Pope Paul VI, "La morale Chrétienne," p. 752. Quoted in Delhaye, "Questioning the Specificity of Christian Morality," p. 257.

99. As the Second Vatican Council says in *Lumen Gentium*, "The followers of Christ are called by God, not according to their accomplishments, but according to his own purpose and grace. They are justified in the Lord Jesus, and through baptism sought in faith they truly become children of God and sharers in the divine nature. In this way, they are really made holy. Then, too, by God's gifts they must hold on to and complete in their lives this holiness which they have received. They are warned by the apostle to live 'as becomes saints' (Eph

5:3) and to put on 'as God's chosen ones, holy and beloved, a heart of mercy, kindness, humility, meekness, patience' (Col 3:12) and to possess the fruits of the Spirit unto holiness (cf. Gal 5:22; Rom 6:22)." Cf. *Lumen Gentium*, no. 40.

100. Delhaye, "Questioning the Specificity of Christian Morality," p. 258.

101. Ibid., pp. 259–60.

102. "Among the pagans prudence is a purely intellectual virtue that is equal to knowledge. Christians have made it a practical virtue that judges the conformity of an action with the demands of the gospel. Among the pagans relations with others depended on justice or friendship. Christianity completely changed the conditions of intersubjectivity by placing in the foreground love as the bestowal of a gratuitous gift. The change was of such a character that Proudhon was to reproach Christianity for forgetting the objectivity of justice to the advantage of the subjectivity of charity. To be sure, he had put his finger on a transient deformation but the fact remains that the social justice of the Christian is encompassed by and saturated with charity. The virtue of religion, in Cicero, has the ceremony of the cult as its object. In many Christian authors, such as St. Augustine and St. Bonaventure, it is faith, hope, charity. Magnanimity, in Aristotle's view, was the sense of honor and of dignity. The Christians preserved these formulas but thenceforth they were to designate the strength to live and, if need be, to die as a martyr. The patience of the Stoic was submission to an implacable fate; for the Christian it has become the courageous awaiting of the hour of God in communion with the passion of Christ. Humility was little known or, at all events, little prized. It has become one of the most characteristic Christian attitudes." Delhaye, "Questioning the Specificity of Christian Morality," p. 261.

103. MacNamara, *Faith and Ethics*, p. 96. See also Bernard Häring, *Free and Faithful in Christ*, pp. 82, 87.

104. James M. Gustafson, *Christ and the Moral Life* (New York: Harper & Row, 1968), p. 240.

105. Richard A. McCormick, "Does Faith Add to Ethical Perception," *RMT* 2, p. 166.

106. Paulinus I. Odozor, "Richard A. McCormick and Casuistry: Moral Decision-Making in Conflict Situations" (Th.M. thesis, University of St Michael's College, University of Toronto, 1989), p. 42.

chapter five
Scripture and Ethics

1. Lisa Sowle Cahill, "The Bible and Christian Moral Practices," in *Christian Ethics: Problems and Prospects*, edited by Lisa Sowle Cahill and James F. Childress (Cleveland: Pilgrim Press, 1996), p. 4.

2. See Lisa Sowle Cahill, *Between the Sexes: Foundations for a Christian Ethics of Sexuality* (Philadelphia: Fortress Press, 1985), pp. 15–16.

3. See, for example, Harold Lindsell, *The World, the Flesh and the Devil* (Washington, D.C.: Canon Press, 1973). Also, *The Bible for the Bible* (Grand Rapids, Mich.: Zondervan, 1976).

4. Brevard Childs, *Biblical Theology in Crisis* (Philadelphia: Westminster Press, 1970).

5. Raymond Brown, *The Critical Meaning of the Bible* (New York: Paulist Press, 1981), pp. 30–31.

6. Ibid., p. 30.

7. Luis Alonso Schökel, "Inspiration," in *Sacramentum Mundi*, edited by Karl Rahner (New York: Herder and Herder, 1968), p. 147.

8. Ibid., p. 150.

9. Richard Gula, *Reason Informed by Faith: Foundations of Catholic Morality* (New York: Paulist Press, 1989), p. 116.

10. Jack Sanders, *Ethics in the New Testament* (Philadelphia: Fortress Press, 1975).

11. Elisabeth Schüssler Fiorenza, "'You Are Not to Be Called Father': Early Christian History in a Feminist Perspective," in *The Bible and Liberation: Political and Social Hermeneutics*, edited by Norman Gottwald (New York: Orbis Books, 1983), p. 397.

12. Elisabeth Schüssler Fiorenza, *Bread Not Stone: The Challenge of Feminist Biblical Interpretation* (Boston: Beacon Press, 1984), p. 5.

13. Elisabeth Schüssler Fiorenza, "The Will to Choose or to Reject: Continuing Our Critical Work," in *The Feminist Interpretation of the Bible*, edited by Letty M. Russell (Philadelphia: Westminster Press, 1985), p. 127.

14. Ibid.

15. Elisabeth Schüssler Fiorenza, *In Memory of Her: A Feminist Theological Reconstruction of Christian Origins* (New York: Crossroad, 1983), p. xviii.

16. Fiorenza, *Bread Not Stone*, p. 5. See also "The Will to Choose," p. 130.

17. Fiorenza, *Bread Not Stone*, p. 8.

18. Ibid., p. 53.

19. Ibid., p. 84.

20. Fiorenza, "The Will to Choose," pp. 130–31.

21. Fiorenza, *In Memory of Her*, p. xx.

22. Fiorenza, *Bread Not Stone*, p. 85.

23. Fiorenza, *In Memory of Her*, p. 27.

24. Cf. Fiorenza, *In Memory of Her*, p. 29. See also *Bread Not Stone*, p. 85.

25. Cf. Fiorenza, "The Will to Choose," p. 130. See also *Bread Not Stone*, p. 15.

26. Cf. Fiorenza, *Bread Not Stone*, pp. 15–20.

27. Fiorenza, "The Will to Choose," p. 131.

28. Ibid.

29. Ibid., p. 132.

30. Fiorenza, *Bread Not Stone*, p. 19. See also "The Will to Choose," p. 133.

31. Fiorenza, *Bread Not Stone*, p. 19.

32. Fiorenza, "The Will to Choose," p. 133.

33. Ibid., p. 135.

34. Fiorenza, *In Memory of Her*, p. 33.

35. Ibid., p. 34.

36. Fiorenza, *Bread Not Stone*, p. 45.

37. Anne E. Carr, *Transforming Grace: Christian Tradition and Women's Experience* (San Francisco: Harper & Row, 1988), p. 80. See also Fiorenza, *In Memory of Her*, pp. 245–342. Also, Fiorenza, "'You Are Not to Be Called Father,'" pp. 394–497.

38. Elisabeth Schüssler Fiorenza, "Toward a Feminist Biblical Interpretation and Liberation Theology," *RMT4*, p. 375.

39. Sandra M. Schneiders, *The Revelatory Text: Interpreting the New Testament as Sacred Scripture*, 2nd ed. (Collegeville, Minn.: Liturgical Press, 1999), p. 175.

40. Ibid., pp. 175–76.

41. Ibid., p. 177.

42. Cahill, "The Bible and Christian Moral Practices," p. 3.

43. Ibid., p. 4.

44. Ibid.

45. Cahill, *Between the Sexes*, p. 36.

46. Roland E. Murphy, "Christian Understanding of the Old Testament," *Theology Digest* 18 (1970), p. 327.

47. Edouard Hamel, "Scripture: The Soul of Moral Theology," *RMT4*, p. 111.

48. Ibid., p. 112.

49. Ibid.

50. Ibid., p. 113.

51. Ibid., p. 115.

52. Second Vatican Council, *Dei Verbum*, no. 11.

53. The conquest theory as a model for the reconstruction of Israel's origin argues that Israel acquired its place in Palestine mostly by a bloody invasion which took place around the thirteenth century B.C., and which resulted in massive destruction of Canaanite populations. The invasion was swift, brief, and energetic, and took place on three fronts: Transjordan, the south, and the north. It was to a large extent the work of the twelve tribes, or at least of the nucleus of the twelve tribes, and culminated with Joshua sharing the captured land among the tribes (Jos 13ff.). Though initiated by Moses in Transjordan, the work was

to a large extent Joshua's. The descent of the Israelites into Palestine is often thought by the proponents of the conquest theory to be part of a wave of general migrations to the Fertile Crescent around this period. Says the late Yohanan Aharoni, "The invasion is not an isolated phenomenon; it is related to the great wave of expansion by Hebrew and Aramaean tribes which exerted pressure in this period on all the lands of the Fertile Crescent. . . . The Israelites belonged to this broad ethnic migration coming from the Eastern and Southern wilds" (Yohanan Aharoni, *The Land of the Bible* [Philadelphia: Westminster Press, 1967], pp. 177–78.)

54. The immigration theory is in many ways a direct refutation of the conquest model. In its broadest outline it runs thus: Israel's occupation of the land did not ensue from a swift and violent encounter between it and the earlier inhabitants of the land in question. Where any such violent encounters occurred they were negligible and happened only much later in the course of Israel's settlement in the land. Instead, Israel's settlement in the land was a fairly quiet, peaceful, and drawn-out exercise which took place without any quick or radical change in the demographic situation in Palestine. The occupation was by a group of seminomads (Israel's ancestors) who "probably first set foot on the land in the process of changing pastures, and in the end began to settle for good in the sparsely populated areas of the country and then extended their territory from their original domains as occasion offered, the whole process being carried through, to begin with, by peaceful means and without the use of force. The occupation was thus not the unified action Conquest theorists take it to be. Rather, it consisted of geographically distinct movements lasting over a long period of time—beginning from about the second half of the fourteenth century and ending in about 1100 B.C." (Martin Noth, *The History of Israel,* 2nd ed. (New York: Harper & Row, 1960), p. 69.

55. For Noth, the approach was a form-critical study of strands in Joshua and Judges aimed at deriving the individual histories of the different tribes of Israel. Part of his conclusion from this exercise was the now famous assertion that Israel was a conglomeration of twelve tribes with diverse backgrounds and histories who arrived from various places at different times in Palestine where they settled and became united into an amphyctionic union, which became the basis of their later identity as the nation of Israel. See Noth, *The History of Israel,* p. 81.

56. For Alt, the approach was the investigation of the territorial divisions of Canaan from about 2000 B.C., completely independently of the histories of the tribes. Albrecht Alt, *Essays on Old Testament History and Religion* (Garden City, N.Y.: Doubleday, Anchor Books, 1968), p. 178ff.

57. George E. Mendenhall, "The Hebrew Conquest of Palestine," in *Biblical Archaeologist Reader,* vol. 3, edited by E. Campbell and D. Freeman (New York: Anchor Books, 1970), p. 107.

58. Ibid., p. 108. See also Norman Gottwald, *The Tribes of Yahweh* (Maryknoll, N.Y.: Orbis Books, 1979), p. 210.

59. Mendenhall, "The Hebrew Conquest," p. 107.

60. Gottwald, *The Tribes of Yahweh*, p. xxii.

61. Allen Myers, "*The Tribes of Yahweh:* A Review," in *The Bible and Liberation*, edited by N. Gottwald (Maryknoll, N.Y.: Orbis Books, 1983), p. 168.

62. Cf. Gottwald, *The Tribes of Yahweh*, p. 212.

63. Alt, *Essays*, pp. 183–84.

64. Gottwald, *The Tribes of Yahweh*, p. 212. See also John Bright, *A History of Israel* (London: SCM Press, 1981), p. 138. Also Alt, *Essays*, p. 184.

65. Alt, *Essays*, p. 187.

66. See *Biblical Archaeologist Reader*, vol. 3 (New York: Anchor Books, 1970), pp. 66–68.

67. Gottwald, *The Tribes of Yahweh*, p. 401.

68. Mendenhall, "The Hebrew Conquest," p. 105.

69. Ibid., p. 63. Also see Gottwald, *The Tribes of Yahweh*, p. 401.

70. Mendenhall, "*The Hebrew Conquest,*" p. 108.

71. *Gottwald*, The Tribes of Yahweh, p. 437.

72. Ibid., pp. 474–75.

73. Ibid., p. 489.

74. Mendenhall, "The Hebrew Conquest," p. 108.

75. Norman Gottwald, "Israel's Emergence," interview in *Bible Review* 5:5 (Oct. 1989), p. 33.

76. Gottwald, *The Tribes of Yahweh*, p. 491.

77. William C. Spohn, *What Are They Saying About Scripture and Ethics?* Rev. and expanded ed. (New York: Paulist Press, 1995), p. 56.

78. Allen Verhey, "The Use of Scripture in Ethics," *Religious Studies Review* 4:1 (Jan. 1978), p. 32.

79. Secundo Galilea, "Liberation Theology Began with Medellin," *Ladoc* (May 1975), pp. 1–6.

80. Richard A. McCormick, *NMT*1, p. 620.

81. Verhey, "The Use of Scripture in Ethics," p. 28.

82. William C. Spohn, "Jesus and Christian Ethics," *Theological Studies* 56 (1995), p. 96.

83. Spohn, *What Are They Saying,*" p. 21.

84. Ibid., p. 32.

85. Charles E. Curran, "The Role and Function of the Scriptures in Moral Theology," *R MT*4, p. 205.

86. Ibid., p. 206.

87. Verhey, "The Use of Scripture in Ethics," p. 28.

88. See William Spohn, "Jesus and Ethics," *Catholic Theological Society of America Proceedings* 49 (1994) 40–57; "Jesus and Christian Ethics," 92–106; *Go and Do Likewise: Jesus and Ethics* (New York: Continuum, 1999).

89. See Spohn, "Jesus and Ethics," p. 46; "Jesus and Christian Ethics," p. 101; and *Go and Do Likewise*.

90. See Spohn, *Go and Do Likewise*, esp. pp. 74–187.

91. Ibid., p. 10.

92. See Spohn, "Jesus and Christian Ethics," pp. 103–4; "Jesus and Ethics," pp. 50–51; *Go and Do Likewise*, p. 186.

93. Spohn, "Jesus and Christian Ethics," p. 104.

94. Ibid., p. 105.

95. Spohn, *Go and Do Likewise*, p. 163.

96. Ibid., p. 165.

97. Gula, *Reason Informed by Faith*, p. 185.

98. See Spohn, *What Are They Saying*.

99. Bruno Schüller, "A Contribution to the Theological Discussion of Natural Law," *RMT 7*, p. 82.

chapter six
Natural Law in the Catholic Moral Tradition

1. Joseph Gremillion, *The Gospel of Peace and Justice: Catholic Social Teaching Since Pope John* (New York: Orbis Books, 1976), p. 11.

2. Pope Leo XIII, *Rerum Novarum*, no. 5, in *Catholic Social Thought: The Documentary Heritage*, edited by David J. O'Brien and Thomas A. Shannon (Maryknoll, N.Y.: Orbis Books, 1998), p. 16.

3. Pope Leo XIII, *Rerum Novarum*, no. 9.

4. Pope John XXIII, *Pacem in Terris*, no. 11, in *Catholic Social Thought*, edited by O'Brien and Shannon.

5. Ibid., no. 12.

6. Ibid., no. 13.

7. Ibid., no. 14.

8. Ibid., no. 15.

9. Ibid., no. 18.

10. Ibid., no. 23.

11. Ibid., no. 26.

12. Ibid., no. 27.

13. It is not my intention here to present a comprehensive picture of the human rights doctrine of Pope John XXIII in this encyclical. I mention these rights here as an example of the extensive natural law foundation of the human rights teaching of this encyclical.

14. *Pacem in Terris*, no. 28. Italics added.

15. *Gaudium et Spes*, no. 79.

16. Jean Porter, *Natural and Divine Law: Reclaiming the Tradition for Christian Ethics* (Grand Rapids, Mich.: Eerdmans, 1999), p. 29.

17. Pope Pius XI, *Casti Connubii*, no. 54, in *The Papal Encyclicals: 1903–1939*, edited by Claudia Carlen (Raleigh, N.C.: McGrath, 1981).

18. Pope Pius XII, "Remarks to the Congress of Hematologists (September 12, 1958)," *RMT*8, p. 171. Also, Pope Pius XII, "Address to the 4th International Convention of Catholic Physicians (September, 1949)," *RMT*8, p. 223.

19. Pope Paul VI, *Humanae Vitae*, no. 11, in *RMT*8.

20. Ibid., no. 12.

21. Ibid., no. 4.

22. Josef Fuchs, "The Natural Law in Church Testimony," *RMT*7, p. 5.

23. Porter, *Natural and Divine Law*, p. 29.

24. Ibid., p. 52.

25. Joseph Boyle, "Natural Law," in *The New Dictionary of Theology*, edited by Joseph Komonchak, Mary Collins, and Dermot Lane (Collegeville, Minn.: The Liturgical Press, 1987), p. 703.

26. Thomas Aquinas, *ST*, 1a-IIae, q.90, a.4.

27. See Appendix 2, by Thomas Gilby, in Aquinas, *Summa Theologiae*, vol. 28 (1a2ae 90–97): *Law and Political Theory*, edited by Thomas Gilby (Cambridge, Eng.: Blackfriars, 1966), p. 162.

28. *ST*, 1a-IIae, q.91, a.3.

29. Ibid., a.2&4.

30. Ibid., 9.94, a.2.

31. Ibid.

32. Ibid.

33. 2 *Sentences*, d.24, q.2, a.3.

34. Ibid.

35. Ross Armstrong, *Primary and Secondary Precepts in Thomistic Natural Law Teaching* (The Hague: Martinus Nijhoff, 1966), p. 29.

36. Ibid., p. 30.

37. *De Veritate*, q.16, a.1, 2 & 3.

38. *ST*, 1a-IIae, q.94, a.2.

39. Germain G. Grisez, "The First Principle of Practical Reason: A Commentary on the *Summa Theologiae*, 1–2, Question 94, Article 2," *Natural Law Forum* (1965), p. 175.

40. *ST*, 1a-IIae, q.94, a.2.

41. Grisez, "The First Principle of Practical Reason," p. 177.

42. Ibid.

43. Ibid., p. 184.

44. Ibid.

45. Armstrong, *Primary and Secondary Precepts*, p. 39.

46. At least this is an impression one gets from reading his article on the first principle of practical reason which has been cited many times in this section.

47. Jacques Maritain, *The Range of Reason* (New York: Scribner's, 1952), pp. 26–29. See also *Man and the State* (Chicago: University of Chicago Press, 1951), p. 81.

48. Eric D'Arcy, *Conscience and Its Right to Freedom* (London: Sheed and Ward, 1960), pp. 52–57.

49. Frederick Copleston, *Aquinas* (Harmondsworth, Middlesex: Penguin, 1955), p. 223.

50. Armstrong, *Primary and Secondary Precepts*, p. 50.

51. John Macquarrie, "Rethinking Natural Law," in *Readings in Moral Theology*, no. 1, *Moral Norms and Catholic Tradition*, edited by Charles E. Curran and Richard A. McCormick (Mahwah, N.J.: Paulist Press, 1979), pp. 121–45.

52. See Appendix 2, by Thomas Gilby, in Aquinas, *Summa Theologiae*, vol. 28.

53. Jacques Maritain, "Natural Law in Aquinas," *RMT7*, p. 114.

54. Johannes Gründel, "Natural Law," in *Encyclopedia of Theology: The Concise Sacramentum Mundi*, edited by Karl Rahner (New York: Seabury Press, 1975), p. 1017.

55. Maritain, "Natural Law in Aquinas," *RMT7*,. p. 116.

56. Bruno Schüller, "A Contribution to the Theological Discussion of Natural Law," *RMT7*, p. 81.

57. Ibid.

58. John Courtney Murray, "The Doctrine Lives: The Eternal Return of Natural Law," *RMT7*, p. 214.

59. *Gaudium et Spes,* 16.

60. Boyle, "Natural Law," p. 704.

61. Bruno Schüller, "Zur theologischen Diskussion über die Lex naturalis," *Theologie und Philosophie* 41(1966), 481–503.

62. Battista Mondin, "Faith and Reason in Roman Catholic Thought from Clement of Alexandria to Vatican II," *Dialogue and Alliance* 1:1 (Spring 1987), p. 20.

63. St. Thomas Aquinas, *ST,* 1, 1, art. 2. The translation here is from *The Basic Writings of Saint Thomas Aquinas,* vol. 1, edited by Anton C. Pegis (New York: Random House, 1945).

64. *ST,* 1, 32, art. 1.

65. "It was necessary for man's salvation that there should be a doctrine revealed by God, besides the philosophical disciplines investigated by human reason. First because man is directed to God as to an end that surpasses the grasp of his reason: Even as regards those truths about God which human reason can investigate, it was necessary that man should be taught by a divine revelation. For the truth about God, such as reason can know it, would only be known by a few, and that after a long time, and with the admixture of many er-

rors; whereas man's whole salvation, which is in God, depends upon the knowledge of this truth. Therefore in order that the salvation of men might be brought about more fitly and more surely it was necessary that they be taught divine truths by divine revelation." Thomas Aquinas, *ST*, 1, 1, art. 2.

66. Thomas Aquinas, *Contra Gent.* 1, 7. See Mondin, "Faith and Reason," p. 20.

67. Thomas Aquinas, *De Trinitate*, 1, 7.

68. Mondin, "Faith and Reason," p. 21.

69. Porter, *Natural and Divine Law,* p. 30.

70. Boyle, "Natural Law," p. 706.

71. Brian V. Johnstone, "From Physicalism to Personalism," *Studia Moralia* 30 (1992), p. 72.

72. Charles E. Curran, "Natural Law and Moral Theology," in *Contraception, Authority and Dissent* (New York: Herder and Herder, 1969), p. 153.

73. Ibid., p. 157.

74. Ulpian was a Roman lawyer who died in A.D. 228. His particular interpretation of natural law was different from that of Cicero, who was the architect of the other view of natural law as deriving from human rationality. Both of these views, as is evident from *ST*, I-IIae, q.94, art. 2, were taken over, amplified, and refined by Thomas Aquinas. For a more detailed discussion of these and other related issues, see Richard Gula, *What Are They Saying About Moral Norms?* (New York: Paulist Press, 1982), pp. 34–53. Also see Charles E. Curran, *Directions in Fundamental Moral Theology* (Notre Dame, Ind.: University of Notre Dame Press, 1985), pp. 127–33.

75. Curran, "Natural Law in Moral Theology," *RMT* 7, p. 258.

76. Curran, "Natural Law and Moral Theology," p. 161.

77. Curran's position on *Humanae Vitae* is very well known and will form part of the topic of study in a different chapter.

78. Cf. Curran, *Directions in Fundamental Moral Theology,* pp. 127–33.

79. Cf. Karl Rahner, "The Man of Today and Religion," in *Theological Investigations,* vol. 6, translated by Cornelius Ernst (New York: Seabury Press, 1974), p. 8.

80. Pope Pius XI, *On Christian Wedlock* (New York: Barry Vail, 1931), p. 26.

81. John Ford and Gerald Kelly, *Contemporary Moral Theology,* vol. 2, *Marriage Questions* (Westminster, Md.: Newman Press, 1963), p. 286.

82. Richard A. McCormick, *Health and Medicine in the Catholic Tradition* (New York: Crossroad, 1984), p. 89.

83. Ibid., p. 90.

84. Cf. McCormick, *Health and Medicine,* pp. 86–104.

85. Cf. *Gaudium et Spes (GS),* in *Documents of Vatican Council II,* edited by Walter M. Abbott (New York: America Press, 1966), p. 256. Also, see *Schema constitutionis pastoralis de ecclesia in mundo huis temporis: Expensio Modorum*

partis secundae (Rome: Vatican Press, 1965), pp. 37–38. See also Richard A. McCormick, *NMT2*, p. 52; and *The Critical Calling* (Washington, D.C.: Georgetown University Press, 1989), p. 212.

86. McCormick, *The Critical Calling*, p. 212.

87. Charles Curran, "Official Catholic Social and Sexual Teachings: A Methodological Comparison," *RMT8*, pp. 536–58.

88. Richard P. McBrien, *Catholicism*, vol. 2 (Minneapolis, Minn.: Winston Press, 1980), p. 609.

89. Ibid., pp. 941–42.

90. Ibid., p. 942.

91. Quoted in Curran, "Official Catholic Social and Sexual Teachings," p. 550.

92. According to Curran, indications of classicism are evident elsewhere, including the "Declaration on Sexual Ethics" (Dec. 29, 1975); the "Letter to the Bishops of the Catholic Church on the Pastoral Care of Homosexual Persons" (Oct. 1, 1986); the "Instruction on Respect for Human Life in Its Origin and on the Dignity of Procreation" (Feb. 22, 1987).

93. Henry Davis, *Moral and Pastoral Theology*, vol. 1, *Human Acts, Law, Sin, Virtue* (New York: Sheed and Ward, 1935), p. 130.

94. Germain Grisez, *The Way of the Lord Jesus*, vol. 1 (Chicago: Franciscan Herald Press, 1983), p. 840.

95. Ibid., p. 847.

96. See Paulinus I. Odozor, *Richard A. McCormick and the Renewal of Moral Theology* (Notre Dame, Ind.: University of Notre Dame Press, 1995), p. 60.

97. Frank Mobbs, *Beyond Its Authority?: The Magisterium and Matters of Natural Law* (Alexandria, N.S.W., Australia: E. J. Dwyer, 1997), pp. 2–3.

98. Ibid., p. 294.

99. Porter, *Natural and Divine Law*, p. 27.

100. Germain Grisez, *The Way of the Lord Jesus*, vol. 1 (Chicago: Franciscan Herald Press, 1983), p. 180.

101. *Veritatis Splendor*, no. 48.

102. Ibid., no. 49.

103. Ibid., no. 48.

104. Ibid., no. 50.

105. Boyle, "Natural Law," p. 706.

106. Ibid., p. 707.

chapter seven
Magisterium and Morality

1. Richard A. McCormick, *The Critical Calling: Reflections on Moral Dilemmas Since Vatican II* (Washington, D.C.: Georgetown University Press, 1989), p. 19.

2. John Mahoney, *The Making of Moral Theology: A Study of the Roman Catholic Tradition* (Oxford: Clarendon Press, 1989), p. 289.

3. "Dogmatic Constitution on the Church" (*Lumen Gentium*, no. 18), in *Vatican Council II: The Conciliar and Post Conciliar Documents*, vol. 1, rev. ed., edited by Austin Flannery (Northport, N.Y.: Costello, 1984).

4. Flannery, *Vatican Council II*, p. 379.

5. Ibid., p. 756.

6. Avery Dulles, "Doctrinal Authority for a Pilgrim Church," *RMT3*, p. 251.

7. Francis A. Sullivan, *Magisterium: Teaching Authority in the Catholic Church* (New York: Paulist Press, 1983), pp. 25–26.

8. Yves Congar's views can be found in two articles, "A Semantic History of the Term Magisterium" and "A Brief History of the Forms of the Magisterium and Its Relation to Scholars," both of which are published in *RMT3*, pp. 297–331.

9. Congar, "A Semantic History," p. 298.

10. Congar, "A Brief History," p. 315.

11. Ibid., p. 316.

12. Ibid., p. 317.

13. Ibid., p. 318.

14. Ibid., pp. 322–25.

15. "Eorum [referring to theologians] est iudicare qua ratione ea quae a vivo magistero docenture, in Sacris Litteris et in divina 'traditione' sive explicite, sive implicite inveniantur" (DS 3886; quoted also in Congar, "A Brief History," p. 325).

16. Germain Grisez, *The Way of the Lord Jesus*, vol. 1, *Christian Moral Principles* (Chicago: Franciscan Herald Press, 1983), p. 865, note 20.

17. Ibid., p. 842.

18. Richard A. McCormick, "The Teaching Role of the Magisterium and of the Theologians," *CTSA Proceedings* 24 (June 1969), p. 247.

19. Bruno Schüller, "Remarks on the Authenticd Teaching of the Magisterium," *RMT3*, p. 16.

20. Ibid., p. 19.

21. Richard Gula, *Reason Informed by Faith* (New York: Paulist Press, 1989), p. 205.

22. Avery Dulles, "Authority and Conscience," *RMT6*, p. 97.

23. Paulinus I. Odozor, *Richard A. McCormick and the Renewal of Moral Theology* (Notre Dame, Ind.: University of Notre Dame Press, 1995), p. 192.

24. Richard A. McCormick, "The Removal of a Fetus Probably Dead," (S.T.D. diss., Rome, Pontifica Universitas Gregoriana, 1957), pp. 239–40.

25. Dulles, "Authority and Conscience," p. 100.

26. Ibid., p. 104.

27. Ibid.

28. Ibid., p. 105.

29. Cf. Odozor, *Richard A. McCormick and the Renewal of Moral Theology,* p. 65.

30. Richard A. McCormick, *NMT*1, pp. 205–6.

31. Schüller, "The Authentic Teaching of the Magisterium," p. 21.

32. Dulles, "Authority and Conscience," p. 106.

33. Congregation for the Doctrine of the Faith, "Instruction on the Ecclesial Vocation of the Theologian," *Origins* 28 (July 5, 1990), n. 30.

34. Ibid., n. 31.

35. Karl Rahner, "Theology and the Magisterium: Self-Appraisal," *RMT*6, p. 39.

36. See John T. Noonan, Jr., "The Amendment of Papal Teaching by Theologians," in *Contraception, Authority and Dissent,* edited by Charles E. Curran (New York: Herder and Herder, 1969), pp. 41–75. See also John T. Noonan, Jr., "The Development of Doctrine," in *The Context of Casuistry,* edited by James F. Keenan and Thomas A. Shannon (Washington, D.C.: Georgetown University Press, 1995), pp. 188–204.

chapter eight
The Debate on Moral Norms

1. Paulinus Ikechukwu Odozor, "Casuistry and AIDS: A Reflection on the Catholic Tradition," in *Catholic Ethicists on HIV/AIDS Prevention,* edited by James F. Keenan, Jon D. Fuller, Lisa Sowle Cahill, and Kevin Kelly (New York: Continuum, 2000), p. 297.

2. Richard M. Gula, *Reason Informed by Faith: Foundations of Catholic Morality* (New York: Paulist Press, 1989), p. 283.

3. Joseph T. Mangan, "An Historical Analysis of the Principle of Double Effect," *Theological Studies* 10 (March 1949), pp. 41–62. See also J. Ghoos, "L'acte à double effet, étude de théologie positive," *Ephemerides Theologicae Lovanienses* 27 (1951), pp. 30–52.

4. Richard A. McCormick, "The Removal of a Fetus Probably Dead to Save the Life of the Mother" (S.T.D. diss., Rome, Pontifica Universitas Gregoriana, 1957). Peter Knauer, "The Hermeneutic Function of the Principle of Double Effect," *RMT*1.

5. Joseph Selling, "The Problem of Reinterpreting the Principle of Double Effect," *Louvain Studies* 8 (1980), pp. 47–62.

6. Mangan, "An Historical Analysis of the Principle of Double Effect," p. 42.

7. *ST,* II-II, q.64, a.7.

8. Lucius Iwejuru Ugorji, *The Principle of Double Effect: A Critical Appraisal of Its Traditional Understanding and Its Modern Reinterpretation* (Frankfurt am Main and New York: Peter Lang, 1985), pp. 29–30.

9. Mangan, "An Historical Analysis of the Principle of Double Effect," p. 43.

10. See Paulinus I. Odozor, *Richard A. McCormick and the Renewal of Moral Theology* (Notre Dame, Ind.: University of Notre Dame Press, 1995), p. 92.

11. Ibid., pp. 92–93.

12. Selling, "The Problem of Reinterpreting the Principle of Double Effect," p. 53.

13. McCormick, "The Removal of a Fetus Probably Dead."

14. Richard A. McCormick, "Ambiguity in Moral Choice," in *Doing Evil to Achieve Good: Moral Choice in Conflict Situations,* edited by Richard A. McCormick and P. Ramsey (Chicago: Loyola University Press, 1978), pp. 11–12.

15. Odozor, *Richard A. McCormick and the Renewal of Moral Theology,* p. 96.

16. Germain Grisez, *Abortion: The Myths, the Realities, and the Arguments* (New York: Corpus Books, 1970). See pp. 330–34.

17. Ibid., p. 330.

18. Ibid., p. 331.

19. Richard A. McCormick, *NMT2,* pp. 16–17.

20. Grisez, *Abortion,* p. 331.

21. James J. Walter, "The Foundation and Formulation of Norms," in *Moral Theology, Challenges for the Future: Essays in Honor of Richard A. McCormick, S.J.,* edited by Charles E. Curran (New York: Paulist Press, 1990), p. 121.

22. Louis Janssens, "Ontic Evil and Moral Evil," *RMT1,* p. 60.

23. Richard A. McCormick, *Health and Medicine in the Catholic Tradition* (New York: Crossroad, 1984), p. 46.

24. Janssens, "Ontic Evil and Moral Evil," p. 69.

25. James J. Walter, "The Foundation and Formulation of Norms," p. 132.

26. Janssens, "Ontic Evil and Moral Evil," p. 55.

27. Ibid., p. 57.

28. Richard A. McCormick, *Doing Evil to Achieve Good* (Chicago: Loyola University Press, 1978), p. 44.

29. Ibid., p. 46.

30. Ibid.

31. This section depends to a large extent on my previous work on Richard McCormick. See Odozor, *Richard A. McCormick and the Renewal of Moral Theology,* p. 105 ff., for a more detailed discussion on McCormick's position on the criteria for determining proportionate reason.

32. Louis Janssens, "Norms and Priorities in a Love Ethic," *Louvain Studies* 6 (1977), p. 219.

33. Ibid., p. 229.

34. Jean Porter, "The Moral Act in *Veritatis Splendor* and in Aquinas's *Summa Theologiae:* A Comparative Analysis," in *Veritatis Splendor: American Responses,* edited by Michael E. Allsopp and John J. O'Keefe (Kansas City, Mo.: Sheed and Ward, 1995), p. 282.

35. Richard A. McCormick, "Some Early Reactions to *Veritatis Splendor,*" *RMT*11, p. 27.

36. *VS,* 52.

37. Alasdair MacIntyre, "How Can We Learn What *Veritatis Splendor* Has to Teach?" *The Thomist* 58:1 (1994), p. 177.

38. McCormick, *NMT*2, p. 64.

39. Lisa Sowle Cahill, "Accent on the Masculine," *RMT*10, p. 89.

40. Josef Fuchs, "The Absoluteness of Moral Terms," *RMT*1, p. 120.

41. Richard A. McCormick, *NMT*1, p. 710.

42. Ibid.

43. Ibid., pp. 710–11.

44. F. S. Carney, "Deciding the Situation: What Is Required?" in *Norm and Context in Christian Ethics,* edited by Gene H. Outka and P. Ramsey (New York: Charles Scribner's Sons, 1968), p. 4.

45. James M. Gustafson, "Context Versus Principles," *Harvard Theological Review* 58 (1965), p. 191.

46. Richard Gula, *What Are They Saying About Moral Norms?* (New York: Paulist Press, 1982), p. 55.

47. Timothy O'Connell, *Principles for a Catholic Morality* (New York: Seabury Press, 1978), p. 160.

48. Janssens, "Norms and Priorities in a Love Ethic," p. 207.

49. McCormick, *NMT*1, pp. 578–79.

50. Bruno Schüller, *Wholly Human* (Washington, D.C.: Georgetown University Press, 1986), pp. 24–25.

51. William E. May, "Aquinas and Janssens on the Moral Meaning of Human Acts." *The Thomist* 48:3 (1984), p. 571.

52. Janssens, "Norms and Priorities in a Love Ethic," p. 217.

53. Richard A. McCormick, "Killing the Patient," in *Considering "Veritatis Splendor,"* edited by John Wilkins (Cleveland, Ohio: Pilgrim Press, 1995), p. 19.

54. See Odozor, *Richard A. McCormick and the Renewal of Moral Theology,* p. 116.

55. See Jean Porter, *The Recovery of Virtue: The Relevance of Aquinas for Christian Ethics* (Louisville, Ky.: Westminster/John Knox Press, 1990), pp. 14–15. See also Janssens, "Ontic and Moral Evil."

56. Ross Armstrong, *Primary and Secondary Precepts in Thomistic Natural Law* (The Hague: Martinus Nijhoff, 1966), p. 50.

57. Thomas Aquinas, *Supplement to the Summa,* q.65, a.1.

58. Thomas Aquinas, *ST,* 1a-IIae, q.94, a.4, 5, 6.

59. Armstrong, *Primary and Secondary Precepts,* p. 93.

60. *ST,* 1a-IIae, q.100, a.1.

61. Francis Sullivan, *Magisterium: Teaching Authority in the Catholic Church* (New York: Paulist Press, 1983), p. 138.

62. *ST,* 1a-IIae, q.91, a.3.

63. Ibid., 1a-IIae, q.94, a.4.

64. Louis Janssens, "Saint Thomas Aquinas and the Question of Proportionality," *Louvain Studies* 9 (1982), pp. 27–46.

65. Thomas Aquinas, *De Veritate,* q.23, a.7.

66. Thomas Aquinas, 1a-IIae, q.18, a.6, quoted in Janssens, "Saint Thomas Aquinas and the Question of Proportionality," p. 31.

67. Janssens, "Saint Thomas Aquinas and the Question of Proportionality," p. 45.

68. Jean Porter, "Moral Rules and Moral Actions: A Comparison of Aquinas and Modern Moral Theology," *Journal of Religious Ethics* (1989), pp. 123–24.

69. Odozor, *Richard A. McCormick and the Renewal of Moral theology,* p. 172.

70. William K. Frankena, "McCormick and the Traditional Distinction," in *Doing Evil to Achieve Good,* edited by Paul Ramsey and Richard A. McCormick (Chicago: Loyola University Press, 1978), p. 145.

71. Mangan, "An Historical Analysis of the Principle of Double Effect," p. 43. Gerald Kelly formulates the principle this way: "1) that the action itself is not morally bad. 2) that the evil is effect is sincerely not intended, but merely tolerated. 3) that the evil is not the means for obtaining the good effect. 4) that the good effect is sufficiently important to balance or outweigh the harmful effect." See Gerald Kelly, *Medico-Moral Problems* (St. Louis: Catholic Hospital Association of the United States and Canada, 1949), p. 12. Also see Benedictus Henricus Merklebach, *Summa Theologiae Moralis,* vol. 1 (Brugis Belgia, 1956), p. 258; E. F. Regatillo and Marcelino Zalba, *Theologica moralis summa,* vol. 1. (Matriti: Editoria Católica, 1952), p. 211. None of these authors mentions the "direct/indirect" term in their presentation of the principle of double effect.

72. Selling, "The Problem of Reinterpreting the Principle of Double Effect," p. 53.

73. Pope Pius XI, *Casti Connubii,* in *The Papal Encyclicals, 1903–1939,* edited by Claudia Carlen, p. 401.

74. *AAS* 50 (1958).

75. Pope Pius XII, "Remarks to the Congress of Hematologists (September 12, 1958)," *RMT8,* p. 171.

76. Pope Paul VI, *Humanae Vitae* (London: Catholic Truth Society, 1968), no. 14.

77. Pope John Paul II, *Evangelium Vitae* (Vatican City: Libreria Editrice Vaticana, 1995), no. 62.

78. Bruno Schüller, "Direct/Indirect Killing," *RMT*1, p. 138.

79. Janssens, "Ontic Evil and Moral Evil," p. 60.

80. Schüller, "Direct/Indirect Killing," pp. 142–43.

81. Ibid., p. 152.

82. Richard A. McCormick, "A Commentary on the Commentaries," in *Doing Evil to Achieve Good*, edited by Richard A. McCormick and P. Ramsey (Chicago: Loyola University Press, 1978), p. 41.

83. Bruno Schüller, "The Double Effect in Catholic Thought: A Reevaluation," in *Doing Evil to Achieve Good*, edited by Richard A. McCormick and P. Ramsey (Chicago: Loyola University Press, 1978), p. 181.

84. McCormick, "Ambiguity in Moral Choice," p. 30.

85. Ibid., p. 32.

86. McCormick, "Commentary on the Commentaries," p. 257.

87. John R. Connery, "Morality of Consequences: A Critical Appraisal," *RMT*1, p. 245.

88. Ibid., p. 247.

89. Bruno Schüller, "Neuere Beiträge zum Thema 'Begründung sittlicher Normen,'" *Theologische Berichte* 4 (1974), pp. 109–81.

90. Connery, "Morality of Consequences," p. 249.

91. McCormick, *NMT*1, p. 541.

92. Ibid., p. 708.

93. Germain Grisez, *Christian Moral Principles,* vol. 1 of *The Way of the Lord Jesus* (Chicago: Franciscan Herald Press, 1983), p. 141.

94. Ibid., pp. 142–43.

95. Ibid., p. 178. Here Grisez is quoting St. Thomas: "Hic est ergo primum praeceptum legis, quod 'bonum est faciendum et prosequendum, et malum vitandum'" (*ST,* 1a-IIae, q.94, a.2).

96. *ST,* 1a-IIae, q.94, a.2.

97. Grisez, *Christian Moral Principles,* p. 180.

98. Ibid., p. 144.

99. Ibid., p. 122. See also Germain Grisez, Joseph Boyle, and John Finnis, "Practical Principles, Moral Truth, and Ultimate Ends," *American Journal of Jurisprudence* 32 (1987), p. 107.

100. Germain Grisez and Russell B. Shaw, *Beyond the New Morality* (Notre Dame, Ind.: University of Notre Dame Press, 1988), p. 69.

101. Grisez, *Christian Moral Principles,* p. 181.

102. Ibid., p. 229.

103. Grisez, Boyle, and Finnis, "Practical Principles, Moral Truth, and Ultimate Ends," p. 106.

104. See Odozor, *Richard A. McCormick and the Renewal of Moral Theology,* p. 99. See also Grisez, *Abortion,* p. 315.

105. Grisez, *Christian Moral Principles,* p. 184.

106. Ibid., p. 186.

107. Ibid., p. 189.
108. Ibid., p. 191.
109. Ibid., pp. 205–26.
110. Jean Porter, "'Direct' and 'Indirect' in Grisez's Moral Theory," *Theological Studies* 57 (1996), p. 614.
111. Grisez, *Christian Moral Principles*, p. 255.
112. Ibid.
113. See Richard A. McCormick, "Ambiguity in Moral Choice," in *Doing Evil to Achieve Good*, p. 25; Grisez, *Abortion*, p. 28; Odozor, *Richard A. McCormick and the Renewal of Moral Theology*, pp. 100–101.
114. See for example, Richard A. McCormick, *Notes on Moral Theology* (2 vols.), and Bernard Hoose, *Proportionalism: The American Debate and Its European Roots* (Washington, D.C.: Georgetown University Press, 1987), among many others.

chapter nine
Two Alternative Approaches: Virtue Ethics and Casuistry

1. Richard M. Gula, *The Good Life: Where Morality and Spirituality Converge* (New York: Paulist Press, 1999), p. 4.
2. James F. Keenan, "Virtue Ethics," in *Christian Ethics: An Introduction*, edited by Bernard Hoose (Collegeville, Minn.: Liturgical Press, 1998), p. 84.
3. Gula, *The Good Life*, p. 5.
4. William C. Spohn, "The Return of Virtue Ethics," *Theological Studies* 53 (1992), p. 61.
5. Robert Wokler, "Projecting the Enlightenment," in *After MacIntyre: Critical Perspectives on the Work of Alasdair MacIntyre*, edited by John Horton and Susan Mendus (Notre Dame, Ind.: University of Notre Dame Press, 1994), p. 108.
6. Alasdair MacIntyre, *After Virtue: A Study in Moral Theory*, 2nd ed. (Notre Dame, Ind.: University of Notre Dame Press, 1984), p. 50.
7. Ibid.
8. Stanley Hauerwas, *A Community of Character: Toward a Constructive Christian Social Ethic* (Notre Dame, Ind.: University of Notre Dame Press, 1981), pp. 214–15.
9. MacIntyre, *After Virtue*, p. 52.
10. Ibid., p. 119.
11. Ibid., p. 118.
12. Alasdair MacIntyre, *Whose Justice? Which Rationality?* (Notre Dame, Ind.: University of Notre Dame Press, 1988), p. 402.
13. Ibid., p. 208.

14. Ibid., p. 222.

15. Jean Porter, *The Recovery of Virtue: The Relevance of Aquinas for Christian Ethics* (Louisville, Ky.: Westminster/John Knox Press, 1990), p. 13.

16. Ibid., p. 15.

17. Ibid., p. 16.

18. Ibid., p. 50.

19. Ibid., p. 63.

20. *ST,* I-II, q.55, a.4; Also, *Sent.* D 27, a.2.

21. Ibid., I-II, q.63, a.3.

22. Ibid., I-II, q.55, a.4.

23. Ibid., I-II, q.58, a.3.

24. Ibid., I-II, q.57, a.5.

25. Ibid., I-II, q.60, a.4.

26. Ibid., I-II, q.61, a.3.

27. Porter, *Recovery of Virtue,* p. 121.

28. *ST,* I-II, q.56, a.6.

29. Ibid., II-II, q.58, a.1, 2.

30. Porter, *Recovery of Virtue,* p. 124. See also *ST,* II-II, q.58, a.5, 6.

31. Porter, *Recovery of Virtue,* p. 126.

32. Jean Porter, *Moral Action and Christian Ethics* (Cambridge: Cambridge University Press, 1995), pp. 167–68.

33. Ibid., pp. 168–69.

34. Ibid., p. 169.

35. Ibid., p. 170.

36. Ibid., p. 174.

37. Ibid., p. 179.

38. Ibid., p. 180.

39. Ibid., p. 182.

40. Ibid., pp. 182–83.

41. Ibid., p. 187.

42. Ibid., p. 196.

43. Ibid., pp. 198–99.

44. Keenan, "Virtue Ethics," p. 84.

45. Ibid., p. 92.

46. Ibid., p. 93.

47. Robert L. Stivers, *Christian Ethics: A Case Method Approach* (Maryknoll, N.Y.: Orbis Books, 1989), p. 3.

48. Richard A. McCormick, *Health and Medicine in the Catholic Tradition* (New York: Crossroad, 1984), p. 46.

49. Ibid.

50. Ibid.

51. Edouard Hamel, "Casuistry," in *New Catholic Encyclopedia,* vol. 3 (San Francisco: Catholic University Press, 1967), p. 195.

52. Ibid.

53. Cf. Geoffrey W. Bromiley, "Casuistry," in *Baker's Dictionary of Christian Ethics* (Grand Rapids, Mich.: Baker Book House, 1967), p. 86.

54. Hamel, "Casuistry," p. 196.

55. Ibid.

56. John T. McNeil, "Casuistry in the Puritan Age," *Religion and Life* (Winter 1942/1943), p. 77.

57. Aristotle, *Nichomachean Ethics,* translated by Martin Oswald (Indianapolis: Bobbs-Merrill, 1962), VI, III, 315ff.

58. Ibid., VI, V, 25ff.

59. Ibid.

60. See Albert R. Jonsen and Stephen Toulmin, *The Abuse of Casuistry: A History of Moral Reasoning* (Berkeley: University of California Press, 1988).

61. See, for example, *The Context of Casuistry,* edited by James F. Keenan and Thomas A. Shannon (Washington, D.C.: Georgetown University Press, 1995), among many others.

62. James F. Keenan, "The Return of Casuistry," *TS* 57 (1996), p. 125.

63. Paulinus I. Odozor, "Casuistry and AIDS: A Reflection on the Catholic Tradition," in *Catholic Ethicists on HIV/AIDS Prevention,* edited by James F. Keenan, Jon D. Fuller, Lisa Sowle Cahill, and Kevin Kelly (New York: Continuum, 2000), p. 298.

64. Richard A. McCormick, "Bioethics and Method: Where Do We Start?" in *On Moral Medicine: Theological Perspectives in Medical Ethics,* edited by Stephen E. Lammers and Allen Verhey (Grand Rapids, Mich.: Eerdmans, 1987), p. 45.

65. See Richard A. McCormick, *How Brave a New World? Dilemmas in Bioethics* (Garden City, N.Y.: Doubleday, 1981), pp. 21–28.

66. Ibid., p. 22.

67. Ibid., p. 23.

68. Ibid., p. 27.

69. See Odozor, "Casuistry and AIDS," pp. 294–302.

chapter ten
Catholic Moral Tradition in an Age of Renewal

1. Eugene LaVerdiere, "The Witness of the New Testament," in *Dimensions of Human Sexuality*, edited by Dennis Doherty (Garden City, N.Y.: Doubleday, 1979), pp. 21–38.

2. Ibid., p. 31.

3. John R. Donahue, "The Challenge of the Biblical Renewal to Moral Theology," in *Riding Time Like a River,* edited by William J. O'Brien (Washington, D.C.: Georgetown University Press, 1993), pp. 75–76.

4. Allen Verhey, "The Use of Scripture in Ethics," *Religious Studies Review* 4:1 (January 1978), p. 28.

5. Henry Davis, *Moral and Pastoral Theology*, vol. 1 (New York: Sheed and Ward, 1946), p. viii.

6. Eduard Génicot, *Theologiae Moralis: Institutiones*, 3rd ed., vol. 1 (Lovanii: Typus Polleunis et Ceutercik, 1900), p. 9.

7. Pope John Paul II, *Fides et Ratio* (Boston: Pauline Books and Media, 1996), no. 13.

8. See Joseph Sittler, *The Structure of Christian Ethics* (Baton Rouge: Louisiana State University Press, 1958).

9. See, for example, Lisa Cahill, *Sex, Gender and Christian Ethics* (Cambridge: Cambridge University Press, 1996). See especially chapter 6.

10. Lisa Cahill, "On Richard McCormick: Reason and Faith in Post–Vatican II Catholic Ethics," *Second Opinion* 9 (Nov. 1988), p. 111.

11. Andrew Greeley, *The Catholic Imagination* (Berkeley: University of California Press, 2000), pp. 6–7.

12. Ibid., p. 1.

13. Pope John Paul II, *Fides et Ratio,* no. 16.

14. *Gaudium et Spes,* no. 59.

15. Ibid., no. 58.

16. William C. Spohn, *What Are They Saying About Scripture and Ethics?* (New York: Paulist Press, 1995), p. 44.

17. James M. Gustafson, "Roman Catholic and Protestant Interaction in Ethics: An Interpretation," *Theological Studies* 50 (1989), p. 49.

18. Thomas Aquinas, *ST*, I-II, q.109, a.2.

19. Brian V. Johnstone, "From Physicalism to Personalism," *Studia Moralia* 30 (1992), p. 71.

20. John T. Noonan, Jr., *Contraception* (Cambridge, Mass.: Harvard University Press, Belknap Press, 1986), p. 573.

21. Some of the main features of the anthropology of Vatican II are as follows. First is that human beings are created in the image of God, are capable of knowing and loving God, and are appointed by God to master all the earth for the sake of God's glory. Human beings are created as essentially social and not solitary beings. We are created male and female. Although God made human beings in a state of holiness, human life is characterized by sin as well because at the dawn of history human beings abused their liberty, at the urging of personalized evil. As a consequence, the human person is split within himself. Human life manifests the dramatic struggle between good and evil, between light and darkness. The call to grandeur and the depths of misery are both a part of human experience. Though made of body and soul, the human person is not a duality. He is one. In his body, he gathers to himself the elements of the material world. Thus they reach their crown through him, and through him raise their voices in

free praise of the creator. We cannot, therefore, despise our bodies nor the created world in which we find ourselves in spite of the stirrings of rebellion which are in our bodies as a result of our being wounded by sin. Human beings are superior to bodily concerns for by their interior qualities they outstrip the sum of mere things. The Council also speaks of the human person as a spiritual being who encounters God in the innermost recesses of the human heart wherein human beings meet God, who awaits them there. Human beings are endowed with intelligence which is capable of knowing truth and moving beyond merely observable data to arrive at metaphysical certitude, "though in consequence of sin, that certitude is partly obscured and weakened. Wisdom and knowledge go hand in hand. That is why, our world is in great danger, unless wiser men are forthcoming" (15).

The Council teaches that each human person possesses a conscience. In the depths of his conscience each person detects a law which he does not impose upon himself, but which holds him to obedience. Conscience is the most secret core and sanctuary of the human person. There he is alone with God, whose voice echoes in his depths. In fidelity to conscience, Christians are joined with the rest of humanity in the search for truth, and for the genuine solution to numerous problems, which arise in the life of individuals and from social relationships (16). The human person is created free. Only in freedom can he direct himself toward goodness. Freedom is not license. But since our freedom has been damaged by sin, only with the help of God's grace can we bring our relationship with God and thereby with the whole of creation to full flower. The reality of death is also part of human existence. In the face of death the riddle of human existence becomes even more acute. Technology cannot calm our anxieties about death, for the prolongation of biological life cannot satisfy that desire for a higher life which is inescapably lodged in the human heart (18). Although the mystery of death utterly beggars the imagination, the Church has been taught by divine revelation, and herself firmly teaches, that man has been created by God for a blissful purpose beyond the reach of earthly misery (18).

22. Arthur C. Danto, "Persons," in *The Encyclopedia of Philosophy,* vols. 5 and 6, edited by Paul Edwards (New York: Macmillan, 1967), p. 110.

23. Joseph Fletcher, "Four Indicators of Human-hood: The Enquiry Matures," in *On Moral Medicine: Theological Perspectives in Medical Ethics,* edited by S. Lammers and A. Verhey (Grand Rapids, Mich.: Eerdmans, 1987), pp. 275–78.

24. See Max Muller and Alois Hadler, "Person," in *Encyclopedia of Theology: The Concise Sacramentum Mundi,* edited by Karl Rahner (New York: Crossroad, 1986), pp. 1206–13.

25. Marjorie Reiley Maguire, "Personhood, Covenant, and Abortion," in *Abortion and Catholicism: The American Debate,* edited by Patricia Beattie Jung and Thomas A. Shannon (New York: Crossroad, 1988), p. 103.

26. Paulinus I. Odozor, *Richard A. McCormick and the Renewal of Moral Theology* (Notre Dame, Ind.: University of Notre Dame Press, 1995), p. 77.

27. Richard A. McCormick, "The Judeo-Christian Tradition and Bioethical Codes," in his *How Brave a New World? Dilemmas in Bioethics* (Garden City, N.Y.: Doubleday, 1981), p. 12.

28. Maguire, "Personhood, Covenant, and Abortion," p. 103.

29. Louis Janssens, "Artificial Insemination: Ethical Considerations," *Louvain Studies* 8 (1980), pp. 3–29.

30. Johnstone, "From Physicalism to Personalism," p. 81.

31. Ibid., p. 83.

32. Dolores L. Christie, *Adequately Considered: An American Perspective on Louis Janssens' Personalist Morals,* Louvain Theological and Pastoral Monographs 4 (Louvain: Peeters, 1990), p. 118.

33. Bernard Häring, "Dynamism and Continuity in a Personalistic Approach to Natural Law," in *Norm and Context in Christian Ethics,* edited by Gene Outka, Paul Ramsey, and Frederick Smith Carney (New York: Scribner's, 1968), p. 206.

34. Richard A. McCormick, *The Critical Calling* (Washington, D.C.: Georgetown University Press, 1989), pp. 15–16.

35. See *Donum Vitae* on this issue.

36. Jean Porter, *Natural and Divine Law* (Grand Rapids, Mich.: Eerdmans, 1999), p. 225.

37. Ibid., p. 226.

38. See, James B. Nelson, *Embodiment: An Approach to Sexuality and Christian Theology* (Minneapolis: Augsburg, 1978), pp. 70–80.

39. See, for example, United States Catholic Conference, *Human Sexuality: A Catholic Perspective for Education and Life-Long Learning,* among many other sources.

40. André Guindon, *The Sexual Creators* (Lanham, Md.: University Press of America, 1986). Cf. Eric Fuchs, *Sexual Desire and Love* (New York: Seabury Press, 1983), pp. 9–32.

41. Klaus Demmer, *Shaping the Moral Life: An Approach to Moral Theology* (Washington, D.C.: Georgetown University Press, 2000), p. 41.

42. *Veritatis Splendor,* no. 107.

43. Ibid., no. 109.

44. See John Gallagher, *Time Past, Time Future* (New York: Paulist Press, 1990).

45. See Porter, *Natural and Divine Law.*

46. Cf. Joseph T. Mangan, "An Historical Analysis of the Principle of Double Effect," *Theological Studies* 10 (March 1949).

47. Peter Knauer, "The Hermeneutic Function of the Principle of Double Effect," *RMT1.*

48. See endnotes to chapter 8 for citations of the work of these authors.

chapter eleven
Pope John Paul II on Postconciliar Moral Theology:
An Epilogue and a Beginning

1. Pope John Paul II, *The Splendor of Truth* (Boston: St. Paul Books and Media, 1993), no. 115.

2. Six years were to elapse between the announcement by the pope and the appearance of the encyclical. The pope explains in his letter that the delay was necessary to allow for the prior publication of the *Catechism of the Catholic Church*, which would provide a more complete presentation of the moral doctrines of the Church. *VS*, no. 5.

3. *VS*, no. 4.

4. Ibid., no. 11.

5. Oliver O'Donovan, "A Summons to Reality," in *Considering "Veritatis Splendor,"* edited by John Wilkins (Cleveland, Ohio: Pilgrim Press, 1994), p. 42.

6. James P. Hanigan, "*Veritatis Splendor* and Sexual Ethics," in *"Veritatis Splendor"*: *American Responses*, edited by Michael E. Allsopp and John J. O'Keefe (Kansas City, Mo.: Sheed and Ward, 1995), p. 210.

7. *VS*, no. 93.

8. Hanigan, "*Veritatis Splendor* and Sexual Ethics," p. 211.

9. *VS*, no. 32.

10. Ibid., no. 35.

11. Ibid., no. 84.

12. Ibid., no. 89.

13. See Ronald R. Burke, "*Veritatis Splendor*: Papal Authority and the Sovereignty of Reason," in *"Veritatis Splendor"*: *American Responses*, edited by Michael Allsopp and John J. O'Keefe (Kansas City, Mo.: Sheed and Ward, 1995), esp. pp. 120–25.

14. Pope John Paul II, *Centesimus Annus*, no. 36.

15. *VS*, no. 88.

16. Pope John Paul II, *Centesimus Annus*, no. 44.

17. Ibid.

18. *VS*, no. 31.

19. Pope John Paul II, *Fides et Ratio: On the Relationship Between Faith and Reason* (Boston: St. Paul Books and Media, 1996), no. 2.

20. Ibid., no. 14.

21. Ibid., no. 15.

22. *VS*, no. 32.

23. Ibid., no. 35.

24. Ibid., no. 40.

25. Ibid., no. 39.

26. Ibid., no. 106.

27. *EV,* no. 20.

28. Ibid., no. 69.

29. Ibid., no. 70.

30. *VS,* no. 115.

31. Ibid., no. 52.

32. Alasdair MacIntyre, "How Can We Learn What *Veritatis Splendor* Has to Teach?" *The Thomist* 58:1 (1994), p. 177.

33. *VS,* no. 50.

34. According to the pope, these threats to life are taking on vast proportions. "They are not only threats coming from outside, from the forces of nature or the 'Cains' who kill the 'Abels.' They are rather *scientifically and systematically programmed* threats coming from significant sectors of the human society." The perpetrators of this threat include legislators who "departing from the basic principles of their constitutions," have determined not to punish the rampant practices against life but rather have sought to legalize them. Others who share more or less in the prevalence of the culture of death include the men who not only directly pressure women into having abortions, but also indirectly encourage such a decision by leaving the woman alone to face the problems of pregnancy. Blameworthy also are those women themselves who decide upon the death of the child in the womb. Other participants in the threat against life are those doctors and nurses who "place at the service of death skills which were acquired for promoting life" and those who create and foster a climate of sexual permissiveness and a lack of esteem for womanhood. "Finally, one cannot overlook the network of complicity which reaches out to include international institutions, foundations and associations which systematically campaign for the legalization and spread of abortion in the world, giving the life issue a highly social dimension. We are indeed facing an immense threat to life: not only to the life of individuals but also to that of civilization itself. We are facing what can be called a *structure of sin,* which opposes human life not yet born."

35. *EV,* no. 12.

36. Ibid., no. 14.

37. Ibid.

38. Ibid., no. 15.

39. Ibid., no. 16.

40. Ibid., no. 17.

41. Ibid., no. 22.

42. Ibid., no. 20.

43. See, for instance, the pope's position in *Redemptoris Missio,* on the good for the Church to re-evangelize what he refers to as the modern areopaguses—modern cultures.

44. Maura Anne Ryan, "'Then Who Can Be Saved?': Ethics and Ecclesiology in *Veritatis Splendor,*" in *"Veritatis Splendor": American Responses,* edited by

Michael E. Allsopp and James J. O'Keefe (Kansas City, Mo.: Sheed and Ward, 1995), p. 3.
  45. *VS*, no. 8.
  46. Ibid., no. 29.
  47. Hanigan, "*Veritatis Splendor* and Sexual Ethics," p. 214.
  48. *VS*, no. 4.
  49. Ibid., no. 36.
  50. Ibid., no. 37.
  51. Ibid., no. 4.
  52. Ibid., no. 110.
  53. Ibid., no. 29.
  54. Ibid., no. 75.
  55. Ibid.
  56. Ibid., no. 76.
  57. Ibid., no. 77.
  58. Ibid., no. 78.
  59. Ibid.
  60. Ibid., no. 80.
  61. Ibid., no. 83.
  62. Ibid., no. 96.
  63. Ibid., no. 101.
  64. Ibid., no. 104.
  65. Ibid., no. 105.
  66. Germain Grisez, "Revelation Versus Dissent," *RMT* 10, pp. 35–46.
  67. Ibid., p. 41.
  68. Bernard Häring, "A Distrust That Wounds," in *Considering "Veritatis Splendor,"* edited by John Wilkins (Cleveland, Ohio: Pilgrim Press, 1994), p. 9.
  69. Ibid., p. 12.
  70. Richard A. McCormick, "Killing the Patient," in *Considering "Veritatis Splendor,"* edited by John Wilkins (Cleveland, Ohio: Pilgrim Press, 1994), pp. 14–20.
  71. Ibid., p. 19.
  72. Ibid., p. 18.
  73. Hanigan, "*Veritatis Splendor* and Sexual Ethics," p. 219.
  74. Ibid., pp. 219–20.
  75. Lisa Sowle Cahill, "Accent on the Masculine," *RMT* 10, p. 86.
  76. Vincent MacNamara, *Faith and Ethics* (Dublin: Gill and Macmillan; Washington, D.C.: Georgetown University Press, 1985), p. 44.
  77. See James Gustafson's classic treatment of this issue in his two books *Christ and the Moral Life* (New York: Harper & Row, 1968), esp. pp. 238–71; and *Can Ethics Be Christian?* (Chicago: University of Chicago Press, 1975).
  78. *VS*, no. 88.

bibliography

Unless otherwise stated, quotations from the *Summa Theologiae* of St. Thomas Aquinas are taken from the translation published by the Fathers of the English Province of the Order of Preachers in 1920 (5 vols.). Various sources have been used for the papal encyclicals. These sources are acknowledged in the text. However, I have also found the following compilations of the papal encyclicals useful: Claudia Carlen, *A Guide to the Encyclicals of the Roman Pontiffs from Leo XIII to the Present Day (1879–1937)* (New York: H. Wilson, 1939); Claudia Carlen, *The Papal Encyclicals (1939–1958)* (Wilmington, N.C.: McGrath, 1981).

Abbott, Walter M., ed. *Documents of Vatican II.* New York: America Press, 1966.

Aharoni, Yohanan. *The Land of the Bible.* Philadelphia: Westminster Press, 1967.

Allsopp, Michael E., and John J. O'Keefe. *"Veritatis Splendor": American Responses.* Kansas City, Mo.: Sheed and Ward, 1995.

Alonso Schökel, Luis. "Inspiration." In *Sacramentum Mundi,* edited by Karl Rahner. New York: Herder and Herder, 1968.

Alt, Albrecht. *Essays on Old Testament History and Religion.* Garden City, N.Y.: Doubleday, Anchor Books, 1968.

Aristotle. *Nicomachean Ethics.* Translated by Martin Oswald. Indianapolis: Bobbs-Merrill, 1962.

Armstrong, Ross. *Primary and Secondary Precepts in Thomistic Natural Law Teaching.* The Hague: Martinus Nijhoff, 1966.

Aubert, Jean-Marie. "Debats autor de la morale fondementale." *Studia Moralia* 20:2 (1982):195–222.

Auer, Alfons. *Autonome Morale und Christlicher Glaube.* Düsseldorf: Patmos, 1984.

―――. *Pastorale Konstitution über die Kirche in der Welt von Heute. Erster Hauptteil. Kommentat zum III. Kapitel, in LTK. Das Zweite Vatikanische Konzil,* t.3, 1968: 377–97.

Augustine, Saint. *De Spiritu et Littera.* Chap. 24; *PL,* vol. 44, col. 225.

Baitu, Juvenalis, ed. *The Gospel As Good News for African Cultures: A Symposium on the Dialogue Between Faith and Culture.* Nairobi: Catholic University of Eastern Africa, 1999.

Baum, Gregory. "Faith and Liberation: Development Since Vatican II." In *Vatican II: Open Questions and New Horizons,* edited by Gerald M. Fagin, 75–104. Wilmington, Del.: Michael Glazier 1984.

Berger, Peter L. *A Rumor of Angels: Modern Society and the Rediscovery of the Supernatural.* Expanded ed., with new introduction by the author. New York: Anchor Books, 1990.

Bouquillon, Thomas J. "Moral Theology at the End of the Nineteenth Century." In *Readings in Moral Theology,* no. 11, *The Historical Development of Fundamental Moral Theology in the United States,* edited by Charles E. Curran and Richard A. McCormick, 91–114. New York: Paulist Press, 1999.

Boyle, Joseph. "Natural Law." In *The New Dictionary of Theology.* Edited by Joseph Komonchak, Mary Collins, and Dermot A. Lane, 703–8. Collegeville, Minn.: The Liturgical Press, 1987.

―――. "The Place of Religion in the Practical Reasoning of Individuals and Groups." *American Journal of Jurisprudence* 43 (1998): 1–24.

Boyle, Joseph, Germain Grisez, and John Finnis. "Practical Principals, Moral Truth, and Ultimate Ends." *American Journal of Jurisprudence* 32 (1987): 99–151.

Breznik, Victor B., ed. *One Hundred Years of Thomism.* Houston: Center for Thomistic Studies, 1981.

Bromiley, Geoffrey W. "Casuistry." In *Baker's Dictionary of Christian Ethics.* Grand Rapids, Mich.: Baker Book House, 1967.

Brown, Raymond Edward. *The Critical Meaning of the Bible.* New York: Paulist Press, 1981.

Bühlmann, Walbert. *The Chosen Peoples.* Maryknoll, N.Y.: St. Paul Publications, 1982.

Burke, Ronald R., *"Veritatis Splendor:* Papal Authority and the Sovereignty of Reason." In *"Veritatis Splendor": American Responses,* edited by Michael E. Allsopp and John J. O'Keefe, 120–25. Kansas City, Mo.: Sheed and Ward, 1995.

Cahill, Lisa Sowle. "Accent on the Masculine." In *Readings in Moral Theology*, no. 10, *John Paul II and Moral Theology*, edited by Charles E. Curran and Richard A. McCormick, 85–91. New York: Paulist Press, 1998.

———. *Between the Sexes: Foundations for a Christian Ethics of Sexuality.* Philadelphia: Fortress Press, 1985.

———. "The Bible and Christian Moral Practices." In *Christian Ethics: Problems and Prospects*, edited by Lisa Sowle Cahill and James F. Childress, 3–17. Cleveland: Pilgrim Press, 1996.

———. "On Richard McCormick: Reason and Faith in Post–Vatican II Catholic Ethics." *Second Opinion* 9 (Nov. 1988): 108–30.

———. *Sex, Gender, and Christian Ethics: New Studies in Christian Ethics.* Cambridge: Cambridge University Press, 1996.

Campbell, E., and D. Freeman, eds. *Biblical Archaeologist Reader.* Vol. 3. New York: Anchor Books, 1970.

Carney, F. S. "Deciding the Situation: What Is Required?" In *Norm and Context in Christian Ethics*, edited by Gene H. Outka and P. Ramsey. New York: Scribner's, 1968.

Carr, Anne E. *Transforming Grace: Christian Tradition and Women's Experience.* San Francisco: Harper & Row, 1988.

Childs, Brevard S. *Biblical Theology in Crisis.* Philadelphia: Westminster Press, 1970.

Christie, Dolores L. *Adequately Considered: An American Perspective on Louis Janssens' Personalist Morals.* Louvain Theological and Pastoral Monographs 4. Louvain: Peeters, 1990.

Collins, Thomas Aquinas, and Raymond Brown. "Church Pronouncements." In *The Jerome Biblical Commentary.* Englewood Cliffs, N.J.: Prentice-Hall, 1968.

Congar, Yves. "A Brief History of the Forms of the Magisterium and Its Relation to Scholars." In *Readings in Moral Theology*, no. 3, *The Magisterium and Morality*, edited by Charles E. Curran and Richard A. McCormick, 314–31. New York: Paulist Press, 1982.

———. "A Semantic History of the Term Magisterium." In *Readings in Moral Theology*, no. 3, edited by Charles E. Curran and Richard A. McCormick, 297–313. New York: Paulist Press, 1982.

Congregation for the Doctrine of the Faith. "Instruction on the Ecclesial Vocation of the Theologian." *Origins* 28 (July 5, 1990): 119–26.

———. Instruction on Respect for Human Life in Its Origin and on the Dignity of Procreation." In *Religion and Artificial Reproduction: An Inquiry into the Vatican: "Instruction on Respect for Human Life in Its Origin and on the Dignity of Human Reproduction,"* edited by Thomas A. Shannon and Lisa Sowle Cahill, ix, 201. New York: Crossroad, 1988.

Connery, John R. "Morality of Consequences: A Critical Appraisal." In *Readings in Moral Theology*, no. 1, *Moral Norms and Catholic Tradition*, edited by

Charles E. Curran and Richard A. McCormick, 244–66. New York: Paulist Press, 1979.

Copleston, Frederick Charles. *Aquinas.* Harmondsworth, Middlesex: Penguin, 1955.

Curran, Charles E. *Directions in Fundamental Moral Theology.* Notre Dame, Ind.: University of Notre Dame Press, 1985.

———. *History and Contemporary Issues: Studies in Moral Theology.* New York: Continuum, 1996.

———. "Is There a Catholic and/or Christian Ethic?" In *Readings in Moral Theology,* no. 2, *The Distinctiveness of Christian Ethics,* edited by Charles E. Curran and Richard A. McCormick, 60–89. New York: Paulist Press, 1980.

———. *Moral Theology: Challenges for the Future: Essays in Honor of Richard A. McCormick.* New York: Paulist Press, 1990.

———. "Natural Law and Moral Theology." In *Contraception, Authority and Dissent.* New York: Herder and Herder, 1969.

———. "Official Catholic Social and Sexual Teachings: A Methodological Comparison." In *Readings in Moral Theology,* no. 8, *Dialogue About Catholic Sexual Teaching,* edited by Charles E. Curran and Richard A. McCormick, 536–58. New York: Paulist Press, 1993.

———. *Ongoing Revision in Moral Theology.* Notre Dame, Ind.: Fides Publishers, 1975.

———. "The Role and Function of the Scriptures in Moral Theology." In *Readings in Moral Theology,* no. 4, *The Use of Scripture in Moral Theology,* edited by Charles E. Curran and Richard A. McCormick, 178–212. New York: Paulist Press, 1984.

Danto, Arthur C. "Persons." In *The Encyclopedia of Philosophy,* vols. 5 and 6, edited by Paul Edwards. New York: Macmillan, 1967.

D'Arcy, Eric. *Conscience and Its Right to Freedom.* London: Sheed and Ward, 1960.

Davis, Henry. *Moral and Pastoral Theology.* 5th rev. and enlarged ed., Heythrop series, II. New York: Sheed and Ward, 1946.

Delhaye, Phillipe. "The Contribution of Vatican II to Moral Theology." *Concilium* 75 (1972).

———. "Les points fort de la morale à Vatican II." *Studia Moralia* 24 (1986): 5–40.

———. "Questioning the Specificity of Christian Morality." In *Readings in Moral Theology,* no. 2, edited by Charles E. Curran and Richard A. McCormick, 234–69. New York: Paulist Press, 1980.

Demmer, Klaus. *Shaping the Moral Life: An Approach to Moral Theology.* Moral Traditions and Moral Arguments Series. Washington, D.C.: Georgetown University Press, 2000.

Donahue, John R. "The Challenge of the Biblical Renewal to Moral Theology." In *Riding Time Like a River: The Catholic Moral Tradition Since Vatican II,* edited by William J. O'Brien, 59–80. Washington D.C.: Georgetown University Press, 1993.

Dulles, Avery. "Authority and Conscience." In *Readings in Moral Theology*, no. 6, *Dissent in the Church*, edited by Charles E. Curran and Richard A. McCormick, 97–111. New York: Paulist Press, 1988.

———. "Doctrinal Authority for a Pilgrim Church." In *Readings in Moral Theology*, no. 3, edited by Charles E. Curran and Richard A. McCormick, 247–71. New York: Paulist Press, 1982.

Emercke, G. "Christlichkeit und Geschichtlichkeit der Moraltheologie." *Catholica* 26 (1972): 193–211.

Ferin, Jacques, and Louis Janssens, "Progestogènes et morale conjugale." *Bibliotheca Ephemeridum Theologicarum Lovaniensium* 22, 9–48. Louvain: Publications Universitaires; Gembloux: Duculot, 1963.

Fiorenza, Elisabeth Schüssler. *Bread Not Stone: The Challenge of Feminist Biblical Interpretation*. Boston: Beacon Press, 1984.

———. *In Memory of Her: A Feminist Theological Reconstruction of Christian Origins*. New York: Crossroad, 1983.

———. "Toward a Feminist Biblical Interpretation and Liberation Theology." In *Readings in Moral Theology*, no. 4, edited by Charles E. Curran and Richard A. McCormick, 354–82. New York: Paulist Press, 1984.

———. "The Will to Choose or to Reject: Continuing Our Critical Work." In *The Feminist Interpretation of the Bible*, edited by Letty M. Russell. Philadelphia: Westminster Press, 1985.

———. "'You Are Not to Be Called Father': Early Christian History in a Feminist Perspective." In *The Bible and Liberation: Political and Social Hermeneutics*, edited by Norman Gottwald. New York: Orbis Books, 1983.

Flannery, Austin. *The Basic Sixteen Documents: Constitutions, Decrees, Declarations: A Completely Revised Translation in Inclusive Language, Vatican Collection. The Basic Volume*. Northport, N.Y.: Costello, 1996.

———. *Vatican Council II: The Conciliar and Post Conciliar Documents, Vatican Collection*. Vol. 1. Northport, N.Y.: Costello Publishing, 1984.

Fletcher, Joseph. "Four Indicators of Human-hood: The Enquiry Matures." In *On Moral Medicine: Theological Perspectives in Medical Ethics*, edited by Stephen E. Lammers and Allen Verhey, 275–78. Grand Rapids, Mich.: Eerdmans, 1987.

Ford, John C., and Germain Grisez. "Contraception and the Infallibility of the Ordinary Magisterium." *Theological Studies* 39 (1978): 259–311.

Ford, John C., and Gerald A. Kelly. *Contemporary Moral Theology*. Westminster, Md.: Newman Press, 1963.

Frankena, William K. "McCormick and the Traditional Distinction." In *Doing Evil to Achieve Good: Moral Choice in Conflict Situations*, edited by Paul Ramsey and Richard A. McCormick, 145–64. Chicago: Loyola University Press, 1978.

Fuchs, Josef. "The Absoluteness of Moral Terms." In *Readings in Moral Theology*, no. 1, edited by Richard A. McCormick and Charles E. Curran, 94–137. New York: Paulist Press, 1979.

———. *Christian Ethics in a Secular Arena*. Washington, D.C.: Georgetown University Press; Dublin: Gill and Macmillan, 1984.

———. "A Harmonization of the Conciliar Statements on Moral Theology." In *Vatican II: Assessment and Perspectives: Twenty-five Years After (1962–1987)*, edited by René Latourelle. New York: Paulist Press, 1988.

———. *Human Values and Christian Morality*. Dublin: Gill and Macmillan, 1970.

———. "Is There a Specifically Christian Morality?" In *Readings in Moral Theology*, no. 2, edited by Charles E. Curran and Richard A. McCormick, 3–19. New York: Paulist Press, 1980.

———. "The Natural Law in the Testimony of the Church." In *Readings in Moral Theology*, no. 7, edited by Charles E. Curran and Richard A. McCormick, 5–16. New York: Paulist Press, 1991.

———. *Personal Responsibility and Christian Morality*. Dublin: Gill and Macmillan; Washington, D.C.: Georgetown University Press, 1983.

Galilea, Secundo. "Liberation Theology Began with Medellin." *Ladoc* (May 1975): 1–6.

Gallagher, John. "Magisterial Teaching, from 1918 to the Present." In *Readings in Moral Theology*, no. 8, edited by Charles E. Curran and Richard A. McCormick, 71–92. New York: Paulist Press, 1993.

———. *Time Past, Time Future: A Historical Study of Catholic Moral Theology*. New York: Paulist Press, 1990.

Gaziaux, Éric. *Morale de la foi et morale autonome: Confrontation entre P. Delhaye et J. Fuchs, Bibliotheca Ephemeridum theologicarum Lovaniensium, 119*. Leuven: Leuven University Press; Leuven: Uitgeverij Peeters, 1995.

Génicot, Eduard. *Institutiones theologiae moralis*. 3rd ed. Lovanii: Typis Polleunis et Ceutercik, 1900.

Ghoos, J. "L'acte à double effet, étude de théologie positive." *Ephemerides Theologiae Lovanienses* 27 (1951): 30–52.

Giddens, Anthony. *The Consequences of Modernity*. Stanford, Calif.: Stanford University Press, 1990.

Gilby, Thomas. Appendix 2, "The Theological Classification of Law," to *Summa Theologiae*, vol. 28 (1a2ae 90–97), *Law and Political Theory*, by Saint Thomas Aquinas, edited by Thomas Gilby, p. 162. Cambridge, England: Blackfriars, 1966.

Gilleman, Gérard. *The Primacy of Charity in Moral Theology*. Trans. William F. Ryan, S.J., and André Vahon, S.J. Westminster, Md.: Newman Press, 1959.

Gottwald, Norman K. *The Bible and Liberation: Political and Social Hermeneutics*. Maryknoll, N.Y.: Orbis Books, 1983.

———. "Israel's Emergence." Interview in *Bible Review* 5:5 (Oct. 1989).

Greeley, Andrew M. *The Catholic Imagination*. Berkeley: University of California Press, 2000.

————. "The Failures of Vatican II After Twenty Years." *America* 146 (Feb. 6, 1982): 86–89.

————. "Going Their Own Way." *New York Times Magazine* (Oct. 10, 1982).

Gremillion, Joseph. *The Gospel of Peace and Justice: Catholic Social Teaching Since Pope John*. Maryknoll, N.Y.: Orbis Books, 1976.

Grisez, Germain G. *Abortion: The Myths, the Realities, and the Arguments*. New York: Corpus Books, 1970.

————. "The First Principle of Practical Reason: A Commentary on the *Summa Theologiae*, 1-2, Question 94, Article 2." *Natural Law Forum* (1965): 168–201.

————. "Revelation Versus Dissent." In *Readings in Moral Theology*, no. 10, edited by Charles E. Curran and Richard A. McCormick, 35–41. New York: Paulist Press, 1998.

————. *The Way of the Lord Jesus: A Summary of Catholic Moral Theology*. Vol. 1, *Christian Moral Principles*. Chicago: Franciscan Herald Press, 1983.

Grisez, Germain G., Joseph Boyle, John Finnis, and William E. May. "NFP: Not Contralife." In *Readings in Moral Theology*, no. 8, edited by Charles E. Curran and Richard A. McCormick, 126–34. New York: Paulist Press, 1993.

Grisez, Germain G., and Russell B. Shaw. *Beyond the New Morality: The Responsibilities of Freedom*. 3rd ed. Notre Dame, Ind.: University of Notre Dame Press, 1988.

Gründel, Johannes. "Natural Law." In *Encyclopedia of Theology: The Concise Sacramentum Mundi*, edited by Karl Rahner, 1017–23. New York: Seabury Press, 1975.

Guindon, André. *The Sexual Creators: An Ethical Proposal for Concerned Christians*. Lanham, Md.: University Press of America, 1986.

Gula, Richard M. *The Good Life: Where Morality and Spirituality Converge*. New York: Paulist Press, 1999.

————. *Reason Informed by Faith: Foundations of Catholic Morality*. New York: Paulist Press, 1989.

————. *What Are They Saying About Moral Norms?* New York: Paulist Press, 1982.

Gustafson, James M. *Can Ethics Be Christian?* Chicago: University of Chicago Press, 1975.

————. *Christ and the Moral Life*. New York: Harper & Row, 1968.

————. "Context Versus Principles." *Harvard Theological Review* 58 (1965).

————. "Roman Catholic and Protestant Interaction in Ethics: An Interpretation." *Theological Studies* 50 (1989): 44–69.

Hamel, Edouard. "Casuistry." In *New Catholic Encyclopedia*. San Francisco: Catholic University Press, 1967.

————. "The Foundations of Human Rights in Biblical Theology Following the Orientations of *Gaudium et Spes.*" In *Vatican II: Assessment and Perspectives: Twenty-five Years After (1962–1987),* edited by René Latourelle. New York: Paulist Press, 1988.

————. "Scripture: The Soul of Moral Theology." In *Readings in Moral Theology,* no. 4, edited by Charles E. Curran and Richard A. McCormick, 104–32. New York: Paulist Press, 1984.

Hanigan, James P. "*Veritatis Splendor* and Sexual Ethics." In *"Veritatis Splendor":American Responses,* edited by Michael E. Allsopp and John J. O'Keefe, 208–23. Kansas City, Mo.: Sheed and Ward, 1995.

Häring, Bernard. "A Distrust That Wounds." In *Considering "Veritatis Splendor,"* edited by John Wilkins. Cleveland, Ohio: Pilgrim Press, 1994.

————. "Dynamism and Continuity in a Personalistic Approach to Natural Law." In *Norm and Context in Christian Ethics,* edited by Gene H. Outka, Paul Ramsey, and Frederick Smith Carney. New York: Scribner's, 1968.

————. "The Inseparability of the Unitive-Procreative Functions of the Marital Act." In *Contraception: Authority and Dissent,* edited by Charles E. Curran. New York: Herder and Herder, 1969.

————. *Sin in a Secular Age.* Garden City, N.Y.: Doubleday, 1974.

Hauerwas, Stanley. *A Community of Character: Toward a Constructive Christian Social Ethic.* Notre Dame, Ind.: University of Notre Dame Press, 1981.

Hebblethwaite, Peter. *The Runaway Church: Postconciliar Growth or Decline?* New York: Seabury Press, 1975.

Hehir, Brian J. "The Social Role of the Church: Leo XIII, Vatican II and John Paul II." In *Catholic Social Thought and the New World Order: Building on One Hundred Years,* edited by Oliver F. Williams and John W. Houck. Notre Dame Center for Ethics and Religious Values in Business, xiv, 383. Notre Dame, Ind.: University of Notre Dame Press, 1993.

Highfield, Ron. *Barth and Rahner in Dialogue: Toward an Ecumenical Understanding of Sin and Evil.* American University Studies, Series 7, Theology and Religion, vol. 62. New York: Peter Lang, 1989.

Hildebrand, Dietrich von. "The Meaning of Marriage and the Principle of Superabundant Finality." In *Readings in Moral Theology,* no. 8, edited by Charles E. Curran and Richard A. McCormick, 111–25. New York: Paulist Press, 1993.

Hillman, Eugene. "Evangelism in a Wider Ecumenism: Theological Grounds for Dialogue with Other Religions." *Journal of Ecumenical Studies* 12 (Winter 1975).

Hoose, Bernard. *Proportionalism: The American Debate and Its European Roots.* Washington, D.C.: Georgetown University Press, 1987.

Hürth, Franz, and Pedro Abellan. *De Principiis, de virtutibus et praeceptis.* Rome: Pont. Univ. Gregoriana, 1948.

Janssens, Louis. "Artificial Insemination: Ethical Considerations." *Louvain Studies* 8 (1980): 3–29.

————. "Morale conjugale et progestogènes." *Ephemerides Theologicae Lovanienses* 39 (1963): 787–826.

————. "Norms and Priorities in a Love Ethic." *Louvain Studies* 6 (1977): 207–38.

————. "Ontic Evil and Moral Evil." In *Readings in Moral Theology*, no. 1, edited by Charles E. Curran and Richard A. McCormick, 40–93. New York: Paulist Press, 1979.

————. "Saint Thomas Aquinas and the Question of Proportionality." *Louvain Studies* 9 (1982).

John XXIII, Pope. "Pacem in Terris." In *Catholic Social Thought: The Documentary Heritage*, edited by David J. O'Brien and Thomas A. Shannon, 131–62. Maryknoll, N.Y.: Orbis Books, 1998.

John Paul II, Pope. *Evangelium Vitae*. Vatican City: Libreria Editrice Vaticana, 1995.

————. *Fides et Ratio: On the Relationship between Faith and Reason*. Boston: St. Paul Books and Media, 1996.

————. *The Splendor of Truth*. Boston: St. Paul Books and Media, 1993.

Johnstone, Brian V. "From Physicalism to Personalism." *Studia Moralia* 30 (1992): 71–96.

Kaiser, Robert Blair. *The Politics of Sex and Religion: A Case History in the Development of Doctrine*. Kansas City, Mo.: Leaven Press, 1985.

Kasper, Walter. "Absoluteness of Christianity." In *Sacramentum Mundi: An Encyclopedia of Theology*, vol. 1, edited by Karl Rahner. New York: Herder and Herder; London: Burns and Oates, 1969.

Kasper, Walter Cardinal. "On the Church." *America* 184 (April 23–30, 2001): 8–17.

Keenan, James F. "Virtue Ethics." In *Christian Ethics: An Introduction*, edited by Bernard Hoose, 84–94. Collegeville, Minn: Liturgical Press, 1998.

Keenan, James F., Jon D. Fuller, Lisa Sowle Cahill, and Kevin Kelly, eds. *Catholic Ethicists on HIV/AIDS Prevention*. New York: Continuum, 2000.

Kelly, Gerald A. *Medico-Moral Problems*. St. Louis, Mo.: Catholic Hospital Association of the United States and Canada, 1949.

Knauer, Peter. "The Hermeneutic Function of the Principle of Double Effect." In *Readings in Moral Theology*, no. 1, *Moral Norms and the Catholic Tradition*, edited by Richard A. McCormick and Charles E. Curran, 1–39. New York: Paulist Press, 1979.

Langan, John. "Catholic Moral Rationalism and the Philosophical Bases of Moral Theology." *Theological Studies* 50 (1989): 25–43.

Latourelle, René. *Vatican II: Assessment and Perspectives: Twenty-five Years After (1962–1987)*. Vol. 2. New York: Paulist Press, 1989.

LaVerdiere, Eugene. "The Witness of the New Testament." In *Dimensions of Human Sexuality*, edited by Dennis Doherty, 21–38. Garden City, N.Y.: Doubleday, 1979.

Leo XIII, Pope. *One Hundred Years of Thomism.* Houston: Center for Thomistic Studies, 1981.

Lindsell, Harold. *The Bible for the Bible.* Grand Rapids, Mich.: Zondervan, 1976.

———. *The World, the Flesh and the Devil.* Washington, D.C.: Canon Press, 1973.

Luigi, M., Franco Imoda, and Joyce Ridick. "Anthropology and the Christian Vocation: Conciliar and Postconciliar Aspects." In *Vatican II: Assessment and Perspectives: Twenty-five Years After (1962–1987),* edited by René Latourelle. New York: Paulist Press, 1988.

MacIntyre, Alasdair C. *After Virtue: A Study in Moral Theory.* 2nd ed. Notre Dame, Ind.: University of Notre Dame Press, 1984.

———. "How Can We Learn What *Veritatis Splendor* Has to Teach?" *The Thomist* 58:1 (1994): 171–95.

———. *Whose Justice? Which Rationality?* Notre Dame, Ind.: University of Notre Dame Press, 1988.

Mackin, Theodore. *Divorce and Remarriage.* Marriage in the Catholic Church Series. New York: Paulist Press, 1984.

MacNamara, Vincent. *Faith and Ethics: Recent Roman Catholicism.* Dublin: Gill and Macmillan; Washington, D.C.: Georgetown University Press, 1985.

Macquarrie, John. "Rethinking Natural Law." In *Readings in Moral Theology,* no. 7, edited by Charles E. Curran and Richard A. McCormick, 221–46. New York: Paulist Press, 1991.

———. *Thinking About God.* New York: Harper & Row, 1975.

Mahoney, John. "The Challenge of Moral Distinctions." *Theological Studies* 53 (1992): 663–82.

———. *The Making of Moral Theology: A Study of the Roman Catholic Tradition.* Oxford: Clarendon Press, 1987.

Mangan, Joseph T. "An Historical Analysis of the Principle of Double Effect." *Theological Studies* 10 (March 1949): 41–62.

Maguire, Marjorie Reiley "Personhood, Covenant, and Abortion." In *Abortion and Catholicism: The American Debate,* edited by Patricia Beattie Jung and Thomas A. Shannon. New York: Crossroad, 1988.

Maritain, Jacques. *Man and the State.* Charles R. Walgreen Foundation Lectures no. 1. Chicago: University of Chicago Press, 1951.

———. "Natural Law in Aquinas." In *Readings in Moral Theology,* no. 7, edited by Charles E. Curran and Richard A. McCormick, 114–23. New York: Paulist Press, 1991.

———. *The Range of Reason.* New York: Scribner's, 1952.

May, William E. "Aquinas and Janssens on Moral Meaning of Human Acts." *The Thomist* 48:3 (1984): 566–607.

McBrien, Richard P. *Catholicism.* 2 vols. Minneapolis: Winston Press, 1980.

McCarthy, Timothy. *The Catholic Tradition: The Church in the Twentieth Century.* Rev. and expanded 2nd ed. Chicago: Loyola University Press, 1998.

McCormick, Richard A. "Ambiguity in Moral Choice." In *Doing Evil to Achieve Good: Moral Choice in Conflict Situations*, edited by Richard A. McCormick and P. Ramsey, 7–53. Chicago: Loyola University Press, 1978.

———. "Bioethics and Method: Where Do We Start?" In *On Moral Medicine: Theological Perspectives in Medical Ethics*, edited by Stephen E. Lammers and Allen Verhey. Grand Rapids, Mich.: Eerdmans, 1987.

———. "A Commentary on the Commentaries." In *Doing Evil to Achieve Good: Moral Choice in Conflict Situations*, edited by Richard A. McCormick and P. Ramsey, 193–267. Chicago: Loyola University Press, 1978.

———. "Conjugal Love and Conjugal Morality." *America* 110 (1964): 38–42.

———. *Corrective Vision: Explorations in Moral Theology.* Kansas City, Mo.: Sheed and Ward, 1994.

———. *The Critical Calling: Reflections on Moral Dilemmas Since Vatican II.* Washington, D.C.: Georgetown University Press, 1989.

———. "Does Faith Add to Ethical Perception?" In *Readings in Moral Theology*, no. 2, *The Distinctiveness of Christian Ethics*, edited by Charles E. Curran and Richard A. McCormick, 156–73. New York: Paulist Press, 1980.

———. "Family Size, Rhythm, and the Pill." In *The Problem of Population*, 58–84. Notre Dame, Ind.: University of Notre Dame Press, 1964.

———. *Health and Medicine in the Catholic Tradition: Tradition in Transition, Health/Medicine and the Faith Traditions.* New York: Crossroad, 1984.

———. *How Brave a New World? Dilemmas in Bioethics.* Garden City, N.Y.: Doubleday, 1981.

———. "Human Significance and Christian Significance." In *Norm and Context in Christian Ethics*, edited by Gene Outka and Paul Ramsey, 26–37. New York: Scribner's, 1968.

———. "Killing the Patient." In *Considering "Veritatis Splendor,"* edited by John Wilkins, 14–20. Cleveland, Ohio: Pilgrim Press, 1994.

———. "Moral Theology 1940–1989: An Overview." In *Readings in Moral Theology*, no. 11, *The Historical Development of Fundamental Moral Theology in the United States*, edited by Charles E. Curran and Richard A. McCormick, 46–72. New York: Paulist Press, 1999.

———. "The Moral Theology of Vatican II." In *The Future of Ethics and Moral Theology*, edited by Don Brezine and James V. McGlynn, 7–18. Chicago: Argus Communications, 1968.

———. *Notes on Moral Theology, 1965–1980.* Washington, D.C.: University Press of America, 1981.

———. *Notes on Moral Theology, 1981 through 1984.* Lanham, Md.: University Press of America, 1984.

———. "The Removal of a Fetus Probably Dead to Save the Life of the Mother." S.T.D. diss., Rome, Pontifica Universitas Gregoriana, 1957.

————. "Some Early Reactions to *Veritatis Splendor.*" In *Readings in Moral The-ology*, no. 10, edited by Charles E. Curran and Richard A. McCormick, 5–35. New York: Paulist Press, 1998.

————. "The Teaching Role of the Magisterium and of the Theologians." In *CTSA Proceedings* 24 (June 1969): 239–54.

McDonagh, Enda. *The Making of Disciples: Tasks of Moral Theology.* Theology and Life Series, 3. Wilmington, Del.: Michael Glazier, 1982.

McNeil, John T. "Casuistry in the Puritan Age." *Religion and Life* (Winter 1942/1943).

Mendenhall, George E. "The Hebrew Conquest of Palestine." In *Biblical Archae-ologist Reader*, vol. 3, edited by E. Campbell and D. Freeman. New York: Anchor Books, 1970.

Merklebach, Benedictus Henricus. *Summa Theologiae Moralis.* Vol. 1. Brugis Belgia, 1956.

Mobbs, Frank. *Beyond Its Authority? The Magisterium and Matters of Natural Law.* Alexandria, N.S.W., Australia: E. J. Dwyer, 1997.

Modras, Ronald. "The Implications of Rahner's Anthropology for Fundamental Moral Theology." *Horizons* 12 (1985): 70–90.

Mondin, Battista. "Faith and Reason in Roman Catholic Thought from Clement of Alexandria to Vatican II." *Dialogue and Alliance* 1:1 (Spring 1987): 18–26.

Moser, Antonio, and Bernardino Leers. *Moral Theology: Dead Ends and Alterna-tives.* Theology and Liberation Series. Maryknoll, N.Y.: Orbis Books, 1990.

Muller, Max, and Alois Hadler. "Person." In *Encyclopedia of Theology: The Con-cise Sacramentum Mundi,* edited by Karl Rahner, 1206–13. New York: Cross-road, 1986.

Murphy, Roland E. "Christian Understanding of the Old Testament." *Theology Digest* 18 (1970).

Murray, John Courtney. "The Doctrine Lives: The Eternal Return of Natural Law." In *Readings in Moral Theology,* no. 7, edited by Charles E. Curran and Richard A. McCormick, 194–220. New York: Paulist Press, 1991.

Myers, Allen. "*The Tribes of Yahweh:* A Review." In *The Bible and Liberation,* edited by N. Gottwald. Maryknoll, N.Y.: Orbis Books, 1983.

Nelson, James B. *Embodiment: An Approach to Sexuality and Christian Theology.* Minneapolis: Augsburg, 1978.

Niermann, E. "Secularization." In *Encyclopedia of Theology: The Concise Sacra-mentum Mundi,* edited by Karl Rahner. New York: Crossroad, 1986.

Noonan, John T., Jr. "The Amendment of Papal Teaching by Theologians." In *Contraception: Authority and Dissent,* edited by Charles E. Curran, 41–75. New York: Herder and Herder, 1969.

————. *Contraception: A History of Its Treatment by the Catholic Theologians and Canonists.* Enlarged ed. Cambridge, Mass.: Harvard University Press, Belk-nap Press, 1986.

———. "The Development of Doctrine." In *The Context of Casuistry,* edited by James F. Keenan and Thomas A. Shannon, 188–204. Washington, D.C.: Georgetown University Press, 1995.

———. "Permitted and Disputed Means of Controlling Conception." In *Readings in Moral Theology,* no. 8, edited by Charles E. Curran and Richard A. McCormick. New York: Paulist Press, 1993.

Noth, Martin. *The History of Israel.* 2nd ed. New York: Harper & Row, 1960.

O'Brien, David J., and Thomas A. Shannon, eds. *Catholic Social Thought: The Documentary Heritage.* Maryknoll, N.Y.: Orbis Books, 1998.

O'Brien, William J., ed. *Riding Time Like a River: The Catholic Moral Tradition Since Vatican II.* Washington, D.C.: Georgetown University Press, 1993.

O'Connell, Timothy E. *Principles for a Catholic Morality.* New York: Seabury Press, 1978.

O'Donovan, Oliver. "A Summons to Reality." In *Considering "Veritatis Splendor,"* edited by John Wilkins, 41–45. Cleveland, Ohio: Pilgrim Press, 1994.

Odozor, Paulinus Ikechukwu. "Casuistry and AIDS: A Reflection on the Catholic Tradition." In *Catholic Ethicists on HIV/AIDS Prevention,* edited by James F. Keenan, Jon D. Fuller, Lisa Sowle Cahill, and Kevin Kelly, 294–302. New York: Continuum, 2000.

———. "How Can the Gospel Be Heard in the Secular Culture of Africa's Cities?" In *The Gospel As Good News for African Cultures: A Symposium on the Dialogue Between Faith and Culture,* edited by Juvenalis Baitu, 63–84. Nairobi: Catholic University of Eastern Africa, 1999.

———. "Richard A. McCormick and Casuistry: Moral Decision-Making in Conflict Situations." Th.M. thesis, University of St. Michael's College, University of Toronto, 1989.

———. *Richard A. McCormick and the Renewal of Moral Theology.* Notre Dame, Ind.: University of Notre Dame Press, 1995.

———. *Sexuality, Marriage, and Family: Readings in the Catholic Tradition.* Notre Dame, Ind.: University of Notre Dame Press, 2001.

O'Keefe, Mark. "Purity of Heart and the Christian Moral Life." In *Method and Catholic Moral Theology: The Ongoing Reconstruction,* edited by Todd A. Salzman. Omaha, Neb.: Creighton University Press, 1999.

Paul VI, Pope. *Humanae Vitae.* In *Sexuality, Marriage and Family: Readings in the Catholic Tradition,* edited by Paulinus I. Odozor, 464–84. Notre Dame, Ind.: University of Notre Dame Press, 2001.

———. "La morale Chrétienne: Une manière de vivre selon la foi." *Documentation Catholique* (1972): 752.

Pinckaers, Servais. *Morality: The Catholic View.* South Bend, Ind.: St. Augustine's Press, 2000.

———. *Le renouveau de la morale: Études pour une morale fidèle à ses sources et à sa mission présente.* Cahiers de l'actualité religieuse; collection dirigée par le collèe dominicain de théologie à la Sarte-Huy, 19. Tournai: Casterman, 1964.

————. *The Source of Christian Ethics*. Washington, D.C.: Catholic University of America Press, 1995. Originally published in French as *Les sources de la morale Chrétienne*. Fribourg: University of Fribourg Press, 1985. This translation by Sr. Mary Thomas Noble, O.P., is from the third edition of the French original.

Pius XI, Pope. *Casti Connubii*. In *Seven Great Encyclicals*. Glen Rock, N.J.: Paulist Press, 1939.

Pius XII, Pope. "Address to the 4th International Convention of Catholic Physicians (September 1949)." In *Readings in Moral Theology*, no. 8, edited by Charles E. Curran and Richard A. McCormick. New York: Paulist Press, 1993.

————. *Divino Afflante Spiritu*. In *The Papal Encyclicals 1939–1958*, edited by Claudia Carlen. Wilmington, N.C.: McGrath, 1981.

————. *Magnificate Dominum*. AAS 46 (Nov. 2, 1954): 561–62.

————. "Remarks to the Congress of Hematologists (September 12, 1958)." In *Readings in Moral Theology*, no. 8, edited by Charles E. Curran and Richard A. McCormick, 171. New York: Paulist Press, 1993.

Porter, Jean. "'Direct' and 'Indirect' in Grisez's Moral Theory." *Theological Studies* 57 (1996): 611–32.

————. "The Moral Act in *Veritatis Splendor* and in Aquinas's *Summa Theologiae*: A Comparative Analysis." In *Veritatis Splendor: American Responses*, edited by Michael E. Allsopp and John J. O'Keefe, 278–95. Kansas City, Mo.: Sheed and Ward, 1995.

————. *Moral Action and Christian Ethics*. Cambridge: Cambridge University Press, 1995.

————. "Moral Rules and Moral Actions: A Comparison of Aquinas and Modern Moral Theology." *Journal of Religious Ethics* (1989): 123–49.

————. *Natural and Divine Law: Reclaiming the Tradition for Christian Ethics*. Saint Paul University Series in Ethics. Grand Rapids, Mich.: Eerdmans, 1999.

————. *The Recovery of Virtue: The Relevance of Aquinas for Christian Ethics*. Louisville, Ky.: Westminster/John Knox Press, 1990.

Rahner, Karl. "Anonymous Christians." In *Theological Investigations*, vol. 6. London: Darton, Longman and Todd, 1969.

————. "Anonymous and Explicit Faith." In *Theological Investigations*, vol. 16. London: Darton, Longman and Todd, 1979.

————. "Christianity and Non-Christian Religions." In *Theological Investigations*, vol. 5. London: Darton, Longman and Todd, 1966.

————. *Foundations of Christian Faith: An Introduction to the Idea of Christianity*. New York: Crossroad, 1984.

————. "History of the World and Salvation-History." In *Theological Investigations*, vol. 5. London: Darton, Longman and Todd, 1966.

————. "The Man of Today and Religion." In *Theological Investigations*, vol. 6. New York: Seabury Press, 1974.

————. "Observations on the Problem of the Anonymous Christian." In *Theological Investigations*, vol. 14. London: Darton, Longman and Todd, 1976.

————. "Theology and the Magisterium: Self-Appraisal." In *Readings in Moral Theology*, no. 6, edited by Richard A. McCormick and Charles E. Curran, 35–41. New York: Paulist Press, 1988.

Ramsey, Paul, and Richard A. McCormick, eds. *Doing Evil to Achieve Good: Moral Choice in Conflict Situations*. Chicago: Loyola University Press, 1978.

Regatillo, Eduardo Fernández, and Marcelino Zalba. *Theologiae moralis summa: Iuxta constitutionem apostolicam "Deus scientiarum Dominus."* Biblioteca de autores cristianos, 93, 106, 117. Matriti: Editorial Católica, 1952.

Rigali, Norbert. "On Christian Ethics." *Chicago Studies* 10 (1971): 227–47.

Robertson, Roland. *Globalization: Social Theory and Global Culture*. Thousand Oaks, Calif.: Sage, 1992.

————. "Globalization, Modernity and Postmodernism: The Ambiguous Position of Religion." In *Religion and the Global Order: Religion and the Political Order*, edited by Roland Robertson and William R. Garret. New York: Paragon House, 1991.

Rodgers, Charles, and Drostan Maclaren. *The Social Teaching of Vatican II: Its Origin and Development*. Oxford: Plater Publications, 1982.

Russell, Letty M., ed. *The Feminist Interpretation of the Bible*. Philadelphia: Westminster Press, 1985.

Ryan, Maura Anne. "Then Who Can Be Saved?" In *"Veritatis Splendor": American Responses*, edited by Michael E. Allsopp and John J. O'Keefe, 1–15. Kansas City, Mo.: Sheed and Ward, 1995.

Sanders, Jack T. *Ethics in the New Testament: Change and Development*. Philadelphia: Fortress Press, 1975.

Schillebeeckx, Edward. *Church: The Human Story of God*. New York: Crossroad, 1991.

————. *Jesus: An Experiment in Christology*. New York: Seabury Press, 1979.

Schindler, Franz M. *Lehrbuch der Moraltheologie*. Wien: A. Opitz Nachf., 1907.

Schneiders, Sandra Marie. *The Revelatory Text: Interpreting the New Testament as Sacred Scripture*. 2nd ed. Collegeville, Minn.: Liturgical Press, 1999.

Schüller, Bruno. "Autonomous Ethics Revisited." In *Personalist Morals: Essays in Honor of Professor Louis Janssens*, edited by Joseph A. Selling, 61–70. Leuven: University Press; Leuven: Uitgeverij Peeters, 1988.

————. "A Contribution to the Theological Discussion of Natural Law." In *Readings in Moral Theology*, no. 3, edited by Charles E. Curran and Richard A. McCormick. New York: Paulist Press, 1982.

————. "Direct/Indirect Killing." In *Readings in Moral Theology*, no. 1, edited by Charles E. Curran and Richard A. McCormick, 138–57. New York: Paulist Press, 1979.

———. "The Double Effect in Catholic Thought: A Reevaluation." In *Doing Evil to Achieve Good,* edited by Paul Ramsey and Richard A. McCormick, 165–92. Chicago: Loyola University Press, 1978.

———. "Neuere Beitrage zum Thema 'Begründung sittlicher Normen.'" *Theologische Berichte* 4 (1974): 109–81.

———. "Remarks on the Authentic Teaching of Magisterium." In *Readings in Moral Theology,* no. 3, edited by Charles E. Curran and Richard A. McCormick, 14–33. New York: Paulist Press, 1982.

———. *Wholly Human: Essays on the Theory and Language of Morality.* Trans. Peter Heinegg. Dublin: Gill and Macmillan; Washington, D.C.: Georgetown University Press, 1986.

———. "Zur theologischen Diskussion über die Lex naturalis." *Theologie und Philosophie* 41 (1966): 481–503.

Selling, Joseph. "The 'Meanings' of Human Sexuality." *Louvain Studies* 23 (1998).

———. *Personalist Morals: Essays in Honor of Professor Louis Janssens.* Bibliotheca Ephemeridum theologicarum Lovaniensium 83. Leuven: Leuven University Press, 1988.

———. "The Problem of Reinterpreting the Principle of Double Effect." *Louvain Studies* 8 (1980): 47–62.

Shannon, Thomas A., and Lisa Sowle Cahill, eds. *Religion and Artificial Reproduction: An Inquiry into the Vatican: "Instruction on Respect for Human Life in Its Origin and on the Dignity of Human Reproduction."* New York: Crossroad, 1988.

Shannon, William H. *The Lively Debate: Response to "Humanae Vitae."* New York: Sheed and Ward, 1970.

Sittler, Joseph. *The Structure of Christian Ethics.* Baton Rouge: Louisiana State University Press, 1958.

Spohn, William C. *Go and Do Likewise: Jesus and Ethics.* New York: Continuum, 1999.

———. "Jesus and Christian Ethics." *Theological Studies* 56 (1995): 92–106.

———. "Jesus and Ethics." *Catholic Theological Society of America Proceedings* 49 (1994): 40–57.

———. "The Return of Virtue Ethics." *Theological Studies* 53 (1992).

———. *What Are They Saying About Scripture and Ethics?* Rev. and expanded ed. New York: Paulist Press, 1995.

Stivers, Robert L. *Christian Ethics: A Case Method Approach.* Maryknoll, N.Y.: Orbis Books, 1989.

Stöckle, B. *Wörterbuch der christlichen Ethik.* Freiburg: Herder, 1975.

Stout, Jeffrey. *Ethics After Babel: The Languages of Morals and Their Discontents.* Boston: Beacon Press, 1988.

Sullivan, Francis Aloysius. *Magisterium: Teaching Authority in the Catholic Church*. New York: Paulist Press, 1983.

Tettamanzi, Dionigi. "Is There a Christian Ethics?" In *Readings in Moral Theology*, no. 2, *The Distinctiveness of Christian Ethics*, edited by Charles E. Curran and Richard A. McCormick, 20–59. New York: Paulist Press, 1980.

Thiselton, Anthony. "Knowledge, Myth and Corporate Memory." In *Believing in the Church: The Corporate Nature of Faith: A Report by the Doctrine and Faith Commission of the Church of England*, 45–78. Wilton, Conn.: Morehouse-Barlow; Toronto: Anglican Book Centre, 1982.

Thomas Aquinas, Saint. *Basic Writings of Saint Thomas Aquinas*, edited by Anton Charles Pegis. New York: Random House, 1945.

———. *De Veritate.*

———. *Summa Theologiae.*

———. *2 Sentences* d.24, q. 2, a. 3.

Tremblay, Réal. "Par dela la 'morale autonome' et l' 'ethique de la foi': À la recherche d'une 'via media.'" *Studia Moralia* 20:2 (1982): 223–37.

Ugorji, Lucius Iwejuru. *The Principle of Double Effect: A Critical Appraisal of Its Traditional Understanding and Its Modern Reinterpretation*. European University Studies, Series 23, Theology, vol. 245. New York: P. Lang, 1985.

Verhey, Allen. "The Use of Scripture in Ethics." *Religious Studies Review* 4:1 (Jan. 1978): 28–39.

Walter, James J. "The Foundation and Formulation of Norms." In *Moral Theology, Challenges for the Future: Essays in Honor of Richard A. McCormick, S.J.*, edited by Charles E. Curran, 123–54. New York: Paulist Press, 1990.

Waters, Malcolm. *Globalization, Key Ideas*. London: Routledge, 1995.

Wilkins, John, ed. *Considering "Veritatis Splendor."* Cleveland: Pilgrim Press, 1995.

Wokler, Robert. "Projecting the Enlightenment." In *After MacIntyre: Critical Perspectives on the Work of Alasdair MacIntyre*, edited by John Horton and Susan Mendus. Notre Dame, Ind.: University of Notre Dame Press, 1994.

index

abortion, 10, 213, 223; decision about, 115, 116; and definition of personhood, 288, 289; and denial of absolute norms, 320; direct vs. indirect, 50, 212, 232; encouragement of, 369 n.34; Grisez on, 213–14; for population control, 220–21; widespread, 311; wrongness of, 134, 324

Absolute: self-realization before, 110–11. *See also* God

absolute evil, rejection of idea of, 317

absolute truth: denial of, 320. *See also* moral absolutes; truth

abstinence, sexual: effects of, 58; periodic, 69; unwillingness to tolerate, 66

act(s)/action(s): circumstances affecting evaluation of, 222–23; concrete, 225; desire and aversion influencing, 258; direct vs. indirect, 212; enjoined by formal norms, 224; eternal implications of, 115–16, 277, 298; evil, 212, 215; experience needed for deliberation about, 263; external, lessened emphasis on, 84, 95; of faith, 89; and fundamental option, 95, 111; good life determined by, 254; human, 37; human person as active agent of, 252–53; ideal order relating to,

173; identification of with physical process, 179, 291; innerworldly, 114; intrinsically evil, 242, 316; judged by intention or consequences, 317; lessened emphasis on in virtue ethics, 248; magisterium's judgment on, 316; morality of, 37, 219–20, 316–19; morally good at all times, 292; movement from potential to, 250; natural, resulting from virtue, 248; as not meaningless, 238; object(s) of, 220, 223, 318; as part of narrative, 251; permitted vs. chosen as means, 234; proportionate to ends, 227; realization of values in, 110; relationship with human goods, 185, 239; rightness or wrongness of, 111, 113–14, 209; Scripture as guide for, 161–62; *Veritatis Splendor* on, 219, 316–19; voluntary, 198, 229, 230. *See also* choice(s); conduct; sexual act(s)

actualization. *See* self-realization

act-utilitarianism, 236, 237

Adam, fall of, 91

adultery, 64, 111, 179, 214, 221, 224, 225, 239; response of Jesus to woman taken in, 263; and rhythm method, 62, 63; stealing to commit, 230

388

PAULINUS IKECHUKWU ODOZOR, C.S.Sp., is a visiting associate professor of Christian Ethics at the University of Notre Dame. Two of his previous
books, include Sexuality, Marriage, and Family and Richard McCormick and the Renewal of Moral Theology, which are also published by the University of Notre
Dame Press.